A CHINESE PIONEER FAMILY

Taiwanese country scene, late eighteenth century (National Central Library, Taipei).

A CHINESE PIONEER FAMILY

The Lins of Wu-feng, Taiwan
1729-1895

Johanna Menzel Meskill

PRINCETON UNIVERSITY PRESS
Princeton, New Jersey

Copyright © 1979 by Princeton University Press

Published by Princeton University Press, Princeton, New Jersey

In the United Kingdom: Princeton University Press,
Guildford, Surrey

Library of Congress Cataloging in Publication Data will
be found on the last printed page of this book

Publication of this book has been aided by
The Andrew W. Mellon Fund of Princeton University Press

Printed in the United States of America
by Princeton University Press, Princeton, New Jersey

Designed by Laury A. Egan

TO
JEREMY INGALLS
AND
ISABEL R. ABBOTT

Acknowledgments

In preparing this study I have received advice, information, and support from many individuals and institutions. It is a pleasure to thank them here.

Lin Chen-chuang first took me to see the Lin mansions and made many helpful contacts later on, in particular with Yeh Jung-chung, an old friend of the Lin family, who introduced me to the Lins and who himself gave many hours of illuminating conversation as well as essential research materials such as the Lin genealogy.

Among the members of the Lin family, I owe a particular debt to Lin P'ei-ying, Lin P'an-lung, and Lin Hsin-ch'ien, representing the three major branches of the family in Wu-feng. All three made themselves available for extended discussions; the first two also made family papers available, as did Lin Hao-nien of the Upper House (second branch). In addition, I discussed aspects of family history with many other members of the family, both men and women. In the wider circle of Lins descended from the pioneer ancestor, I received much helpful information from the branches now residing in T'ai-p'ing, T'u-ch'eng, and Fan-tzu-liao, as I did from the more distantly related Lin families of Ta-li (the descendants of Lin Ch'iu-ch'in) and of Shu-tzu-chiao. Among the latter, Lin T'ang-p'an gave most generously of his time and of materials in his possession. In the penumbra of the Lins, I had productive conversations with representatives of families who were allied to the Lins by marriage, such as the Wus (descendants of Wu Te-kung) and Yangs (descendants of Yang Chih-shen) of Chang-hua and the Wus of Hsin-chuang-tzu.

Outside the family circle I received indispensable encouragement and advice from Hung Min-lin of the Taiwan Historical Commission (*T'ai-wan-sheng wen-hsien wei-yüan-*

hui), a specialist in the history of mid-Taiwan, whose own family history was intertwined with that of the Lins. Mr. Hung not only made his genealogy available but gave generously of his time and ample knowledge. Our joint field trips in the Upper Valley are among the most pleasant memories of my research stay. In Taichung, Chang Yao-ch'i and Chang Shen-ch'ieh shared information and materials, as did several other residents of that city and of Chang-hua. In Ta-she, near Feng-yüan, P'an Che-chou allowed me access to the papers of his ancestors, the tribal An-li chieftains.

Among local organizations in mid-Taiwan, several provided background information as well as access to data in their files. I recall particularly the staffs of the Chang-hua and Taichung Historical Commissions, of the Feng-jung and Ts'ao-t'un Irrigation Offices (*shui-li-hui*), of the Wu-feng branch of the Provincial Land Bureau (*T'ai-wan-sheng ti-cheng-chü*), and of the local township offices (*hsiang-kung-so*) in Ta-li and Wu-feng. Tunghai University provided me with lodging during my mid-Taiwan stay, as well as with the congenial company of its faculty and students.

In the Taipei area, I owe much to a number of individuals in governmental or academic positions who called my attention to relevant materials or who made data in their custody available. Among them Shen Shih-k'o, director of the Provincial Land Bureau, Lai Yung-hsiang and Ts'ao Yung-ho of the Taiwan University Library, and Wang Shih-ch'ing and the late Ch'en Han-kuang of the Taiwan Historical Commission were especially helpful. At Taiwan University, I also benefitted from discussions with the late Ch'en Shao-hsing. At Academia Sinica, Lin Heng-tao and Inez de Beauclair answered many questions while Liu Chih-wan shared generously of his vast knowledge of Taiwanese history and of the holdings of his library.

Also in Taipei, the staffs of the Taiwan Museum, the Taipei Historical Commission, and the National Central Library, including its Taiwan Branch Library, made me welcome and facilitated my use of their holdings. I am grateful to the Taiwan Museum and the National Central Library for permission to reproduce materials in their custody. Dennis Ch'en helped with photographing some of the special materials in these collections.

No American scholar in Taipei at the time could function without the good offices of Robert Irick and his staff at the Chinese Materials and Research Aids Service Center. He helped me obtain materials, provided introductions, and was helpful in countless other ways. James Leonard, formerly of the American Embassy, and William Whitson, then of the U.S. Army Language School, also gave assistance in a variety of ways. Harriet Mills generously provided a home base in her house in Taipei and added greatly to the enjoyment of my stay.

Neither in Taiwan nor in the United States could I have functioned effectively without the expertise, linguistic and otherwise, of a number of research assistants and translators. Among them, my Taiwanese assistant, Lin Hsin-hsiung, stands out for his unflagging devotion, his patience and good cheer, and his thorough performance of every assignment. Yung Ying-yue and Yao-chung Li each assisted me during one summer's intensive translation work while Eddie Wang, Abraham Shen, and Kyoko Selden helped with smaller projects.

Among American scholars in the field of Chinese and Taiwanese studies, Marc Mancall and William Speidel provided helpful leads at an early stage of my exploration. C. Martin Wilbur gave me much quiet encouragement over the years; he and John K. Fairbank read and commented on portions of an earlier draft. Myron Cohen shared his insights from years of field work in Taiwan, while Randle Edwards provided help in matters of Ch'ing law. Fang Chao-ying assisted me with some knotty problems of textual interpretation and Jeremy Ingalls gave advice on matters of style. Invitations to read papers—at a conference on family and kinship in Chinese society, at the American Historical Association, and at the Modern China Seminar (Columbia)—produced constructive criticism and an opportunity to clarify my analysis. John Meskill provided perceptive comments on successive drafts, help with translation, particularly from the Japanese, and a welcome in our home for those invisible yet real presences, the Lins of Wu-feng.

Jeanette Hsu of Columbia's East Asian Library did the calligraphy.

Financial support came from a number of sources. My research stay in Taiwan was financed by a faculty fellowship from Vassar College and by a grant from the American Council of Learned Societies—Social Science Research Council. In 1971 and 1972, Herbert H. Lehman College gave support through two grants from the George N. Shuster Fellowship Fund while the City University of New York awarded me a Faculty Research Grant in 1973-1974.

Last but not least, the dedication records my thanks to two great teachers who helped me, indirectly, to write this book: Jeremy Ingalls by shaping my interest in China and in history, and Isabel R. Abbott by first introducing me to the craft, and the pleasure, of historical research.

Note on Proper Names and Source Citations

Personal names have been transcribed in their mandarin form and according to the Wade-Giles system. Lin wives are referred to by their maiden name, but with the title Mrs. Thus, "Mrs. Ch'en," "Mrs. Lo," etc.

Place names are also given in their mandarin form and according to the Wade-Giles romanization, except for a few better-known place names which follow the postal atlas spelling. For easier recognition, I have used the modern name, "Tainan," throughout to designate the prefectural capital then called "T'ai-wan-fu." The name for Wu-feng is also given in this, its modern and most familiar form; it has been substituted for A-chao-wu, used in the Ch'ing period, and Atammu, used by the Japanese. "Chang-hua district" refers to the administrative unit set up in the Yung-cheng reign and not to the smaller entity that emerged from the various administrative redistrictings of the late nineteenth century.

Source citations are consolidated at the end of the text.

Contents

List of Illustrations

List of Maps

List of Figures

A CHINESE PIONEER FAMILY

"Wu-feng is located in the mountains of Chang-hua district. It adjoins barbarian territory and the people therefore all love arms. The Lin family was able to control and bridle them. Armor and sword achieved their purpose and achievements under the military flag were numerous. It was all a matter of selecting great leaders. After several decades, the Lin descendants delighted in the *Rites* and the *Music*, revered the *Odes* and the *History*, and became elegant and skillful in the arts, inspired as they were by the rivers and mountains. Possessed of a supernatural spirit, they combined the arts of war with the arts of peace."

—Lien Heng, *T'ai-wan t'ung-shih*

Introduction

I came across the Lins of Wu-feng on a summer afternoon in 1962. A Taiwanese friend had asked a group of us— American college professors on a summer study tour— whether we cared to step off the bus at the next village to take a look at an old gentry mansion. As I laid eyes on the two Lin houses, the first of their kind I had ever seen, it was in reality the mansions themselves which took hold of me. Perhaps I responded to their decayed grandeur, to the myriad signs of a once mighty family now down at its heels, a melancholy theme which the study of history and of my own family history had long impressed on me. Or it may have been the intellectual frustration of our early weeks in Taiwan which explained my immediate interest in the Lin houses—our initial inability, as humanists steeped largely in the "great tradition" of old China, to make much sense of the peasant culture around us, to link this swiftly modernizing frontier-land to the main currents of Chinese history as we knew them. In the Lin mansions I had found, at last, a relic of a Chinese past familiar from the history books. With their low pavilions around rain-washed cobble-stone yards, children at play behind the lattice work of interior doors, the mansions must have stirred deeper emotions as well, half-forgotten memories of life in other great houses which I had vicariously enjoyed, the world of Pao-yu in his Yung-kuo-fu, of Chiang Yee's childhood, and, yes, even the world of Nora Waln's *House of Exile*, a favorite book of my teens which I had discovered in my grandmother's library.

Touched by the encounter, I revisited the mansions several times on my own. Once, a film crew was shooting a period film in one of the outer courtyards; some image makers, it seemed, had sensed the possibilities of the site. The sheer chanciness of my find began to haunt me. In the mid-Hudson Valley, where I then lived, almost every colonial gristmill had been lovingly restored and was attracting hundreds of tourists a year. Could not the Lin mansions be restored to their former splendor, a reminder to Taiwanese children and foreign visitors alike of the world they had lost? Surely, a government which spoke so eloquently of guarding the traditional culture would be interested in such a project. And the Lins, I naively thought, should feel flattered if their ancestral home became a museum.

By the end of the summer, my project had been dashed. The government professed other priorities and the family, I was told, could not let go of the much-needed living quarters. Even if other space could be found for the family members and for all the flotsam and jetsam which recent history had washed ashore (mustered-out veterans in makeshift cubicles in the once stately hall), property claims on behalf of various individuals and family branches would prove too difficult to disentangle. No one in Taiwan was ready, it seemed, to go into the stately homes business.

As I returned to America and to teaching that fall, I accepted the decision for what it seemed, the end of a lighthearted summer infatuation. But the memory of the houses would not let me go. If the structures themselves could not be preserved in the way I had hoped, preservation of another kind was still possible. During my inquiry about the houses, I had picked up bits of family lore, hints of fortunes won and lost, of fame and infamy. Would it not be possible to reconstruct and preserve the *history* of the Lin family? Armed with two research grants, I returned to Taiwan for a second and much longer stay during the academic year 1964-1965.

My topic proved more rewarding than I could have hoped. The Lins, it developed, had led unusually vigorous lives, far more eventful than one might have thought possible in a sleepy provincial backwater. In turn peasant pioneers, petty rural traders, landlords, local strongmen, military officers, and gentry, they ran the gamut of social status. Their lives intertwined with rebellion and rural violence, with clan vendettas and blood revenge; their deaths were often violent and ugly. If nothing else, the family history I had undertaken was proving to be an exciting story of fast-paced and colorful action.

But there was far more, for the lives of the Lins were touched as well by the less melodramatic, the quieter currents which were reshaping a rude frontier into a recognizable part of late imperial China. Here I found the raw materials of social history, the story of the settling of a new land, of the jostling of many newcomers in an ill-governed frontier region, of the patterns of local power and class differentiation that emerged. The family history I had set out to reconstruct could serve as the key to the history of an entire region.

Much as I welcomed this broader perspective on my subject, I realized that it would impose additional research. For there was no ready-made social history of Taiwan at hand into which I might simply fit the family chronicle. Nor would the general framework of Ch'ing society do, spliced together as it was from data on various regions of the Chinese mainland. Too much in the setting of the Lin family history was proving to be specifically Taiwanese and would have to be understood on its own terms. That I found such abundant materials on the local history of mid-Taiwan was my second stroke of good fortune.

There can be few other areas of China where an American scholar will have such rich local sources at his disposal. Far more open than the mainland is likely ever to be in our lifetime, Taiwan offers opportunities for field study and for the exploration of monumental sources *in situ*—an entire region with its temples, water channels, and stelae from which the contours of local settlement and society can be read. Local informants shared their libraries and sometimes their private papers and made themselves available for unhurried interviews, free from intrusive official guides and interpreters. If some held back on sensitive issues, they were at least free of the rigid stereotypes that have settled on the mainland population's view of their past. In Taiwan I was treated to a rich variety of local views on the Lins and their rivals, on ancient feuds and rebellions, and on the merits of particular landlords and rural strongmen.

In yet other ways, Taiwan turned out to be a uniquely favored setting for local historical research. Local historical societies had rendered much painstaking labor to update the old gazetteers and in Taiwanese intellectual circles there was a lively interest in the island's past. The research department of the Taiwan Bank had compiled splendid modern editions of over three hundred primary sources, materials without which my work would have been wellnigh impossible. Then there were certain accidents of recent history from which I benefited, ironic legacies of an earlier colonialism which had created public records of a kind that exist in only one or two other regions of China. I am thinking of the land surveys and population censuses undertaken by the Japanese around 1900 and the many other compilations which conscientious Meiji proconsuls commissioned in the first flush of their colonial venture. Here was a mine of detailed information on late Ch'ing Taiwan, its laws and customs, its landlordism and family structure.

Having plunged into Taiwanese historical waters on impulse, as it were, I felt the need to justify my project in broader terms. Local history, I knew, had a respected place in the historical traditions of both China and the West, stirring pride and pleasure in native sons, satisfying the curiosity of outsiders and antiquarians. But to establish its intellectual credentials in my own eyes, local history needed to do more. It had to shed light on some of the larger problems of a civilization. Could the Lin story contribute at all to a better understanding of China as a whole, illuminating the range of its regional variants, the dynamics of its expansion, or the decay of its traditional order? At a time when sinologues appear less sure of the sweeping generalizations they once embraced ("Confucian society," "hydraulic society," "gentry society," "traditional society," etc.), no one local study can singlehandedly make new patterns. But it may suggest questions that need asking before we devise a new set of concepts about the Chinese past. What is more, the new skepticism concerning the older concepts has itself helped to establish the local and regional approach as a key tool for a new assessment of Chinese society. If the earlier generalizations now seem premature, a fuller inventory of all the local and temporal variations must surely precede any new effort at conceptualization. In the last few years, students of China have in fact moved in this direction. Not only among the disciplines traditionally committed to the local approach—such as anthropology and sociology, with their emphasis on field work and community studies—but among historians as well, a variety of problems have begun to be studied in the limited yet promising framework of local history.

Once the importance of the local or regional approach has been granted, it remains to suggest the value of an investigation centered on a single family. It is only fair to say at the outset that this book is not an exercise in family history as that term is now understood. While historians have much to contribute to an understanding of the Chinese family as an institution—until now the almost exclusive province of the behavioral sciences—my contributions to family history are incidental. Instead, I would argue that the history of a family such as the Lins provides a unique vantage point for the study of local society.

Since so much historical writing in China was inspired by the needs of government, the record reflects the interests and ignorances of the officials, always outsiders to the area in their charge. To write about local society from the vantage point of a magistrate's *yamen* (his official residence) is to miss nine-tenths of what went on in a local community; such a view exposes local developments only at that point, often late in time and in moments of crisis, when they have begun to impinge on official responsibilities; it means seeing social reality through official spectacles, the locals neatly divided into the loyal and the disloyal, the docile and the troublesome. It means, in short, to miss the complexity of local social configurations. To write about local society from the vantage point of a local family, on the other hand, gives the historian some of the advantages of the insider: a sense of place, a growing familiarity with a changing community over the generations and with the memories of its people, a steady concern for one small corner of the world in times both turbulent and seemingly uneventful.

To take a specific family as the framework for this local study has had, for me, yet another advantage. It has forced me to write about concrete individuals and to realize how they imposed their personal stamp on their social milieu. It has kept me from writing about institutions and "impersonal forces" as if they functioned from some seemingly innate rationale, one which requires no further elucidation and yet all too often, on closer inspection, simply mirrors the ideological assumptions of its creator. It has shown me the interplay of individual initiative and creativity with the established patterns of a society. And it is precisely this multiplicity of individual temperaments and wills even within a single family—impossible to contain within the simple framework of a "modal personality"—which stands out in my mind as an important, if perhaps obvious, truth about China's past.

If the Lin story reminds us of the particularity of person, place, and time, the larger problems which the book illuminates are also implicit in its locale and timing. To position ourselves in Taiwan during the centuries of its rapid sinicization, especially from 1683 to 1895, should help us to clarify the place of the island in the Chinese polity, a subject often obscured by the a-historical and one-sidedly juridical treatment in recent discussions. Since my study concludes in 1895, it obviously cannot speak directly to the question of Taiwanese nationhood today. But in clarifying Taiwanese beginnings and the islanders' own sense of their past, the book gives us clues to their self-definition as a people. And even as the progressive sinicization of the island emerges as a major theme of these two centuries, it seems that Taiwan's integration into the Chinese empire was never so thorough as to preclude the emergence of a separate identity in the twentieth century.

The story of Taiwan's colonization by Chinese settlers allows us to glimpse a further, and very large, topic. For Taiwan in the Ch'ing period was merely the newest of China's many frontier areas. It was by settling and sinicizing one such area after another that China has grown outward, and southward, over the centuries. While Taiwan's colonization involved an unusual expansion across open water, in other respects it may have resembled the earlier settlement process on contiguous land frontiers. That this expansion is a subject of immense importance—and not only to historians—few would deny; yet few have taken the trouble to study it.

Contributing as it does to this larger topic, the Lin story also suggests that we may have to broaden our concept of Chinese frontier history. Chinese expansion involved far more than the actions of government—its military arrangements for aborigine control or the ministrations of civilian officials spreading the sweetness and light of Chinese culture among benighted savages. For all Chinese frontiers, we must reexamine the role of voluntary associations and private enterprise and the often uncoordinated efforts of thousands of individuals acting without reference to government (indeed in the teeth of official prohibitions) to colonize and sinicize a new land.

If the first part of this book contributes to the larger topic of Chinese expansion and the integration of newly colonized lands with the older parts of the empire, the second part deals with some major problems of the nineteenth century. In analyzing Taiwanese patterns of local violence and rebellion, it suggests new perspectives on the genesis of Chinese rebellions, and especially of those great upheavals of the third quarter of the century which almost destroyed the Ch'ing state. It may have required such a narrow scope as mine to focus on the highly localized patterns of group violence out of which many later rebellions grew. But in deemphasizing the broader, China-wide causes of rebellions—long-term impoverishment, dynastic decay, foreign encroachment—and in focussing on their local, private, and a-political origins, we may come to understand better some of the puzzling features of Chinese rebellions, their tendency to fission, their proneness to failure on the larger national stage, their inability to present an alternative vision of society.

The Lin story also suggests that local violence cannot be understood in terms simply of institutions and groups (clans, speech groups, secret societies, not to mention classes) without reference to those specific energetic individuals, the local strongmen (*t'u-hao*), who organized this violence and benefited from it. That they were ubiquitous in the Chinese countryside far beyond Taiwan or the southeastern littoral may be gathered from the writings of their keenest competitor and close student in the twentieth century. Mao Tse-tung spent almost twenty years of his life organizing local armed power for class struggle; thus he inevitably clashed with local strongmen who had built their power on the solidarity of speech group, lineage, or clan. Mao's frequent vituperation of the *t'u-hao* proves their significance even as it requires us to study the phenomenon in a more systematic and even-handed manner.

My focus on the strongman as a key figure in local power configurations may even reopen basic questions about the nature of local, especially local rural, society in recent centuries. Was the Chinese countryside as pacified and orderly as we have assumed? Was local violence not far more endemic than we thought? And was it really the "local gentry" (presumably urban-based) which mediated between the formal government and the various social groupings in the magistrate's bailiwick, as most accounts have it? Did not village-based rural strongmen perform this function in much of the rural hinterland, remote from the district seat? And can we understand social stratification on the local level in terms only of wealth and education, factors which may make sense at the national level? Did not private armed power play as large a role in many areas?

Following the Lins' adroit transformation from strongmen into gentlemen in the last quarter of the nineteenth century, the book's final part touches on some of the broader questions concerning the Chinese gentry. Since this was such an important group—the reservoir of potential officeholders, an unofficial elite in their home communities—the gentry has been studied quite thoroughly already, and from various angles. Lacking the grand statistical sweep of some of the earlier gentry studies, the Lin story must make its points on the basis of its specificity in time and place. It deals not with the gentry as a timeless social category, but with the responses of specific gentrymen, the late nineteenth-century Lins, to a time of travail for Taiwan and for China.

Once of marginal concern to China's rulers, Taiwan moved into the forefront of self-strengthening during the last quarter of the nineteenth century. Set in motion by the state, this reform effort had important implications for the gentry as well, giving them additional political leverage while testing their capacity for leadership in a fragmented society. How did the newly "gentrified" Lins rise to this challenge? More broadly, what resources and what vision did China's traditional local elite bring to the solution of her modern problems at the local level?

We have come to think of the period as one of gathering cultural crisis as well, one in which China's boldest gentry-members (spiritual ancestors to her modern intelligentsia) had begun to question long-established political and social arrangements while the bulk of the gentry obviously remained a vast reservoir of conservatism. What did it mean for a family to seek entrance into the gentry at such a time? Did they become gentry members in any but the most external sense, by virtue of legal standing and status privilege? Or did the older gentry ideal—community service and Confucian self-cultivation, moral leadership in the area of private and domestic life—still exercise some shaping power over the children and grandchildren of rude strongmen?

PART ONE

PIONEERS ON
A CHINESE FRONTIER

CHAPTER 1

THE SOLITARY ISLAND

Taiwan Before
the Chinese Annexation (1683)

A tiny place beyond the pale,
Taiwan is a haven for outlaws.[1]

When the Chinese annexed Taiwan in 1683, they found it
a crude and lawless place and such it remained despite all
the changes China introduced in the next two centuries. A
land of opportunity for countless Chinese settlers, to the
officials it proved one of the empire's least governable
areas. Taiwan's turbulence will be a central theme in our
story, for it was in its midst that the Lins of Wu-feng
reached out for wealth and power.

Geography and early history provide some clues to
Taiwan's restless character.[2] Geographically, Taiwan belongs to a vast chain of islands that stretch along the east
coast of Asia from the Kuriles in the north to the Philippines in the south. Near the center of the chain, Taiwan is
only some one hundred miles from the China coast, yet
marginal to the great subcontinent on which Chinese history unfolded. While Taiwan's mountain peaks are visible
from the Fukien coast on a clear day,[3] the island was to
prove less accessible, or attractive, to the early Chinese than
its physical proximity might suggest; China was late in no-
ticing, much less annexing, Taiwan.

It was not only that Taiwan's coastline—treacherous sandbanks in the west, steep rock in much of the east—was hazardous to the early mariners; the land itself, with its narrow plain in the west backed by high mountains in the east, held scant promise for a people that was still settling the great river valleys of central and south China.

Not that China remained entirely indifferent. The short-lived Sui dynasty (589-618) sent an expedition to a "Liu-ch'iu" island in the eastern sea which most modern historians identify with Taiwan.[4] Burning and plundering aborigine villages, the Sui force gave Taiwan a place in the Chinese annals; most Chinese still hail the event as the starting point of their country's sovereign rights over Taiwan. Yet there was no follow-up to this atrocity, no conquest, much less an extension of Chinese government to the island. Even the Chinese nomenclature for Taiwan remained confused for several centuries more as bits of information bearing on Taiwan, on the modern Liu-ch'iu islands, and even on the Philippines were filed away under the capacious rubric "Liu-ch'iu."

This lack of precision is not really surprising when we remember how slowly the Chinese established themselves in Fukien, the mainland province opposite Taiwan, and how they remained preoccupied with problems of the northern land frontier. Only towards the year 1000 did the south begin to fill with Chinese settlers and only during the Sung dynasty (960-1279) did the government develop a maritime interest in the southern seas.[5]

China's greatest maritime achievement of early modern times, the Ming expeditions to south Asia and Africa (1405-1433) which did so much to broaden her geographic horizon, passed Taiwan by, although the leader of the voyages, Admiral Cheng Ho, is said to have visited the island.[6] Taiwan would remain beyond the Chinese pale as long as neither her merchants and mariners nor her rulers had reason to visit or control the island.

Fukien Takes to the Sea

The outward movement of a regional sub-culture finally drew Taiwan into the Chinese orbit. For sheer survival, the Fukienese turned increasingly to the sea after 1500. By that time, the mountainous province had less cultivated land per person than any other in China, Fukien's half acre per capita being roughly half the national average.[7] Even with the widespread use of double-cropping and of dry crops on marginal land, subsistence farming could no longer support the population. To survive, the Fukienese developed a specialized economy based on sea-faring and trade, manufacture, and the growing of cash crops for export.[8]

During the sixteenth century, entire coastal communities turned to the sea for their livelihood. Fukienese pilots were the finest in East Asian waters, as even Portuguese mariners testified.[9] Farmers took acreage out of rice cultivation and planted it with the higher-paying sugarcane. Fukienese merchants distributed the sugar, along with such other local products as textiles, metal wares, and porcelain. The new economy brought wealth to many communities—by 1600, Chang-chou was known as "little Soochow"—and a marked cosmopolitan flavor to all of south Fukien. For while many products went to domestic markets, a large part went overseas, especially to Japan, the Liu-ch'ius, the Philippines, and southeast Asia.

The long-term consequences of this commercial revolution remain to be explored, yet its immediate impact on the social order must have been obvious even to contemporaries. A predominantly mercantile society, its upper classes deep in foreign trade and commercial profit, was hard to square with the Confucian vision of the good society, defined as agrarian and self-sufficient. Traders were sure to encounter disturbing notions overseas. In going abroad, moreover, they violated specific dynastic statute.

Unorthodoxy and illegality commingled in Fukien's turn to the sea.

In 1371, the first emperor of the Ming dynasty (1368-1644) had forbidden all private overseas trade, a ban maintained until 1567 when a system of licensed private trade replaced it.[10] In the intervening two centuries, any Chinese merchant who ventured beyond coastal waters made himself, literally, an outlaw. The emperor expected foreign trade to be carried in foreign ships, handled by the nationals of China's tributary states. Concerned with security, the policy ignored the economic realities of coastal Fukien. The provincials therefore defied the ban from the start. Buying the silence of most of the local officials, they conducted their foreign trade as one vast smuggling operation. On the other hand, it also happened that merchants were harassed and blackmailed upon their return. Barred from legitimate society, such outlaws often turned to outright piracy. Organized in bands, they engaged in smuggling and piracy at sea and even took to raiding defenseless coastal settlements.[11]

It was this underworld of free-wheeling, lawless trader-pirates that first found a use for Taiwan. Since the island was a no-man's land—except for the aborigines, and they could be intimidated or bought off with trinkets—it became the trader-pirates' lair: a place to rest and refit one's ships, store booty, await the monsoon, and plot the next venture. From the 1560's, we hear of bands under specific leaders on Taiwan.

Taiwan might have lost its appeal to the mariners of Fukien after 1567 when private overseas trade was legalized. The pirate scourge did in fact subside. By then, however, a trade link between Taiwan and the mainland had developed. There was a small market in China for Taiwanese goods, particularly the deer horns which, ground up, yielded an aphrodisiac.[12] Moreover, Chinese mariners had opened a sea-route to the Philippines and Borneo via Taiwan.[13] By 1600, a small colony of year-round Chinese residents lived in Taiwan, serving the needs of the traders in Taiwanese goods and the merchants in transit. The new links between Fukien and Taiwan had not grown in a vacuum. Chinese trader-pirates had no sooner staked out a claim to the island than men of other nations too were attracted to Taiwan. The first, probably showing an interest as early as the Chinese, were the Japanese.[14] Having discovered Taiwan on their far-flung voyages to southeast Asia, Japanese merchants used it as an entrepôt for trade with China, from whose ports they were barred during most of the sixteenth century. Japanese pirates, too, used it as a base. Around 1600, the Japanese government even considered laying formal claim to the island, but its overtures to the aborigines were rebuffed, and the effort lapsed shortly. Without benefit of formal government except for their pirate chiefs, Chinese and Japanese learned to coexist on the island, especially in its most frequented corner in the southwest, a place they called Ta-yüan.[15]

Grafted in the first place onto China as part of her underworld, her hidden world of piracy and illegal trade, Taiwan grew in the seventeenth century as the twig had been bent. Had Chinese officials paid Taiwan much attention, they might have found the island going from bad to worse, for it soon harbored profit-seekers of a novel kind, the Fu-lan-chi, or Europeans. They had arrived in East Asian waters in the sixteenth century and combined trading and raiding in somewhat the same proportion as did the Chinese and Japanese.[16] In the long run, they would inject a keener sense of national and religious rivalry into the East Asian scene, but, at the outset, Portuguese fidalgos and Dutch captains had much in common with their Asian counterparts and they soon entered into profitable deals.

Earliest among the Europeans, the Portuguese took note of Taiwan on their voyages up and down the China coast and to Japan. They were struck by its beauty—the semitropical vegetation in the plain, snow-capped mountains in the distance—and gave it the name Formosa (*Ilha Hermosa*, Beautiful Island) by which it is still known to many Westerners. But the Portuguese needed no foothold on Taiwan, having one already in Macao, and left the island alone. Not so the Spanish and Dutch. Locked into their European hostilities, they entered into fierce competition over Taiwan in the 1620's, each wanting it as a base to trade with China and to harass the other's shipping. China was drawn into their contest when the Dutch in 1623 seized the Pescadores, a Chinese-held island group in the Taiwan Strait. Forced by China to relinquish the Pescadores, the Dutch went to Taiwan instead, where the Chinese promised to trade with them.[17] At Ta-yüan, the Dutch built a fort in the harbor and made it the headquarters for their East Asian trade. By the end of the decade, they had expelled the Japanese. Only Spain remained to challenge the Dutch position. She had a foothold in north Taiwan and was constructing forts and sending missionaries among the aborigines, much as the Dutch did in the southwest. In the end, the Dutch prevailed and forced their rivals out. From 1642, theirs was the only major force on Taiwan. Ironically, it was during the ascendancy of these Europeans that the most durable links yet between Taiwan and China were forged.

The Growth of a Chinese Community on Taiwan

Ensconced on Taiwan for purposes of trade, the Dutch helped in a variety of ways to bring more Chinese to the island. Barred from regular access to Chinese ports, they relied on Chinese traders to bring the bulk of Chinese wares to the island and to take back the goods bought in return. Commercial traffic between island and mainland thus grew in the Dutch period. The Dutch, moreover, encouraged the Chinese to exploit Taiwan itself. They looked with favor on the Chinese trade in aborigine products, taxing it to their own advantage. Growing numbers of Chinese learned the aborigine languages, intermarried with the tribes, and soon dominated the trade in deerskins, Taiwan's most lucrative product. Less to the Dutch liking were the many Chinese who came directly across the Taiwan Strait, bypassing the Dutch control points and customs houses in the southwest. Other Chinese performed a multitude of services for which the Dutch lacked the personnel and the aborigines the skills. In the Dutch core area in the southwest and in the outlying mission stations, we hear of Chinese contractors, masons, carpenters, smiths, and other craftsmen doing the hauling and building and repairing for the Dutch.

Most numerous and in the end decisive were the Chinese peasants. Here again the Dutch created the opportunities to attract these permanent immigrants.[18] Exactly when the first Chinese cultivators had arrived is unclear. Some were already there when the Dutch took over, but they did not produce enough food for themselves and for the Dutch soldiers and traders. Hoping to make themselves self-sufficient in foodstuffs, the Dutch encouraged Chinese peasants to settle in Taiwan. They offered cash subsidies, made draft animals available, and built the first irrigation works. Land, probably taken from rebellious and recently subdued tribes, was assigned to Chinese settlers.

The policy was a resounding success. With their background in Fukien's highly commercialized farming region, the settlers not only provided Taiwan with an adequate food supply but produced cash crops for export. From the 1650's, rice and sugar were sent to the Chinese mainland. Even the "Indian districts" (presumably the Dutch East Indies) received food from Taiwan.[19] The intensive agriculture of the Chinese required, and permitted, a much denser population than the island had ever known before. Numbering at most a few thousand at the beginning of the Dutch era, the Chinese population climbed to around 50,000 by 1660.[20]

The Dutch in fact grew apprehensive about the Chinese

genie they had released from its bottle. Not only did the Chinese vastly outnumber the few hundred Dutch, but they spread farther afield, as hunters and farmers in the western plain. The Dutch complained about the many shady characters that always flock to a frontier, the adventurers and get-rich-quick artists, but also about the "distinguished and wealthy subjects," the "elders," the "distinguished men [with a] following of farmers, tradesmen, and others."[21] If the former cut into Dutch profits, the latter could raise a challenge to the very presence of the Dutch. In 1652 a Chinese uprising against the heavy Dutch poll-tax had been put down only with the help of friendly aborigines. Thereafter, Dutch records spoke with growing exasperation of the "Chinese rabble" that was everywhere defying Dutch controls and of an island "simply swarming with all kinds of Chinese." Events on the Chinese mainland would soon end Dutch rule altogether.

China's mid-century crisis—the fall of the Ming and the establishment of the new Ch'ing dynasty by Manchu invaders in 1644—finally brought Taiwan into the mainstream of Chinese political life. When champions of the fallen Ming house found refuge in Taiwan, the new rulers of China could no longer ignore the island. The central figure in this episode is Cheng Ch'eng-kung or Koxinga (1624-1662).[22] A product of that mestizo world of Chinese adventurers who had first made Taiwan their home, Cheng was the son of a Japanese mother and of a famous Fukienese trader-pirate who had dominated parts of Taiwan before the Dutch era. In 1628 the father had made his peace with the Ming government and joined its drive against coastal pirates. Showered with honors by a grateful throne, he saw to it that his son was groomed for an official career. In 1645 Cheng Ch'eng-kung was presented to a Ming court-in-exile in Foochow, where the dynastic surname, Chu, was bestowed on him. This later gave rise to his name *Kuo-hsing-yeh* (Lord of the Imperial Surname; in Fukienese, *kok-sèng-iâ*), which on Western tongues became Koxinga.

Koxinga proved worthy of the name, for when his father surrendered to the victorious Ch'ing dynasty in 1646, he remained steadfastly on the Ming side. Inheriting men and ships from his father and recruiting others on his own, he dominated the Amoy region where his family lived, and denied it to the advancing Ch'ing troops. Defeated when he tried to recover the old Ming capital, Nanking, in 1658, Koxinga withdrew to Amoy and from there planned the conquest of Taiwan. He saw it as a base for his anti-Ch'ing campaign and as the nucleus for a future maritime empire.

Attacking Taiwan in the spring of 1661 and enjoying the support of the local Chinese, Koxinga soon swept the Dutch from the island. The first part of the Ming loyalists' scheme had succeeded, but their long-range plans collapsed with Koxinga's death a few months later. There would be no maritime empire of the Chengs ruled from Taiwan; still, the family retained control of Taiwan for another twenty years and was able to contribute in important ways to the island's internal development.

Economically, the Chengs built on earlier foundations. Large numbers of new settlers came, most of them from the enclaves on the Fukien coast held by Cheng forces. By 1680, the Chinese population in Taiwan reached well over 100,000.[23] Cash crops, primarily rice and sugar, were grown for export; cultivated acreage and irrigation expanded. The government promoted sugar refining, salt production, and ship building. Despite strenuous Ch'ing efforts to interdict trade with the mainland, it continued, as did the commercial ties with the Philippines, Japan, and the Liu-ch'iu islands.

Politically, the Cheng family broke new ground in Taiwan. As enfeoffed princes of the Ming house, they brought the regular Chinese territorial administration to the island, along with a group of classically trained scholars to staff the civil service. Administrative arrangements foreshadowed those later imposed by the Ch'ing, for the conquerers themselves adopted the Ming pattern. At the old center of

Dutch power, the Chengs laid out their prefectural capital on the site of the modern Tainan; under it, there were two districts, the basic units of local administration. Taxes were levied and officials recruited, as under the Ming. At their capital, the Chengs maintained the court of a Ming feudatory, complete with Ming ritual and a calendar based on Ming reign dates. Schools were established, an academy catered to more advanced intellectual needs, and civil service examinations were held.[24]

The bulk of the Cheng forces were kept in the southwest, where the Chinese population was concentrated, but a chain of garrisons, reaching up and down the western plain, extended deep into aborigine territory. Toward the tribes, the Chengs maintained a kind of "divide and rule" policy. Sinicized tribes were assimilated, the wild ones kept at a distance or, if they attacked, beaten into submission.

By 1683 a more complex society had grown up in Taiwan's southwest. Officials, soldiers, and literati had a place in it alongside the traders and peasants who had formed the earliest Chinese settlements. Taiwan was not yet Chinese, but the demographic and institutional bases for sinicization had been established.

While the contours of this more settled society were coming into view, Taiwan still bore all the traces of its crude beginnings: the contempt for law, the lust for wealth, and the ready recourse to violence. With all its pretensions to Ming rectitude, the Cheng government clearly had its roots in the freebooter regime of Koxinga and his father. The Chengs' staunch defense of the Ming cause had implanted an anti-Manchu tradition which the island was slow to lose. Settlers came by stealth and in defiance of Chinese law, swelling a population that had never been known for its law-abiding habits. Composed of large numbers of males without immediate family ties in Taiwan, even the farming population was mobile and restless, not to mention the hunters, the traders in aborigine goods, and the seasonal migrants from the mainland. Along with most settlers, the government showed an unbecoming interest in gain, and the economy was based on cash crops, not subsistence farming. There was only smuggling trade with the mainland; its other trade linked Taiwan with the larger, non-Chinese world.

In sum, Taiwan abounded with precisely those groups which any good Chinese ruler would approach warily—restless adventurers, cosmopolitan merchants, illegal migrants, anti-dynastic malcontents, not to mention unruly and savage natives. How the Ch'ing rulers shaped this rather wayward member of the Chinese *oikumene*, the setting for the Lin family history, must now be examined.

CHAPTER 2

REASONS OF STATE

The Ch'ing Government and Taiwan, 1683-1770

If Taiwan is pacified, then the four provinces* are pacified; if the four provinces are pacified, then All-under-Heaven is at peace.[1]

China's new rulers, the Manchus, had security uppermost in their minds as they framed a policy for Taiwan. The issue became acute in 1674 when Koxinga's son joined the great anti-Ch'ing rebellion of the Three Feudatories, disgruntled satraps in the south, and retook some stretches of the Fukien coast. For the Ch'ing rulers, it was now plain that the Cheng family would have to be dislodged from its island stronghold. The emperor's larger plans also required that something be done. Before K'ang-hsi undertook his planned campaign against Russia, this thorn in the empire's southern flank would have to be removed. As soon as the rebellion in the south had been put down and a fleet readied, China attacked. In July of 1683, Admiral Shih Lang[2] defeated the Cheng forces in the Pescadores; the way to Taiwan lay open. Rejecting last-minute counsels that he pack up and seize the Philippines, Koxinga's grandson surrendered to imperial forces in September.

The career of Shih Lang illustrates the close links be-

* Kiangsu, Chekiang, Fukien, and Kwangtung; together, they make up the east and southeast coast of China.

tween public policy and private purpose which we shall encounter so frequently in this story. As a native of Fukien,
his life had been deeply intertwined with Koxinga's. Once a
lieutenant in the pirate forces of Koxinga's father, he had
quarreled with Koxinga, left the Cheng camp, and in the
retribution that followed saw many of his relatives slaughtered. After he·surrendered to the Manchus, he pursued
the campaign against Koxinga's house with a vengeance.
As commander-in-chief of Fukien naval forces, he helped
dislodge the Chengs from the mainland in the early 1660's
and submitted the first plan for an attack on Taiwan in
1664. The surrender of Koxinga's grandson was his personal triumph.

The island's political future was next debated at the
Ch'ing court. Some thought it was enough to have dislodged the Chengs, but Shih Lang argued that Taiwan, a
providential shield for the southeast coast, must remain in
Chinese hands. K'ang-hsi agreed. For the first time in its
history, Taiwan slipped under the heavy, if sometimes un-
sure, hand of Chinese officialdom.

K'ang-hsi was concerned about two groups in Taiwan
whom he considered dangerous: the remnants of Koxinga's army and the aborigines. To make Taiwan secure, the
soldiers were removed and sent to the Russian front.[3] As
for the tribes, K'ang-hsi decided to make them docile by
placing a strong garrison on Taiwan and by safeguarding
tribal lands and hunting grounds.[4] A fateful decision, this
dictated the most stringent limits on Chinese settlement: a
total ban on Chinese emigration to the island and a prohibition of Chinese purchases or rentals of aborigine lands.[5]
Much like the Ming ban on private overseas trade, these
prohibitions ran counter to the economic interests of the
coastal population. They were similarly defied, then relaxed and, after two centuries, abandoned, but not before
they had done a grave disservice to the cause of real security in Taiwan. For as K'ang-hsi tried to perpetuate the
status quo, he only invited the illegal settlement of the is-

land and thereby intensified that atmosphere of lawlessness which had long hovered over Taiwan.

The Administrative Framework

As a military district (*chen*) and a prefecture (*fu*) of Fukien, Taiwan was placed under parallel hierarchies of military and civilian officials. Both the military district commander, a brigade general, and the prefect reported to the Amoy-Taiwan intendant (*tao-t'ai*), a high functionary in the provincial government of Fukien.

The military component, some 8,000 soldiers of the provincial Army of the Green Standard (*lü-ying*), was far more numerous than the civilian, as was customary in China.[6] While the bulk of the forces were stationed in the capital area around Tainan, chains of garrisons (called *pei-lu* and *nan-lu*, north road and south road) projected far into the western plains. Interspersed among the many small garrison units, other soldiers manned a network of postal relay stations.

Reflecting tactical needs, the dispersal of the troops in many small units had unintended side effects. It brought the soldiers into closer contact with the society than was common in most mainland areas. Particularly during the early decades of Ch'ing rule, when war between settlers and aborigines was endemic, scattered settler groups sought shelter with local garrisons. Commanders dabbled in land speculation[7] and military posts became nuclei for Chinese settlements. Beyond the shared danger from aborigine raids, a common origin linked the colonists and many of the soldiers. Many officers and the bulk of the common soldiers were Fukienese and hence, literally, on close speaking terms with the settlers themselves.[8]

The army did not only undermine the settlement ban; it became a force for disorder in its own right.[9] Poor pay left many soldiers disgruntled and prone to mutiny, easy targets for malcontents who exploited their grievances. Such troops were useless against Chinese rebels, as the early eighteenth century would already show. Nor were they adept at jungle or mountain warfare against the aborigines. The government therefore recruited loyal aborigines to serve as an auxiliary force. In sum, the military dispositions which looked so adequate on paper turned out quite otherwise; in time, their shortcomings encouraged the formation of private armed forces and all the violence that went with them.

On the civilian side, the prefecture was divided into three districts (*hsien*), one centered at the prefectural capital at Tainan, one in the south (Feng-shan), and one in the north (Chu-lo).[10] Below the district level, smaller units or tithings, the *li* and *pao*, handled the police and tax administration. The hills and mountains in the east, beyond the area of Chinese settlement, were excluded from government control, though the authorities claimed the right to enter and chastize disobedient savages.

Based on mainland precedent, these arrangements were sensible enough for the moment. The central district, for example, resembled an average mainland district in size while being below average in population.[11] The two outlying districts, however, and particularly Chu-lo in the north, which encompassed the entire northern two-thirds of the plain, were bloated in size and underpopulated. Administrative readjustments would be in order after a time.

If the administrative subdivisions made sense, the full set of local governmental institutions (schools, public granaries, etc.) took time to develop, particularly in the areas beyond the capital district.[12] Chu-lo, for instance, remained without a permanent capital for twenty years. It took another two decades before the traditional symbol of government, the city wall of the district capital, was completed. Until 1723, a hedge of live thorny bamboo and a wooden palisade served in place of a regular wall, a vivid reminder of the simplicity of Chinese institutions beyond the prefectural seat.

Legend

⊙ Prefectural Capital
● District Capital
--- District Borders established 1684
•••• District Borders established 1723
▓ Approximate Area of Chinese Settlement
░ Area above 500 m.

Tan-shui

Chang-hua

Chu-lo

Tainan

Feng-shan

0 10 20 30 km.

Peking ·

Nanking ·   · Shanghai

Foochow ·

Canton ·

—— 200 km.

MAP 1: TAIWAN IN THE EARLY EIGHTEENTH CENTURY

There have been so many, and apparently well-deserved, condemnations of Ch'ing officialdom in Taiwan that it is hard to know whether the caliber of the magistrates was poor to begin with or whether it deteriorated later on. Given the hazards of the voyage, the malarial climate, and the lack of cultural amenities, posts in Taiwan were unpopular from the start. Absenteeism was therefore high and poorly educated men had to be appointed to the posts in Taiwan.[13] The frequency of rebellion suggests that the majority of the officeholders were indeed a sorry lot, venal and lackadaisical. The occasional competent official stood out all the more clearly, as did the Chu-lo magistrate of the mid-1710's who encouraged irrigation projects, built roads, oversaw relief work, and sponsored a district gazetteer.[14]

Treatment of the aborigines followed earlier precedent under the Chengs and was, like it, derived from administrative experience in the minority areas of south China.[15] The tribes were divided into the "raw" (*sheng*) and the "cooked" (*shu*). The former, most unlike the Chinese in skills and social organization, were not integrated into Chinese institutions, nor was their assimilation pursued at first. The latter, already somewhat sinicized, were brought under Chinese overlordship. K'ang-hsi inherited forty-two such tribes and added eleven more during his reign, a fact suggesting a slow pace of sinicization. The land rights of these tame tribes were recognized and their chiefs given Chinese titles. The tribes paid no land tax, but were subject to tribute, often rendered in the form of deerhides. The emperor bestowed gifts in return. He also appointed an interpreter (*t'ung-shih*) for each tribe as an intermediary between the chief and Chinese officialdom. Recruited from among bilingual Chinese or aborigines, these men often took unfair advantage of the tribes, conspired to bring their lands under Chinese control, and added to the anger that erupted in frequent tribal revolts.[16]

Near the end of the K'ang-hsi reign, in 1721, a major rebellion cast a glaring light on misgovernment and social tension in Taiwan. Abuses by a local official had fanned popular discontent in the south, where Chu I-kuei,[17] a resident of Feng-shan and recent arrival on Taiwan, exploited the tension. Sharing the surname of the fallen Ming house, Chu manipulated the people's residual loyalty toward that dynasty. Leader of a secret society, he unleashed an island-wide rebellion. His forces seized Tainan in May of 1721 and proclaimed him king. The two other district capitals fell as well but when dissension broke out in the rebel camp, imperial forces brought in from the mainland gained the upper hand. Chu was captured late in the summer but it took another year and a half before the whole island was pacified.

Meanwhile thoughtful men had occasion to diagnose the more general sources of discontent. The most searching analysis came from Lan Ting-yuan[18] (better known by his literary name, Lu-chou), a private scholar come to Taiwan in the company of a relative, a general in the expeditionary force. Lan's essay on the pacification of Taiwan called attention to the serious shortcomings of government: the low caliber of the officials, the abuses in the interpreter system, the mutinous spirit of the troops. But he also spoke of certain deformities in the social order which had, he thought, contributed to the rebellion. He dwelt on the corruption that arose from the unrealistic ban on immigration, the severe population pressure and unemployment around Tainan, the lopsided sex ratio among the settlers—a high proportion of unattached males who were easily drawn into a shiftless and immoral life.

Lan's essay revealed the single largest failing of the K'ang-hsi years in Taiwan: the exclusive concern with security in the narrowest sense, the futile attempt to prevent change, the failure to guide it in orderly channels. In the light of Taiwan's first great rebellion and the malaise it revealed, K'ang-hsi's successor would have to readjust the older policies.

Reforms of the Yung-cheng and Early Ch'ien-lung Reigns

A vigorous ruler, Yung-cheng (r. 1723-1735) tightened the administration of the whole country. Using both carrot and stick, he sought to stem corruption by giving officials more adequate salaries while also putting them under closer supervision. For Taiwan, he decreed bi-annual inspections by visiting censors and readjusted the administrative units.[19] Chu-lo district was divided; a new district, Chang-hua, and a new sub-prefecture, Tan-shui, were carved out of its northern portions. Sub-magistracies were established in the older districts and the Taiwan Intendancy was separated from the Amoy office, making each into a more manageable post.

Most important were Yung-cheng's reforms in matters of migration and land-holding.[20] He relaxed the earlier ban on immigration, allowing wives and children of men already on Taiwan to join them. He also sanctioned the renting of aborigine lands by Chinese cultivators, legalizing a widespread practice. He probably foresaw that renting might become the entering wedge for a complete Chinese takeover, and so forbade outright land sales. A few years later, his government assigned specific areas to the pacified tribes, allotting 500, 300, and 200 *chia** to large, medium, and small tribes for farming and hunting. Ostensibly a pro-aborigine measure, the decision must have freed much land for Chinese occupance as well.[21]

While these were considerable innovations, they did not begin to satisfy the land hunger of the immigrants. Their pressure on tribal lands continued and provoked frequent aborigine uprisings. Along the *pei-lu*, major ones occurred in 1726, 1729, and 1731. When Chinese in Feng-shan also revolted in 1731, more drastic action followed. Yung-cheng increased the garrison to about 12,000 men, making

* The unit of land measure in Ch'ing Taiwan. The *chia* varied locally until it was standardized in the 1880's at .9025 *ha* or approximately 2.2 acres.

it the largest for any military district in the empire, and introduced the *pao-chia* system of mutual surveillance.[22]

That all these reforms did not fundamentally pacify the island—another serious aborigine rebellion broke out in 1735—is not surprising. The conflict over land was bound to keep Taiwan in turmoil for years and the measures to improve officialdom worked at best for a time. Corruption in the passport system spread once more as non-relatives of settlers attempted to migrate. The imperial guarantee of tribal lands must have irked many settlers, who simply seized what the tribes could not defend nor the government protect. Yung-cheng had not yet arrived at a formula that would pacify the restless island.

Inheriting no major crisis on Taiwan as had his father, Ch'ien-lung (r. 1736-1795) could dispense with a broad reform program. He kept the garrison as he found it, but permitted the *pao-chia* to lapse. As population increased, he authorized sub-magistracies in several districts. Although he appointed better educated officials, the caliber of government showed no improvement.

In time, certain major issues nevertheless required attention. The passport system for the limited migration of kinsmen did not work well, but an alternative was slow to emerge. The government blew hot and cold, revoking the system from 1739 to 1744, then reinstituting it, only to revoke it again from 1747 to 1760.[23] In fact, these new prohibitions did not stop the steady stream of migrants, as we shall see from the life of the first Lin ancestor who crossed over during the last phase of prohibition. In the end, Ch'ien-lung adopted a more liberal policy, which broadened the passport system to include people who had no relatives in Taiwan. Though soon entangled in fresh corruption, this new arrangement helped to swell the tide of migration which poured into the island in the final decades of the eighteenth century.

With the number of settlers growing, the land problem also clamored for fresh solutions, but the government merely continued its old policy of confirming aborigine land titles and allowing Chinese rentals. To forestall wide-spread abuse, Chinese loans to aborigines were forbidden (the tribes had lost much land through foreclosures). The loans continued, however, as did direct sales of land to Chinese, a practice which the government itself may have encouraged when it retroactively sanctioned earlier, illegal purchases.[24]

The assimilation of the friendly tribes was pushed with greater vigor than before. To this end, the government employed time-tested methods from the aborigine areas of south China.[25] Beginning with the tribal leadership, it sought to remake the social and ritual life of the tribes along Chinese lines. Chinese surnames, genealogies, and inheritance laws were introduced, as was Chinese clothing and the Manchu-imposed hair style (shaven forehead and queue). Tribal chiefs had to participate in Chinese cere-monial life and received honorific distinctions from the emperor.

The An-li tribe in northeastern Chang-hua, the district we are concerned with in this book, illustrates the change.[26] A Chinese ally since K'ang-hsi days, the tribe's braves served in the aborigine militia. In the 1750's the tribal chiefs took the surname P'an, started keeping a Chinese-style genealogy, received imperial plaques for valiant serv-ice, and travelled to Foochow to celebrate the emperor's birthday. Tastes of the tribal elite had visibly changed by the latter part of the century. In 1771 we find the chieftain recruiting a gardener to tend his orchids, in the manner of a Chinese gentleman with an expensive hobby.

Successful policies have their less welcome side effects. If the assimilation of the aborigines worked well at times, the sinicization of the few often brought the ruination of the many. As the tribal elite became more sinicized, it lived more expensively and needed new sources of income. Many chieftains could raise money only by renting or sell-ing tribal lands to the Chinese, a process that often ended in the complete loss of the tribal allotments.

As the plains filled with Chinese settlers and the danger

from the tribes there receded after mid-century, the government sought to demarcate the pacified plains from the unsubdued mountains.[27] This was done as much to guard the plains from the wild mountain tribes as to protect the latter from further encroachments, for when Chinese advances goaded the tribes into rebellion, it was the government which had to bear the burden of the ensuing campaign. Since it was impossible to build a solid wall the length of the island, the government established barriers only in the big river valleys, the traditional access routes for generations of Chinese prospectors and pioneer settlers. Made from earth and guarded by aborigine militia, these "earth cows" (*t'u-niu*) defined the limits of legal Chinese settlement. Old maps and modern place names still disclose their locations, as does an occasional stone marker which survives near the site of the vanished *t'u-niu* to recall the imperial ban on entering the mountain region.[28]

By the end of the 1760's, policy on such varied matters as migration, land-taking, and the assimilation of the aborigines had assumed final shape. To handle the complex relations between settlers and tribes, a new specialized post, a sub-prefect for barbarian control (*li-fan t'ung-chih*), was created in 1767.[29] At this mid-point in Ch'ien-lung's long reign, the Ch'ing framework for the governing of Taiwan was complete. There were a few adjustments near the end of the reign, in response to another big rebellion. But, in essence, the policies and institutions that had emerged by 1770 were to stand for another century. Only in the 1870's, when they saw Taiwan threatened by a new set of barbarians, did the Chinese once more embark on a period of major reform in Taiwan.

With its mutinous garrison and its slovenly administration, Taiwan was anything but the pacified region K'ang-hsi had envisaged. Unrealistic policies and the low caliber of most officials aggravated rather than solved the problems of a raw frontier region. The continued turbulence on the island cannot, however, be laid solely at the doorstep of the government. The very society from which the settlers came posed an exceptional challenge to any ruler. Southeast China had a native tradition of violence which sustained ceaseless private feuds and the anti-Ch'ing activities of many secret societies. Less tightly integrated into the Chinese state on account of their distance from the center and their mountainous terrain, Fukien and neighboring Kwangtung were difficult to govern in the best of times. When their unruly people had further removed themselves to the outer fringes of the empire, ruling them well would have taxed the powers of a government far more competent and less venal than that of Ch'ing Taiwan.

A century of markedly poor government, punctuated by an occasional show of force, had established the superstructure of imperial authority. For Taiwan to become truly pacified, more was required. Much would depend on the settlement process and whether it could turn lawless frontiersmen into law-abiding subjects. To understand the forces at work in the society, we must now turn to a particular microcosm of the Taiwanese frontier. In examining eighteenth-century Chang-hua, we will also familiarize ourselves with the setting in which the Lin family history would unfold after mid-century.

CHAPTER 3

BRAVE NEW WORLD

Chang-hua Society in the Eighteenth Century

At that time, Chang-hua had not been settled long. The soil was rich and the springs sweet. The first ancestor was confident that success was within his grasp.[1]

Like other newcomers to Taiwan, the ancestor of the Wu-feng Lins chose a place whose promises, to him, outweighed its problems. In chosing as he did, each man revealed something of himself. One who came to the Chang-hua grasslands in the 1750's, as did Lin Shih, opted against the more settled area in the southwest, with its older towns, its wider business opportunities, its docile aborigines. He chose the edge of the frontier, not its backwater.

Yet in one man's lifetime, a frontier district underwent many changes. From a raw beginning early in the century, Chang-hua had by its end become a complex society. The patterns of its growth, of settlement, land tenure, urbanization, and social stratification, must now be examined. They not only molded each pioneer life but determined what kind of Chinese society would in the end emerge in Taiwan.

Established by Yung-cheng in 1723, Chang-hua was carved out of the middle section of the old Chu-lo district.

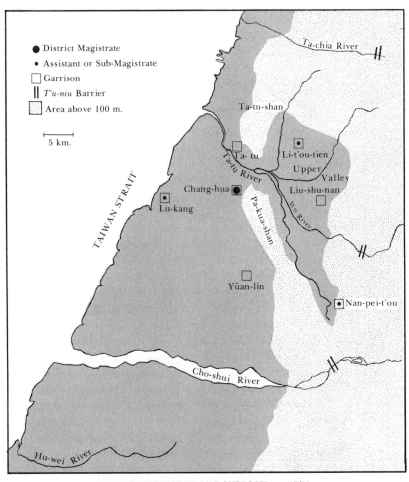

Legend on map:

- ● District Magistrate
- • Assistant or Sub-Magistrate
- □ Garrison
- ‖ *T'u-niu* Barrier
- ▦ Area above 100 m.

5 km.

Ta-chia River

Ta-tu-shan

Ta-tu

Li-t'ou-tien

Upper Valley

TAIWAN STRAIT

Ta-tu River

Chang-hua

Lu-kang

Liu-shu-nan

Hu River

Pa-kua-shan

Yüan-lin

Nan-pei-t'ou

Cho-shui River

Hu-wei River

MAP 2: CHANG-HUA DISTRICT, ca. 1770

It was bounded by rivers, the Ta-chia in the north and the
Hu-wei in the south, and by the Taiwan Strait in the west;
in the east it rose, ill-defined, toward the mountainous core
of the island. Low mountains that run parallel to the coast
divide the district into two parts: the coastal plain in the

west and the valley of the district's major river, the Ta-tu, in the east. Abutting the high mountains farther east, this valley was called *nei-shan* (inner mountain, within the mountains). Center stage for the Lin family history, I shall call this the Upper Valley.

Like all Taiwanese rivers, the Ta-tu played an important role in Chinese settlement.[2] Descending from the high mountains to the coast in less than a hundred miles, it cuts deep gorges into the mountains before abruptly entering the plains. Meandering slowly now, it deposits debris as it carves many channels and builds an alluvial fan into the sea. During the heavy monsoon rains of the summer, the river becomes a torrent and overflows its bed; during the dry winter and spring, it shrivels and trickles to the sea in an enormous boulder-strewn river bed.

Such a river was both help and hindrance to the settlers. Its bed gave access to the high mountain region which was elsewhere sheltered by the impenetrable jungle of the lower hills. It also provided a year-round link with the coastal ports since shallow rafts could travel on it even in the dry season. On the other hand, north-south connections were impeded by the rivers, particularly during the rainy season, when the major road through the western plain was barely passable in many spots even in the late nineteenth century.

On balance, the Ta-tu had created a valley to beckon the settler in search of fertile land. Climatically, it belonged to the southern, semitropical zone of Taiwan, with long hot summers, short mild winters, and abundant rainfall. Given its natural endowment, Chang-hua eventually attracted a dense Chinese population. But when the district was established in 1723, it looked as it had to a Dutchman in the 1600's, "intersected by many beautiful rivers, containing abundance of fish, and . . . full of deer, wild swine, wild goats, hares and rabbits, with woodcocks, partridges, doves and other kinds of fowl. . . . The land is exceedingly rich and fertile, though very little cultivated."[3]

Aborigines and First Settlers

According to the Chu-lo gazetteer of 1717, the Chang-hua area counted a single Chinese village and two to three dozen aborigine tribes.[4] While the figures appear low for both groups, the numerical advantage during the first half of the eighteenth century was certainly with the tribes. What is more, few of the Chang-hua tribes had yet been influenced by Chinese ways. They lived as they always had, with only limited trade contacts to the larger Chinese world.

Among themselves, the aborigines were divided into several speech groups and, within these, into tribes that numbered anywhere from a few dozen to a few hundred persons.[5] The Chinese settlers saw a basic distinction between the plains and mountain tribes. Only the former lived a recognizably human life, combining, as they did, agriculture with the hunt. Still, their failure to develop the potential of their land puzzled the Chinese. Without permanent fields or fertilizer, their crops were poor and supported only a sparse population. Like the Dutch before them, the Chinese invariably criticized the tribes' indolent, lilies-in-the-field approach ("Only after it gets cold do they seek [warm] clothing; only after they get hungry do they look for food; they do not plan in advance").[6] From such heights, the Chinese quickly concluded that in displacing the aborigines they were putting a better way in place of an inferior one.

If the plains tribes had rudiments of a settled life, though hardly of civilization as the Chinese understood that term, the denizens of the mountain seemed entirely savage, akin more to the beasts of the forest than to human beings. "With their nimbleness in climbing, in ascending to the peaks, getting past the creepers and crossing the wilds, they can pursue and frighten the apes, chase and terrify the wild beasts. . . . When they have returned to their nests, no one can get near them."[7] What made them more terrifying still was their head-hunting. "The barbarians of the plains live in dread of them and do not dare to enter their territory. But the wild barbarians in their ferocity from time to time emerge to plunder, burning their huts and killing people. . . . When they kill a person, they immediately take his head back with them. They cook it upon their return, strip the flesh off the skull, daub it with red plaster and set it at the door. One whose fellows see many skulls at his house is esteemed a brave."

In time, when the Chinese encroached on the mountain fastnesses, they, too, would suffer from the head-hunters. But initially it was the plains tribes who bore the brunt of the Chinese advance. For, however inefficiently they farmed, the tribes valued their land and resisted the new settlers by force.

Chinese deer hunters and traders in aborigine goods had begun to visit the Chang-hua area in the Dutch period. Under Koxinga's house, the *pei-lu* garrison first reached the area. In 1670 its northernmost outpost was established near the lower Ta-tu River. Named after a nearby tribe, Pan-hsien would later become the site of Chang-hua city.[8] Under the Ch'ing, the *pei-lu* was extended farther north and Pan-hsien became its headquarters. Encouraged by the local garrison, the first Chinese farmers settled nearby; next came traders to serve the needs of the soldiers and settlers. In 1717 the Chu-lo gazetteer identified Pan-hsien's triple function: a military garrison, a Chinese settlement, and a market.[9]

In the opening years of the eighteenth century, settlers were moving into the Chang-hua area from two directions. Some came up from the south, a spillover from the more crowded area around Tainan. Many of them settled in the southwestern part of the future Chang-hua, where an extensive irrigation facility, the *pa-pao-chün* (irrigation canal of the eight tithings), completed in 1719 after forty years of labor, promised good crops.[10] Other settlers arrived by sea, directly across the Taiwan Strait.[11] Some settled near Lu-kang, a small port just south of the mouth of the Ta-tu River. Everywhere, the attitude of the local tribes mattered, for they could rent or sell land or else repulse the small early settler parties. Relations with the tribes were particularly important in the Upper Valley, far from the protective shield of the garrisons. In its northern part, the friendly An-li tribe welcomed Chinese settlers after 1715.[12]

When the district was established in 1723, Chinese settlements were few. Officials who visited the area at the time of the Chu I-kuei rebellion urged that it be settled to relieve the overcrowding around Tainan.[13] Indeed, Chang-hua began to grow more steadily from the 1720's on. A worsening land shortage in Fukien, Yung-cheng's partial relaxation of the migration ban, and the growth of government personnel which promised greater security may explain this trend. Growth was slow at first, though, and quickened only in the last third of the century, when the aborigines were in retreat and when Lu-kang's brisk traffic with the mainland gave many would-be settlers a chance to slip into Taiwan unobserved.

Since so much migration was illegal and secret, we have no record of the numbers who came in any one year or decade. The 1811 census showed a district population of almost 350,000, out of a total Chinese population in Taiwan of almost two million.[14] Given the rate of population growth at the time and the lop-sided sex ratio in the early settlements, it is clear that most of this growth came, not from a natural increase, but from fresh in-migration. Some idea of the growth curve of the district may be derived from the various gazetteers of the eighteenth and early nineteenth century:[15]

Number of Villages in Chang-hua District

1717	1
1742	110
1763	132
1834	1,108

The bulk of the Taiwanese settlers, over 80 percent, came from Ch'üan-chou and Chang-chou, two prefectures in Fukien that had contacts with Taiwan back in the pirate days.[16] Most of the rest came from adjoining areas in Kwangtung province and they were mainly Hakkas, a distinct minority even on the mainland. In Chang-hua, the two Fukienese groups seem to have been evenly balanced, at perhaps 45 percent, and the Hakkas somewhat less numerous than in other Taiwan districts.

Political opposition to the Manchus may have driven some to Taiwan in the Dutch and Koxinga periods, but the majority in Ch'ing days came in order to better themselves economically. While this much is clear, we know little of the economic background of the settlers, except that they included men from all walks of life. There were officials and their private secretaries and military men who came to Taiwan in an official capacity; they saw the promise of the island, left their posts, and stayed on. There also were wealthy entrepreneurs from the southeast coast, men with capital and experience who saw an opportunity to make money from land speculation and frontier trade. The great majority of the settlers, however, were men of modest or no means who came from dire need, a love of adventure, or the hope of improving their lot. Some went directly from mainland farms to farms in Taiwan; others worked for a while in some city, either on the mainland or in Taiwan, saving their wages to buy into the emerging Taiwanese land tenure system.

Whatever their occupation or status before the move, the newcomers included a disproportionate share of young single males, particularly during the early part of the century when almost all migration was illegal. Facing the obstacles they did—the official ban, the aborigines, the malarial climate—they must have been a particularly lawless, venturesome, and hardy lot. Nothing less would do. As in the Chinese migration to southeast Asia, the move to Taiwan was selective, sorting out the "galloping guests" from the "rice-pot keeping turtles," as the stay-at-homes were called.[17] Last but not least, they all shared the distinctive skills and values of their native region, "the drive, industriousness, and thrifty habits of the Chinese peasant, and, in addition, commercial experience and a heightened appreciation of the value of money."[18]

Land-Opening and Land Tenure

In the opening of a district like Chang-hua, the so-called *k'en-shou* (literally, settler-chief) played a key role. The meaning of the term is best captured by a free translation such as "land developer" or "frontier entrepreneur." From local gazetteers, where their biographies hold an honored place, we obtain portraits of four such men that will illuminate the land-opening process:

(1) Orphaned early but in possession of some means, Yang Chih-shen[19] and his brothers had grown up in Tainan, descendants of Ch'üan-chou immigrants. In the late 1680's, the brothers moved to the Pan-hsien area and rented land from nearby tribes. They improved it through hard work and the building of irrigation facilities. With a growing income, they rented more land and built more *chün* (irrigation canals) toward the north. When the district was formally established, the Yangs were already wealthy and moved to the district city. Yang Chih-shen became a philanthropist and gave land to build a school and a temple. One of his sons bought the rank of prefect, joined the local gentry, and gained merit during the great rebellion of the 1780's. The family remained prominent through the nineteenth century and began to intermarry with the Wu-feng Lins after they, too, had prospered.

(2) A mainlander and perhaps a relative of Admiral Shih Lang, Shih Shih-pang[20] was a lower degree-holder who had served as an educational official in Fukien and in the Peking city administration. Already wealthy, he came to Taiwan and lived first in Feng-shan, where he became a pil-

lar of the community. By 1719 he had moved to Chang-hua and was busy opening land. He gathered large parties of vagrants from the crowded south and moved them to virgin land in southern Chang-hua district. The irrigation facilities he built became part of the *pa-pao-chün* and are said to have provided the Shih family with immense water rents.

(3) A Hakka from Kwangtung, Chang Ta-ching[21] came to Taiwan at the age of twenty, around 1710. A "guest" of the An-li tribe, he married the chief's daughter and became the tribal interpreter (*t'ung-shih*). In the 1720's he acquired land in the northern tip of the Upper Valley, presumably from the An-li tribe, which had received huge extra allotments as a reward for military service. Chang and the An-li chieftain rented land to Chinese settlers and constructed irrigation works, including the Hu-lu-tun *chün*. Among the newcomers were two of Chang's brothers and probably many other Hakkas, for the area soon became a Hakka enclave. Rice was grown for export, the Hu-lu-tun brand acquiring fame throughout Taiwan. The Chang family became very wealthy and maintained their influence with the tribal leadership beyond Chang Ta-ching's death in 1773.

(4) A degree-holder from Ch'üan-chou, Wu Lo[22] came to Taiwan around 1750 in the entourage of an official. Impressed by Chang-hua's potential, he turned frontier entrepreneur, acquired large tracts of land, probably through illegal purchase from hard-pressed tribes, summoned tenants, and built irrigation works. His effort centered in the middle and southern part of the Upper Valley. When he had become a rich man, he retired to Chang-hua city, where he built a clan temple, edited the family genealogy, and busied himself with other good works for his clansmen and for higher education. All his thirteen sons were educated men and several earned or purchased degrees.

The admittedly flattering portraits reveal certain com-

mon features. The entrepreneurs were well-off or well-
connected before they turned to land-opening and they
became rich as a result of it. Their main task was to bring
together the three basic elements in land-opening: the land
itself, manpower, and capital. Liquid funds were needed to
pay the tribes for the land, purchase seed grain and live-
stock, make cash loans to the settlers, and finance the irrigation projects.

When an area was first opened, relations between the entrepreneur and the settlers were most likely close; each depended on the other for success. But later, when the entrepreneur moved on to new ventures or retired to a life of
leisure in the district city, he took a less personal interest in
the settlements he had launched. Relations between him
and the settlers became those customary between an absen-
tee landlord and his tenants.

In the early eighteenth century, most settlers must have
come to Chang-hua under the aegis of such *k'en-shou*. But
even then, and particularly toward mid-century, others
came on their own. Middling men, they banded together
on the basis of a common background in the old country.
Thus, we hear of "Chang-chou people," of "Hungs," of
"Hakkas," of "Lis" first establishing a certain village or
opening an area.[23] As long as land could be taken from the
tribes outright or obtained at a small price, such middling
men working in groups did well for themselves. The middle decades of the century were their golden age. Later,
when land was more expensive and the average immigrant
poor, he had to make do with a far more modest place in
Taiwan's emerging land tenure system.

Land tenure arrangements in Chang-hua evolved from
the traditional tenure system of Fukien and the dynamics
of the settlement process.[24] As in mainland Fukien, three
individuals could establish a claim to a given parcel of land.
A kind of chief owner, called the *ta-tsu* (literally, "big rent,"
after the rent he received) paid taxes to the government
and received rent from a secondary owner who was initially

his chief tenant. In Taiwan, *ta-tsu* rights became vested in the tribes or in the frontier entrepreneurs who had bought land from the tribes or been assigned land that became vacant when the tribes were confined to their allotments. At first illegal, Chinese *ta-tsu* ownership spread rapidly in Chang-hua from the 1740's, sanctioned by magistrates who wanted to fatten their tax rolls or perhaps line their own pockets. Individual *ta-tsu* holdings ranged from as much as 300 *chia* in the case of an entrepreneur like Wu Lo to around three *chia*, still a tidy little farm by mainland standards.[25] Mostly, *ta-tsu* titles remained in the families that had initially acquired them, though they could be bought and sold.[26] Tribal *ta-tsu* rights were less stable. The chiefs often mismanaged and finally lost tribal lands. While government insisted that tribal landlords receive the same land rent as Chinese *ta-tsu* owners, and many nineteenth-century land deeds still recognize tribal *ta-tsu* claims, we may doubt that rent was always paid.[27]

Moving down one step in the three-tier system, the secondary owners (called *hsiao-tsu*, "small rent," after the rent they received) were originally the *ta-tsu*'s tenants. They rented directly from a tribe or a frontier entrepreneur. But in the course of the eighteenth century such men acquired most of the attributes of full ownership: their right to the land became permanent, subject only to the payment of *ta-tsu* rent, and they could sell their *hsiao-tsu* titles or sublet the land to others.[28] This upgrading of the initial tenant to almost full ownership must have occurred after the entrepreneurs moved away or retired or when the tribal landlords retreated.

In contrast to the *ta-tsu* rights, the *hsiao-tsu* titles changed hands constantly as these tenures were freely bought and sold. This made the system flexible and allowed it to adapt to the changing needs of the settlers. Early on, for instance, *hsiao-tsu* titles could be obtained by poor but hard-working settlers simply in return for cultivating the land and paying the *ta-tsu* rent. The tribes, it is true, often charged a fee for allowing the settlers to cultivate their land, but such cultivation permits for virgin land were reasonably priced before the last third of the century, costing twelve to fifteen *Taels** per *chia* when land prices in Fukien were ten times as high.[29] As the district became more crowded and the virgin land was converted to paddy, however, *hsiao-tsu* titles rose in price. From the 1770's, we find such tenures selling for over 100 *Taels* per *chia*.[30] Such a sum was beyond the means of the ordinary immigrant, and *hsiao-tsu* titles were now more often bought by wealthy businessmen or officials who sought a safe and respectable investment.

It was the poor immigrants of the late eighteenth century who rented land from the now upgraded *hsiao-tsu* landlords. Working farmers, they became the tenants (*tien-jen*) at the bottom rank of the three-tier ladder.[31] The parcels available were often quite large (five *chia* was a standard size in portions of the Upper Valley) and came with houses, sheds, stables, seedbeds, gardens, bamboo palisades, and tools. Three-year leases were customary and could be had for a small rent deposit and a rent of about half the crop. Onerous as it was, tenant status provided a livelihood for the great number of migrants who poured into the district in the last third of the century. A Japanese scholar dates it from the 1770's.[32]

The tenants' labor provided handsome incomes for the landlords. The after-tax income of a *ta-tsu* holder was about five *Taels* per *chia*, while the *hsiao-tsu* owner cleared ten to twenty *Taels* per *chia*. From his nearly 300 *chia* a land developer like Wu Lo might collect a net income of about 1,500 *Taels*, while a *hsiao-tsu* owner could retire to a life of leisure if he owned as much as a tenth of such an estate. The sheer size of such incomes must be stressed. In a country where the per capita income of commoners was

---

* The *Tael* was a Chinese unit of account equivalent to an ounce of monetary silver.

around six *Taels* per year, Chang-hua's frontier landlordism provided princely incomes for a few, moderate com-
fort for many.[33]

Self-Reliance and Group Solidarity

Since government frowned on Taiwan's rapid colonization,
the initiative for settlement was, perforce, private. Defying
government writ, invading forbidden territory, despoiling
the tribes by hook or crook, the settlers were a hardy and
self-reliant lot. But theirs was the self-reliance of the
group, not of the individual. Only by working with his
fellow-settlers could the pioneer succeed.

Safety was a case in point. As the tribes fought back
against the Chinese onslaught, the settlers found safety only
in organized self-defense. Joining together to fortify their
villages with bamboo palisades,[34] they patrolled and stood
watch for each other. To work in the fields, too, the men
went in groups, and armed with knives, daggers, and
matchlocks.[35] Except during major tribal uprisings when
government troops intervened, the settlers were on their
own. Little wonder that they valued martial skills and
group cohesion!

Settlers also worked together to build the irrigation facilities that made their land productive. Government did little
to provide Taiwan with its exceptionally high ratio of irrigated land; it neither built nor owned the facilities nor did
it mobilize corvée labor for their construction.[36] At best,
government provided a legal framework within which private initiative flourished. While the earliest irrigation facilities were often built by frontier entrepreneurs using hired
labor, after mid-century most such construction work was
done by settler groups who pooled their labor.

Where success and even survival depended on such close
cooperation, neighborhoods were not formed by chance
associations of strangers. Rather, new frontier communities grew out of older loyalties developed on the main-

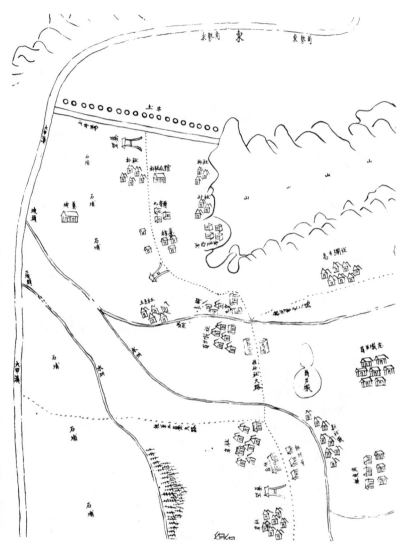

Fig. 1 Irrigation and defense works in northeastern Chang-hua, with "earth cows" and irrigation canals tapping the Ta-chia River. Eighteenth century (Taiwan Museum, Taipei).

land. In the settlers' homeland, Fukien and northeastern Kwangtung, it was the large localized lineage which commanded a man's strongest loyalty, though there was also a tight cohesion based on one's dialect group (Hakka vs. native [*pen-ti*] speakers, for example). Against this mainland background, we note that the large localized lineage did not survive the move to Taiwan.[37] Settlers came as individuals or in small family groups, splinters at most of the larger lineages. In Taiwan they joined with others of the same surname or from the same district or prefecture. The chief bond of solidarity in a frontier district like Chang-hua was therefore not the lineage but the common surname or the common place of origin.

To its bearers, the common surname implied a common, if no longer demonstrable, descent from a joint ancestor and hence a kinship only slightly less close than that of the lineage with its demonstrated descent lines. As a framework for organizing common tasks on the frontier, the surname group or clan was institutionalized in much the same way as the Chinese lineage, through clan temples and endowments to underwrite clan rites or the education of the young. In the Upper Valley, the earliest surname clusters appeared by the middle of the eighteenth century.[38] Lins, for example, gathered in the central sector, around Ta-li-chi, and Hungs farther south, astride the Wu River where it entered the plain. Such clustering did not produce completely homogenous (single-surname) villages, but groups of adjacent villages in which bearers of one surname formed the majority, while other surnames made up lesser segments of the population. In time, people sorted themselves out further and solid surname "turfs" developed.

Surname clusters usually formed within larger groupings based on a common place of origin which I shall call communal groups.[39] As in other parts of Taiwan, such communalism produced a three-way division in Chang-hua. People from Ch'üan-chou predominated along the

coast, those from Chang-chou inland, while Hakkas initially formed small splinters here and there before they
pulled back to a larger enclave in the Upper Valley's northeast. Communal groups, too, became institutionalized early
on. In Chang-hua city itself, communal temples, often dedicated to the patron god of the settlers' native prefecture,
first appeared in the 1730's.[40]

An important source of support for individual settlers,
the surname and communal groups also generated much
tension with their competing claims to land or water. From
the late eighteenth century, they engaged in frequent
armed feuding,[41] a development to which the frontier tradition of armed self-help and the mainland legacy of private feuding no doubt contributed.

The Growth of Trade and Towns

Commerce and manufacturing grew apace with the settlement of Chang-hua. In many Chinese-run shops in tribal
territory, the aborigine trade flourished.[42] The trade in
cash crops expanded even more dramatically. Already in
1741, rice had been exported from Lu-kang. As the Chinese
peasants in the district multiplied, the export of agricultural surpluses became big business. By the early 1780's,
Lu-kang was an official port and sent rice to Fukien and the
Yang-tze delta.[43] In the mountains, Chinese prospected for
gold, silver, and sulphur. Wood-felling became a sizeable
industry; special woods went to the luxury markets of the
mainland, the rest yielding charcoal for local use. In the
plains villages, small entrepreneurs turned out straw
goods, cooking oil, bricks, and natural dyes.[44]

Given the state of the roads, most of the trade went by
water. Products of the interior were floated to the coast on
rafts. In this fashion, even upland areas like the Pu-li basin
in the hill country, settled by the Chinese before the end of
the century, were in touch with the trading centers downstream. Along these trade channels, the number of market

towns grew rapidly and reached almost three dozen early in the nineteenth century.[45] Chang-hua and Lu-kang were in a class by themselves, major commercial centers with several specialized markets. In all these towns, a distinct urban society developed, composed of hundreds of shop-keepers and clerks and the various professions associated with the handling of cargo. At its upper levels, it included the wealthiest businessmen and shipowners, retired *ta-tsu* rentiers, and the members of officialdom.

Had it been a Chinese custom to celebrate such anniver-saries, there might have been no little pointing with pride as Chang-hua celebrated its fiftieth anniversary in 1773.[46] Various public buildings—a modest *yamen*, a Confucian temple, an academy, a variety of Buddhist, Taoist, and primarily communal temples—gave the city an air of dig-nity and permanence. The wall, to be sure, was still the simple bamboo palisade built in 1734. Just over 9,000 feet long, it had four gates and encompassed a space of a third of a square mile. Not until the nineteenth century would Chang-hua receive a masonry wall.

Another measure of the district's urbanity, the growth of a native literati class was a slow business. The examination system had been set up in Chang-hua in 1726 and low-level degree-holders were no doubt graduated. But the district produced few higher literati, no *chin-shih** in the eight-eenth century and only two *chü-jen*† before the 1770's. Thereafter, *chü-jen* graduated with some frequency, though the total pool of native degree-holders remained small compared with an average mainland district.[47]

Chang-hua's urban elite also differed from its mainland counterpart in the private philanthropy it dispensed. Works of filial piety and clan loyalty abounded, as among the retired *ta-tsu* holders we have mentioned. Communal sanctuaries also benefited from the donations of an urban elite that retained close links to the district's basic solidarity

---

* A graduate of the highest, or metropolitan, examination in the Chinese examination system.
† A graduate of the provincial examinations.

groups.[48] By contrast, there were few exertions on behalf
of higher learning and the arts. The city's one academy
had been founded by the magistrate, not by private
donors.[49] Intellectual and artistic endeavors must have
seemed frivolous to an upper class that was still little removed from the pragmatism and materialism of the wider
society. For the educated outsider, like the district magistrate, Chang-hua was no doubt still a cultural wasteland.
Only its earliest pioneers could measure how far it had
come in a few decades.

Chang-hua's growth repeated the developmental cycle
of the older Taiwanese districts, and perhaps of districts
along the entire southern frontier in centuries past. In a
process as old as Chinese history, this "race of pioneers"
(the phrase is René Grousset's)[50] has always displaced or
assimilated alien groups. As new communities grew up,
they diversified. An upper class, grounded in landlordism
and trade, began to participate in the empire's higher culture. Contributing native sons to the empire's pool of
higher degree-holders, a new district slowly fused with the
older regions of China. Peasant-settlers, on their part,
brought terraced fields and wayside shrines to sinicize the
frontier landscape.

But to say that Chang-hua became more Chinese in the
course of the eighteenth century is not to say that it became
more orderly or peaceful. The locale and timing of the
frontier experience, not to mention the legacy of turbulence from the southeast coast, worked against such stabil-
ity. On an island, the outreach of the central government
was bound to be weaker, the settlers' penchant for direct
action less restrained. No sooner had the plains tribes been
subdued than the settlers began to fight among themselves.
Nor would the native elite become a stabilizing power as
long as it retained its links to the divisive forces of clanship
and communalism. The prospect, hardly glimpsed at the
time but clear in hindsight, was for continued turbulence.
How the Lin ancestor made out in this land of promise and
peril must now be told.

CHAPTER 4

THE PIONEER

The Rise and Fall of Lin Shih, 1729-1788

*For riches and profit
he came to Taiwan.*[1]

The pioneer ancestor of the Lins was one of the many obscure men who came to Chang-hua in the mid-eighteenth century. We would know nothing of his life had it not been for his famous descendants, who decided to compile a genealogy with suitable ancestral biographies. For even as such men turned this frontier land into a recognizably Chinese landscape, their lives were not remembered in the local gazetteers.

We know little of Lin Shih's beginnings. He was born in 1729 in P'ing-ho district in Chang-chou prefecture, back from the sea and on the Kwangtung border.[2] It was a raw enough district by mainland standards (only two hundred years old), whose turbulence foreshadowed that of the Taiwan frontier. P'ing-ho's mountainous terrain bristled with fortified settlements and "every man [was] a warrior";[3] each lineage occupied "a well-marked piece of land and the clansmen [fought] and [robbed] one another from generation to generation." While Shih's native village, "Fifth Stockade Market" in P'u-p'ing-she, cannot be identified, it was most likely a localized lineage village.

Shih's forebears had lived in Chang-chou prefecture for centuries, yet his immediate family was undistinguished enough, though probably not poor. They made the boy help with farm chores, but could spare enough to give him a simple education. Then disaster struck. Both parents died, between Shih's tenth and twelfth year, leaving him and two younger brothers in the care of the paternal grandmother. In a family of modest means, such a loss plunged the survivors into poverty. The next few years were hard, though Shih took the setbacks well and matured quickly. "In his relations to those above and below him [the grandmother and the brothers], he surpassed even an adult."

While he discharged family duties faithfully enough, Shih, like many orphan boys, yearned to escape from his straitened circumstances. In a district that was tied to the trading network of the southeast coast, he had no doubt ample opportunity to learn about the fortunes that could be made overseas. Clearly, though, there was a conflict between his urge to go and his duty to stay. His descendants plainly admired both his independence and his filial piety. "When seventeen years old, he teamed up with companions and crossed over to Taiwan. . . . He was planning to open land and settle down. Later, a letter from [the grandmother] arrived and he immediately returned home." For another few years, he took care of her and the brothers, but he resisted all attempts to tie him down, refusing, for example, to marry. When the grandmother died, nothing could hold him any longer. "Ordering his two brothers to guard the family tomb, he went forth alone, full of determination." The year was 1754.

Shih's repeated crossings to Taiwan—in 1754, and again in 1757, when he went back to fetch his brothers, the migration was banned—underline the futility of the official prohibitions. But though it was possible to evade the ban, the voyage held other perils, as a Ch'ing folk ballad reveals

> He heads straight for the seashore
> To sneak across from the province
> Undaunted by the tiny boat

Since life and death are predestined.
He carries dry food
Sweet potatoes, dried turnips;
Of ten men aboard
Nine are seasick.
They beg for water, rinse their mouths,
The captain flies into a rage.
With Heaven's help
They soon reach Taiwan
And climb ashore under cover of night.[4]

Once safely ashore, a newcomer set out in search of friends or relatives who helped him get a start. Unlike the wretched fellow in the ballad ("In the four directions, not a relative; hungry and cold, he is in sore need."), Lin Shih must have had help, for he was soon on his feet. He spent some time in Chang-hua city,[5] perhaps in day labor that allowed him to accumulate savings. In the sparsely populated district, wages were good and attracted many a newcomer whose ultimate aim was to own his own farm.

Years of Fulfillment

Before long, surely by 1757 when he fetched his brothers, Shih had moved on and found the land he wanted. It was in Ta-li-chi in Sung-tung tithing, a new village near the center of the Upper Valley which probably already contained more Lins (including several from P'ing-ho) than people of other surnames.[6] The setting and Shih's mood are deftly sketched in his biography: "Just beyond the village, the high mountains rose and the rivers criss-crossed; the native aborigines owned [the land] and each time they came down, they killed people. Shih bought land and tilled it, regulated the ditches and dikes, and established dividing strips. He tilled his fields and used his weapons as a pillow."

The reference to Shih's land acquisition is perhaps intentionally vague, or else the details had become blurred in

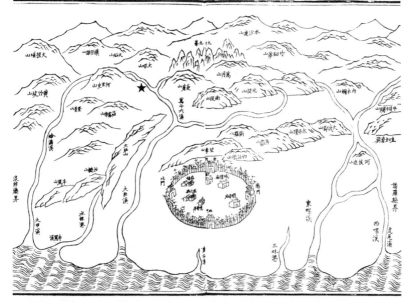

Fig. 2 Chang-hua district at the time of Lin Shih's first visit. The approximate location of Ta-li-chi has been starred (*T'ai-wan fu-chih*, 1747, Library of Congress).

the minds of the twentieth-century authors. We know that the villagers of Ta-li-chi were an aggressive lot, encroaching on the lands of even the mighty An-li tribe which extended to the vicinity.[7] Shih may well have acquired his land by seizure or through some form of "squatting" rather than through formal purchase. Whether he ultimately established *ta-tsu* rights or worked out *hsiao-tsu* arrangements with the aborigines is uncertain, but he was clearly not of tenant status.

Almost from the start, things worked out well for Lin Shih. When he brought his brothers over, the finality of the move to Taiwan was underlined: the brothers took their parents' bodies along with them for reburial in Taiwan. Three young men in their prime, the Lin brothers must have been able to seize, guard, and till more land. Briefly, they maintained a common household and may have held their land jointly. But this arrangement broke up when they married, starting with the eldest, Shih. For once, the genealogy provides us with a marriage date (1760), probably because Shih's advanced age of thirty-one appeared noteworthy to the early-marrying descendants who compiled his life story. Shih's wife, a Miss Ch'en, was fourteen years his junior, but whether she was Taiwan-born or from the mainland we do not learn. "The two brothers also took wives, one after another. Each managed his own affairs, and their property grew from day to day." The brothers' prospects must have looked good indeed if all three of them found wives so quickly in an age when bachelors still outnumbered eligible girls on the frontier.

The 1760's and 1770's were the golden years of Lin Shih's life. Strong and determined, he worked his land and overcame all obstacles. "He was strong and would not yield," the descendants report. "In the end, he had success."

Lin Shih's success had several dimensions. For one, he became exceedingly prosperous in a thriving corner of the district. By the late 1770's, he owned enough land to rent much of it to tenant farmers[8] and he probably withdrew from work in the fields himself. If his income was even a tenth of what the genealogy reports (a round ten thousand piculs* of rice, equivalent to ten thousand *Taels*), he must have been able to live most comfortably on his rental income. Following a suggestion by his eldest son, he "summoned merchants to come,"[9] and traded with them, probably in grain. For this, too, Ta-li-chi was a promising spot. Located on a tributary of the Ta-tu river, it became a trans-shipment point and by the 1780's was one of the Upper Valley's four major villages and a flourishing market.[10] The term "chi" in the place name refers to a stake that was driven into the ground at the river edge where boats tied up while loading and unloading.

---

* The picul was a unit of weight equivalent to 133⅓ lbs.

With wealth came esteem in the eyes of Lin Shih's peers. Typically, the genealogy attributes both the wealth and the good name to a sterling character that was not spoiled by success. "The harvest entering the granary reached 10,000 piculs. At the same time, [Shih] was charitable and by nature kind. When it unfortunately happened that a crop was poor, he would at once open his granary and extend aid. Among the people in the neighborhood, there was not a one whom he failed to help." He also became a moneylender, perhaps again under the influence of his sharp-eyed eldest son, and this inevitably made him enemies as well as friends; but their baleful influence would not become apparent for some time.

Another dimension of Shih's success was the steady growth of his family. Six sons were born between 1762 and 1776 and perhaps several daughters as well, though the agnatically oriented genealogy tells us nothing about them. The survival of the mother and of so many children in the disease-ridden island—the genealogy records no deaths at an early age—testifies to their good fortune if not their stamina.

There are few additional facts to flesh out the bare bones of this story. We may wonder what Shih wanted for his sons. Were they to become well-to-do frontier landlords? Were they to aim higher? Among the sons, the genealogy emphasizes the eldest, Sun, reportedly the father's favorite.[11] Since it was Sun's descendants who compiled the genealogy, this emphasis is not surprising; but Shih may well have preferred this son, whose business acumen and foresight balanced Shih's own more stolid nature. Sun appears as an adroit, resourceful young man in the few episodes that tell of his brief life. The other sons and Shih's wife remain shadowy characters. Only the turbulent 1780's were to reveal some facets of their character.

Shih's brothers also fade into the background. Nothing more is heard of them in Shih's biography and they have no biographies of their own. Even the birth and death dates of their offspring are not preserved in the genealogy beyond a generation or two, suggesting that the families of the brothers drifted apart, though not perhaps in Shih's own lifetime. If the genealogy loses sight of the brothers, it provides a clue to the kinds of families with which Shih's offspring intermarried. Already a father at eighteen, Lin Sun must have married by 1780. This early marriage would testify to the Lins' affluence even if we know nothing about the background of his bride. But because this matter played a role in family history later, we are told that she was the daughter of a clerk in the sea-defense prefecture in Lu-kang, a member of the powerful sub-bureaucracy.[12] Clearly, Lin Shih's eldest was a most eligible young man.

The Chinese have long thought that good and bad times follow each other in a regular cycle. As if to confirm this belief, the early 1780's brought ominous changes in Lin Shih's world. Tension between Chang-hua's communal groups had been growing for some time and early in the decade it flared into open violence. Ta-li-chi was not directly involved at first. A Hakka element in the village had either moved away earlier or retreated in 1782 when Hakkas and Fukienese came to blows in the neighboring Mao-lo tithing to the south.[13] More serious to the people of Ta-li-chi was the growing strife between the Chang-chou and Ch'üan-chou elements. Though Ta-li-chi appears to have been solidly Chang-chou, other villages nearby were not, and trade with the largely Ch'üan-chou people from the coast also allowed friction to develop. At first, cooler heads in the village prevailed and conflict was avoided. The genealogy credits the young Sun with a valuable initiative: after summoning merchants, it explains, "he took the lead in establishing a local pact. They relied on it to maintain peace." Such community pacts (*hsiang-yüeh*),[14] well-known from the strife-torn southeastern mainland, were sometimes imposed by the government; they were most effective when concluded at the villagers' own initiative, as seems to have been the case here. In the long run, however, such efforts were unavailing. Tension between the two groups mounted after a bloody incident at a gambling spot outside Chang-hua city in 1782.[15] More ominous still, the government intervened on the Ch'üan-chou side, transforming a communal feud into an affair of state. If Chang-chou settlers persisted in armed violence, they would find themselves branded as rebels.

When Lin Shih and his eldest son saw that "the cruel flames had already spread [from the district city] and reason could not extinguish them,"[16] they decided to prepare against the conflagration. At Sun's suggestion, Shih allowed him to return to P'ing-ho with a good many of the family's assets. The idea was "not to risk losing everything in Taiwan" and perhaps to prepare for the family's evacuation. Accordingly, Sun bought land and a house in P'ing-ho. But there disaster struck: "the way of Heaven is inscrutable. He suddenly fell ill and died . . . having attained the age of twenty-one." Shih evidently abandoned plans for a return to the mainland, clinging with his characteristic tenacity to the place that had been good to him. Here, deprived of his eldest son's prudent counsel, he faced the final crisis of his life—entanglement in one of the major rebellions of the eighteenth century.

The Lin Shuang-wen Rebellion

Before examining Lin Shih's unhappy fate in the rebellion, we should provide a brief explanation of its course and background. As the long reign of Ch'ien-lung drew to a close, China entered a time of troubles. The White Lotus Rebellion (1796-1804) is often seen as the overture to a century of anti-Ch'ing rebellion, but the Lin Shuang-wen rising, while smaller in scope, could serve as well. Its magnitude needs to be stressed. To subdue the rebels, 100,000 troops had to be sent to the island, led by some of the empire's renowned commanders, such as Fu-k'ang-an.[17] The emperor himself celebrated the pacification as one of the "ten great triumphs" of his reign, a back-handed compli-

ment for the obscure Ta-li-chi villager who now ranked
with Ch'ien-lung's great foes, the Eleuths, Burmese, and
Gurkhas.[18]

In the history of Chinese rebellions, the rising is often
listed as the earliest in which the *T'ien-ti-hui* (Heaven and
Earth Society, or Triads) played the major role. When
Triad members later joined Sun Yat-sen's revolutionary
movement, Lin Shuang-wen was even enrolled in the
pantheon of modern nationalist heroes,[19] a misleading
perspective not shared by the Lin family chroniclers. The
antecedents of the Lin Shuang-wen rebellion must be
sought not in modern nationalism or class warfare but in
the bloody communal feuds that had begun to trouble the
island. The *T'ien-ti-hui* itself had initially appealed to its
members as a framework for communal self-defense. Immigrants from P'ing-ho had brought it in 1783 to mid-
Taiwan, where the Chang-chou settlers of the Upper Valley espoused it in the aftermath of the recent bloody feud
with the Ch'üan-chou group. Since government had sided
with their rivals, the Chang-chou people took no umbrage
at the anti-dynastic program of the secret society.[20]

The rebel leader's background also underlines the close
nexus between communal feuding and rebellion. A man
from P'ing-ho like Lin Shih, Shuang-wen had become a
wealthy landlord in Ta-li-chi.[21] During the troubles with
the Ch'üan-chou settlers, he led an armed contingent;
later, he was among the first to welcome the *T'ien-ti-hui* to
Chang-hua and became one of its leaders. The mid-1780's
continued to be turbulent in the Upper Valley, a time when
a leader of fighting men like Lin Shuang-wen could attain
great power. Communal groups battled each other and, in
Ta-li-chi, Lins were involved in several armed incidents
which verged on rebellion.[22] Thus, the villagers gave shelter to political outlaws from Chu-lo and killed the official
who attempted to prosecute the case. As the scale of violence widened, the *T'ien-ti-hui* broadened its organization,
particularly while the officials temporarily ignored the so-

ciety and allowed it to grow. Then, as so often with Chinese
rebellions, a belated attempt to suppress the society goaded
it into open revolt.

Rising in late 1786, the rebels quickly seized Chang-hua
and Chu-lo cities. While Chu-lo was recaptured in the
spring (during its subsequent siege, Ch'ien-lung bestowed
the name Chia-yi, Commendable Loyalty, on the city), most
of Chang-hua district remained in rebel hands. The rebel
leaders called for the overthrow of the Ch'ing and the restoration of the Ming, but rebel actions seldom followed
such lofty political maxims. We hear of much burning and
looting of Hakka and Ch'üan-chou villages by the rebels,
another indication that the rebellion merely extended the
communal violence of earlier years. In the entire district,
government forces retained only Lu-kang, the port city
with an overwhelmingly Ch'üan-chou population.[23]

After much bickering among the generals and the despatch of further reenforcements, government troops made
headway against the rebels in late 1787. They lifted the
siege of Chia-yi and then moved against Lin Shuang-wen.
Surrendering Chang-hua, the rebel leader retreated to the
heavily fortified Ta-li-chi. After some time, its triple defenses of wall, moat, and bamboo hedge were breached.[24]
Shuang-wen escaped into the mountains, but was caught
and sent to Peking for execution. The rebellion ended in
the spring of 1788.

To have one's native village turned into a rebel redoubt
and leveled by imperial troops was bad enough; to be a
kinsman of the rebel leader could prove fatal. The precise
relationship between Lin Shih and Lin Shuang-wen cannot
now be ascertained, but everything points to a tie even
closer than the clanship implied in the common surname
and the common P'ing-ho background. Like other rebel
relatives, the Wu-feng Lins may have expunged Shuang-
wen from the genealogy to disguise a relationship that
would have done them little credit when the work was
being compiled. But if the genealogical tables were altered,

Shih's biography hints all the more strongly of a close family tie.[25] Today, many of Shih's descendants admit that the bonds were close, though they differ in calling the rebel leader a younger brother, a nephew, or a generic "cousin" of their ancestor.

As the story unfolds in Shih's biography, the ancestor became entangled through his kinship tie and the denunciation by an envious informer. The sequence of events conveys a sense of doom, as of an inexorable fate frustrating his efforts to escape. These attempts began with an effort to talk Shuang-wen out of rebelling. "When Shih heard about [the plot], he was greatly alarmed and sighed, saying, 'This will destroy our clan [tsu]; it must not be allowed to happen.' He then went to Shuang-wen to stop it, but Shuang-wen would not listen." When Shuang-wen, finally persuaded by Shih, tried to call off the uprising, the ardor of his followers carried him away and he plunged into the rebellion—a detail as unverifiable as Lin Shih's warning itself.[26]

Once the rebellion had broken out, Shih's family decided to escape to the mainland. But this plan, too, went awry. Before taking ship, Shih "ordered all the women to visit their parental homes and take leave of their fathers and mothers. Now the eldest son's widow, Mrs. Huang, had a father who was a clerk in the office of the assistant prefect for sea-defense in Lu-kang. Because his son-in-law had died young, the father could not bear to see his daughter move so far away. He sent in a petition to the assistant prefect to forbid their leaving the harbor."[27] With mid-Taiwan in turmoil, the family was unable to reach other ports because "to the north and south, everywhere there were disturbances, the roads were blocked, and they could not get through." Desperate, Lin Shih went into hiding in loyalist Lu-kang, apparently allowing his family to remain in Ta-li-chi. The logic of this decision is hard to fathom, for as long as his family was in rebel-held territory, Shih himself could not espouse the government side for fear of repris-

als. Yet nothing but an open avowal of loyalty now promised safety to a rebel kinsman during the coming reckoning.[28]

All might have gone well even so, had not a disgruntled
neighbor denounced Shih. Soon after Ta-li-chi was taken
by the imperial forces, one Ho Ao, at odds with Shih over
money matters,[29] "spied out [his] hiding place and told the
investigating authorities about it, saying: 'This Lin is of
the same clan [tsung] as Shuang-wen and has concealed
much property. You can get hold of it to your own benefit.'" Shih was tracked down and arrested. Again un-
verified, the detail rings true, for it was indeed a time when
men settled old scores and informers reaped their rewards.
In central Taiwan, many Lins fell victim to the crackdown
simply because they shared the rebel leader's surname.[30]

The final months of Lin Shih's life were grim. Kept in a
Lu-kang jail, he must have feared for his life and the well-
being of his family. When word of his plight reached them,
his fourteen-year-old son, Ta, joined Shih in prison, a
common arrangement in China which allowed the young
man to minister to his father's need.[31] "He respectfully
served him food and drink and he wailed and wept to
compassionate Heaven. He himself wanted to take the first
ancestor's place. But before many months had passed, Ta
fell ill and died. Without ceremony, they buried him in
Lu-kang-pu."

If this display of filial piety did nothing to soften official
hearts, help of sorts came from an unlikely source, the
rebel leader himself. In another unverifiable detail, the
genealogy reports that Shuang-wen, in his confession,
spoke of Shih's attempt to dissuade him from rebelling.
"The crowd all wanted me to be king and to be rich in
wealth and honor," he is supposed to have said, "only a certain clansman [tsu-jen] reasoned vigorously with me that I
should not [get involved]." As a result, General Fu-k'ang-
an is said to have ordered Shih released and his property
restored. It is an unlikely story, for Fu-k'ang-an was any-

thing but scrupulous or fair.[32] There may have been a more modest vindication when Shih was released from jail—perhaps he bribed his way out of it. But release from prison could at most restore his good name; it could not restore his broken health and spirit. "On the day he left prison, he fell ill and died in an inn. He was given temporary burial outside the district city."

The pioneer's fate epitomized both the opportunities and the dangers of the frontier world in which he chose to make his way. The early days gave him everything that men sought in Taiwan: ample land, great wealth, a healthy and flourishing family. But the very forces that brought a man success—the tight group spirit, the grasping for wealth, the ready use of force against the weak—brought disaster when turned inward, group against group among the settlers. The kinship ties that eased a pioneer's early days proved his undoing in the end.

The pioneer ancestor's life revealed some other unexpected ironies. If Chang-hua developed into a recognizably Chinese society, it was due to men like Lin Shih and what they wrought, usually without government support and often in the teeth of official prohibitions. In a frontier setting where government appeared relatively weak in relation to the vigorous pioneers, Lin Shih's fate warned that the settlers did not have the last word after all. Fitfully exercised though it might be, ultimate authority still rested with the state. When we consider the Lin family's role during Taiwan's next great rebellion, in the 1860's, it seems that Shih's descendants drew some such cautionary lesson from their ancestor's fate. On the morrow of the Lin Shuang-wen rebellion, they faced the very question of survival itself.

CHAPTER 5

A NEW BEGINNING

The Second and Third Generation, 1788-1839

*The orphans endured hunger and cold in order
to rebuild the fortunes of the family.*[1]

Dispersal and recovery marked the family's history during
the next half century. After the swift turns of fortune in
the pioneer ancestor's life, the cycle now turned more
slowly. There was a modest recovery for most of the survivors, wealth for a few. Moreover, Lin Shih's descendants
dispersed over several villages in the Upper Valley. As we
survey them, our attention will come to rest on the Wu-
feng branch. By 1839, these Lins were almost as wealthy as
their ancestor had been. That they had come this far and
nursed yet higher ambitions reflected their own drive as
much as the changing opportunities of the mid-nineteenth
century.

When Shih was first arrested, "the family members became scattered like stars."[2] Emerging from their hiding
places, the survivors found Ta-li-chi in ruins and moved to
T'u-ch'eng, some two miles to the southeast. On higher
ground, it was not as fertile as Ta-li-chi, but for that very
reason still had virgin land.[3] Its closeness to the mountains
must also have attracted a family that was still under a political cloud. If they were wanted by the government, the Lins
could readily slip away into the mountains.

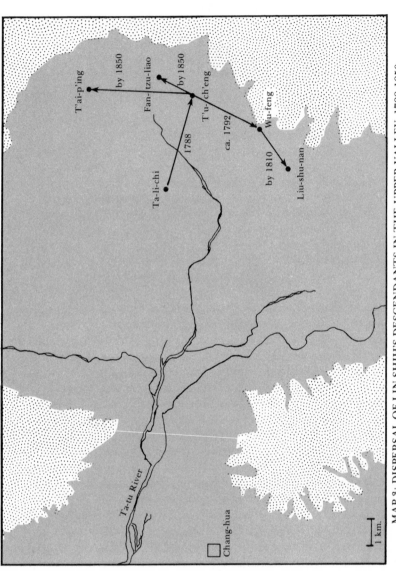

MAP 3: DISPERSAL OF LIN SHIH'S DESCENDANTS IN THE UPPER VALLEY, 1788-1850

The survivors included Shih's widow, forty-five years old, four remaining sons and perhaps some unmarried daughters and daughters-in-law, for the older sons had been old enough, before disaster struck, to have married. There was also the twenty-six-year-old widow of Lin Sun, with her two boys. When the family had fled from Ta-li-chi, she and the children had become separated from the others. They "had stolen away into a deserted valley. When thirsty, they had drunk from the rivers and when hungry, they had gathered wild herbs and sweet potatoes. Out under the open sky, exposed to the elements, they had climbed over mountains and through valleys, wearing out their shoes and bruising their feet."[4] All three survived, as if by a miracle, for "it was a time when nine out of ten perished." Reunited at last in T'u-ch'eng, the survivors made it through the next few years of hardship. There was a food shortage, inflation, and mounting debt in mid-Taiwan, and the Lins must have had their share of these troubles.[5] A new rebellion broke out in 1795, again inspired by the *T'ien-ti-hui*, but it was brought under control without affecting the family directly.

Under the Matriarch's Shadow

From Lin Shih's death in 1788 to her own death nearly forty years later, Mrs. Ch'en was the dominant figure in the family.[6] A woman of strong vitality and deep feelings, she emerged as the first of several formidable matriarchs in the Lin family. Two powerful emotions ruled her long widowhood: a deep hatred for her eldest daughter-in-law and a fierce determination to have her sons recover the wealth that had been lost. In the matriarch's hates and hopes we find a clue to the dispersal and recovery of the survivors.

When young Mrs. Huang first rejoined the others, relations were superficially amicable. The brothers-in-law helped out, "succouring the orphans because Mrs. Huang did not remarry. . . . They set aside a field of thirty piculs and gave it to her."[7] In truth, what the genealogy pictures as a fraternal gesture may well have been a first division of the remaining family estate, a step on the way to independence for all of Shih's offspring. If the others still maintained a common household for some time, Mrs. Huang and her children were no longer part of it. She may have been difficult to live with: "others too had harsh words for her at the time," the genealogy delicately hints. But the driving force behind separation was clearly the matriarch. Here, the genealogy minces few words: "Mrs. Ch'en meanwhile bore Mrs. Huang a deep hatred. . . . Leading her sons, Mrs. Huang thereupon established a separate residence in Wu-feng village." To make the break final, the matriarch decreed a ban on Lin-Huang marriages which her descendants (except for the Wu-feng branch) observed for three generations.[8]

What accounts for the depth of the matriarch's hatred is hard to say. The genealogy states that she blamed Mrs. Huang for her father's intervention, which had frustrated the family's escape plans at the start of the rebellion. But it is as plausible to assume that the two women had already quarreled earlier, and that it was this older tension which had led Mr. Huang to veto his daughter's exodus. Whatever the circumstances, the rift opened by this quarrel was wide and would take long to heal. At the same time, the episode throws light on the moral climate of Taiwan. In a society where men sought blood revenge, the matriarch's open hatred only added to her moral stature.

If she repudiated one branch of the family, the matriarch must have been gratified by the growth of the other branches. Though survived by only one of her six sons, she could, before her death, take pride in her nine grandsons and fourteen great-grandsons. With so many sturdy shoots, the survival if not the greatness of Lin Shih's line was assured.

The matriarch's death in 1826 and the other deaths of older family members (Shih's brothers were long dead, their widows died in 1824 and 1828) made this decade a watershed in family history.[9] All those with personal memories of the early pioneer days—the hard-won affluence, the final disaster—now passed from the scene. Even the second generation was thinning out. Shih's last surviving son died in 1830, and five years later the ancestress of the Wu-feng branch, Mrs. Huang, also died. While the old wounds did not heal right away, the deaths of these immediate participants in the old quarrel offered at least a chance for future reconciliation. When peace was made later, it involved, significantly, the two most prosperous branches among Lin Shih's descendants, those at T'ai-p'ing and at Wu-feng. Before we turn to the Wu-feng branch, we must briefly chart the economic fortunes of the others.

The matriarch's hopes for economic recovery were only partly fulfilled. For some time after the end of the rebellion, the mirage of recovering Shih's confiscated lands haunted the survivors. Some believed that the family could simply rely on Fu-k'ang-an's word; others thought that a bribe would take care of the problem. But after the rebellion and the two funerals (Shih's and Ta's), the family had no funds with which to pay a bribe. The matter thus "dragged on for months and years, the high and the low cheating each other. In the end, the property was not returned."[10]

How much the family lost is hard to say. Some family members and officials in Ta-li-chi believe that Shih owned between seventy and a hundred *chia*, and other estimates go even higher.[11] The lower figure is probably more accurate, but even so the loss was stupendous. It is indirectly confirmed by the unusually high proportion of government-owned land in nineteenth-century Ta-li-chi, land that was initially private property but was confiscated in the wake of the Lin Shuang-wen rebellion. Local officials maintain that as late as the twentieth century the Lins still viewed some of this land as rightfully theirs though they evidently refrained from formally asking for its return.

What remained, then, was some small amount of land that had escaped registration, and hence confiscation,[12] and whatever the sons might win through new pioneer efforts. Under the watchful eye of the matriarch, who "spurred on her sons to concentrate on the recovery of the property," they pursued their fortunes along different lines.[13] The second son, who died young at sea, may have abandoned farming altogether and tried his luck in business or seafaring. The third and sixth sons worked on the land, the latter also dying young. Their descendants remained mostly in T'u-ch'eng and a few later moved to Fan-tzu-liao, a mile farther east. A century after the pioneer ancestor's death, these branches comprised many modest peasant households and a few well-to-do landlords, if we can judge by the concubines that a number of them were able to afford.

Marked success came only to Ti, the fourth son. He must have been wealthy by the 1820's, when a private tutor educated his youngest son.[14] Whether in Ti's lifetime or later, a segment of this branch moved to T'ai-p'ing, a market town some two miles north of T'u-ch'eng. Here, they flourished in various businesses and later in land-opening in the hill-country. Other descendants remained in T'u-ch'eng and also did well in various small enterprises, including the sugar business, peanut-oil pressing, and the camphor trade.

The slow economic recovery of Shih's descendants reflected the changing opportunities of the early nineteenth century. In their various moves, these Lins of the second and third generation illustrated the two major directions in which men sought to improve themselves economically. Some pioneered on the remaining stretches of virgin land. In the district, this meant that they moved to higher ground, up the sides of Ta-tu-*shan* or into the eastern hills. On higher, drier ground, their efforts did not repay as handsomely as had Shih's pioneering earlier. Those who stuck to farming in the nineteenth century did not grow rich. The others moved from the land into the towns and engaged in small manufacturing or trade. Mostly, they did better than their country cousins. In the greater reward of a business career as compared with farming we get one indication that a more crowded Taiwan was beginning to resemble the mainland.

The Founder of the Wu-feng Branch

Of all the branches descended from Lin Shih, it was the one at Wu-feng which eventually brought fame to the pioneer ancestor's line. Yet for quite some time, these Lins too remained undistinguished. They played no part, for example, in the founding of Wu-feng. When Mrs. Huang moved there, probably in the early 1790's, the village had been a Chinese settlement for nearly half a century.[15] Its name at the time, A-chao-wu (the name Wu-feng dates only from the 1880's)[16] recalled the locally dominant tribe, the A-shu. In the south central part of the Upper Valley, where aborigine resistance was fiercest, the Wu-feng area was opened late. Only when the government placed a fortified outpost (*yai*, manned by friendly aborigines) in Liu-shu-nan in 1735, did the Wu-feng area attract Chinese settlers. Many groups contributed to its opening: Hakkas, settlers brought in by the entrepreneur Wu Lo, and individual cultivators to whom the A-shu rented directly. Lins from Ta-li-chi are said to have come early too. From the late 1750's, the fledgling settlement began to benefit from the exertions of another group, the Hungs of Ts'ao-t'un. Settled astride the Wu River where it entered the plain, the Hungs tapped the river water and extended a *chün* as far north as Wu-feng, where the villagers presumably made the usual rental arrangements.[17]

When Mrs. Huang arrived, Wu-feng must have been a solidly Chang-chou village, though of mixed surname. Among its inhabitants, Lins may already have dominated. The villagers' economic mainstay was agriculture, though some felled trees and produced charcoal in the hills. Such produce as the villagers wanted to sell could be taken to either of two markets, Liu-shu-nan to the west or Ta-li-chi to the north.[18] The physical appearance of the village underlined its frontier character. The people clustered in three bamboo palisades to which new ones were added as the village grew. Not until 1900, when the Japanese took the bamboo hedges down, did the separate palisades coalesce into a single continuous village.[19]

Mrs. Huang settled in what was then the most recent, or third, palisade. Later, many would say that she had chosen well, for to the local people it was the geomancy of this site which explained the exceptional fortunes of her descendants.[20] On the northern edge of the modern Wu-feng, this area still forms a separate hamlet today where the bus from Taichung makes its last stop before coming to the center of Wu-feng itself. In recent times, this hamlet has been called Chia-yin-*ts'un*, after Mrs. Huang's second son. Yet when the Lins arrived, a poor family with at best a few local contacts, no one thought of naming anything after them.

Whatever their ultimate good fortune, the Wu-feng branch found the early years difficult. "They built a flimsy cottage to shelter from wind and rain, [and] . . . endured hunger and cold."[21] In moving away, Mrs. Huang may have forfeited the claim to the thirty-picul field that had been assigned to her earlier. Then, too, her sons may have found it hard to get a start. Contemporary records imply that many young men did not readily find work in either farming or a trade.[22] The older of the two, Ch'ung-yao, moved away after some time to the larger Liu-shu-nan. How he fared we do not know; a century later, his descendants were middling farmers or small shopkeepers, on quite a different level from Chia-yin's mighty offspring.[23] Ritual relations between the two sub-branches continued, in keeping with the amicable relations among the brothers of which the genealogy speaks. But these ties were loose at best—there was no joint ritual trust for the common forefather, Sun, no biography for Ch'ung-yao in the genealogy, nor a seat for his descendants on the editorial committee. Ch'ung-yao's seniority yielded to Chia-yin's success.

Chia-yin (born in 1782) had begun humbly enough, as a small-time peddler between Wu-feng and Ta-li-chi.[24] If we follow the genealogy, his rise to wealth began with a miracle. The local soil god appeared to him in a dream one night and promised him the twelve gold pieces that were hidden under his seat in the near-by temple. A reward for the young man's sincerity and filial conduct, the capital helped Chia-yin to broaden his trading ventures. "Wherever he turned, he made a profit." He tried his hand at many things. "When he went up into the mountain region, produce was abundant. He felled trees and produced charcoal, and again reaped a profit." With enough wealth from trade, Chia-yin turned to land-opening in this still backward corner of the district. "At that time, Wu-feng was still aborigine territory. The soil was rich but the barbarians were dull and lazy, unable to till the land. The fields in the plain were rich, but abandoned to grass and wilderness. He bought land and opened it up and his annual income gradually grew."[25]

By the 1830's Chia-yin's wealth and standing nearly rivaled that of his grandfather before the rebellion. "The harvest he reaped was at least four thousand *Taels*." Still, "he remained diligent and frugal, wearing cotton clothes and eating vegetarian food. In his love of virtue he was unceasing. Among the neighbors, there was not a one who did not praise him." His wife, described as a paragon of female virtue, "assisted her husband and taught her sons. Thus they were able to lay a firm foundation for the family."

Chia-yin was indeed the founder of a famous line, though there is reason to believe that his domestic situation was not as placid as the genealogy claims. For one thing, in late 1837 "he ordered all his sons to establish separate

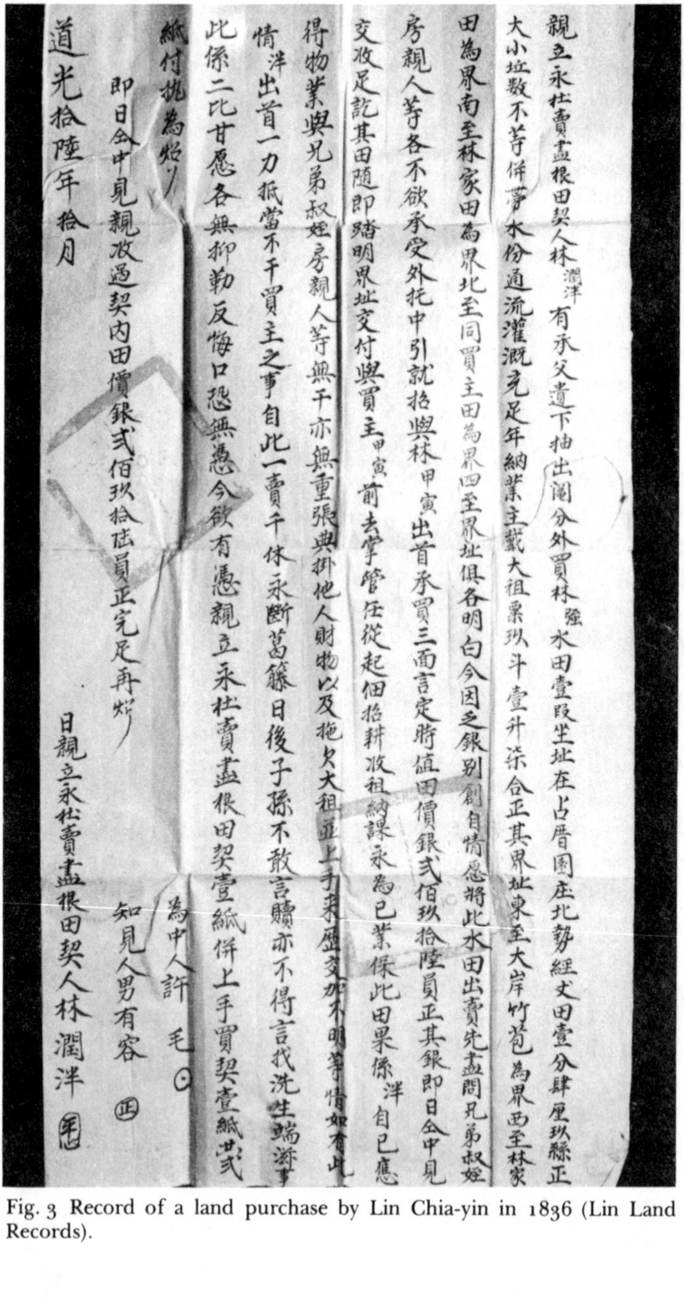

親立永杜賣盡根田契人林潤洋　有承父遺下抽出闊分外買林　強　水田壹段坐址在占厝園庄北勢經丈田壹分肆厘玖縣正

大小址數不等係買水份道流灌溉充足年納業主載大祖栗玖斗壹井添合正其界址東至大岸竹苞為界西至林家

田為界南至林家田為界北至同買主田為界四至界址俱各明白今因乏銀別創自情愿將此水田出賣先盡問兄弟叔姪

房親人等各不欲承受外托中引就招與林甲寅出首承買三面言定時值田價銀式佰玖拾陸員正其銀即日仝中見

交收足記其田隨即踏明界址交付與買主甲寅前去掌管任從起佃招耕收祖納課永為己業保此田果係洋自己應

得物業與兄弟叔姪房親人等無干亦無重張典掛他人財物以及抛欠大祖正上手來歷交加不明等情如有此

情洋出首一力抵當不干買主之事自此一賣千休永斷葛籐日後子孫不敢言贖亦不得言代洗生端滋事

此係二比甘愿各無抑勒反悔口恐無憑今欲有憑親立永杜賣盡根田契壹紙併上手買契壹紙共式

紙付挑為炤／

即日仝中見親改過契內田價銀式佰玖拾陸員正完足再炤

為中人許　毛○

知見人男有容　囲

日親立永杜賣盡根田契人林潤洋　囲

道光拾陸年拾月

Fig. 3 Record of a land purchase by Lin Chia-yin in 1836 (Lin Land Records).

households. Thereby the branches of the clan spread out."
It was not usual for a father to divide his estate in his own
lifetime, and we may surmise that family tensions made
him take this step. The sons were all grown up and married
and may have pressed for independence, or else Chia-yin
feared that they would quarrel over the inheritance unless
he himself made the division. There was in fact trouble
over the matter later when the three eldest sons excluded
the fourth from a share in the ritual trust which they established in Chia-yin's honor.[26]

The existence of this fourth son suggests other tensions
in the household. Listed in the genealogical tables but not
in Chia-yin's biography, he had a clearly marginal status in
the family, as his exclusion from the ritual trust also
suggests. An adopted son, his was not the regular adoption
of a full-fledged son, but the special kind which brought a
lesser, merely economic son (*ming-ling-tzu*) into the family,
one whose duty it often was to take care of a father's concubine during her widowhood. We may tentatively conclude, then, that Chia-yin had a concubine who was not acknowledged in the genealogy and that his three regular
sons had refused to be responsible for her.[27] In short,
Chia-yin's domestic life was neither as modest nor as un-
ruffled as his biographer suggests.

Having been nearly as successful as his grandfather,
Chia-yin aimed higher still. His favorite grandson, who
grew up in Chia-yin's last affluent years, received a classical
education, preparation for an official career.[28] Chia-yin, it
seems, dreamed the ordinary dreams of Chinese social as-
piration. Risen from small peddler to wealthy landlord, he
would launch his descendants into the ruling class.

Chia-yin's aspirations reflected a new range of opportunities. Among several changes in the early nineteenth century, we note the rise of a native scholar-gentry to greater
local prominence. In an era of continued trade expansion,[29] many of the district's affluent citizens began to in-
vest their wealth in the appurtenances of gentry culture.

They gave their sons a classical education and made them compete in the higher examinations. Soon after 1800, the district began to produce at least one *chü-jen* in each of the triennial examinations held at Foochow, and some of these men went on to compete in Peking. In 1823 a native son first gained the *chin-shih*. A second one, three years later, did well enough to be elected into the prestigious Hanlin Academy. Others followed. Soon, several of these higher degree-holders held office on the mainland; others, and the bulk of the lower literati, lived at home, strengthening the higher culture in the district.[30]

Chang-hua's cultural flowering centered around several academies (*shu-yüan*) where eager young men sought the learning which the district's leading lights dispensed. Lu-kang's *Wen-k'ai shu-yüan* played a prominent role, while Chang-hua's older *Pai-sha shu-yüan* gained new vitality from the initiative of an occasional outstanding magistrate. Mainland scholars took up residence in the district and enriched its intellectual and artistic life. At home with scholarship, native literati edited the first district gazetteer in 1834, an enterprise in which several Lu-kang scholars took the lead.[31]

But the examination system with its degree quotas provided too narrow a path for the many upwardly mobile families of the district. Increasingly, wealthy citizens purchased degrees from the financially hard-pressed government.[32] Not eligible for office, such men lived at home and strengthened the rising new district elite. Over and above these degree-holders, Chang-hua had many untitled citizens who contributed to public causes. Their civic spirit if not their formal rank made them members of the local elite. Subscription lists of local schools and temples preserve the names of scores of landlords and other untitled donors in Chang-hua, of dozens of guild chiefs and boat owners in Lu-kang.[33]

Comprising degree-holders and other civic-minded men, this new elite performed many of the functions which we associate with the gentry of the older mainland districts. They organized militia against rebels, funded civic projects, and sponsored temples, granaries, and academies.[34] Characteristically, they remained close to the basic communal groupings into which the district population had divided. In helping to build the Chang-hua walls in 1810, the citizenry contributed through the three major communal groupings, each organized under its own leadership.[35] Though Chia-yin's name does not appear among these worthy citizens, he could feel that his descendants would join this solid elite. When he died on January 30, 1839, his eldest grandson, Wen-ch'a, seemed well launched on his classical studies.

While positions in the elite opened up to the studious and wealthy citizens of Chang-hua, the acquisition of wealth through pioneer farming was itself becoming more difficult. This suggests an almost Turnerian perspective. If Lin Shih's had been the classical story of the frontiersman exploiting an almost virgin land, Chia-yin's generation lived in a more crowded Taiwan. Fortunes could no longer be made in the manner of the pioneer ancestor; keen businessmen stood the best chance of gaining wealth in a single lifetime.

The first Wu-feng Lin was such a man. Frugal and enterprising, he laid the economic foundations of his house. Had the descendants followed his wishes and joined Chang-hua's new elite, they might have contributed to the district's peaceful development. Yet under Chia-yin's sons and grandsons, the family embarked on quite another course. Instead of joining the scholar-gentry, these men enmeshed the family in the rural violence that was spreading in mid-Taiwan. Using Chia-yin's wealth, they joined the dangerous demi-monde of rural strongmen. Such a course would test a family's powers of survival far beyond anything the Lins had yet experienced. Still, in the middle of the nineteenth century, such lives also held out a chance for exceptional success beyond Chia-yin's modest dreams.

The manner and timing of Chia-yin's death are thus symbolic. Luckier than the unfortunate Shih or his own short-lived father, Sun, Chia-yin was one of the few major Lin figures to die peacefully and of natural causes at home. His quiet death, a few months before the outbreak of the Opium War, signaled a final moment of peace, the calm before the storm into which the family, and the country, were heading.

PART TWO

THE LINS AND
THE CRISIS OF
THE CHINESE STATE

Imperial troops defeat Lin Shuang-wen's forces. Eighteenth-century engraving, with poem and calligraphy by the Ch'ien-lung Emperor (Taiwan Branch Library, National Central Library, Taipei).

Portraits of major Lin figures of the nineteenth century. Upper left: Lin Tien-kuo; Upper right: Lin Wen-ch'a; Lower left: Lin Wen-ming; Lower right: Lin Ch'ao-tung (Lin Genealogy).

Portraits of major Lin figures of the late nineteenth century. Upper left: Lin Wen-ch'in; Upper right: Lin Ch'ao-hsüan; Lower left: Mrs. Yang with her youngest son; Lower right: Mrs. Lo with greatgrandsons (Lin Genealogy; Lin Family).

The Lin mansions. Top: the *Kung-pao-ti*, main gate; Bottom: the Upper House (Johanna Meskill).

CHAPTER 6

STRONGMEN

The Lins and
Rural Violence, 1839-1859

*The villagers were all experienced in warfare.
. . . Grandfather knew how to control them and
the young men in the neighborhood were thus all
curbed.*[1]

China's problems of overpopulation and dynastic decay
were aggravated after 1839 by foreign aggression and
widespread rebellion. No part of the country escaped the
turmoil. In a remote frontier district like Chang-hua, the
larger crisis simply accentuated the old turbulence. Communal and clan feuds flared more often; pirates and rob-
bers harassed coast and countryside. Periodically, local and
private violence transmuted into rebellion against the state.
   The economic strains underlying this turbulence were
plain enough. Close to half a million people were now
crowded into Chang-hua district, and the livelihood of
rural communities depended, as never before, on access to
good land and water. Many of the local feuds arose from
competing claims to these scarce resources.[2] In parts of
mid-Taiwan, the population had grown so rapidly that job
opportunities lagged far behind the demand. Hundreds of
bored, unemployed young men threatened the public
order as they banded together for petty violence.[3]

Fig. 4 Fighters in a local brawl employing swords, staves, and pitchfork (*Tien-shih-chai hua-pao*, East Asian Library, Columbia University).

But economic factors alone do not account for the lines of cleavage, nor do they explain the virulence of many of these feuds. Violence not only served economic ends but satisfied personal needs rooted in the moral climate of Taiwan.

From the southeastern mainland, Taiwan had inherited a tradition of private feuding and the cultural values that sustained it, especially an admiration for courage and fighting prowess.[4] The southeast was one of the few regions of China where blood revenge still flourished, and Taiwan inherited this tradition as well. Once begun, local feuds therefore festered. Slain men were worshiped in the temple of their clan or communal group, and their fellows vowed vengeance for the martyrs.[5] On the island, the contest with the aborigines had strengthened this mainland legacy, for it too put a premium on toughness and the use of force.

Among men bred in this culture, feuds ignited easily: from verbal insults traded in an atmosphere of swaggering pride, from the pugnacious temper of young toughs spoiling for a fight, from a zealous defense of sacred symbols or tabus.[6] In a period of increased social strain and governmental incompetence, Taiwan's inherited culture of violence accounted for the near-permanent feuding that overtook the island.

Once people were in the habit of solving conflicts by force, even the defensive efforts of the more peacefully inclined helped to militarize the society. To protect themselves, many villages and merchant groups hired armed guards or trained some of their own members for self-defense. Such fighting men soon had a vested interest in violence, and the lines between defense and offense became blurred when braves hired to protect a merchant convoy developed a regular protection racket.

As in the late eighteenth century, much of the violence took the form of communal or clan vendettas.[7] As more and more aborigine tribes evacuated the plains in the first half of the nineteenth century, their exodus freed space in which the settler-groups contended. It was during the 1830's, for example, that the last Hakka splinters were driven from the Wu-feng area to their enclave in northeastern Chang-hua. Already well demarcated in the district, Chang-chou and Ch'üan-chou groups kept a precarious truce broken by frequent armed clashes.[8]

Within the larger communal demarcations, surname groups established a more clearcut dominance. The arrival of new Lins in the Wu-feng area, for example, caused the Hakka exodus. The whole central section of the Upper Valley was turning into a Lin turf by mid-century, while a clan temple at Nei-hsin, built before 1820, proclaimed the surname's solidarity.[9] Elsewhere "in the vicinity, there were many powerful clans, each occupying a sector."[10] South of the Lins, along the Wu River, the Hungs flourished, while to the north a Lai clan was challenging the Lin expansion. (See Map 4 on p. 100.)

The processes which produced more solid surname turfs were complex. Migrations played a role, strengthening a group here, yielding an exposed position there. Economic pressures also came into play. Where a prominent land-owner of a certain surname controlled an irrigation canal, he might assure that surname's ascendancy in the villages served by that canal.[11] Elsewhere, clan members engaged in selective land sales to squeeze out their rivals. In the area that became the Lin turf, non-Lins had held a considerable amount of land early in the century, but lost ground thereafter as Lins bought from them but sold only to each other.[12] And everywhere, violence was involved.

In this atmosphere of increasing strife, communal and clan groups rallied around vigorous leaders. Assertive and skilled in combat, such men organized groups of fighters for more effective action, whether in self-defense or for aggrandizement. Known as local strongmen (*t'u-hao*), these leaders benefited from the chaos and in turn perpetuated it. In much of Chang-hua's countryside, they formed an alternate, if unstable, system of power, superseding the city-based magistrates and their representatives as *de facto* power-holders. Since it was in their ranks that Chia-yin's sons and grandsons enlisted, we must examine the species briefly before resuming our narrative.

The Local Strongman as a Social Type

What distinguished the local strongman from others who wielded private armed power—the mobile soldier of fortune or the roving outlaw—was his strong tie to local society. The strongman shared its hatreds and loyalties and used his power to protect his group from its rivals. Using local solidarities—whether of surname or communal group—he always had his roots more deeply in the local soil than did the government itself.[13]

Central to a strongman's power was his armed following, his troop of braves. Including both full- and part-time fighters, a strongman's force might number anywhere from a few dozen to a few hundred men. By mid-century, the major strongmen of the Upper Valley had personal armies of two hundred, three hundred, and four hundred men. Since a successful strongman usually belonged to the locally dominant surname group and was his kinsmen's champion, he drew on his clansmen for recruits.

Full-time braves must have received regular pay as well as a part of the booty that all fighters shared.[14] Part-time braves, often tenants on the strongman's land,[15] tended to their farm chores and served in their spare time. All the men lived near the strongman's residence, some in quarters he provided, others in the surrounding villages and hamlets, but all within reach of the gongs and drums that called them to a fight.

The strongman's power, next to his force, rested on his fortified base. Since even the average Taiwanese village was fortified, it took but little else—a cannon or two, a store of food and water, plenty of guns and ammunition, armed guards and a few fierce dogs—to turn a village into a strongman lair. Most rural strongmen used their native villages as lairs, while those who were at home in market towns secured village bases as well, finding the towns apparently too large or socially too heterogeneous to be easily defended.[16]

While most strongmen were wealthy before they turned to careers of private armed power, they multiplied their wealth from the spoliations of their rivals or from protection money they exacted. Yet they were more than simple predators. Deeply enmeshed in local economic life, they often owned a substantial share of the cropland in their turf and dominated the local people through both land-lordism and the control of water. Leading men of their communities, they managed local institutions, sponsored local shrines, and patronized the people of their turfs, both bestowing and receiving favors.

Yet the feelings of the local people toward any given strongman must have been ambivalent. Many gained by joining his force; some were harassed or driven out. No wonder that the image of the strongman in the local literature was contradictory! A monster to his victims and enemies, he was patron and benefactor to his wards. Always he appeared larger-than-life.

These larger-than-life, heroic qualities of the strongman must be appreciated against the background of the local culture, with its admiration for heroes and fighting prowess.[17] The strongman was the living exemplar of that martial type which a dozen battle tales and opera plots had paraded before the villagers' eyes. Little wonder, then, that many a rich man's son preferred the strongman's roisterous career to a humdrum "examination life" or that many a peasant lad chose a job as a brave over toil in the paddy fields. Quite ordinary men—romantic adolescents or small-time toughs—grew in self-esteem when they assumed the role of latter-day knights-errant, glorying in the manly arts of archery or sword-fighting, and perhaps in drinking and whoring as well.

That strongmen flourished because local government was weak goes without saying, yet how the magistrates looked upon the strongmen is less clear. Some no doubt detested the increasing violence they associated with the new species; yet others thought that in working through the strongmen they might get a better grip on a lawless district. If strongmen allowed taxes to be collected in their turfs[18]—they were low enough in mid-Taiwan—the authorities usually left them alone and might even bid for their services in local peace-keeping. In times of crisis, such as rebellion or foreign attack, many a strongman was recruited as *pao-chia* or militia chief. Relations between local government and the strongmen in its jurisdiction were therefore as ambivalent as those between a strongman and the people of his turf. Some strongmen led rebellions; others fought rebels on the government side. As a wielder of private power, the strongman undercut the government; when he supported authority, it in turn legitimized him.

A similar ambivalence must have marked the relations of the strongmen to the new civilian elite of the towns. Here, too, there were tacit alliances, for how else could urban rentier families or grain merchants receive the agricultural surpluses from the hinterland on which they depended?[19] As landlords, the strongmen themselves had an interest in a well-functioning grain trade. The cultural divide between the strongmen and the urban, partly scholarly, elite was also narrower than one might expect. Some humane scholars no doubt recoiled from the brutality of the strongmen, but a great many others accepted the local tradition of armed violence and admired the heroic values. Joint functions, too, drew the two groups together, as when both served the government as militia leaders or when they jointly sponsored a religious festival, the townsman underwriting the expenses, the strongman guarding the procession.

Rural strongmen were, in short, both rivals and colleagues of urban elite figures.[20] They represented an unofficial power in the countryside, but they were always candidates for entrance into the regular local elite. Should a strongman decide to launch his son into the gentry, or should he aspire to official rank himself, neither the local elite nor the local magistrate would stand in his way.

The Lins Become Strongmen

It was through Chia-yin's two eldest sons that the Lins first became local strongmen. Born in 1808 and 1814, Ting-pang and Tien-kuo both have biographies in the genealogy, as befits the founders of the Wu-feng line's two major

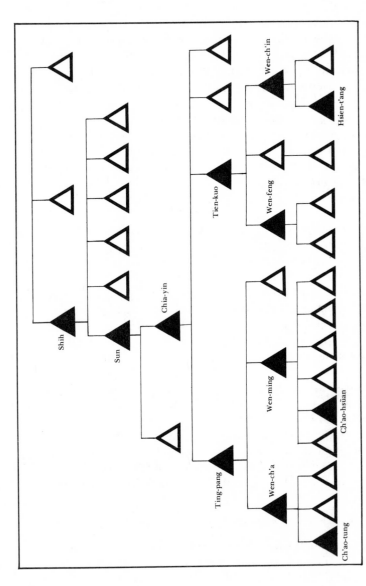

Fig. 5 Genealogical table of Lin Shih's descendants in the male line: the Wu-feng branch. Important figures have been emphasized.

sub-branches. Yet neither these lives nor Tien-kuo's brief biographies in local gazetteers[21]—he was the earliest of the family to merit such recognition—give us more than a few tantalizing fragments of their early history. Of Tien-kuo it is said that he "knew how to control [the turbulent villagers] and the young men in the neighborhood were thus all curbed."[22] The somewhat enigmatic passage must refer to his founding of an armed band, though it does not allow us to date the event.

While Tien-kuo's force of braves can be documented for the 1850's and 1860's, in the 1840's he was probably overshadowed by his older brother, a man "by nature honest and direct"[23] (a euphemism for blunt toughness?). According to his flattering biography, Ting-pang proved himself a peacemaker among several adjoining villages (perhaps the separate Wu-feng palisades) who promptly chose him as their headman (tsung-li).[24] Such tsung-li had extensive police powers and were supposed to be chosen from among "venerable, rich, and learned scholars."[25] If Ting-pang held such an office—a man in his thirties and with no known educational attainments—he was clearly chosen for something other than his age or learning. Most likely, he had established his local dominance through a private army; the tsung-li office merely ratified this power. We know from the neighboring Tan-shui district that tsung-li offices were often held by strongmen who used these posts to justify their keeping men under arms and as a cover for their strong-arm tactics.

That Ting-pang did indeed have a small force of braves may be gathered from several clues. He conducted an armed feud with a local rival and on the morrow of his death, his eldest son already disposed of a following (tang-yü),[26] most likely Ting-pang's legacy. We also note that a friendly historian refers to him as a knight-errant.[27] Derived from the knights-errant of feudal times, the term later denoted a man who used force for high-minded purposes, albeit outside the law. Taiwanese historians have found it a useful euphemism for the strongmen they admire.

If Ting-pang maintained a troop of armed men, his power was quite modest. He took no visible part in the Opium War when some of the district's better-known strongmen were recruited for government service.[28] Just how tiny his turf still was became clear a few years later when he ran into a tough rival little more than a mile from home. This man was Lin Ho-shang, a strongman with a substantial turf to the west and northwest of Wu-feng and a lair at Ts'ao-hu.[29] The two Lin strongmen must have been feuding for some time, over water or other matters (one source reports that Ting-pang had seduced Ho-shang's concubine)[30] or, most likely, over their respective recruiting areas in the Upper Valley's Lin turf. Since Ho-shang's force was organized under a secret society label, the *Kuan-yeh-hui*,[31] Ting-pang, with his quasi-official *tsung-li* title, had grounds for challenging his rival's political loyalty. In the typical strongman tit-for-tat, Ho-shang then took one of Ting-pang's men prisoner, holding him for ransom as a challenge to the other man's power. Stung in turn, Ting-pang marched on Ts'ao-hu and freed his brave. But on the way back to Wu-feng, his party was pursued and he was killed (1848).

Ting-pang's violent death might have precipitated another decline for the family had it not been for his sons, and particularly the eldest. Rising to the challenge of his father's death, Lin Wen-ch'a (1828-1864) became a veritable folk hero in mid-Taiwan and one of the district's major strongmen.

A Chinese hero enters the world under miraculous circumstances. So it was with Wen-ch'a, of whom it is said that "there was a miracle at his birth; as his mother, Mrs. Tai, took a rest because of fatigue, in her dream a giant entered the room, holding in his hand a golden turtle. Startled, she awoke and gave birth."[32]

While still a child, Wen-ch'a already showed the direction of his genius. When at play with the neighborhood children, "he 'played' military campaigns. He piled up stones to build a fortress, cut out paper to make flags, and sat on top of the fort or went in and out, commanding his playmates."[33] Yet the family did not at first take its cue from his evident habit of command. Because Wen-ch'a "did not look like a warrior"[34] (he seems to have been delicately built, unlike his burly brother, Wen-ming) and because Chia-yin had chosen an official career for his favorite grandson, Wen-ch'a was first given a classical education. Taught to write essays and poetry at home, he was, at age twelve, enrolled with a tutor in Chang-hua. But instead of practicing his examination essays, Wen-ch'a hung around the teahouses, listening to stories about the great heroes of the past, Kuan Yü and Yo Fei.* His reading too ran to heroic romances and military treatises. "When some of his fellow-students laughed at his wild ways, he answered them coldly, saying: 'Your goal is the *hsiu-ts'ai*† degree, but mine is different and does not lie in this.' " Failing in a preliminary examination, he gave up the academic life altogether and returned to Wu-feng, probably in the early 1840's.[35] Here, he studied what he truly liked: proficiency in arms, the ruses of war, and the delicate art of gaining and holding his men's loyalty. It must have been at this time too that he indulged his love of sword-fighting and acquired the knowledge of firearms that would stand him in good stead later. On the whole, though, these were unspectacular years for an ambitious youth. They ended abruptly with Ting-pang's death.

Wen-ch'a had not accompanied Ting-pang on the fatal trip to Ts'ao-hu. When he heard of the disaster, and of his brother Wen-ming's wounding and capture, he responded

* Heroic figures of the third and twelfth centuries, respectively. In the Chinese tradition of biography, a person's youthful choice of such models foreshadows his adult development.

† "Flowering Talent," a popular name for the *sheng-yüan* degree that was awarded on the basis of prefectural examinations.

with characteristic ardor: "he jumped up and brandished his pistol, ready to go."[36] His mother restrained him and insisted that he first ransom his father's body and Wen-ming before taking on the solemn duty of blood revenge.

To have his father killed confronted a young man in nineteenth-century Taiwan with a tangle of moral and legal complexities. Centuries ago, the Confucian moral law had insisted on a son's duty to avenge a slain father; many chivalric figures had since observed this code. More recent dynasties had abridged the custom and insisted that the government alone could punish murderers. But while blood revenge may have declined in most of China, it was still common in the strife-torn southeast, where lineage and communal feuds kept the idea alive. In Taiwan, offshoot of this pugnacious culture, blood revenge was a son's sacred duty.[37]

Wen-ch'a's moral duty was thus clear. His self-interest pointed in the same direction, for, to make good his claim to Ting-pang's succession, he would first have to eliminate his father's rival. Still, political caution was indicated. Prudently, Wen-ch'a gave the government a chance to take matters in hand and bring Lin Ho-shang to justice. Only when the magistrate failed to act did Wen-ch'a take the law into his own hands.[38]

As a first step, Wen-ch'a and his younger brother Wen-ming (1833-1870) made sure of their men's loyalty and determination.[39] " 'Our great hatred is not stilled yet and we cannot co-exist with [Ho-shang],' " they said to the assembled men, " 'are there any among you gentlemen who can assist us?' " The men answered, "as if with one voice," that they would follow the brothers, even unto death. The brothers then knelt down and thanked the men; having assured themselves once more of the men's readiness, they slaughtered a cow and sealed the covenant with a feast. Then they all dispersed, wearing mourning clothes. If their intention was to disguise their plan, it failed, for "the enemy too was gathering determined men and building strong fortifications to await [the Wu-feng force]."

In all, the feud lasted for almost three years and raged across the length and breadth of Mao-lo tithing. Wen-ch'a and his followers "battled the enemy on the road four times and attacked him at the theater and at the gambling place twice. Their wounded and killed reached several dozen." Nor were innocent bystanders safe from the fury of Wen-ch'a's attack. Eight cloth peddlers are said to have been killed when they crossed a ford and were mistaken for the enemy.[40]

The Lin brothers finally prevailed. Destroying one after another of Ho-shang's ten lairs, they caught their enemy alive and took him to Ting-pang's grave, where the full ceremonial act of revenge was carried out. In the presence of clansmen and neighbors, "Wen-ch'a killed him with his own hand and then addressed Ting-pang's spirit, saying: 'The deed of this day was not simply done for the sake of revenge but to carry out my father's mission and reduce the depredations of evil men.' They wept and all the people joined in the lamentations until the sound of wailing shook the earth."[41]

No less important than the ethical implications of this ritual were its political consequences. In the competitive world of local strongmen, Wen-ch'a had scored handsomely. His power expanded, perhaps encompassing Ts'ao-hu. The reaction of the government was another matter. Ho-shang's allies went to court and obtained a warrant for Wen-ch'a's arrest.[42] After a family palaver, Wen-ch'a surrendered and threw himself on the magistrate's mercy. His case was suspended after some time, both because the magistrate sympathized with the avenger and because the government needed Wen-ch'a's services. Before long, he regained his freedom.

Wen-ch'a's political caution deserves note. In the highly ambiguous relation between local magistrate and local strongman, appearances counted for something, and Wen-ch'a had saved the appearances. Without sacrificing his independent power, he had acknowledged the authority of government. In the years ahead, this stance would stand him in good stead as he expanded his power base by working with, rather than against, the authorities.

The Rise of Lin Wen-ch'a

During the 1850's, Wen-ch'a developed into one of the most formidable strongmen of the district. His force of braves grew, from perhaps a few dozen at the time of the revenge to several hundred by the end of the decade.[43] It must have included a sizeable number of full-time braves because Wen-ch'a was able to take his force on campaigns far from home, apparently for weeks at a time. To accommodate these larger numbers, the family changed quarters, moving from the northern palisade to a more central location in Wu-feng, on or near the site of the later Lin mansions.[44]

As the force grew, so did Wen-ch'a's recruiting area. By the late 1850's, it included both Mao-lo and Sung-tung tithing,[45] that is to say, a good portion of the Lin surname turf in the Upper Valley. Yet the surname tie was only one of the bonds, albeit probably the strongest, that linked the force together.[46] At the graveside ritual, Wen-ch'a had assembled not only clansmen but also "neighbors," and among his sub-commanders in later years we encounter both Lins and non-Lins.[47] Communal affiliation provided a bond that allowed the strongman to reach out beyond the surname group. We learn that Wen-ch'a intervened, perhaps militarily, in a feud between Chang-chou and Ch'üan-chou groups in neighboring Tan-shui in the early 1850's, and that he extended relief to civilians in distress, presumably fellow-members of the Chang-chou group.[48]

Wen-ch'a reached out to gain local followers in yet other ways. In Ta-li-chi, still the major market town near the edge of his expanding turf, he donated funds for the repair of a Ma-tsu temple in 1855.[49] It was probably at this time, too, that he resumed the ties with the estranged Lin branches, Shih's other descendants in the area north of

Wu-feng. We know that several of his cousins and nephews served under him in the early 1860's and the connection must date back some time.[50] Since several of these men were independently wealthy and prominent in the northern section of the Lin surname turf, around T'ai-p'ing, their support enhanced Wen-ch'a's stature among his clansmen.

As Wen-ch'a's power grew, it intruded on the domains of other strongmen. So did the raids of his uncle Tien-kuo, who, perhaps encouraged by Wen-ch'a's growing power, now fielded his own force and led it against neighboring clans.[51] We hear of feuds between the Wu-feng Lin strongmen and at least three rival surnames in the Upper Valley: Lais to the north, a Tai family in the northwest, and Hungs to the south. The bone of contention was usually land or, in the case of the Hungs, that clan's continued control of the Wu-feng *chün*. But the most formidable rival was another Lin, a strongman from Szu-k'uai-ts'o just west of Wu-feng, with whom Wen-ch'a quarreled over land and, most likely, over their respective recruiting grounds. In alternating battles and truces, these early feuds confirmed Wen-ch'a's growing power without as yet eliminating his rivals.[52]

Grounding his power in local solidarities, Wen-ch'a in turn used this private power base to gain access to public power, the authority of the government. He placed his braves at the disposal of the local magistrates and in the process secured official rank for himself and public funds for his growing army.

To understand why officialdom sought out the services of a man like Wen-ch'a, we must briefly recall the general situation in China during the 1850's. On the mainland, the story was largely that of the Taiping rebellion, which we shall consider in the next chapter in connection with Wen-ch'a's mainland campaigns. But the shock waves of the rebellion had quickly reached Taiwan. To reenforce the mainland, a large part of the Taiwan garrison was with-

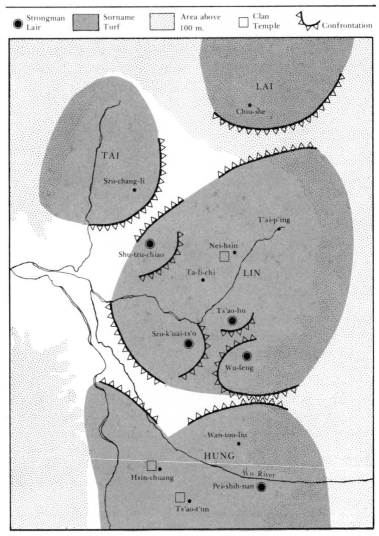

MAP 4: STRONGMAN LAIRS AND SURNAME TURFS IN THE UPPER
VALLEY, ca. 1840-1860

drawn in the early 1850's.[53] At the same time, the early Taiping triumphs emboldened all the rebels and malcontents on the island. As numerous minor rebellions flared during the decade, the officials fell back on irregular forces, including such pre-existing strongman bands as Wen-ch'a's, to strengthen the depleted regular forces.[54]

Wen-ch'a's first service with the government came in 1854, when Small Sword rebels had occupied Keelung, on Taiwan's northern tip. He himself was in the thick of the battle and took no fewer than seven enemy heads. His stratagem is said to have expelled the rebels from the harbor. Four years later, Wen-ch'a fought once more in Tan-shui, and perhaps in Chia-yi as well. His men gave a good account of themselves, and Wen-ch'a was amply rewarded.[55]

For a strongman, the benefits of an association with government were numerous. While on campaign for the government, he could draw on public funds.[56] This surely was the key to Wen-ch'a's wider recruiting by the end of the decade, for to maintain a troop of nearly a thousand braves, as he did, clearly exceeded his private income and Wen-ch'a had no access to the kinds of *t'uan-lien* (militia) bureaus which elsewhere in China raised funds for the irregular forces needed in the emergency. Next to the funds, Wen-ch'a's most important gain was the acquisition of official rank. In a country where government offered the most prestigious positions, he made the crucial transition from commoner to official. His rank, to be sure, was low at first—after the Tan-shui campaign of 1858, he became a major in the Army of the Green Standard[57]—but during a time of crisis, an army career promised exceptional opportunities. There must have been other gains as well: opportunities for graft and personal enrichment that were common in the Chinese military at the time. We do in fact note a more lavish style of life in the Lin family, beginning with the 1850's. Not only were there more spacious quarters for the family, but concubines for Wen-ch'a, Wen-ming, and their uncle Tien-kuo as well.[58]

Like the founder of the Wu-feng Lin line, his sons and grandsons showed a keen sense for the opportunities of the age. Where Chia-yin had taken advantage of the changing economy, they profited from a decaying public order.

Chinese historians have not been kind to the strongman. A person of too much violence and too little culture in the eyes of traditional historians, he has emerged in modern works, if at all, as a scavenger of a dying system. There is some truth in these views, yet they ignore an important dimension: the strongman was neither a simple exploiter nor an outsider preying on the local society. On the contrary, his power arose from local solidarities and his style of life reflected cherished local values. Knight-errantry furnished a personal model and patronage defined his ties to friends and clients. His manpower came from the poverty of the young, his clansmen's loyalty from their need for protection. In a fragmenting social order, the strongmen fashioned a rough and ready system whose only alternative was an even more chaotic war of all against all.

While the strongman's private power, his *shih-li*, undercut the authority of government, in the crisis of mid-century many strongmen found the magistrates bidding for their support. It was Wen-ch'a's good fortune that he was able to make the most of this opportunity. A local hero, a formidable power in the Upper Valley, a supple politician in relation to the local officials, he found at the end of the decade that his services to the Taiwanese government were but the prelude to a larger assignment.

CHAPTER 7

THE YOUNG GENERAL

Lin Wen-ch'a's
Mainland Campaigns, 1859-1863

Rising from an island in the sea
Bursting on to the Central Plain
Riding in the south by boat, on horseback in the north
Fighting for fame in winds and clouds.[1]

Responding to a call from the governor-general of Fukien
and Chekiang, Wen-ch'a left Taiwan in 1859 to help the
government fight rebels on the mainland.[2] On a broader
stage, his mainland years repeated the earlier pattern of his
relationship with government on Taiwan. Working under
higher placed officials, Wen-ch'a was able to draw ampler
government funds, recruit a larger force, win more resounding victories, and obtain higher honors for himself.
From being on the margin of the local elite he became, at
age thirty-three, one of the empire's youngest generals.

Wen-ch'a's contact to the governor-general had probably
been made by one of his patrons in the Taiwan hierarchy.
These included such men as K'ung Chao-tz'u, a Shantung
chin-shih, descendant of Confucius, and former district
magistrate in Taiwan. It was K'ung who had presided over
Wen-ch'a's case in court, had sympathized with the young
avenger, and had set him free. In 1859, he obtained the
important post of Taiwan intendant. Or it may have been
Ting Yüeh-chien who established the link, an Anhui *chü-*

Fig. 6 Braves drilling, observed by officials (*Tien-shih-chai hua-pao*, East Asian Library, Columbia University).

jen who had held the Tan-shui magistracy during Wen-ch'a's fighting in Keelung and who had recommended him for awards.[3] Ting had good contacts in Foochow and was himself back in mainland Fukien for pacification work at the end of the decade. Another possible intermediary was Colonel Tseng Yü-ming, a veteran officer of the Taiwan garrison and *pei-lu* commander during the mid-1850's.[4] It was he who had recommended Wen-ch'a for his first government service, the Keelung campaign, and who remained his friend thereafter.

Asked to bring a larger number of men than he had commanded before, Wen-ch'a took some weeks to recruit and ready his forces. When he crossed over to the mainland, probably in the summer of 1859, the governor-general who had called him, Wang Yi-te, had been replaced by Ch'ing-tuan, a Manchu. But Wen-ch'a's mission was not affected by the change. Ch'ing-tuan himself had

long served in Fukien and may have been familiar with
Wen-ch'a's merits.[5] At any rate, he gave him important assignments and recommended him for promotions and
rewards—the stuff that an ambitious young officer's
dreams are made of.

Serving on the mainland, Wen-ch'a's men became
known as the "Taiwan Braves" (*T'ai-yung*). They were not
the only Taiwanese irregulars fighting there at the time,
but they appear to have been the most distinguished. Unlike other Taiwanese fighters shipped over for the
emergency, Wen-ch'a's force was not an *ad hoc* contingent,
thrown together for the occasion. Built on the long-
standing loyalties of a strongman army, it was better disci-
plined and combat-worthy for longer stretches of time. In
addition, Wen-ch'a's braves became known as superb
marksmen.[6] "Clumsy with words but fierce in battle,"[7] they
must have been a ferocious lot, particularly under the
leadership of an aggressive commander like Wen-ch'a.
Their reputation was such that mainland militia occasionally asked to borrow the Taiwan Braves' uniforms, confident that their very sight would scatter the enemy. Numbering around 2,000 men, the fighters were presumably
drawn from Wen-ch'a's old recruiting grounds in the
Upper Valley. Wu-feng itself had been gone over thoroughly and only a few dozen men remained behind while
Wen-ch'a was away.[8]

Wen-ch'a's larger force and broader mission also required a more elaborate staff organization. We now hear of
various sub-commanders leading portions of his force into
battle. One close associate at this time was his brother,
Wen-ming, who also obtained formal rank in the army and
rose in its hierarchy. His services were special, for he not
only served as a unit commander on the mainland but as
liaison to Wen-ch'a's power base at home. For as the mainland fighting took its toll, Wen-ming would go back to
Chang-hua and gather fresh recruits.[9] There also was now
a private secretary, Hsieh Ying-su, a Fukienese from

Hsing-hua who had long resided in Taiwan. A noted calligrapher and painter of bamboo and orchids, neither his paintings nor the memorials he drafted for Wen-ch'a have survived.[10]

The Taiwan Braves in Fukien and Chekiang

It is sometimes said that a successful military career depends on being in the right war at the right time. For Wen-ch'a, this time was approaching but it had not yet arrived. From 1859 to 1861, he was assigned to Fukien fighting local rebels, a minor theater of war on which he could not expect to win the highest rewards.[11] Still, the time was not lost; he had much to learn—about commanding a larger force, about cooperating with the regular army, about staff work at higher official levels—before he would be ready for the greater challenges to come.

In all, he participated in four separate campaigns during the Fukien phase. In 1859 a rebellion in the northwest, around Chien-yang, had to be put down and Wen-ch'a gained valuable experience in mountain warfare. Biographers praised his sure sense of terrain. In 1860 he campaigned with regular provincial forces in west central Fukien. He was frequently in the thick of battle and took no fewer than two hundred enemy prisoners by himself. The winter of 1860-1861 saw a brief diversion to southwestern Chekiang, where Wen-ch'a helped wrest the district city of Chiang-shan from the Taiping rebels and made his first acquaintance with siege warfare for conventionally fortified towns. The Chekiang authorities esteemed him highly and sought to keep him in their province, but a new emergency called him back to Fukien. In early 1861, he saw action in the mountainous southwest. He fought again alongside regular provincial units and helped to recover Lien-ch'eng, a district city, and the prefectural capital, T'ing-chou. The fighting involved much setting of ambushes and more hand-to-hand fighting, in both of which Wen-ch'a excelled.

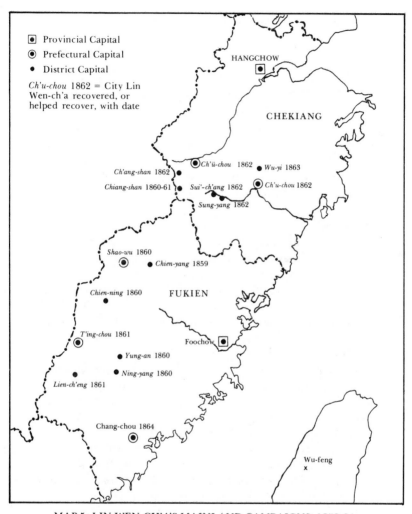

Provincial Capital

Prefectural Capital

District Capital

Ch'u-chou 1862 = City Lin
Wen-ch'a recovered, or
helped recover, with date

HANGCHOW

CHEKIANG

Ch'ang-shan 1862   ⊙*Ch'ü-chou* 1862   *Wu-yi* 1863

Chiang-shan 1860-61   *Sui'-ch'ang* 1862   ⊙*Ch'u-chou* 1862

Sung-yang 1862

Shao-wu 1860   *Chien-yang* 1859

Chien-ning 1860   FUKIEN

T'ing-chou 1861   Foochow

Yung-an 1860

Ning-yang 1860

Lien-ch'eng 1861

Chang-chou 1864

Wu-feng
x

MAP 5: LIN WEN-CH'A'S MAINLAND CAMPAIGNS, 1859-64

His rise in the military hierarchy was swift. In two years he had advanced from major to acting brigade general and had collected a string of decorations as well. But the T'ing-chou campaign also gave the first signs of trouble ahead, for here Wen-ch'a had a falling-out with Ting Yüeh-chien, his former patron. Ting was at this time provisions *tao-t'ai* and active in pacification work in Fukien. We do not know how the quarrel started, but since both men's biographies credit them with the recovery of T'ing-chou, they may have fought over their share of the glory.[12] The incident may also suggest that Wen-ch'a lacked the finesse for operating at the higher levels of provincial officialdom. While the rupture with Ting had no immediate ill effect, it was to haunt his career later.

Toward the end of 1861, Wen-ch'a transferred once more to Chekiang. Here, the next eight months would be the most important in his mainland career. His Taiwan Braves now belonged to a larger force, the so-called Fukien Army (*Min-chün*),* sent north to aid a sister province in distress. Composed of diverse units, the *Min-chün* numbered some 20,000 men and Wen-ch'a became one of its senior commanders.[13]

The transfer to Chekiang took Wen-ch'a into the final campaign against the Taipings.[14] Though past their peak, the rebels were still formidable and had lately overrun the lower Yangtze valley, capturing Soochow, the capital of Kiangsu, in 1860, and Hangchow, Chekiang's capital, in December 1861. It was to defend Hangchow that the *Min-chün* was first rushed into Chekiang. The city fell, however, before the Fukien troops arrived, and the *Min-chün*'s mission was redefined. Its new assignment was to help in the systematic recovery of Chekiang, part of the overall plan for the final assault on the Taipings.

To defeat the Taipings once and for all, it was thought that Kiangsu and Chekiang would first have to be retaken.

* *Min*, from the Min River, its chief waterway, is the classical name for Fukien province.

Only then could Nanking, the rebel capital, be attacked from all sides. Moreover, for the imperial side the two rich downriver provinces were "as important in the battle for funds and supplies as for strategic position,"[15] and Tseng Kuo-fan, special commander for the final campaign, therefore gave high priority to the reconquest of the two provinces. In January 1862, a few weeks after the *Min-chün* had entered Chekiang, Tseng's trusted associate and fellow-Hunanese, Tso Tsung-t'ang, was appointed governor of Chekiang. Henceforth, the *Min-chün* would help Tso to recover his province.

For Wen-ch'a, it was, at last, the right war at the right time, though not yet, as it turned out, under the right commander. For as Tso conceived military strategy, he himself would operate in the north of Chekiang, driving to recover Hangchow, while the *Min-chün* would operate independently in the south.[16] Keeping Wen-ch'a out of the orbit of the distinguished governor, the arrangement actually made good sense. Southern Chekiang had the kind of mountainous terrain with which the Fukien forces were familiar. Supply lines, too, were shorter this way, for the *Min-chün* continued to be paid and supplied from Fukien. Indeed, it reported to, and received orders from, the governor-general at Foochow, not from Tso.[17]

When Wen-ch'a entered Chekiang in December of 1861, the government position was bleak indeed. Imperial forces held only Ch'ü-chou in the south and a few towns in the northwest which were soon lost. Virtually the entire province had to be wrested from the rebels.[18]

On his southern sector, Wen-ch'a first saw action in February 1862. Recovering the district city of Ch'ang-shan, he helped to relieve the pressure on Ch'ü-chou.[19] His services were greatly esteemed, for when a death in the family required him to go into mourning that spring, the governor-general obtained a waiver of his mourning duties to keep him in the field.[20] By April, Wen-ch'a had moved to the Sung-yin valley, where he did his most distinguished

fighting in the next few months.[21] He often fought alongside regular Chekiang forces and at times faced Li Shih-
hsien, a cousin of the famous Li Hsiu-ch'eng, the Taipings'
Chung-wang or Loyal Prince. By May he had recovered the
district city of Sui-ch'ang and was moving on. Ordered to
capture Sung-yang, another district city in the valley,
Wen-ch'a mounted a protracted siege. After seventy days,
the city finally fell. Then the *Min-chün* moved downriver
and recovered the prefectural city of Ch'u-chou in August.

This string of victories brought the *Min-chün* commanders ample rewards. All spring, as Wen-ch'a captured cities
and showed bravery in battle, Governor-General Ch'ing-
tuan had reported his merits to the throne. Even Tseng
Kuo-fan became aware of the dashing young Taiwanese
commander. In late July, Wen-ch'a was made a full brigade

Fig. 7 Taiping rebels and imperial troops in battle (*T'ai-p'ing t'ien-kuo
chan-chi*, East Asian Library, Columbia University).

general and, three weeks later, there followed another promotion, to the acting rank of *t'i-tu*, or provincial commander-in-chief (Rank 1B).[22] Wen-ch'a was suddenly near the pinnacle of the military hierarchy.

Wen-ch'a's steep climb up the military ladder reflected both the government's plight—in the emergency, honors and rewards abounded—and a certain Chinese tradition of generalship which placed daring and cunning ahead of staff work and logistics. What mattered was personal leadership on the battlefield and adroit use of superior intelligence. Close rapport with his men, exemplary bravery in the thick of battle, a clever use of ambushes—these were the marks of the great field commander, and these Wen-ch'a possessed in abundance.

With the end of the summer, something went wrong. After the capture of Ch'u-chou, Wen-ch'a did not campaign for months and when he was transferred to the Wu-yi area, farther north, in early 1863, he had only a few minor victories to his credit and received no further awards or promotions.[23] No doubt his braves deserved a rest after the strenuous summer fighting, but the long inaction and the modest performance that followed had deeper causes. The foundations of Wen-ch'a's success—access to the recruiting ground in Taiwan and favorable command arrangements in Foochow—were slipping.

A rebellion in Chang-hua was drying up his troop supply and threatening his power base at home, indeed the very safety of Wu-feng and his family. We shall recount in the next chapter how Wen-ch'a dealt with this challenge; here we merely note its effect on his Chekiang campaign. Not only were replacements unavailable when most needed after the costly summer campaign. The Taiwan Braves in Chekiang too were affected; they "all thought of home and not of war and proved listless."[24] By fall, Wen-ch'a judged the situation in Taiwan so critical that he detached a portion of his men and sent them home. Wen-ming received official permission to lead them back to assist in pacification at home.[25]

Wen-ch'a's command arrangements were also in disarray. As we have seen, he had never had a personal patron among the high provincial officials, though he had worked well under Governor-General Ch'ing-tuan. Ch'ing-tuan, however, did not please the throne and was dismissed in August of 1862. His successor, another Manchu, proved a disaster for Wen-ch'a. Ch'i-ling had used his previous office, the Kwangtung governorship, to create his own personal army of Kwangtung braves whom he now brought into his new jurisdiction. First squabbling with the outgoing Ch'ing-tuan over troop disposition, Ch'i-ling soon vented his bias against the Fukienese units, disbanding them to find employment for his Kwangtung braves.[26]

Wen-ch'a's long inactivity in the fall and winter of 1862-1863 resulted from these adverse developments. Even when the throne reassured him that Ch'i-ling would not dismiss his unit,[27] he still received no significant assignments. As his mainland career languished, Wen-ch'a's thoughts inevitably turned to the troubles in Taiwan. Sometime that winter, he too asked for a transfer home.[28] Nothing happened at first, but in the spring he had an opportunity to return at least to Fukien. His old friend Tseng Yü-ming, who had recently served on the mainland, became commander of the Taiwan garrison, and Wen-ch'a received Tseng's old job as commander of the Fu-ning military district. About April 1, 1863, he returned to Fukien with his remaining braves.[29]

The appointment was actually one of Ch'i-ling's last official acts for he, too, displeased the higher authorities and was dismissed. In May the throne appointed Tso Tsung-t'ang to be the new governor-general.[30] For Wen-ch'a, it was yet another command change, though one that brought him, at last, in touch with a man of real distinction. With a future of his own, Tso might give a new lift to Wen-ch'a's stalled career.

The Taiwan Command

Because they had fought separate campaigns in Chekiang, Tso was not well acquainted with Wen-ch'a when he took over the governor-generalship in the spring of 1863. What knowledge he possessed had come to him during the preceding fall when he had been asked to examine the *Min-chün's* affairs during the squabbles between Ch'i-ling and Ch'ing-tuan. At that time, Tso had formed a generally favorable view of Wen-ch'a and his braves. He had praised their fighting spirit, though he criticized their opium addiction.[31] On the face of it, then, Wen-ch'a might expect better assignments than under Ch'i-ling.

But it soon developed that Wen-ch'a's new duties depended more on Tso's overall military needs than on the opinion he had formed of the young Taiwanese general. In the early summer of 1863, Tso's forces in Chekiang lay immobilized with malaria, and little campaigning was planned. Since Wen-ch'a was not needed on the Chekiang front, Tso instead found another assignment for him in Fukien: the reform of the badly deteriorated provincial forces.[32] Wen-ch'a probably disliked the job—for one thing, it kept him from returning to Taiwan—but performed it to Tso's satisfaction. He screened the existing units, dismissed the unfit, and retrained the others to fill them with a new fighting spirit. Nor did he neglect the small courtesies of official life. In the summer, he sent a gift of special Ch'üan-chou ginseng to Tso in Chekiang, which seems to have done wonders for the governor-general and his army.[33]

If Wen-ch'a satisfied a far-away Tso, the officials on the spot in Fukien were less pleased with him. Of course, Wen-ch'a's general house-cleaning was bound to make him enemies among the army's vested interests. But there was also resentment of his unruly braves and of some of his associates.[34] In the end, however, it was Tso's opinion that mattered, and Wen-ch'a's performance finally paid off.

Dissatisfied with the snail's pace of pacification in Taiwan, Tso had for some time cast about for a new commander to lead the Taiwan campaign. In September, he proposed Wen-ch'a for the post. This was no hasty decision. Well aware of the problems inherent in such an assignment, Tso had pondered the matter for weeks and had cleared it with the Fukien governor, Hsü Tsung-kan.[35]

To suggest that a man serve in his native area was to touch a raw nerve in the Chinese body politic. Since localism and nepotism would invite abuses of such posts, a special "law of avoidance" forbade a man's holding office in his native province. The military had always applied this law loosely,[36] and the emergency itself had eroded many of the earlier restrictions. While the "law of avoidance" was never revoked, pacification itself created many informal posts in militia and fund-raising bureaus from which local notables could exercise power in their home areas. Tso's own career was a case in point. On the secretarial staff of successive Hunanese governors (all, by law, non-Hunanese), Tso had for years played a vital role in the pacification of his native province. Tso's mentor, Tseng Kuo-fan, moreover had built his famous Hunan Army by inviting the local gentry to raise volunteers and money. Tso, then, it seems, came naturally by his preference for local initiative and the use of native sons.

In recommending Wen-ch'a for the Taiwan command, Tso stressed that the rebellion had grown too big to be suppressed by "guest," that is outside, troops. Since native Taiwanese soldiers would be needed to do the job, Tso thought, "we cannot but use local big gentry as managers. They are familiar with local feelings and can easily establish rapport and control them."[37] In a letter to Wen-ch'a, Tso stressed another point. Since he could provide little money for the campaign, he explained, the ardor of outside soldiers might be affected but not the fighting spirit of the local men who would defend house and home.[38] Psychologically sound as far as it went, the argument also reveals a certain, perhaps willful, naïveté. For if underpaid local soldiers were let loose on local rebels, might they not join the outlaws? Or find compensation for unpaid wages in wholesale looting? In either case, local abuses might well outweigh provincial savings.

Familiar with the inveterate feuding of the Taiwanese, and perhaps with Wen-ch'a's strongman background, officials in Fukien saw the dangers of the appointment more clearly than did the distant Tso. One of these men was Ting Yüeh-chien, whose earlier experience with pacification in Taiwan now moved him to write an essay on the subject. Probably circulated among the high provincial officials in the late summer, it warned against the use of native braves on Taiwan and called attention to their lawlessness. To drive the point home, Ting alluded to Wen-ming's recent poor record in pacification.[39] But the essay came too late to change Tso's mind. A more direct challenge to Wen-ch'a's appointment came from the deputy governor, Chang Yu-chih, who wrote directly to Tso to head off the governor-general's recommendation to the throne. He, too, was too late and Tso refused to reverse himself. But, in replying to Chang, Tso revealed his own uneasiness about the appointment. Wen-ch'a, he said, was "young and high-spirited; he does not know how to select his friends and his shortcomings are of course numerous."[40] He suggested that the Fukien authorities reexamine the situation, to see if Wen-ch'a needed to go at all, now that the news from the island was more favorable.

The upshot of all these doubts and interventions was a decision to let Wen-ch'a proceed, but to curtail his powers. The title of provincial naval commander-in-chief, recently bestowed on him at Tso's request, was taken away so as not "to overburden him."[41] More important, a second man was to share the overall direction of the campaign and serve as a watchdog over Wen-ch'a. This would be none other than Ting Yüeh-chien, who now received the Taiwan intendancy. Since a shared command was not unusual in China, the throne approved both appointments, perhaps unaware of the strain between the two men.[42] On a distant frontier—even an express dispatch to Peking took upwards of four weeks[43]—the arrangement was bound to cause trouble.

Wen-ch'a's ascent from local strongman to imperial general traces an important pattern of upward mobility. Less familiar than the commoner's classic rise through the examination system, upward mobility in the military was significant in many periods of Chinese history and often startling in periods of turmoil.

If Wen-ch'a appeared to be joining an illustrious company, the setbacks he encountered in the autumn of 1862 underline another aspect of elite mobility: the dependence of promotions on personal contacts and sponsors.[44] The military men who rose high in the late nineteenth century almost invariably came from the entourage of the two or three outstanding anti-Taiping fighters, men like Tseng Kuo-fan, Li Hung-chang, and Tso Tsung-t'ang. As Wen-ch'a's first stay on the mainland drew to a close, he had not yet established himself as a personal protégé of one of these mighty men. What counted against him was less his background as a strongman—far more disreputable types rose to high rank[45]—than his provincial origin. For Tseng, Li, and Tso tended to chose their most trusted commanders from among their fellow-provincials, Hunanese in the case of Tseng and Tso, men from Anhui in Li's case. The same parochial loyalties which Wen-ch'a had exploited earlier in the context of Taiwan's communal tensions now worked against him in the larger political arena.

Nor was this all, for doubts about his personal fitness had at last been raised. Was he too small a man for high command? Was he at heart still a local strongman or did he have the makings of the true soldier-statesman? The questions were no less pertinent for having been raised by Wen-ch'a's enemies. The Taiwan assignment would tell whether he deserved the full trust of one of China's great generals.

CHAPTER 8

TESTING TIME

Lin Wen-ch'a and
the Pacification of Taiwan, 1863-1864

*On imperial orders he returned home to punish
the bandits. Public duty and private vengeance
made him ardent.*[1]

When the Chinese elite rallied to the alien Manchu house
against Chinese rebels, many acted from a sense of localism.[2] In fighting rebellion, they were of course defending their own privileges, but it was the old order in their
native districts they sought to safeguard, not the higher
principles of dynasty or ideology. If this was true of
scholar-officials with a broad background in the country's
affairs, little wonder that a man like Wen-ch'a viewed the
issues of the day in local and personal terms. Unfamiliar as
he was with the perspective from the center, the battle for
Chang-hua's Upper Valley loomed larger in his mind than
the contest for the entire Yangtze valley.

Conditions in Taiwan lent support to Wen-ch'a's seem-
ing idiosyncrasy: the Taiwanese rebel leaders were in the
main strongmen from the Upper Valley and old enemies
of the Wu-feng Lins. They therefore threatened Wen-
ch'a's family and power base quite as much as they did the
dynasty and the local magistrate. Embarking on the
Taiwan campaign, Wen-ch'a thus faced a multiple test. His
future in the military would depend on the impression he
made on Tso, hence on his ability to subordinate personal

pique to the larger goal of pacification. Yet his future as a strongman would depend on the very opposite: his ability to wrest personal advantage from his new assignment and to recover, and perhaps expand, his strongman base. A review of the background and early course of the Tai Wan-sheng rebellion will illuminate the mixed motives with which Wen-ch'a returned to Taiwan.

As in the Lin Shuang-wen rebellion, there was a link between insurgency and older patterns of private feuding. We can best understand the connection by tracing the rebel leaders' background in the world of rural violence. The eponymous leader of the rebellion, Tai Wan-sheng, came from a prominent family in Szu-chang-li, a market town some eight miles northwest of Wu-feng.[3] Of Chang-chou background, the Tais had been on the fringes of the local elite for some time and more recently served as clerks in the office of the *pei-lu* garrison commander, a post which must have provided political leverage and opportunities for graft. By mid-century, they had become deeply involved in rural violence as well. Tai Wan-sheng's older brother had quarreled with the Wu-feng Lins, reportedly over land,[4] and kept an armed following to conduct the feud. Under the label of a sworn society (variously called *Pa-kua-hui* or *T'u-ti kung-hui*),* the force appeared as ambiguous as its names, subversive in the eyes of some, an innocuous self-defense corps to others. Tai Wan-sheng's own early career positioned him in a similarly ambivalent stance vis-à-vis the authorities. Inheriting the clerkship from his brother, he became friends with Tseng Yü-ming, the *pei-lu* commander who also patronized Lin Wen-ch'a.[5] Under Tseng's successor, however, Tai fell out with the military. When the new commander sought to shake him down, Tai refused, left his post in a huff, went home, and reassem-

---

* The term *Pa-kua-hui* (Eight Trigram Society) was reminiscent of a major uprising unleashed earlier in the century by the Eight Trigram sect; by comparison, the term *T'u-ti-kung-hui* (Society of the Local Earth God) was harmless.

bled the band of fighters that his brother had once led. Though it now bore the subversive name of the *T'ien-ti-hui*, the force remained politically inoffensive for some time; the magistrate even drafted Tai's men to serve as *t'uan-yung*, "militia braves."[6] But this legalization proved Tai's undoing. Basking in the light of official approval, the society suddenly attracted many malcontents ("bullies and rascals," according to a conservative source)[7] who saw it as a vehicle for both lawlessness and social protest. As Tai lost control of his followers, his truce with the authorities wore thin.

Protest was indeed rife in the district in the spring of 1862 and centered on a rumored new tax which the intendant, Wen-ch'a's old patron, K'ung Chao-tz'u, was said to be planning for the district.[8] As such rumors radicalized the *T'ien-ti-hui*, officials tended to see Tai's organization behind every murmur of protest. Amidst omens of impending rebellion—strange thunderclaps, biological freaks—Intendant K'ung came up from Tainan in early April to take matters in hand. The local officials could not agree on the best course to recommend. Some counselled that Tai be bought off, others that he be suppressed.[9] K'ung chose the tough line but, as military preparations began, Tai decided to strike first. The *T'ien-ti-hui* rose in mid-April and quickly captured Chang-hua city, killing K'ung and many other officials. To make matters worse, Tai was soon joined by another powerful strongman in the district, Lin Jih-ch'eng of Szu-k'uai-ts'o. Summoned to join the government forces assembling for the attack on Tai, he mutinied instead, killed the official under whom he was supposed to serve, and proclaimed himself co-leader of the rebellion.

The background of Crazy Tiger Ch'eng, as Lin Jih-ch'eng was nicknamed, throws further light on the roots of rebellion in mid-Taiwan.[10] While he proclaimed broader political goals such as the independence of Taiwan, his animus came from the private feuds of the

Upper Valley. The official he slew was an old enemy who had once dared to try to arrest him.[11] But Lin's major antagonist (and his immediate target once he had joined the rebels) was Lin Wen-ch'a, a bitter rival during the 1850's when the two men had waged the district's fiercest, though inconclusive, strongman feud.[12] His relations to the local government were much like those of his rival a decade earlier, a blend of defiance and accommodation. Except for the official he had killed at the outset, he got along with the authorities and even enjoyed the favor of some. He had been friendly with Colonel Tseng Yü-ming and more recently a local *tsung-li* had recommended his services to the district magistrate.[13]

While rebellion spread quickly in the spring of 1862, by the summer the two rebel leaders came to a parting of the way. Abler than Tai, Lin Jih-ch'eng must have found it difficult to take orders from the senior leader, and there was political disagreement as well.[14] The Crazy Tiger dreamed of Taiwanese independence, while Tai professed an old-fashioned loyalty to the Ming. Eventually, Tai abandoned Chang-hua city, where he had been crowned rebel king earlier, leaving it to Lin. He moved south, where his adherents already held much of northern Chia-yi district, and laid siege to the district city. Lin Jih-ch'eng on his part tried to carry the rebellion north but got no farther than the Ta-chia River, where loyalist forces offered a spirited resistance.

Settling Old Scores

Everywhere, the alignment of forces reflected the older cleavages in mid-Taiwan.[15] As in the 1780's, the rebels came mainly from among the Chang-chou settlers and they again failed to take Lu-kang, with its largely Ch'üan-chou population. Utilizing the divisions, the government organized the Ch'üan-chou villages along the coast into a protective shield around Lu-kang. As in previous rebellions, the

Hakkas, too, chose the government side. Under a redoubtable strongman from the Feng-yüan area, Lo Kuan-ying, they contributed to Lin Jih-ch'eng's setback at the Ta-chia River.[16]

Elsewhere, old clan feuds reignited. A case in point was the Hung clan of Ts'ao-t'un. For some weeks after the outbreak of the rebellion, the clan's leading family remained torn between dynastic loyalty—some Hung braves served with the government on the mainland—and their old friendship with Tai Wan-sheng. Though officials tried hard to keep them neutral, the clan leader, Hung Ts'ung, and many of his clansmen finally joined the rebel side. Personal animosities rather than political loyalties seem to have inspired the decision; for as Tai Wan-sheng and Lin Jih-ch'eng began to settle old scores with the Wu-feng Lins, the Hungs could not resist joining in.[17]

The Hungs's feud with the Wu-feng Lins had developed over irrigation water, the Wu-feng *chün* on which the Lins depended and which the Hungs controlled. The earlier rental arrangements, dating to the eighteenth century, had broken down, perhaps as Wu-feng under its strongmen challenged the earlier terms. Violence had erupted and a Hung leader, Hung Fan, was killed. Some say that the Hungs had retaliated by blocking the *chün* altogether, but later reopened it when a truce was arranged.[18]

Whatever the specifics of this old feud—and they cannot now be reconstructed—the Hungs were as deeply involved in rural violence as were the Lin strongmen. From before mid-century, they had based their power on a multisurname alliance, the *Szu-ta-hsing* (Four Great Surnames) of Pei-t'ou tithing, which maintained an armed force and had its own temple in Ts'ao-t'un. The Hungs were probably the leading element in the association, secure in their large landholdings, their water control, and with a handsome clan temple of their own near Ts'ao-t'un.[19] Under Hung Fan's brother, Ts'ung, the armed force was reorganized, perhaps in the 1850's. Under a new label (*Wan-an-*

chü,* innocuous enough), it is said to have functioned much as Tai Wan-sheng's *T'ien-ti-hui* did at first, protecting merchants and goods in transit from the Ts'ao-t'un area to the markets downriver, and it controlled a broad swath of territory east of Pa-kua-*shan*. It is unlikely to have been quite so benign as the Hungs picture it, but, like Tai's group in the beginning, enjoyed the tacit approval of the local magistrate.[20] Yet whatever their political skills in the past, in the late spring of 1862 the old grudge got the better of the Hungs's caution and they plunged into the rebellion.

Old feuds shaped not only the basic alignment of prominent rebels but their military moves as well. An object of Tai Wan-sheng's and Lin Jih-ch'eng's hatred, Wu-feng was a natural rebel target. Both the Wu-feng strongmen and the rebel leaders prepared for a siege as soon as the rebellion had broken out. In Wu-feng, the responsibility fell to Lin Tien-kuo. He too had initially been summoned to raise braves for the anti-Tai campaign, but he sensed danger as soon as Lin Jih-ch'eng mutinied. He quickly returned with his braves to Wu-feng and "dug a moat and established fortifications, gathered in rice and salt and sought military equipment, planning to hold out for a long time."[21] He also sent trusted men into the mountains to ask for aborigine help.

The time was indeed short, for no sooner had the rebel leaders met after the initial success of their uprising than they agreed to attack Wu-feng.[22] Under Lin Jih-ch'eng's personal command, more than thirty-thousand rebels began to attack the village. Its manpower depleted from Wen-ch'a's vigorous recruiting, Wu-feng had barely enough men to patrol the palisades. By almost superhuman efforts (to follow the Wu-feng accounts), the defenders beat back the direct assaults by day and the sneak attacks by night. Frustrated, Jih-ch'eng then changed his

* Bureau of Perpetual Peace.

plans, expecting now to starve the village into surrender. With the help of the Hungs, who joined the rebellion at this time, Wu-feng's water supply was cut off and neighboring villages who might have helped their beleaguered kinsmen were attacked. "Wu-feng stood isolated, a lone village among the red [rebel] flags. The defense lasted a whole year. Water in the irrigation canals was cut off . . . and our good fields all dried up and no rice was harvested."

As the siege dragged on, Tien-kuo's eldest son, Wen-feng (1840-1882) proved himself the village's outstanding leader. He organized patrols and issued grain to the villagers from the family's own storehouses. "He kept morale high, planning for final victory." Even so, the villagers could not raise the siege on their own, and they remained in danger. At times, they observed Hung women riding around the village, cheering their men on to a final effort.[23] Still, Wu-feng held out.

Relief of sorts may have come with Wen-ming's arrival in the fall of 1862, but he brought too few men to turn the tide and was himself forced to sneak into Wu-feng in disguise.[24] More substantial aid came the next year with the arrival of two hundred Hakka braves under their leader, Lo Kuan-ying of Tung-shih-chiao, near Feng-yüan, the same group that had aided the loyalist cause at the Ta-chia River earlier.[25] But the arrival of so many strangers posed its own problems. Suspicion between the villagers and their would-be rescuers ran high until Wen-feng, always the diplomat, exhorted his people: "They have come to help us; therefore they cherish us. How can there be an incident?"[26] He then ordered cattle killed and treated both Hakkas and villagers to a great feast in the besieged village. Finally, he ordered treasure from the family storehouse brought out and offered it to the Hakkas, saying: "You gentlemen have come across hills and valleys and you have braved dangers to aid and protect our village. Truly, it is a blessing for us. If you had not helped, surely we would have died. I am offering you this unworthy token, fortunate that the rebels have not taken it." This gesture apparently calmed the tension, for the groups now joined together and guarded the village with their combined forces.

By mid-1863, imperial forces were clearing the Upper Valley and the danger to Wu-feng receded. Clansmen, some four or five hundred strong, were able to reach Wu-feng from T'u-ch'eng and other neighboring villages. Together, they "opened the palisades and went out to fight among the dikes and fields. . . . Each of our men," the Lin genealogy reports, "was worth a hundred of the enemy and we killed hundreds and wounded many tens. Jih-ch'eng suffered a big defeat and hurriedly ran away." By the time Wen-ch'a reached the island, the siege was over.

The New Commanders Take Over

When Wen-ch'a and Ting Yüeh-chien crossed over to Taiwan in the fall of 1863, the rebels were already confined to certain large pockets in Chang-hua and northern Chia-yi district. The back of the rebellion had been broken, though Chang-hua city remained to be captured and the rebel leaders caught. As if to avoid close contact, the two new commanders came ashore on opposite ends of the island. Ting landed in the north, where he had served as a magistrate ten years earlier and where he still had many friends. Contacting his "old followers,"[27] he moved south toward Chang-hua, raising braves as he went along. He reached the district in December and assumed overall command of the attack on the city which the local commanders had been planning—men such as Tseng Yü-ming, the new Taiwan garrison commander, Tseng Yüan-fu, another old officer of the Taiwan command (they were nicknamed Big and Little Tseng, respectively), and Ling Ting-kuo, the acting Chang-hua magistrate. The assault on the city was successful and imperial forces reentered Chang-hua in mid-January 1864.[28]

Wen-ch'a had meanwhile landed in the south with some five hundred braves. Moving up through Chia-yi, he cooperated with local leaders to win defiant villages back to the imperial fold. He, too, recruited along the way and was to have over five thousand braves under his command by spring.[29] While Ting directed the siege of Chang-hua city, Wen-ch'a invested Tou-liu (modern Yün-lin), a town in northern Chia-yi where Tai Wan-sheng had dug in. The town fell to Wen-ch'a about the time that Chang-hua city was recovered, but the chief prize, the rebel leader, got away.[30]

Meeting in Chang-hua in late January, the leading men sat down to map the next phase of the campaign but found time for much personal squabbling as well. Both Ting and Wen-ch'a claimed credit for the recovery of the district city, Wen-ch'a arguing that his siege of Tou-liu had drawn off enough rebels to allow Chang-hua to be taken. Ting countered that it was the Chang-hua operation which had allowed Wen-ch'a to capture Tou-liu.[31] Over the next few weeks, the secondary leaders, too, chose sides. Tseng Yü-ming stayed with Wen-ch'a, true to their old friendship, while Tseng Yüan-fu and Ling Ting-kuo joined Ting's camp. Henceforth, they conducted operations with the Intendant, received his recommendations for rewards, and fed him information hostile to the Wu-feng Lins.[32]

While the court urged the feuding commanders to cooperate,[33] Ting and Wen-ch'a went their own ways. Ting pursued Tai, the rebel leader who had escaped Wen-ch'a; within a few weeks, he had captured and executed him.[34] Ting now could fairly claim that he had achieved the two major feats of pacification: the recovery of the rebel "capital" and the capture of the eponymous rebel leader. As over against such prize catches that would impress the throne, Wen-ch'a gave priority to his own deepest hatreds. Determined to avenge the attack on Wu-feng, he laid siege to Lin Jih-ch'eng's lair in Szu-k'uai-ts'o. A local folk ballad conveys the popular interest in this final battle of the local titans.[35] Wen-ch'a's "troops went forth, attacking big brother Lin of Szu-k'uai-ts'o. But the attack came to nothing." Changing tactics, Wen-ch'a found traitors in the enemy lair who spiked the Crazy Tiger's guns. Then, as the village was being overrun, Lin Jih-ch'eng's elaborate preparations for suicide also went awry and he fell into Wen-ch'a's hands, alive though badly burned. "Crazy Tiger Ch'eng was burned, but not dead; badly burned, his gums exposed. So he fell into Yu-li's [i.e., Wen-ch'a's] hands." When the two met face to face, Wen-ch'a's words appeared to mock the dying man as he urged "Uncle Ch'eng"

> "Drink this tea to soothe the burned skin;
> I will save your life, you will not die."
> When Crazy Tiger Ch'eng heard this [he wondered]
> "For long there's been a feud between our houses
> Over the business of Ch'en Ta-shih [?].
> Why should he spare my life?
> Better to die, biting off my own tongue."
> [Out loud he said] "Do as you like, cut or slice."
> So Crazy Tiger Ch'eng was put to death,
> A fitting death, to die by slicing.
> His limbs torn off, his head put on display.

We may wonder what went through Wen-ch'a's mind as he offered to spare his rival's life. Did he plan to nurse him back only to despatch him to Peking in triumph? Or would this be too bureaucratic a satisfaction for the strongman who had already savored vengeance once? To know the answer would give us a clue to Wen-ch'a's state of mind as he hovered between his two worlds—the bureaucratic world of the imperial government and the direct-action world of the strongman.

With his arch-rival out of the way, Wen-ch'a began his reckoning with the Hung forces. He sent Tseng Yü-ming to attack their lair at Pei-shih-nan which was captured after a prolonged siege. While Hung Ts'ung escaped and remained at large until after Wen-ch'a left the island, the Hung turf lay open to his reprisals.[36]

With the major rebel figures dead or on the run, the rebellion approached its end, but not the quarrel among the imperial commanders. There was renewed feuding over individual merits, for example. Wen-ch'a resented the fact that Ting had not recommended Wen-ming for a reward; furious, he memorialized on his brother's behalf and won him a promotion to colonel.[37] While Wen-ch'a's own reward was beyond Ting's jurisdiction (the throne asked Tso and the Fukien governor, Hsü, to evaluate his record and make appropriate recommendations),[38] Ting still sought to belittle Wen-ch'a's record. He told Tso privately that in Szu-k'uai-ts'o, a "half-dead rebel chief"[39] had fallen into Wen-ch'a's hands, suggesting a less than heroic performance.

Fig. 8 Soldier's medal, a silver plaque awarded by Lin Wen-ch'a and inscribed with his name (Lin Family).

In April, both Ting and Wen-ch'a withdrew from Chang-hua city, Ting to attend to his duties in Tainan, Wen-ch'a to savor victory in Wu-feng. But distance did not abate the quarrel of the two men. In the aftermath of victory, their feud simply shifted to other grounds.

As Wen-ch'a turned to exploit his victory for personal advantage, Ting rose in righteous indignation to challenge his colleague's iniquities. In a series of mounting denunciations to the throne, he almost wrecked Wen-ch'a's career. Clearly, there was much to criticize in Wen-ch'a's conduct. But Ting discharged this particular duty with such zeal[40] as to suggest that for him, no less than for Wen-ch'a, public policy and private grudges had become inextricably intertwined. In very large part, it was the old feud dating back to the T'ing-chou affair and the more recent friction in Taiwan which made Ting so eager to find fault, so ready to listen to denunciations of the Lin family.

Ting's zeal was all the more dangerous since he was an experienced bureaucrat who orchestrated his charges skillfully and with minimal risk to himself.[41] Attacking Wen-ch'a's more vulnerable relatives first, for example, he only slowly focused his attack on the commander himself. By comparison, Wen-ch'a was a novice, wielding the weapons of bureaucratic infighting—memorials, leaks, private letters to superiors—less skillfully. Luckily for him, Tso Tsung-t'ang recognized the personal animus at work and therefore took Ting's charges with a grain of salt.[42] But as Ting conducted his crusade, Tso would not be the final judge.

The charges that Ting raised in the spring and elaborated over the early summer added up to a stark indictment: the Lins were abusing pacification for their own aggrandizement as strongmen.[43] In a memorial of early May, Ting charged that Tien-kuo, Wen-ch'a's uncle, had unleashed a reign of terror against a neighboring Lai clan and had robbed them of their land. Ting's first official accusations against Wen-ch'a were less specific though no less serious, for Ting hinted that Wen-ch'a's pacification methods had injured the innocent and spared the guilty. When Peking ignored Ting's denunciation, the intendant returned to the attack in June. He reiterated the charges against Tien-kuo and added particulars of Wen-ch'a's wrongdoing: that he sat idly at home, wasting precious public monies on his soldiers without helping to "mop up" the last rebels; that partisanship guided his work of pacification; that his braves harassed the people and drove them into the arms of the remaining rebels, and so forth.

After prolonged soul-searching, the throne handed down a decision in late August: Ting was to stop Tien-kuo's depradations and to put him on trial on the charges he had itemized.[44] Since Ting, as intendant, was the chief judicial officer on Taiwan, the imperial edict gave him an almost free hand to do with Tien-kuo as he pleased, provided only he could lay hands on him. The question of Wen-ch'a's transgressions was more delicate. If Ting's charges proved true, the imperial edict stated, Wen-ch'a was guilty of a serious breach of trust. Hence, Governor-General Tso and Governor Hsü would have to examine Ting's accusations. If they proved accurate, Wen-ch'a would have to be impeached. It was an uncomfortable assignment for the two men who had recommended the young general for the Taiwan command and particularly embarrassing for Hsü because Ting was his old protégé as well.

Despatching a special investigator to Taiwan, the two high officials sought to weaken the impact of Ting's charges: a personality clash, they explained, had helped to inspire the accusations. But neither the throne nor Ting was easily deterred; Peking insisted that an examination into Ting's charges must be held; Ting on his part plied Tso with further particulars of Wen-ch'a's misdeeds.[45]

When matters had come to this critical stage in September, further serious charges against Wen-ch'a reached the capital.[46] These had to do with his long-postponed departure from the island. Since the spring, Peking had asked that some of the units sent to Taiwan be returned to the mainland. This, too, had become a bone of contention between Ting and Wen-ch'a. Ting wanted Wen-ch'a and Tseng Yü-ming to go, his own friends to stay. Each side had used, and perhaps manufactured, incidents to support its argument. A brief rebel flare-up in May had been grist to both their mills. Wen-ch'a argued that it proved that his presence was still required for pacification; Ting hinted that it merely proved Wen-ch'a's inept pacification, if the incident had not indeed been artificially blown up to provide him with a pretext for staying on.[47] Since an order for Wen-ch'a's departure had been issued months ago, the throne reacted sharply to the new denunciation; the appropriate board was asked to assess Wen-ch'a's penalty.[48] Perhaps getting wind of these developments, Wen-ch'a now prepared his departure in earnest. Claiming that Taiwan was now truly pacified, he returned to mainland Fukien, probably in mid-September just as the throne ordered him punished for the delay.[49]

The Spoils

If Wen-ch'a treated imperial orders with some nonchalance, it was because he found his true satisfaction not in pleasing the throne but in the spoils of victory: new, immense wealth and an unchallenged dominion over the Upper Valley. Wen-ch'a thus proved Ting's charges correct even as he lived up to the strongman code of honor. For after the rebel siege of Wu-feng, there could be only revenge, not reconciliation, and all his official powers must be bent toward that end.

The extent of Wen-ch'a's spoliations can only be suggested since Ting's accusations were never subjected to an impartial review. Oral traditions from the district, gathered by a folklorist in the twentieth century, largely confirm the intendant's charges while adding much gory detail.[50] Further circumstantial evidence comes from the official land surveys taken at the turn of the century; these show such exceedingly high concentrations of Lin land-ownership in the villages around Wu-feng as to suggest a massive take-over by force, not a slow accumulation by purchase. Moreover, Lin holdings were most extensive in precisely those locations where the rivals-turned-rebels, especially Lin Jih-ch'eng and the Hungs, had once been major owners.[51] Then, too, the hatred which several local families bore the Wu-feng Lins in the late 1860's suggests an injury which we can associate most easily with Wen-ch'a's abuses during pacification. Last but not least, today even members of the Lin family concede the substance of Ting's charges, although some insist that it was Lin tenants, not their masters, who despoiled the victims.

Who, then, were the major victims and how were they despoiled? To the south, the Hungs lost all their lands between Wu-feng and the Wu River.[52] This gave Wen-ch'a and his family almost ninety-eight percent of the crop land in Wan-tou-liu and, more strategic, access to the river's precious water. Control of the Wu-feng *chün* passed to the Lins.[53] To the west, the family seized the lands of Lin Jih-ch'eng and his followers.[54] This gave them more than three-quarters of the crop land in Wu-ts'o (the survey unit which encompassed Szu-k'uai-ts'o) and Liu-shu-nan. To the west and northwest, there may have been further spoliations of the lands of the family's first great enemy, the dead Lin Ho-shang, but the specifics are less clear.[55] Straight north were the lands of the Lai clan, many of which Tien-kuo had seized.[56]

Most of the major victims, then, were old enemies of the Lins, rivals who would treat them with an equal measure should the tables ever be turned. We need not, perhaps, extend overmuch sympathy to them. In another category were the many random victims, forced to yield cash or land to pay "donations" or "fines," ostensibly for pacification but in reality to line Wen-ch'a's own pocket.[57] Among them we find a hapless city-man, one "millionaire" (*Ch'ien-wan*, i.e., ten million) Wang, who lost his Chang-hua mansion to Wen-ch'a. Here, too, belong the government-owned fields, particularly in Ta-li-chi, whose rents Wen-ch'a seized;[58] it may have given him a grim satisfaction to collect what had once belonged to his great-great-grandfather, Shih.

Not only Wen-ch'a but a whole host of his sub-commanders and underlings descended on the Upper Valley. Since most of them were natives and deeply enmeshed in the Upper Valley's private violence, they too were no doubt settling old scores. Some of Wen-ch'a's T'ai-p'ing and T'u-ch'eng cousins took advantage of their illustrious relative's power. They seized lands and manipulated "donations" and "fines" for personal enrichment.[59] Further down, many soldiers must have simply looted.

The spoliations were no doubt undertaken with varying degrees of finesse. Wen-ch'a, triumphant in his headquarters at Wu-feng, several thousand soldiers at his beck and call, had no need to observe legal niceties. Yet here and there, the law itself provided cover for spoliations. Rebel lands could be seized by law and portions awarded to informers. Ting's charges suggest that Wen-ch'a confiscated some rebel land, as was proper, and then incorporated it into his own holdings.[60] Tien-kuo was said to have bought land at rock-bottom prices from frightened rebels whose only alternative was outright confiscation.[61] In the case of the Hung lands, a happy accident came to the Lins' aid. Some time back, before the rebellion, a Lin daughter had been married to a Hung, probably in the kind of political match that was meant to seal a truce. When the rebellion neared its end, the Hungs sent this woman back to Wu-feng with the bulk of their land deeds, a desperate tactic to avoid confiscation. It quickly backfired, for the Lins simply pocketed what they were asked to safeguard.[62]

Mostly, though, the methods were cruder. Boundary markers "walked" mysteriously overnight to expand Lin holdings. Wen-ch'a's soldiers and Tien-kuo's bullies simply occupied what their masters wanted, forcing tenants at gunpoint to deliver the rental grain to the Wu-feng Lin storehouse.[63] Ting charged that Wen-ch'a lingered in Taiwan precisely to assure that the land rent from the seized fields would be delivered to the Lin storehouse, not to the former masters.[64]

In most cases, the Lin takeovers displaced only the former *hsiao-tsu* owners, leaving the rights of the *ta-tsu* and the tenants intact. The number of the aggrieved parties was thus held to a minimum and the Lins could more easily establish their claims to the new land. That they did establish title, whatever the dubious mechanisms of the takeover, can be in no doubt. The land surveys of the 1880's and of the 1900's showed them to be owners of immense holdings such as were rare in China at the time.[65]

The end of the Taiwan campaign found Wen-ch'a in possession of unprecedented power in the Upper Valley; yet in the imperial firmament his star had begun to set. His accomplishments in the field had been meager and he received no awards for the Taiwan mission. His official prospects were in fact more clouded than ever before, for even if one took Intendant Ting's charges with a grain of salt, as Tso was inclined to do, Wen-ch'a's feud with his colleague spoke poorly of his political skills. After the Taiwan campaign, neither Tso nor any of the senior leaders in the empire were likely to invite Wen-ch'a into their entourage or to open any doors to him. Still, this was perhaps after all as Wen-ch'a wished it. To judge from his conduct in Taiwan, the mainland years had given him a new arrogance but no broader concept of public service. At heart he was still the strongman he had always been.

The question was rather whether he had not already over-reached himself. With a disciplinary penalty due and the threat of impeachment hanging over him, he would be lucky to emerge from the Taiwan venture with his wealth and his power base intact, to say nothing of the dimmed prospects of an official career. Nor was it only the long arm of the imperial government which seemed to be reaching out to chastize Wen-ch'a. His "pacification" left a whole host of enemies in its wake, both among the local rivals whom he despoiled and the local officials who had stood helplessly by as he wreaked his vengeance. The hatred of these men would long haunt the family.

CHAPTER 9

THE SCAPEGOAT

The Era of
Lin Wen-ming, 1864-1870

Lin Wen-ming was by nature coarse, overbearing, and quite incapable of following the rules. Yet his reputation . . . was half owing to the fact that he and his elder brother, Lin Wen-ch'a, pacified the Tai Wan-sheng rebellion and brought under constraint local gangs hostile to them; thus he was slandered by vengeful families.[1]

As Lin Wen-ch'a returned to mainland Fukien in September of 1864, he found himself possessed of unexpected leverage at the provincial capital. A new military emergency forced the provincial authorities to turn to him for assistance. One final time, he could play his old card and, by aiding government, advance his own cause.

Taiping remnants had fled south after the fall of Nanking (June 1864) and had occupied several prefectures in southern Fukien.[2] Wen-ch'a's help was needed to dislodge them. Governor Hsü received him and, before sending Wen-ch'a into battle, asked that the penalty for the dilatory commander be waived. Hsü argued that not only had typhoons delayed Wen-ch'a's departure but that his earlier merits should be weighed in the balance. No doubt much to Wen-ch'a's relief, the throne agreed to set the yet undetermined penalty aside.[3] Since Ting's graver charges still hung over his head, he needed not penalties but new laurels on the battlefield. With Tso's and Hsü's blessing, Wen-ch'a threw himself into a new Fukien campaign.

Yet he was in some ways ill-prepared for the assignment. All but two hundred of his braves had chosen to remain behind. Recruiting a motley troop of mainland Fukienese and mustered-out Hunanese braves, Wen-ch'a would find this new mixed force less vigorous than his veteran Taiwan Braves when he reported for action in November.[4]

Wen-ch'a's first target was the rebel-held city of Chang-chou. To lay siege to the city, he decided first to capture Wan-sung pass, some seven miles from the prefectural capital. But the rebels proved as determined in defending the strategic position as Wen-ch'a was in attacking it. Rebels engaged the imperial forces before the soldiers had time to dig in, and a furious fight ensued. Outnumbered, Wen-ch'a's force could neither retreat nor be reenforced. After some hours of desperate combat, the ammunition for their superior foreign rifles ran out and the soldiers succumbed, along with their youthful commander. The date was December 1, 1864.[5]

Wen-ch'a's last hours have been variously described. The Lin genealogy reports a final talk with Tien-kuo, the uncle who had followed him into the campaign.[6] As the fight neared its end, Wen-ch'a urged the older man to retreat. "As a general, I belong to the country," he is supposed to have said, "I must die for righteousness' sake. You, uncle, can break out . . . and get away. You do not all have to die." After some hesitation, Tien-kuo and some braves managed to retreat, leaving Wen-ch'a to perish on the battlefield. Another source reports that Wen-ch'a himself attempted to flee, on foot, but was recognized and captured. The manner of his death, too, is variously described. Official accounts say that he died quickly, from a gunshot wound, but others have him falling into enemy hands alive, only to die after torture and mutilation.[7]

If Wen-ch'a's death was gruesome, as seems likely, the imperial government could make up for it, after a fashion. It bestowed lavish honors on the fallen hero, raising him to the exalted rank of Junior Guardian of the Heir Apparent and giving him a temple name and the hereditary rank of *ch'i-tu-wei* which passed automatically to his eldest son. Temples in Wen-ch'a's memory were authorized in Chang-chou and in his native district. To ensure immortality, the government further ordered that his biography be included in the standard compendium of generals' lives. For Wen-ch'a's next-of-kin, there were the customary money donations and, for some of his forebears, posthumous honors.[8]

The awards had special significance in view of the still unsettled question of Wen-ch'a's impeachment. Not only were his posthumous honors exceptionally lavish, but they evidently brought to a halt the inquiry into his wrongdoings. At least we hear no more of the investigation which Tso and Hsü had been asked to undertake. In the eyes of government, the final year of Wen-ch'a's life thus left an ambiguous legacy: his conduct in Taiwan invited censure, yet his death conferred immunity. His private enemies would have to seek vindication elsewhere.

The New Leaders

After Wen-ch'a's death, his branch of the family passed under the leadership of his younger brother, Wen-ming (1833-1870). Closely associated with Wen-ch'a during his strongman years, Wen-ming had the authority and experience to step into his brother's shoes. He inherited Wen-ch'a's position as the Upper Valley's premier strongman as well as the headship of the large, still joint household of Ting-pang's descendants.

The black sheep of the family, Wen-ming has no biography in the Lin genealogy. We therefore lack the anecdotal detail that evokes a man's personality, even though scraps of information bearing on his life turn up in the biographies of his relatives. Wen-ming seems to have been a man much after Wen-ch'a's heart, inured to the rough life of the self-styled soldier and endowed with superb courage, a powerful physique, and the strongman's haughty and vengeful bearing. He may have lacked his brother's tactical gifts and his initial political prudence in dealings with government, yet Wen-ming was no mindless bully. His role in local society went beyond simple intimidation to include the shrewd use of clan ties and of capital investments to gain influence.

His picture in the public record, particularly in the court case that developed out of his death, is distorted. It speaks only of the neighbors he robbed, the houses he burned, the fields he stole, and the women he ravished. *This* Wen-ming served as the scapegoat for his brother's many sins. When Wen-ch'a joined the pantheon of heroes, Wen-ming had to bear the burden of all the hatreds which the family had aroused. Admittedly, his temper suited the role; even family friends who insisted that he was much maligned allow that he was "coarse, overbearing, and quite incapable of following the rules."[9] In the end, however, it was not so much the man as the times in which he led the family that set his career apart from that of his brother.

Soon after Wen-ming took over the senior branch, the family's second branch also came under a new leader. Tien-kuo, who may have hoped that battlefield merits in Fukien would shield him against the charges brought by Intendant Ting, saw his calculation go awry. His escape from Wan-sung pass was hardly heroic and the authorities soon caught up with him and threw him into a Foochow jail. The family appealed, but the case had not yet been resolved when Tien-kuo died, still in jail, in 1880.[10]

Leadership of his branch of the family passed to his eldest son, Wen-feng (1840-1882), an obvious choice in view of his merits during the siege and the youth of his two brothers, Wen-tien (born 1852) and Wen-ch'in (born 1854). But Wen-feng succeeded only to Tien-kuo's headship of a large and wealthy household; he did not continue Tien-kuo's strongman role. While he was competent in battle—as in the siege or during an aborigine raid later— he did not maintain his father's following of braves. He preferred to use money and persuasion, not force, to get his way.[11]

From early on, Wen-feng had shown a keen sense of what money could achieve, as in his gifts to the Hakka braves during the siege. After the rebellion, he began a custom of making regular small money gifts to the villagers at New Year's, in recognition of their loyalty during the siege. It was he, too, alone among family members, who thought that Tien-kuo should solve his legal problems through bribery.[12] Less wealthy than Wen-ming and conscious of the power of money, Wen-feng hoarded it in the interest of family power. His domestic arrangements were miserly; he kept his household in shabby clothes and poor food.[13] With the money he saved he bought additional land and cemented political alliances.

Money aside, Wen-feng had a personal presence that made him a good negotiator. He therefore represented the family in dealings with the government, attending "to all the official business in the district city that he was aware of." This was in marked contrast to Wen-ming, who shunned the district *yamen*—and not only because a fortune-teller had warned that he would die in it.[14] At the higher levels, too, in Foochow and perhaps even in Peking, Wen-feng represented his father's case. His political style, in short, was more that of the gentry member than that of the strongman. Through the 1860's, it is true, he had Wen-ming's cruder forms of power to fall back on, but he himself did not wield, and probably did not desire, such power. And while he did not always succeed in what he attempted, his more cautious approach at least prevented setbacks for his branch of the family. In all, his prudence and clear sense of the possible stood the family in good stead.

His contacts with the *yamen* led Wen-feng to appreciate

the advantage of a classical education. Himself without degrees, he came to realize how useful scholarly status was in dealings with the government. He therefore gave his two brothers a classical education, hiring a tutor from Changhua while he himself supervised the young men's lessons.[15] Neither Wen-ch'a nor Wen-ming did anything of the sort for the young men in their charge. Wen-feng thus became the first Wu-feng Lin in more than a quarter-century (since Chia-yin had sent Wen-ch'a to study for the examinations) to encourage conventional gentry skills. Along with his turn away from the cruder bully-tactics, this too was a portent for the future.

While Wen-feng's innovations had significance for the future, he could not alter the family's dominant style overnight. It continued to be set by Wen-ming, that is to say, by the strongman tradition with its reliance on a force of braves, a lair, and a turf.

After he was shorn of all pacification duties (in late 1864, at Ting's behest),[16] Wen-ming's force was again a purely personal army. With no government funds available as they had been to Wen-ch'a, the force may have numbered no more than a few dozen full-time braves, while the part-time fighters numbered many hundreds, if not thousands.[17] The uses to which Wen-ming put his men were personal and private, too: the expansion and consolidation of the immense turf he had inherited from his brother. Well past 1864, Wen-ming mounted raids on people who stood in his way or whose property he coveted. While such spoliations were less frantic than in 1864, they now lacked the excuse of "pacification" which had served Wen-ch'a so well.[18]

Wu-feng too remained a fortified base, complete with walls of thorny bamboo, gun towers, and caches of arms. The villagers even manufactured their own rifles. At the end of the decade, Wen-ming may have placed cannon in the hillsides overlooking Wu-feng to command the approaches to the village.[19]

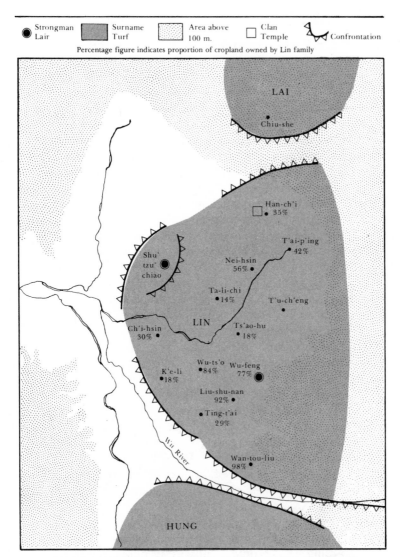

LAI

Chiu-she

Han-ch'i
● 35%

T'ai-p'ing
● 42%

Shu'
tzu'
chiao

Nei-hsin
56% ●

Ta-li-chi
● 14%

T'u-ch'eng
●

LIN

Ts'ao-hu
● 18%

Ch'i-hsin
30% ●

K'e-li
● 18%

Wu-ts'o
● 84%

Wu-feng
77% ●

Liu-shu-nan
92% ●

● Ting-t'ai
29%

Wu River

Wan-tou-liu
98% ●

HUNG

MAP 6: LIN WEN-MING'S STRONGMAN TURF, LATE 1860'S

His turf, too, was an impressive affair. In the shape of a triangle, its base ran some ten miles along the foothills and its apex extended about five or six miles west. Encompassing some thirty square miles, this was the kingdom over which the Lins were sovereign; here Wen-ming recruited his braves, gave asylum to lawbreakers from beyond,[20] and reigned supreme. On the margins, to be sure, there still lurked opponents, though they were shorn of their former power. Beyond the Wu River in the south, the Hungs retained their land and local influence. Toward the northwest, an independent small strongman, also surnamed Lin, flourished in Shu-tzu-chiao and even dared offer refuge to the surviving relatives of Lin Ho-shang. Elsewhere, the boundaries of the turf may well have been contested as late as 1870.[21]

A strongman's power or *shih-li* was a blend of many things: sheer coercion by armed force, economic power, social prestige, and personal dominance. Nor was such power evenly diffused through the length and breadth of a strongman's domain. Wen-ming's hand rested most heavily on Wu-feng itself and on the villages attached to the Wu-feng *chün*. Here, his family controlled the entire water supply and virtually all the land. Few other families of note survived. We can call this the core of his strongman turf. Farther north, the family owned lesser percentages of land and did not control the irrigation water. Local notables of independent means survived. While Wen-ming's power extended to this area as well, his ascendancy rested as much on political alliances, on kinship ties, and on business investments.

The clan tie was central, for it furnished the basis for the most durable political alignment. By the late 1860's, Wen-ming had become an important figure in his clan organization, the formal group whose temple in Nei-hsin dated from early in the century. When that temple collapsed and the clansmen decided to rebuild it in Han-ch'i, they chose Wen-ming to head the project; the wealthy Lin Wu-hsiang from T'ai-p'ing became his deputy.[22]

Lin Wu-hsiang may stand as one example of the kind of minor rural notable who supported the Lins in the northern part of their turf. Descended from Lin Shih's successful fourth son, he was well-off at birth and later added to his wealth by many shrewd business ventures. His family controlled the T'ou-pien-k'eng *chün*, the major irrigation facility in the area. In the pacification of 1864, he had worked with Wen-ch'a, had shared in the spoils, and been awarded rank on his nephew's recommendation.[23] Later, he headed local militia and sponsored community projects.

Other friendly notables in the northern part of the Lin turf came from outside the surname group. Here, political alliances could be buttressed by intermarriage. A case in point was Wu Ching-ch'un, a landlord from the Ta-tun area and leader of his own fighting men.[24] He had married a sister of Ting-pang and fought with his nephew Wen-ch'a on the mainland and later in Taiwan. The alliance of the two families was sealed when he shared Wen-ch'a's martyrdom. The Wus remained prominent in the area and close to the Lins through further intermarriages and joint service on local projects.

Wen-ming sought influence not only at the hub of his kinship network and among rural notables, but in the major market town of his turf, Ta-li-chi. In 1869, he "provided capital, opened shops, summoned merchants, and tried to revive trade,"[25] an enterprise which launched the town on three decades of prosperity before the rising new city of Taichung eclipsed it early in the twentieth century. That the Lins sought economic rather than military power in Ta-li-chi may have been due to the small garrison stationed in the town. Within the walls, even a strongman paid minimal respect to this token of the imperial presence, however much he defied it elsewhere.

Under Wen-ming, as under Wen-ch'a, the sources of family power in the Upper Valley were thus varied. Quite as complex were the feelings of the turf's people toward the mighty Lins. There were loyal kinsmen, friendly notables, and grateful protégés. Their fortunes were bound up with Wen-ming's; their loyalty brought tangible benefits. Men serving under Wen-ming shared in the spoils of his raids; the awe his name inspired rubbed off on them too. Many local people must have benefited from the safety which a strongman could assure to the people of his turf, on the road to market or against aborigine attack. In the winter of 1867-1868, for example, Wen-feng and Wen-ming were singularly successful in warding off an aborigine attack and destroying the tribesmen in the plain.[26]

But we must not sentimentalize the relations between the people of the turf and their strongman. The Lins inspired both loyalty and fear. Hence there existed, in the turf, along with the loyal and the docile, the merely prudent and the sullen, men who were lying low only because to do otherwise would bring swift reprisals, a raid on one's homestead, a loss of land or life. Active enemies of the family had long since been crushed or driven out. Only from outside the turf could they challenge the mighty lord of the Upper Valley.

Challengers

By the late 1860's the Lins had numerous enemies, all desiring retribution but at a loss how to obtain it. An outright military challenge was out of the question. No private army was a match for Wen-ming's force and the local garrison was even feebler—a few old men with rusty spears.[27] The Lin enemies would have to shift the battle to other ground.

A legal challenge looked hardly more promising at first. When the despoiled relatives of Lin Ho-shang tried to sue in the local magistrate's court for restitution of their property, they were turned away.[28] The magistrate had either been bribed or refused to tangle with the Lins. Rebuffed in the district, a plaintiff could take an appeal to a higher tribunal, thus outflanking the Lins's powerful position at home. Yet this route, too, was not inherently promising. Litigation beyond the district level was expensive and justice in Tainan or Foochow proverbially slow. Even at these higher levels, a lawsuit against the family of one of the empire's heroes must have seemed a hopeless undertaking, except for one thing: some officials there were themselves anxious to give the Lins their comeuppance. An alliance of private plaintiffs and hostile bureaucrats just might bring the Lins down.

The most resourceful among these hostile officials was Ling Ting-kuo, the acting Chang-hua magistrate during Wen-ch'a's Taiwan campaign.[29] Already in 1864, he had supported Intendant Ting's anti-Lin crusade, and for a very personal reason: his own bitter quarrel with Lin Wen-ch'a. It had begun as a clash of two proud, high-spirited men, sometime during the spring of 1864. When Ling had failed to extend the courtesies due a commander-in-chief, Wen-ch'a retaliated by punishing Ling's father, an officer in the expeditionary corps. Then it was Ling's turn. He joined the intendant's vendetta and also charged Wen-ch'a with other improprieties (such as taking a rebel woman as concubine), but allowed Wen-ch'a to buy him off. In the autumn, Wen-ch'a paid Ling back; in his talk with Governor Hsü, he pointedly criticized Ling's conduct in office, and Ling shortly lost his Chang-hua post. Though he obtained another magistracy, at Feng-shan, he resented the transfer and the humiliation of his father, and nursed a bitter hatred.

More tenuously linked to the unfolding scheme was Intendant Ting himself, Wen-ch'a's old nemesis. Not content with having almost brought about Wen-ch'a's impeachment, he continued his vendetta against the Lins, removing Wen-ming from pacification work as soon as Wen-ch'a had left Taiwan, and securing the arrest of Tien-kuo.[30] During the late 1860's, both Ling and Ting were in a position to help the Lin family's commoner-enemies. Ling held the Feng-shan post until 1869 and then returned to Foochow, where he belonged to a pool of provincial officials (*wei-yuan*) available for special assignment.[31] Ting held the

Taiwan intendancy until 1866, retired from the post with honors, and after an audience at Peking also returned to Foochow. His position there is not known, but two accounts imply that he held office there when he influenced the anti-Lin case.[32]

When and how the two parties—the private plaintiffs and the hostile officials—made contact and who took the initiative is not clear. One source maintains that Magistrate Ling personally arranged for the plaintiffs to take their case to Foochow. Another tells of a chance encounter between an aggrieved Lin victim, seeking justice in Foochow, and the vengeful Magistrate Ling.[33] Whatever the circumstances, their coming together need not surprise us. In 1864 both Ting and Ling had been in contact with Wen-ch'a's victims and with other local people who informed on the commander's misdeeds. Later, Ting had secured Tien-kuo's arrest. It can have been no secret to the various aggrieved parties that Ting and Ling were receptive to accusations against the Lins and prepared to act on them.

In 1867 one Lin Ying-shih, formerly a wealthy landlord in Ts'ao-hu but more recently a Lin victim, sued Wen-ming in a Foochow court.[34] As best we can reconstruct the charge, he accused Wen-ming of having seized his land on the pretext of fining a rebel. The merits of his case are hard to substantiate at this time. While the Wu-feng Lins would later admit that the property of the Ts'ao-hu Lins *had* been confiscated, they insisted that this had been a *bona fide* confiscation, justified because Lin Ying-shih's brother, presumably a co-owner of the land, had been a rebel.[35] Much later, too, the authorities seem to have accepted this defense, for the original form of the accusation was dropped. Nevertheless, we need not take the Lin position at face value. The plaintiff very likely had a case, for during 1864 Wen-ch'a had been able to affix the dreaded label of "rebel" to his enemies almost at will. We learn, moreover, that Lin Ying-shih was related to the slain Ho-shang,[36] a connection which suggests that both the Foochow lawsuit and the spoliation earlier were merely new rounds in the old feud between the two families.

Whatever the merits of Lin Ying-shih's accusations, the tactics and timing of his suit seem to have been carefully chosen, perhaps by an experienced bureaucrat such as Ling. To minimize the risk to the plaintiff, the charge bypassed the martyred Wen-ch'a and focused on his more vulnerable brother. The timing is also suggestive, for the suit followed close on the heels of important personnel changes in Foochow which favored the plaintiff. Intendant Ting had recently returned to the city while two high officials who might have helped the Lins had departed.[37] In September 1866, Tso Tsung-t'ang had been appointed to a governor-generalship in West China, and three months later Hsü Tsung-kan had died. While neither man had been a personal patron of the Lins, both had furthered Wen-ch'a's career and their earlier support gave them a stake, as it were, in the Lin family's reputation. Both had been scrupulous while handling Ting's charges against Wen-ch'a in 1864 and Tso at least was aware of Ting's personal animus against Wen-ch'a. Neither man would have lent himself to a scheme of personal revenge against the Lins. The same could not be said of their successors.

Since no contemporary record of the litigation exists, the stages of the suit and how it was guided to the Lin family's discomfiture must be pieced together from later references. After an initial delay, the case took an unusual turn. In appeals, the provincial authorities could either remand the case to its original jurisdiction or else delegate an officer from the provincial capital to conduct a special inquiry. Foochow chose the second option. What made the case unusual was the choice of the special hearing officer: none other than Ling Ting-kuo, hardly a neutral fact-finder. Two sources claim that Ling received the assignment through Ting, one that he got it through bribery.[38]

Whatever the truth, the appointment was hardly a coincidence; it raises questions about the man who formalized it, the new governor-general in Foochow. A Manchu, Ying-kuei had for years served as the commander of the local banner force before assuming the governor-generalship in 1868.[39] While he probably knew Wen-ch'a, and perhaps Wen-ming, we have no evidence of bad feelings between him and the Lins. Most charitably, we may conclude that Ying-kuei was unaware of the personal hatreds below the surface and that he lent himself, unwittingly, to the schemes of others.

Sometime before the fall of 1869, Ling completed his mission of inquiry in Chang-hua. We do not know how he conducted the investigation—whether secretly or in open court—but his findings, not surprisingly, confirmed the plaintiff's charges. The governor-general then rendered a verdict: Lin Wen-ming was to make restitution of the ill-gotten gains. It was left to the new acting Taiwan intend-ant, Li Chao-t'ang, who was about to depart for the island, to enforce the judgment.[40] Since this was Li's first assign-ment in Fukien, he almost certainly had no prior connec-tion with any of the principals. But though he was not a partisan, he was easily influenced by the locally knowledge-able Ling and would prove to be the kind of hatchetman who gladly cooperated in Ling's scheme. In fact, Li found Ling's methods so attractive that he applied them before long to an enemy of his own, with equally deadly conse-quences.[41]

The Trap

The events of the next few months—late 1869 and early 1870—can best be understood if we assume that Ling Ting-kuo was carefully building a trap[42] for the Lins. He had guided the litigation to the point where he might achieve his main goal: not to restore the property of the Lins's victims but to avenge the family's misdeeds against his father and himself. The verdict now in hand gave him his leverage against the Lins.

Evidence for conspiracies is usually indirect. In this case, it is twofold: first, Ling Ting-kuo's presence at so many of the key moments of the unfolding drama, a fact pointing to design, not coincidence. Secondly, as we learn from an independent source,[43] Ling had once before confronted a defiant local strongman and had devised a way of trapping and executing him. The parallels to the Wen-ming case are striking and suggest that Ling not only had the courage and guile to see such a scheme through but that he drew on the earlier case to plan his moves against Wen-ming.

Sometime during that winter, Ling had himself reassigned to Chang-hua, where he practically superceded the regular magistrate, Wang Wen-ch'i, in masterminding the Wen-ming affair.[44] He was in a position to observe Wen-ming's moves and to report them, distorted if need be, to his superior, Intendant Li, in Tainan. He also contacted members of the two major local families who had grudges against the Lins: the Hungs of Ts'ao-t'un and the Lins of Ts'ao-hu, the relatives of Lin Ying-shih, the plaintiff, and of the slain Lin Ho-shang. He signed some of them up as *yamen* guards, giving them a chance to be in on the kill.[45]

Wen-ming's state of mind is harder to fathom. A local source reports that he had no inkling that the lawsuit against him had taken a turn for the worse nor, indeed, that the governor-general had made a decision at all. He still pursued his defense in the local court, albeit in a desultory manner.[46] Ling's despatches to Tainan painted a different picture: a Wen-ming preparing to defy the restitution order at all costs, parading troops about in a show of strength, even contacting an aborigine tribe to plot resistance and, perhaps, rebellion.[47] While Ling Ting-kuo may simply have manufactured such charges to suit his purpose, it would not have been out of character for Wen-ming to strengthen his defenses.

The precise events in the Upper Valley mattered less, in any case, than the version of these events which Intendant Li came to believe. Informed by Ling of Wen-ming's sev-

eral acts of defiance, on February 15 Li wrote out a proclamation which called for Wen-ming's execution as a felon
while holding out mercy to his misguided followers. He
sent this to Ling and Wang in Chang-hua, but told them
not to tip their hand and to conceal the explosive order
until the time came to enforce it.[48] From Ling's point of
view—and he probably inspired the tenor of the document—the proclamation had one simple purpose: it gave
him *carte blanche* to put Wen-ming to death.

That an intendant could issue such a sweeping order and
remain within the letter of the law is noteworthy.[49] Chinese
law has sometimes been praised for having had its own
versions of "due process." While not foolproof, these procedural safeguards required that all capital cases be automatically reviewed in Peking by the empire's highest judicial bodies. Before a felon could be put to death, the
emperor himself would, in effect, have to sign his death
warrant.[50]

The case of Lin Wen-ming underlines what students of
Ch'ing law appear to have overlooked: that these safeguards had been largely abandoned by the second half of
the nineteenth century. As rebellion swept the land, the
government had set aside many of the due-process clauses.
Intendants and prefects were authorized to summarily
execute broad classes of offenders on their own authority.
A common enough response to crisis in all societies, these
emergency provisions were not revoked after the major
rebellions had been put down. As late as 1873, when a censor proposed that the country return to the earlier, procedurally more careful, approach, governors and governors-general objected with rare unanimity; the tough
emergency provisions stayed in force.[51]

Bureaucratic abuses eroded many of the remaining
safeguards. According to the emergency provisions, sen-
tences of summary execution had still to be rendered in a
court and confirmed by an intendant or prefect before
being carried out. In case of doubt, the reviewing official

was to consult the provincial authorities. In fact, however, court trials and consultations were often dispensed with. Men were put to death "without the examination of witnesses . . . on the simple fiat of a district or department magistrate,"[52] or, as in the Wen-ming case, on the basis of an advance authorization by an intendant.

It was against this legal background, and the discretion it gave to Intendant Li, that Ling Ting-kuo had evidently planned his moves during the winter. But before he could enforce the ominous proclamation, one more hurdle remained. Wen-ming had to be lured out of the safety of his Wu-feng lair, a task to tax the ingenuity of the guileful Ling.

Ling employed two ruses to lull Wen-ming into a false sense of security. First, he staged an elaborate charade.[53] He persuaded Magistrate Wang to cancel a local religious festival, a procession honoring the goddess Ma-tsu which regularly took place in the district in the spring. Wang explained that public order was too fragile, the gathering of large crowds too dangerous. When the expected protest arose, Wang relented and promised to let the procession take place if Wen-ming, the district's major strongman, guaranteed the public peace. Wen-ming agreed; his braves guarded the procession, and the festival went off peacefully, as scheduled. The whole episode relaxed his vigilance, as had been intended. He had left his lair and his turf, and all had gone well. The authorities trusted him; a measure of cordiality had even been restored between the district office and the district's major strongman.

In this propitious atmosphere, Magistrate Ling made his second, and boldest, move a day or two later. He paid a personal call on Wen-ming in Wu-feng, hoping to persuade him to come to court in Chang-hua on the morrow.[54] What mixture of threats and blandishments he employed is still impossible to disentangle, so varied are the descriptions of what transpired. He may well have presented himself as a friend of the family, ready to protect the Lin interests for a consideration or out of regard for a fellow-official. To drive home the urgency of the case, Ling seems to have tipped his hand and shown Wen-ming the ominous proclamation. While Wen-ming remained suspicious enough to seize the document (the Lins later pointed to it as proof of an official conspiracy to kill him), his arrogance caused him to misjudge the situation as a whole. Sure of his rank and power, he agreed to come to court.

The next morning, April 17, Wen-ming donned his official robes, his colonel's uniform and military decorations, as was proper for a formal court appearance.[55] Then, in the company of numerous braves, he mounted his sedan chair and was carried to the *Pai-sha shu-yüan*, the Chang-hua academy that served as the temporary district *yamen*.

The events in the *yamen* that morning are still not entirely clear, as family and officialdom have offered sharply conflicting accounts. The most nearly independent source, a local folkstory,[56] is much closer to the family version, but it also contains some literary, and perhaps unhistorical, *topoi*. It relates that Magistrate Ling welcomed the distinguished visitor at the gate of the *yamen*. As the two men proceeded through the several courtyards, one after another door fell shut. Behind each remained some of Wen-ming's braves, until, arriving in the rear audience hall, he had only four or five men with him. Suddenly, a command rang out: "This is the place of imperial law. Why do you not kneel down?" It was Hung Hou of Ts'ao-t'un, one of the specially hired *yamen* guards, giving the signal for attack. He caught Wen-ming by surprise and plunged a knife into his chest. Wen-ming changed color and screamed out in pain, now fully aware of the trap into which he had blundered, and of the man who had set it. "You dog of a Ling," he is supposed to have shouted, "in that case, I am going to get your dog's life, too."

As the wounded Wen-ming threw himself against Ling, the magistrate retreated to the back of the *yamen*, crying for help and shouting, "Kill, kill, kill." At this, apparently prearranged, signal, *yamen* guards rushed into the audience hall, turning it into a battlefield. For quite some time, "silver daggers flashed, scarlet blood flowed, and shouts of 'kill, kill' rose above the groans of the wounded." When the melée was over, Ling reemerged to inspect the pile of bodies, among them Wen-ming's huge corpse. He ordered the strongman's head cut off and displayed on the city wall, a punishment in death reserved for the vilest criminals.[57] Then he posted a new proclamation to the effect that a local bandit had attacked the *yamen* and that the garrison had been called out to protect the city.[58]

Fig. 9 A melée in a *yamen* (*Tien-shih-chai hua-pao*, East Asian Library, Columbia University).

As news of Wen-ming's death spread, Chang-hua was plunged into chaos.[59] Expecting a full-scale attack from the Lin forces, frightened citizens hid in their houses and storekeepers boarded up their shops. Normal city life came to a standstill and soldiers milled around nervously. The city gates were shut and martial law proclaimed. With reenforcements in the city, Ling was confident he could meet the challenge.

If Wen-ming's death satisfied some higher justice, as an atonement for the family's past outrages, the circumstances of his dying hardly vindicated the rule of law in Chang-hua district. Try as the officials might to disguise it, they had triumphed only by adopting the family's own unsavory methods. Where Wen-ch'a had exploited his command authority for private advantage, the family's enemies had abused the judicial power to settle a personal score. The next few weeks would show that Wen-ming's death had been an act of vengeance, not of justice. So far from working for the restoration of the victims' property, the officials sought only to cover their own tracks and to rewrite the account of Wen-ming's final hours so that it would retroactively justify his murder.[60] The new proclamation charging him with an assault on the city—the act of a rebel—was but the first step on this slippery path.

That strongmen drove officials to despair, and sometimes to the use of extra-legal methods, need not surprise us. Nor should strongmen who built their power outside the law expect "due process" whenever it suited them. But that a civilian official could commit a judicial murder to settle a personal score hinted at an even more insidious corruption of public life than did the open rule of the strongmen. It remained to be seen if Ling and his accomplices would be called to account. In the meantime, the Lin family stood once more on the brink of disaster.

CHAPTER 10

THE TRYING YEARS

The Lins in Court, 1870-1882

In cases involving human life, if there is bias and protection of subordinates and colleagues, we fear that even if the court can be deceived and the common people cheated, in the end there is no escape from Heaven's principle, no denying one's conscience.[1]

The braves who had survived their master's death in the *yamen* fled back to Wu-feng and as they spread their grisly news, "the villagers were all very angry. Carrying spears and clubs, they gathered, their number reaching several thousand in no time. Their mood was violent and they thirsted for revenge."[2] But cooler heads prevailed and the men were persuaded—some say by Wen-feng, others by Wen-ming's mother—that to march on Chang-hua was to court destruction. According to yet others, the troop turned back only after having marched within sight of the city walls.[3] Whatever the differences of detail, all accounts suggest that this was an important turning point in family history: it symbolized a retreat from the strongman tradition, from a quarter-century of direct action, violence, and blood revenge.

In accounting for this important turn, we find a clue in the composition of the family on the morrow of Wen-ming's death. The soldierly leaders who had dominated the recent past were all gone: Ting-pang slain at age forty; Wen-ch'a and Wen-ming dead in their mid-thirties; Tien-kuo, now in his mid-fifties, was in prison. The remaining senior members, especially the older women, inclined to caution, well aware of the high cost of violence. After a quarter-century of strongmanship, there survived but one experienced male adult (Wen-feng), yet many widowed wives and concubines and many children, hostages to fortune as the family took thought for the future. Could one risk a confrontation when the weak and vulnerable far outnumbered the strong and competent and when an untried young man presided over the senior branch?

The leadership of the senior branch had gone to Ch'ao-tung (1851-1904), Wen-ch'a's oldest son.[4] While he would in time become one of the family's most illustrious leaders, in the spring of 1870 he was a nineteen-year-old youth of no particular accomplishments. It may have been the title he inherited from his father more than his seniority which had tipped the scales in his favor and against his cousin Ch'ao-ch'ang (1853-1914), the seventeen-year-old eldest son of Wen-ming. If the family faced dangerous times, far better to be led by the son of a hero than the offspring of a criminal.

Though he had neither skill nor experience to offer, Ch'ao-tung's personality suited his family's needs. He was self-confident, yet without his father's and uncle's arrogance. His education had run to the military classics, such as *Sun Tzu*, itself a lesson in prudence. His interest in military affairs would come to the fore again later; what mattered now was his political skill. Though lacking the literary education that shaped the common culture of China's ruling class, Ch'ao-tung had a link to the local gentry through his wife, the remarkably educated and strong-willed daughter of a notable Chang-hua family. Through her and her well-connected brothers and in-laws, Ch'ao-tung must have learned his first lessons in gentry skills and political favor-trading. An apt pupil, he would soon move to the mainland, where he continued his political self-education in circles which the family had never frequented before.

Taking Stock

Once the Lins had decided against armed revenge and in favor of Ch'ao-tung's headship, the dimensions of the crisis could be assessed, the remaining alternatives explored. One matter of grave concern was the governor-general's decision of the previous autumn, ordering the restitution of Lin Ying-shih's property. Inexplicably, however, officialdom did not move to implement this verdict, nor did the private plaintiffs insist on immediate satisfaction.[5] This, then, turned out to be one issue which the Lins could best handle by leaving it in limbo.

Not so the far more serious matter of Wen-ming's rebel status, with its potentially deadly consequences. As we have seen, Ling Ting-kuo had quickly pinned the dreaded label on the dead man. Wen-ming's alleged military preparations in the spring (the fortifying of Wu-feng, the contacting of an aborigine tribe) were now interpreted as a prelude to rebellion, and the events of his last day were drastically rewritten. According to the official version, Wen-ming had marched on Chang-hua with a huge force and had been the first to raise arms in the *yamen*.[6] The exposed head on the wall, the tenor of the proclamations splashed all over town, the official report to the governor-general, all proclaimed Wen-ming to have been that most execrable creature, a rebel against imperial authority. The danger to the family was thus extreme, for the law's dire punishment for rebel relatives—death or castration for males, slavery for the women—was no dead letter in the 1870's.[7] If the issue of the land seizure could be ignored for the moment, Wen-ming's rebel status could not. For the sake of survival, if not for Wen-ming's good name, the stigma of rebellion must be removed.

Towards that end, the Lins committed themselves to a dual course of action, one legal, the other political. Through the appeals process, they would attempt to overturn the verdict on Wen-ming; simultaneously, they would mount a campaign to seek friends in high places and to gain the political leverage which alone could insure a favorable outcome in court.

The Lins's search for highly placed friends extended from Chang-hua district to the capital in Peking. In the nature of the enterprise, the full scope of their activities cannot be reconstructed. Favors and bribes—and these must surely have been part of the story—would hardly be recorded even in private papers. Enough bits of evidence nevertheless survive to suggest the range of the family's efforts.

At the highest level of government, in Peking, where the Lins would present their four appeals, Ch'ao-tung installed himself for a number of years, the better to watch over family interests. He obtained a minor post on the Board of War, which, together with his inherited title, gave him the needed entrée into official circles.[8] To judge from the kind of men who later put in a good word for the family, he cultivated two groups in particular: metropolitan officials, primarily censors and Hanlin academicians, and higher degree-holders, perhaps Taiwanese or Fukienese, who may have been in the capital to await assignment or to take examinations.

To pursue influential backers in Peking was a novelty for a family which had played no political role outside Fukien before. But the Lins did not neglect the provincial and lower levels of government. Wen-ming's mother, Mrs. Tai (1808-1883), and later his second son, Ch'ao-hsüan (1859-1909), betook themselves to Foochow to cultivate office-holders there.[9] Mrs. Tai spent a good part of the 1870's at the provincial capital, where this ancient mother of a martyred hero must have cut a touching figure. At the same time, she did not spurn the use of money to open doors and to obtain audiences. Family sources report that she pawned or sold much of her jewelry to finance these expenses.

During the early 1880's, we can trace efforts to secure the backing of other high officials in Taiwan itself, such as the intendant, Liu Ao, and the Fukien governor, Ts'en Yü-ying, who made periodic visits to the island.[10] Ch'ao-tung, for instance, contributed lavishly to a public-works project dear to the governor's heart, gained his ear, and immediately spoke to him of the family's lawsuit.

Whether the Lins sought out any of Wen-ch'a's former superiors is not clear. An obvious choice was Tso Tsung-t'ang, but there is no evidence that he was approached or that he interceded on the family's behalf.[11] A distinguished senior officer who did intercede for the Lins, P'eng Yü-lin, was, like Tso, a Hunanese and a veteran anti-Taiping fighter, but whether he had been an acquaintance of Wen-ch'a's during mainland days, or whether his support was first gained much later, remains unclear.[12]

In addition to cultivating men in office, the Lins also sought the good will of others who had the prospect if not yet the reality of power. In 1874, for instance, the family granted travel money to an aspiring scholar on his way to Peking for the examinations.[13] Such a gift, a familiar "social investment" to gain a promising man's favor, was a first for the Lins also. The man in question, Ch'en Wang-tseng, a *chü-jen* from Tainan, did not disappoint his patrons. He won the *chin-shih*, one of two men on the Taiwan quota, and then served in the cabinet (*nei-ko*). While we have no evidence of specific favors that he did for the Lins, he and the family remained friends for many decades and we can assume that the amenities were observed and favors returned.

On the local level, in Chang-hua itself, the Lins acted to establish a new and more respectable image for the family. They discontinued, or at least sharply curtailed, their private fighting force.[14] Raids and spoliations came to an end and the military side of family power was played down, even though the Wu-feng palisades remained and Ch'ao-tung kept a small bodyguard, as was common among local notables.

The Lins also sought ties with the local gentry, men without formal power but with prestige and influence in mid-Taiwan. We note, in particular, an increasing number, of Lin marriages with gentry families.[15] Rare before 1870, such marital ties became common thereafter. At the same time, the Lins sought peace with some of their old enemies. In at least one documented case, they paid compensation to a family from whom they had earlier bought land, apparently at rock-bottom prices and under the threat of force.[16] Then, in 1874, both major Wu-feng branches and their T'ai-p'ing cousins contributed to the repair of a temple near the present-day Taichung, making donations jointly with many members of the Lai clan.[17] The shrine's location near the border of the two surname groups who had previously been feuding suggests that this venture, too, may have been an act of reconciliation.

To understand the Lins's need for well-connected friends, and the legal maneuvers they soon undertook, a brief introduction to the Ch'ing appellate system is needed. A little-known aspect of Ch'ing law, it allowed private parties to appeal the ruling of a lower court. As it worked in the late nineteenth century, however, the system was unlikely to satisfy most appellants, as the Lins would discover to their dismay.[18]

An appellant's major problem arose from certain procedural features of the system. A case that had been duly appealed upwards through successive levels of the bureaucracy—the prefecture, the province—was no sooner received at the highest level in Peking, the Censorate or the Board of Punishment, than it was once more sent down to the provincial authorities. Often not even specifying what elements of the earlier verdict required review, Peking returned the appeals cases to the governors and governors-general and charged them with holding personal hearings and then reporting their findings back to the capital. Actually, of course, these busy officials delegated much of the review work to the provincial judicial commissioners (*an-ch'a-shih*), who in turn drew on men further down the hierarchy—often the very officials in whose jurisdiction the case had begun—to assist them in their task.

A system less likely to secure relief from an earlier miscarriage of justice is hard to imagine. Yet, despite severe criticism from censors, the procedures were retained. Imperial mandates not to resubmit cases to the officials who had tried them in the first instance went unheeded.[19] Even if implemented, such admonitions could not have corrected another major weakness of the system: the tendency for officials to shield each other and to uphold the original verdict out of concern for their colleagues. As a censor explained in 1875, "where grave irregularities exist in the earlier stages of a case, the number of persons through whose hands it has passed is likely to be considerable, and they mutually stand by each other in their own interest. . . . Either, evidence is fabricated with a view to forcing withdrawal from further proceedings, or false statements are laid before the superior authority in order to hoodwink him into dismissing the case."[20]

Such abuses must have given pause to appellants like the Lins whose success in court would mean the disgrace and punishment of several officials. For, under the disciplinary rules of the bureaucracy, abuses of power for personal gain or from personal malice were considered grave offenses.[21] Ling Ting-kuo and those who had knowingly assisted him were therefore in danger and even those who had unwittingly helped Ling stood to be called to account. Such men would clearly do everything in their power to prevent Wen-ming's vindication.

To these difficulties we must add others which appellants faced: unhealthy lockups where they and their witnesses might be confined, the risk of torture, and of punishment, should the appeal fail.[22] Such risks could be minimized, to be sure, depending on the social status and the motives of the appellant. It was probably with this precaution in mind that the Lins chose to make old Mrs. Tai the formal appellant. As a gentlewoman and mother of a martyr, she was less likely to suffer such indignities. To be quite safe, she also exaggerated her age so that she would enjoy the freedom from torture which Chinese law held out to the very old.[23]

She would hardly escape the financial strains of litigation, the costs for herself and her witnesses or proxies while at court, the bribes to *yamen* personnel and various underlings who handled documents and court calendars. Indeed, the lawsuit was to prove a severe financial burden to the family, aggravated by the immense delays in judicial proceedings that seem to have been common in the 1870's.[24]

Finally, an appellant had to consider the broader political setting in which the courts functioned. It tended to give pause to all but the most determined—or well-connected. Their search for highly placed friends makes clear that the Lins understood this side of the matter very well. Unlike other legal traditions, the Chinese did not aspire to the independence of the judiciary. Judges were not a separate order of officials, protected in their independence by lifetime tenure and other safeguards. For the most part, they were the all-purpose officials who also handled taxes, the census, flood relief, local defense, and many routine matters. Far from being technicians of an impersonal law, they were expected to bring the sum total of their moral perceptions to bear on the judging of cases. In only a few instances (when a party to a suit was his relative, former teacher, or administrative superior) was a judge excused from sitting on a case.[25] Other personal relationships did not require, or justify, that an official disqualify himself on account of a conflict of interest.

On the contrary, magistrates habitually discussed their

cases outside the courtroom and received private petitions on behalf of one or the other litigant. Enmeshed in their own web of loyalties and obligations, they were hard put to ignore the pleas of old friends when they recalled past favors or invoked old friendships. The fictional literature of recent centuries shows that few Chinese went to court without approaching the judge through some such personal connection.[26] In seeking recourse to law, then, the Lins had to weigh their own and the opposing side's leverage outside the courtroom. Who one was, whom one knew,

Fig. 10 Scholar-officials in conversation (*Tien-shih-chai hua-pao*, East Asian Library, Columbia University).

and who could be persuaded to intercede on one's be-half—these would determine the outcome of the case even more than the evidence itself.

The First Appeal

In the autumn of 1871, when almost all the office-holders connected with Wen-ming's death had left their Fukien offices,[27] the Lins took their case to one of the highest tribunals in Peking. By proxy, Mrs. Tai appealed to the Censorate, charging that Ling Ting-kuo, together with the Taiwan intendant and brigade general, had engineered her son's murder.[28] For proof, she pointed to the two proclamations: the first, of mid-February, she argued, revealed a long-standing intention to put Wen-ming to death, while the second foisted posthumous charges of rebellion on him in order to justify his death *ex post facto*. The appeal was received in routine fashion and duly forwarded to Foochow for the customary rehearing before the provincial authorities.[29]

In Foochow, the case was soon stalled in the labyrinth of provincial government. Many factors contributed to the delay, some *bona fide* and others probably not: the need to summon witnesses who had now been transferred to posts elsewhere in China, the high turnover in the judicial commissioner's office and other provincial posts, the delaying tactics of some of the implicated officials.[30] Early in the summer of 1874, before the Lin case had been completed, the provincial establishment was plunged into the crisis of the Japanese punitive expedition to Taiwan (see Ch. 11). Officials had their hands full with emergency measures; routine legal cases such as the Lin appeal receded into the background.

Still, the case had not simply gathered dust. Some witnesses had been heard, some testimony reviewed. Tentative at best, the results gave the Lins a foretaste of things to come. On the hopeful side, the family learned that the governor-general, Li Hao-nien, the highest official to handle the case in Foochow, had twice rejected the explanations proffered by the implicated officials.[31] On the grimmer side, the Lins discovered that these officials and their colleagues had already begun to tamper with the record.[32] They had drawn up a new and more innocuous version of the first proclamation and substituted it for the original. Omitting Wen-ming's name and calling for the execution of the unnamed ring-leader, the document was now more compatible with Ling Ting-kuo's version of Wen-ming's death in which he described himself as surprised by Wen-ming's attack on the *yamen* and reluctantly ordering the execution of the assailant.[33] Not content with undercutting one of Mrs. Tai's chief arguments, the implicated officials also dug up an old, unresolved case of multiple murder and pinned it on the dead man.[34]

That the Wen-ming issue was politically sensitive may be seen from the way in which a high official, not concerned with the appeal in the line of duty, nevertheless injected himself into the case, and anonymously at that. In a memorial from the autumn of 1874 which dealt primarily with coastal defense, the anonymous memorialist added a plea for a "fair" review of the Wen-ming case.[35] At first glance, the phrase suggests that the author was one of the new Lin patrons, putting in his expected good word for the family. But we may read his remark as an anti-Lin argument as well, presented directly to the throne over the head of the governor-general. If the governor-general was indeed rejecting the explanations of the implicated officials (as the Lins maintained), a patron of these officials would argue to the throne precisely as the anonymous memorialist did.

If the Lin case was stalled by the mid-1870's, this probably reflected the balance of the forces arraigned against each other: the Lins and their new patrons on one side, the implicated officials and their friends on the other. Though we cannot document the steps which these officials took to prevent Wen-ming's vindication, we can demonstrate their powerful political connections, confident that they, no less than the Lins, would leave no stone unturned to prevent an unfavorable outcome in court.

Though not charged by name in the Lins's suit, the former governor-general, Ying-kuei, was the highest official to be implicated. He had, probably unwittingly, lent himself to the schemes of others, had sent the unsuitable Ling Ting-kuo to handle the case, had given his subordinates sweeping powers, and had reported their doctored version of Wen-ming's death to the throne. His negligence would bring censure, should the Lins prevail.[36] While he was no longer in Foochow to handle the case, his promotion to higher office gave him enough leverage to influence the litigation from a distance. From 1872, he served as president of the Board of War, and after 1875 he held the same post at the Board of Personnel. Along with Jung-lu, the empress dowager's favorite, he served as comptroller of the Imperial Household, and in 1875 was made a grand secretary. Clearly, Ying-kuei had become one of the most prestigious senior Manchu officials.[37]

Next in rank and directly implicated in the Lins's charges, Li Chao-t'ang, too, had risen to an impregnable position.[38] At first, it is true, his career in Taiwan had taken a strange turn. Charged with stubbornness and bias for his fellow-provincials from Kwangtung, he was found unfit for office and dismissed from the Taiwan post. Returning to Kiangsi, the province on whose waiting list he originally belonged, Li nevertheless retained eminent friends in Foochow, in particular his oldest patron, Shen Pao-chen. A native Fukienese, Shen had since 1867 served as director of the Foochow Naval Yard, a major self-strengthening venture of the time. As a protégé of Li Hung-chang, the most powerful Chinese official, Shen gathered more power in Fukien in the 1870's when he was appointed a special imperial commissioner to handle the 1874-1875 Taiwan crisis.[39] At the same time, Shen continued to place extraordinary trust in his old friend Li Chao-t'ang and asked that

Li be returned to Fukien to help him handle the crisis.[40] Conceivably, it was Shen, too, who had written the anonymous memorial of 1874 on his friend's behalf.

In any event, Li returned to Fukien only briefly. His future lay with an even more eminent patron, Li Hung-chang himself. In 1875 he moved to Tientsin, Li's seat as governor-general of the metropolitan province, where he became customs commissioner.[41] Controlling the revenues of this important northern port, the post was so crucial to Li Hung-chang's empire that he always assigned it to a close confidant. In short, by the mid-1870's, Li Chao-t'ang not only had a powerful patron in Foochow but had also moved into the inner circle of the most powerful official of the empire. Famous for his loyalty to friends and servitors,[42] Li Hung-chang was obviously quite capable of shielding Li from the attacks of such relative non-entities as the Lins of Wu-feng.

Even Ling Ting-kuo, the *bête noire* of the Lin family, had found a patron in Foochow. By the mid-1870's, he too seems to have moved into the circle around Shen Pao-chen. When Shen strengthened the Taiwan defenses in the wake of the Japanese expedition, Ling received a post in Tainan. Now with the rank of prefect and expectant *tao-t'ai*, he was to oversee the building of harbor defenses at the Taiwanese capital.[43]

The positions and connections of the implicated officials, then, were formidable enough. But this was not all. Aside from the governor-general in Foochow, who remained skeptical of their explanations, other Fukienese officials who sat in judgment on the Lin case had ties with the implicated officials, either directly or through common patrons such as Shen Pao-chen and Li Hung-chang. This was true of the men who held the governorship and the Taiwan intendancy and prefecture in the early and mid-1870's.[44] That balance of opposing forces which had produced an initial stalemate was thus precarious. It would not require much to tilt it against the Lins.

Further Appeals and a Counter-Attack

To break the deadlock, the Lins returned to the charge in the second half of the decade. In March of 1876 and once more in December of 1877, Mrs. Tai's proxies again went to the Censorate, repeating the charges of the first appeal and adding new accusations of a cover-up.[45] Each time, Peking referred the appeals back to the province. The case even drew public attention when the *Shen-pao*, most prestigious of the new breed of private newspapers, devoted an editorial to it in the spring of 1878. Without taking the Lins's charges at face value, the paper nevertheless supported the family's most serious accusations and called attention to the obvious weaknesses in the officials' case: the misproportion between the death meted out and the offense initially charged against Wen-ming; the failure to try him on the multiple murder charge that was now, posthumously, being raised against him; the suspicious first proclamation; Ling Ting-kuo's evident manipulation of the case, and the apparent collusion later.[46]

If the *Shen-pao*'s support was heartening, it could not disguise the weakness of the fourth estate in Ch'ing China. Favorable publicity mattered less than the composition of the provincial bureaucracy which would sit in judgment on the new rehearings. And here the Lins's position, instead of firming, had drastically weakened. The neutral Li Hao-nien was replaced by Ho Ching, a vigorous partisan of the implicated officials.[47] As a native of Shun-te district in Kwangtung, Li Chao-t'ang's home district, and a *chin-shih* classmate of Li Hung-chang, Li's powerful patron, the new governor-general had a double bond to the implicated ex-intendant. As if this was not enough, in 1879 Li Chao-t'ang himself became a power in his own right in Foochow when he took over the directorship of the Naval Yard.[48]

As they gained strength, the Lins's opponents first tried to pressure the family into dropping their appeal.[49] When this failed, they counter-attacked. As in the late 1860's, private litigants and officials worked in concert. In the late 1870's, either in 1878 or in early 1879, the Lins's commoner-enemies in Taiwan renewed their litigation. Led by the veteran plaintiff Lin Ying-shih, they sued in Peking for a restoration of their property and the righting of other wrongs.[50] But the main blow came from an anonymous memorial. Late in 1878, it charged that Wen-ming's gang was still on the loose and that Wen-feng had taken part in its spoliations.[51]

These new charges effectively threatened the two major branches of the family, putting the senior branch on the defensive and implicating the second branch in Wen-ming's alleged crimes. The stakes rose higher for all the Lins. As if this was not enough, the examination of the new charges was entrusted to a zealous prosecutor, the Taiwan intendant, Hsia Hsien-lun. Whether because of a personal grudge, as the Lins later charged,[52] or because of his connection with the Shipyard circle, Hsia developed a broad catalogue of Wen-ming's crimes that was more devastating to the family than anything charged against him before: not only the offenses of which Wen-ming had been accused in his lifetime and the multiple murder charge hung on him since, but additional rapes, robberies, arsons, and murders were now laid at Wen-ming's doorstep. Wen-feng, too, was found guilty as charged and the intendant's findings were reported to Foochow and thence to Peking.[53]

Duly sworn to, the evidence Hsia presented was hard to refute, at least by persons remote from the scene, as the Peking authorities inevitably were. Yet Hsia's findings were also tendentious and incomplete. In Wen-ming's contests with other local power-holders, there were inevitably two sides to every story, but Hsia presented each incident in a one-sided way, solely from the Lin enemies' point of view, leaving out the complexities and mutual provocations.[54]

By the summer of 1879, the family's position had become desperate. The second branch spirited Wen-feng away, perhaps out of the country, while his brother protested in Peking that his branch had been maliciously drawn into the case.[55] Mrs. Tai filed another appeal in Peking, her fourth, repeating her earlier charges and protesting the new accusations. Then, just as the case against the family seemed to move to a climax—the genealogy records that Hsia had already obtained an order for the confiscation of all their property[56]—a stroke of good fortune saved the Lins. Already suffering from malaria, the elderly Hsia had a particularly nasty crossing to Taiwan, caught a fever, and suddenly died on August 10, 1879.[57] The Lins heaved a sigh of relief; the genealogy records that Hsia's death "stopped the trouble for a while."[58] Others found the death too much of a coincidence and rumors soon sprouted that the Lins themselves had encompassed their enemy's death by pulling away the gangplank when he alighted from the boat, causing him to drown. Far from the scene of the intendant's death, in Chang-hua, it made a credible story which is still told to this day.[59]

However timely the reprieve, it could last only for a while. The litigation moved forward of its own momentum, albeit more slowly, and other officials, especially Governor-General Ho Ching, took almost as dim a view of the family's record as had Intendant Hsia. This was not surprising in view of Ho's ties to Li Chao-t'ang and his reliance on Lin Ying-shih, the plaintiff, and on Ling Ting-kuo to corroborate the sworn depositions.[60] In one of his periodic reports, Ho concluded in the autumn of 1879 that Mrs. Tai's latest appeal was worthless. According to the governor-general, it was merely a maneuver to counter the charges of the private litigants.[61] Ho, in short, accepted all of Hsia's findings and none of Mrs. Tai's arguments. Clearly, there would be no satisfaction for the Lins as long as Ho handled the case in Foochow.

In the spring of 1880, the Lins therefore tried to get the case moved out of Ho's jurisdiction. On the family's behalf, friendly literati requested the Censorate to have the case transferred to Peking.[62] But a change of venue would have

Fig. 11 An audience with a high official in Foochow (*Tien-shih-chai hua-pao*, East Asian Library, Columbia University).

implied that the throne found fault with Ho Ching's handling of the case, and this it would not concede.[63] While the Censorate may still have been friendly to the family, elsewhere in Peking opinion against them had hardened. An imperial decree of May 1880 accepted Ho Ching's findings and ordered that the case be settled on the governor-general's terms as soon as Wen-feng was apprehended.[64]

The decision dealt the final blow to the Lins's hopes, and once more the family took stock. The increasing financial strain of the litigation, the new danger to the second branch, the powerful position which Li Chao-t'ang had gained in Foochow—all these swung opinion in favor of a settlement short of victory. Not that family counsels were unanimous. Mrs. Tai, still in Foochow to seek justice, would not hear of compromise, but she was old, and perhaps senile, and her opinion mattered less. The decisive voice was Ch'ao-tung's, and he overrode his grandmother's wishes.[65] Without telling her, he began to bargain for the best settlement that could still be had. The second branch, on its part, also decided to negotiate, particularly now that nothing more could be done for Lin Tien-kuo. He had died in prison in July 1880.

Toward a Settlement

The proceedings which now ensued are not known in detail, but they must have involved negotiations among several parties: the Lins and their patrons, the private plaintiffs, the implicated officials and their friends, as well as the judicial authorities. The highly placed P'eng Yü-lin is said to have intervened on the Lins's behalf, as did some of the family's patrons in the Hanlin Academy and the Censorate.[66] Ho Ching, too, perhaps aware of some of the weaknesses in the implicated officials' case, proved more flexible than might have been expected. While the fiction of an august government dispensing justice was maintained, it was hard bargaining and the intercession of mediators which finally produced a settlement.[67]

The final terms of the compromise were hammered out by the summer of 1882.[68] Set forth in a memorial by Ho Ching and ratified by the emperor, they were as follows: Wen-ming stood convicted of the murders, rapes, arsons, and robberies that Hsia Hsien-lun had certified. The local officials' version of the events of April 17, 1870 was also upheld, but with a significant concession: the charge that Wen-ming had been a rebel was withdrawn, the crucial phrase declared "excessive."[69] As between the private parties, the Lins undertook to pay compensation to Lin Ying-shih. All plaintiffs agreed to cease litigation.

The formula was judicious if not, perhaps, altogether just. The moral authority of the imperial government had been upheld. If Wen-ming was not, after all, a rebel, his many other crimes fully justified his ignominious death. Between the private parties, the settlement made good Lin Ying-shih's losses without crippling the Wu-feng Lins. Once the indemnity was paid—14,700 *Yüan*,* about a sixth of the senior branch's annual income, and some additional land—the bitterness between the estranged families slowly disappeared.[70]

Just as diplomatically, the final formula endorsed the conduct of the implicated officials in proportion to their political leverage. Ying-kuei, who had died some years ago as a respected elder statesman, received praise as a far-sighted public servant. Li Chao-t'ang, still riding high in his Naval Yard post, also emerged unscathed.[71] Neither man was even criticized for poor judgment in the affair and Li remained so proud of his role in it that the Wen-ming episode was included in his biography in the gazetteer of his native district.[72] At the lower levels of the bureaucracy, Ling Ting-kuo and the former Chang-hua magistrate, Wang Wen-ch'i, were upheld in their treatment of Wen-ming but criticized for not carrying out the order to restore the Lins's ill-gotten gains to the rightful owner. But since Ling had already been disgraced on another count, and Wang was dead, the emperor graciously refrained from punishing their offense.[73]

For the Lins, the settlement naturally brought many disappointments. The failure to get Wen-ming's good name restored weighed heavily, particularly on his descendants. Nor did Mrs. Tai ever agree to the compromise. She re-

* The *Yüan* was a silver dollar, originally of Spanish and later of Mexican coinage, that circulated widely in Taiwan and in Chinese coastal areas that traded with the West. It was worth approximately .7 *Taels*.

mained ignorant of what Ch'ao-tung had conceded and died, a year later, still seeking justice in Foochow.[74] But there were gains as well, and in time they would outweigh the losses. If Wen-ming's name remained tarnished, the stigma of rebellion had been removed and with it immense danger to the family. On the financial side, the settlement also favored the Lins. They held onto the bulk of their property, paying a large but not crushing sum to the plaintiff. The compensation payment very likely was smaller than would have been the cost of continued litigation. In a triumph of realism, Ch'ao-tung had settled for safety at the price of Wen-ming's good name.

The terms were made more palatable all around, thanks to a few imperial grace notes. Reasserting the moral order after the complex bargain had been struck, the emperor distributed suitable tokens of moral approbation.[75] One of Wen-ming's rape victims had committed suicide from shame; an honorary tablet was now bestowed on her. Ironically, the rapist's mother received a similar honor. For having dissuaded the family from violence in 1870, for having raised her grandsons well, and in memory of Lin Wen-ch'a, Mrs. Tai was granted an honorary portal. As for her stubborn litigation, she was granted the benefit of extenuating circumstances; mother love and concern for the family's good name, honorable sentiments all, were held to excuse her repeated presentation of baseless charges at Peking. The second branch's appeals on Tien-kuo's behalf were similarly excused because it was filial piety which had inspired them.[76]

If financial strain and the adverse political climate in Foochow impelled the Lins to settle far short of the original goal, they had compromised reluctantly. No sooner had family members gained fresh laurels in the imperial service in 1885 than they asked to have the Wen-ming case reopened, not as a matter of law, but in a request for imperial grace. Though they had an impressive new patron—no less a personage than the new Taiwan governor, Liu Ming-ch'uan—the effort came to nought. Peking stood by the 1882 terms.[77] Henceforth the family had to reconcile itself to the stain that would always remain on Wen-ming's name. As late as the 1930's, when they published the genealogy, the Lins could not bring themselves to include a biography of Wen-ming. He remained the black sheep, the only major male figure in the family without this memorial in the genealogy.

But while the sense of shame lingered, the end of the litigation nevertheless brought an immense relief. After a dozen years of anguished maneuver and lavish expenditure, the Lins were free from the dangers they had faced. They not only survived, they held on to the bulk of their property. More important, in working themselves free from the tangles of the past, the new leaders of the family had left the strongman tradition behind. They had developed new political skills and connections, stepping-stones to a spectacular political comeback in the 1880's and 1890's. The trying decade after Wen-ming's death thus worked a decisive change in the family's political style, one which happily coincided with major developments in Taiwan as a whole.

PART THREE

THE MAKING OF A TAIWANESE GENTRY FAMILY

CHAPTER 11

RENEWAL

The Lins in a Changing Taiwan,
1882-1895

*Suddenly, the fame of the Lin family spread to
north and south.*[1]

Burdened with the cares and costs of litigation, the Lins
had not participated in the affairs of Taiwan for over a
decade. With the end of the lawsuit in 1882, they returned
to public life, though not to the strongman role they had
played earlier. It was not the circumstances which had
changed—communal conflicts, private violence, and the
power of strongmen continued to the end of the century—but the family itself. Its leading men now acted more
like members of the gentry and thereby established a new
image for their tarnished house. While some were active
locally, in Chang-hua district, others acted on a broader
stage and became deeply involved in the island-wide reform efforts which marked the last years of Ch'ing Taiwan.
This was particularly true of Lin Ch'ao-tung, the family's
most prominent member in the late nineteenth century.

From the mid-1870's, public life in Taiwan was dominated by foreign crises and by the many self-strengthening
activities which made the island a showcase of progressive reform. In this setting, Lin Ch'ao-tung had not only
broader opportunities for service than his father ever had;
he also found what had always eluded Wen-ch'a: a per-

sonal patron in the highest ranks of officialdom. Liu Ming-ch'uan, the first governor of the new province of Taiwan, gave him unique opportunities for service and the family now approached that eminence which they secured fully only in the twentieth century: that of being, quite simply, the island's first family.

To appreciate the opportunities which lay at hand as the Lins emerged from their self-imposed hibernation, we must regress briefly and review some of the major developments which had begun to influence Taiwan in the meantime.[2] Like other parts of China, Taiwan was now subject to foreign encroachments. From the early 1860's, there were treaty ports in north and south and a growing trade with the wider world which looked to Taiwan for tea, camphor, and sugar. Christian missionaries reappeared on the island. While traders and preachers posed no territorial threat, they provoked many incidents with the people of Taiwan. Gunboats intervened to enforce Western treaty rights. A Taiwanese specialty among such typical nineteenth-century incidents were aborigine attacks on shipwrecked foreigners whose lives and property Chinese officials appeared unable to protect.

It was out of just such an incident that the crisis of 1874 arose.[3] Claiming jurisdiction over the Liu-ch'iu (Ryu-kyu) islands as she now did, Japan protested the massacre of shipwrecked Ryu-kyuans by Taiwanese aborigines. Informed that the offending savages lived outside the pale of Chinese jurisdiction, Tokyo quickly seized on this admission: if China refused to assume responsibility for the island as a whole, Japan would send her own forces to chastize the savages; she might even establish a permanent presence on the island. In May of 1874, a Japanese expedition landed in south Taiwan and proceeded to fight and parlay with the tribes. Thoroughly aroused, the Chinese reversed their legal position, declared themselves masters of the entire island, and belatedly strengthened its defenses.

When diplomacy secured the departure of the Japanese at the end of the year, the Chinese remained deeply disturbed over the long-range threat to Taiwan and embarked on a reform program that encompassed a wide range of measures: military reorganization and a technical modernization of its defenses; improved communications with the mainland and within the island itself; the conquest of the unsubdued mountain area and its settlement by new Chinese settlers. Along with such self-strengthening measures, there would be an extensive administrative reorganization; new *hsien* units were to be created and a new prefecture, encompassing the northern half of the island, would provide better oversight. The governor of Fukien was to spend half the year in Taiwan; some champions of reform began to talk of separate provincial status for the island.[4]

By the early 1880's considerable progress had been made. The administrative changes had been easiest to carry out. The new prefectural capital in the north, Taipei, had been built. Other changes proved harder to achieve. Thus, the military strengthening, the subjugation of the aborigines, and the settlement projects in the east lagged behind schedule. Continued corruption undercut many new projects, as did financial shortages. Fiscal reform (beyond the abolition of a few old nuisance taxes) had not been part of the reform program. While a start had been made, the reforming impulse appeared to lose momentum just as the Lins reentered public life. But a new crisis was at hand and sparked a new reform effort.

The Sino-French War

The new crisis arose from French advances in Indochina, an old Chinese satellite. By the spring of 1884, Chinese resistance to the takeover had led to an undeclared state of war which now threatened to spill over into China proper, and into Taiwan in particular.[5]

To handle the expected French threat, the government

sent to Taiwan one of its most distinguished field officers, Liu Ming-ch'uan.[6] Twenty-odd years earlier, he had made his mark as a young general in Li Hung-chang's anti-Taiping force, the Huai Army. From Li's district in Anhui, Liu became one of the pillars of Li's power and gained further laurels in other campaigns. With a background in local strongman feuds similar to Wen-ch'a's,[7] Liu, unlike Wen-ch'a, had the makings of the soldier-statesman. In retirement recently, he had made up for his lack of a conventional education and had also developed plans for the long-term strengthening of China. His military experience, knowledge of Western tactics, and close ties to Li Hung-chang—still China's premier statesman and now placed in charge of the Taiwan defense effort—made Liu the man of the hour when he reached Taipei in mid-July 1884.

Liu had arrived none too early, for in August the French escalated the war. A first landing attempt at Keelung failed, to be sure, but late in the month they destroyed the entire South China Fleet riding at anchor in Foochow. After this spectacular episode, they concentrated on Taiwan, hoping to secure valuable enclaves which might serve as bargaining chips in the talks with China. For several months, from October 1884 to March 1885, Taiwan became the chief theater in the Sino-French war.

In their attack on the island, the French had mixed success. Early in October, they managed to seize Keelung and nearby coal mines, but their attempt to land at Tamsui,[8] on the northwestern tip of the island, was beaten back. Finding the Chinese resistance more spirited than they had expected, the French in late October imposed a blockade, hoping to starve Taiwan into submission. Henceforth, Liu Ming-ch'uan would have to fall back on the island's own resources for defense, especially the local notables with their command of money and manpower.

As urgent calls went out to the Taiwanese notables, inviting them to raise braves, the Lins seized their chance. It was an opportunity fraught with risks, too, for officialdom did not speak with one voice. Besides Liu Ming-ch'uan in Taipei, Intendant Liu Ao in Tainan, the highest regular official on the island, also issued calls for volunteers.[9] Which man to follow? Since the two Lius were soon to clash in a vicious fight—it ended in Liu Ao's disgrace, Liu Ming-ch'uan's triumph—the decision of a notable to join one or the other of these rivals had a bearing on his future.

It may be that the Lins made a deliberate choice to establish a foot in each camp. More likely, individual family members were swayed by the earlier ties which they had formed with particular officials. Thus Lin Wen-ch'in (1854-1899), Tien-kuo's youngest son and head of the second branch after Wen-feng's death in 1882, took his braves south. He had long been a protégé of Liu Ao's.[10] Tied to a waning star and hastening to an area that would see little military action, Wen-ch'in's decision proved a costly mistake. By contrast, Ch'ao-tung took his braves north. While he had as yet no personal ties to Liu Ming-ch'uan, Ts'en Yü-ying, the former Fukien governor whom Ch'ao-tung had impressed favorably some time back, furnished him with an introduction.[11] The move north was easily the most important decision of Ch'ao-tung's life. With major fighting ahead in the north and Liu Ming-ch'uan's star in the ascendant, Ch'ao-tung gained both honor and a patron, and with them the opportunity to restore his family's fame and fortune.

During the six months of war, Ch'ao-tung played a key role in the defense on the outskirts of Keelung.[12] Since Liu had been censured for losing the city, it was important not to yield more ground and he must have been doubly grateful for Ch'ao-tung's aid. The five hundred Lin braves gave an excellent account of themselves and carried a major share of the fighting. Considering the locale (with its constant rain and "pestilential vapors" in the hills, Liu considered it the most difficult battleground he had ever seen) and the fierceness of the French attack, Liu conceived the highest admiration for the young Taiwanese commander,

Fig. 12 The French attack on north Taiwan, autumn 1884 (*Tien-shih-chai hua-pao*, East Asian Library, Columbia University).

a feeling which survived the efforts of others to drive them apart.[13]

When the hostilities ceased in the spring, the French had marched within a dozen miles of Taipei, but the city itself eluded them. The staunch resistance to which Ch'ao-tung had so ably contributed paid off, for as the Chinese fought the French to a virtual draw, they were able to achieve marginally better peace terms.[14] Here lay the significance of Ch'ao-tung's contribution to the larger cause. But it was on his family's behalf that he scored the most signal gain when he won Liu's trust and friendship, the basis of their subsequent relations.

Concrete rewards came in the summer. In a handsome gesture, Liu memorialized the throne on behalf of Wen-ming's vindication, but to no avail, as we have seen. For himself, Ch'ao-tung received a peacock feather and promotion to the rank of intendant (4A).[15] Unlike his father's promotions to regular rank in the army, Ch'ao-tung secured the more usual reward of the gentry member: a civilian brevet (non-office-holding) title. Unburdened by substantive office, he remained free to serve Liu in whatever post his new patron might assign him.

The Governor's Strong Right Arm

After the end of the Sino-French war, Liu Ming-ch'uan remained in Taiwan, responsible for its security and modernization. He revived and expanded the earlier reform program and initiated change in a host of fields: administrative, fiscal, economic and, last but not least, military.[16] From 1886, when Taiwan was established as a province, until his resignation in 1891, Liu presided over the changing island as its first governor. It was Lin Ch'ao-tung's good fortune that Liu employed him on numerous missions and made him, along with Lin Wei-yüan of Pan-ch'iao (the most prominent notable of the Taipei area), his most trusted Taiwanese collaborator.

Ch'ao-tung received a regular position in the island's new defense system. While dismissing most of the local braves who had served during the emergency, Liu retained Ch'ao-tung's units and those of one or two other local notables.[17] With two battalions stationed in the area around Hsin-chu and Hou-lung, Ch'ao-tung commanded the largest contingent of local troops to be retained in the reorganized garrison force. Designated as "Tung" battalions after their commander's name, these units were expanded during subsequent emergencies and were then referred to as the "Tung Army."[18] Deployed on garrison duty or on campaigns, the Tung units were on the public payroll. Ch'ao-tung thus gained much the same benefit from his link with government as had his father: he built a semi-private force[19] with public means. In other respects, too, he proceeded much as had Wen-ch'a. He recruited his men from the old Lin turf and his sub-commanders from among relatives and the lesser notables in the vicinity of Wu-feng.[20]

Alongside this field command, Ch'ao-tung also received a post in the central military administration. When Liu revived an old institution, the *Ying-wu-ch'u* (Governor's Military Secretariat), to carry out the army reforms, he appointed Ch'ao-tung to head its mid-Taiwan branch office.[21] While the exact nature of Ch'ao-tung's duties remains unclear, the position must have given him influence over the affairs of units other than his own.

With Ch'ao-tung's wider duties came a more complex staff organization. We hear of two private secretaries (*mu-yu*) whom he employed to handle Tung Army finances and his enlarged correspondence.[22] For while he was not of high enough rank to memorialize the emperor, he directed much official correspondence to Liu.

In addition to such routine military duties, Ch'ao-tung assumed a key role in the governor's wars on the aborigines. Liu believed that Taiwan would not be safe until the quarter-million tribesmen who roamed the mountains had been subdued.[23] The frequent aborigine raids on Chinese farmsteads and camphor stills—retaliation for the Chinese advance into tribal lands—provided a convenient occasion for the crackdown.

Ch'ao-tung participated in three aborigine campaigns. The first began in the autumn of 1885 and lasted half a year.[24] With the governor advancing from Taipei and Ch'ao-tung from Cho-lan, in the hills near Chang-hua's northern border, the venture resembled a triumphal march into the hills of north Taiwan. Most tribes submitted *en masse*, while the rest vanished into the higher mountains. Employing the surrendered chieftains as emissaries, Ch'ao-tung secured the allegiance of these holdouts, too, and arranged for the ceremonial hair-cuttings that symbolized the tribes's new allegiance.

When the central government criticized the high cost of

Fig. 13 Surrender of "raw" aborigines (*Tien-shih-chai hua-pao*, East Asian Library, Columbia University).

the campaign, Liu and his stalwarts, including Ch'ao-tung, pointed to the huge gains: four hundred tribes, with a total population of some 70,000 persons, had been pacified, thousands of acres of farmland made safe for settlement.[25] But it soon became clear that the victory claims had been exaggerated. Incidents between the tribesmen and the Chinese continued and when Ch'ao-tung demanded that the chiefs surrender the guilty, the aborigines resisted. By the late summer of 1886, many of the newly surrendered tribes were in open revolt. Weeks of costly fighting lay ahead before they were again subdued.

This second campaign, in the fall of 1886, was the most arduous of Ch'ao-tung's career.[26] Lured into the higher mountains, harrassed by ambushes in the jungle, and beset by insurmountable supply problems, the Chinese fought at a disadvantage. When government troops ventured too far, they were often surrounded, cut off from their comrades, and wiped out. Ch'ao-tung himself once barely withstood a ten-day siege on a mountain top and was saved only through the daring intervention of his wife, who, hearing of his plight from an escaped soldier, rallied fresh braves in Wu-feng and personally led them to her husband's rescue. The story of her ride into the hills, on a white horse and wearing a white skirt, is still a staple of the local folklore today.

The Chinese threw their most sophisticated equipment into the battle, using machine guns, land mines, and special fire bombs to destroy the villages at a distance and to defoliate the jungle which sheltered the tribesmen.[27] Even so, it was clear by the end of the year that all this was not enough. With heavy stress on the treachery and perversity of the aborigines, Liu requested further funding for the campaign. Though deserving officers like Ch'ao-tung were rewarded, the whole messy business tarnished Liu's image in Peking and may have contributed to his departure from Taiwan in 1891.[28]

Ch'ao-tung saw action against the tribes a third time, in the fall of 1887.[29] Once more, the advances of Chinese settlers had provoked aborigine reprisals and when Ch'ao-tung secured the chief culprit and sent him to Taipei for execution, the tribes rose again. The challenge never equalled that of the year before and Ch'ao-tung restored order after a brief and vigorous campaign.

The wisdom of the aborigine campaigns has been questioned, for they were costly at a time when there were many other demands on Taiwan's resources. Pacification would not be achieved in Liu's time nor, indeed, for over a generation. Still, a sizeable area was opened for Chinese settlement and exploitation. Not the least of the beneficiaries of this new colonization were families like the Lins

themselves, who gained a dominant role in the production
of camphor, a chief product of the newly opened region. If
Ch'ao-tung's campaigns marked a new, albeit inconclusive,
chapter in a relentless Chinese advance, their greatest
value to Ch'ao-tung personally was to seal his alliance with
Liu.

The Governor and the Local Notables

Even in uneventful times, an official required minimal
cooperation from the local notables. In times of drastic
change, a man like Liu Ming-ch'uan was even more dependent on the local elite for their approval of his innovations, for their financial support and managerial talents,
and for the influence they had on public opinion. Ch'ao-
tung was therefore called upon to serve the governor not
only in military matters, but in a host of other areas.

Cooperation between the governor and the local notables was achieved through the device of the specialized
bureau (chü).[30] Quasi-official bodies, such bureaus were in
charge of specific projects: railroad building, mining, tax
reform, and so forth. Widely used on the mainland earlier,
such agencies mushroomed in Taiwan under Liu, for they
had the advantage of flexibility. They were ad hoc institutions, not bound by statute, and Liu had greater freedom
in choosing bureau personnel than in selecting his regular
subordinates. He thus staffed the bureaus with his personal
followers from the mainland and with his favorites among
the local gentry. For the Taiwanese notables, bureau posts
provided a rare chance of shaping the affairs of their native
area from within a public body.

While the bureau institutionalized the cooperation between officialdom and gentry, the ties between the governor and his local supporters remained highly personal,
following the classical pattern of patron-client relations.
Ch'ao-tung acknowledged this bond by withdrawing from

government service under Liu's successors and some have thought that his life-long veneration for Liu (and not merely dynastic loyalty) inspired his decision to leave Taiwan in 1895.[31]

Where personal loyalties were so important, vendettas between an official and the clients of his rival were common. Of this, too, the Lins gained some experience under Liu, for when Liu impeached his rival, Intendant Liu Ao, soon after the end of the war with France, Liu Ao's followers, including Lin Wen-ch'in, were made to feel their patron's disgrace. Impeached for embezzlement, Wen-ch'in was stripped of such ranks as he possessed and forced to pay back the 16,000 *Taels* he was accused of having taken.[32] Not for some time did he re-emerge into respectability, and his relation to Liu Ming-ch'uan remained distant, precluding a place for him in the governor's reform program. Similarly, much of the south Taiwanese gentry remained aloof from the governor, disgruntled because of the treatment he had meted out to the locally popular Liu Ao.[33]

If Wen-ch'in experienced Liu's vindictiveness, Ch'ao-tung basked in the governor's favor and was entrusted with many tasks. He worked with other gentry members on building roads and bridges, not in the usual pattern of gentry-led local improvements, but as part of a coordinated, province-wide program of improved communications. He seems to have worked on the western spur of the important east-west link through central Taiwan, a job for which his ample manpower and his campaign experience in the mountains had prepared him.[34]

In the late 1880's, he supervised the building of a new provincial capital in the Upper Valley.[35] His men laid out the street grid, built walls, city gates, and *yamens*, and manned the local defenses. Although Ch'ao-tung's use of his own men for the job was supposed to save expenses, the project proved costly, swallowing almost a quarter-million *Taels*.[36] In the end, much of the work proved pointless, for financial shortages forced Liu to abandon the project in mid-course and instead make Taipei the provisional capital. Ch'ao-tung's half-finished project, "government buildings overgrown with wild grass,"[37] became the core of the modern city of Taichung.

Other jobs which the governor entrusted to Ch'ao-tung dealt with the economic exploitation of the newly won mountain areas. In the Miao-li region, Ch'ao-tung headed an office for developing the petroleum resources discovered there.[38] Without much success during his tenure, the venture was later turned over to private entrepreneurs. Ch'ao-tung was also in charge of the mid-Taiwan sub-bureau of the Pacification and Reclamation Bureau, the agency responsible for oversight of the pacified tribes and for the development of natural resources in hill and mountain.[39] Among these resources, camphor occupied an important place; it was much in demand on the world market and a duty on its export promised to yield a handsome income for the government. There was ample room for private profit as well, since the gentry managers often dealt on their own accounts in the commodities over which their bureaus had jurisdiction. Thus, Ch'ao-tung became one of the leading camphor producers, while Lin Wei-yüan of Pan-ch'iao became the island's chief tea grower, another industry under the control of the all-Taiwan Pacification and Reclamation Bureau which he headed.

Gentry positions which combined public authority with a chance for private gain existed also in the field of tax reform. A Tax Reform Bureau oversaw the ambitious land survey and tax reform program which Liu conducted in 1886-1888. There is no evidence that Ch'ao-tung held a post in this bureau, although Wen-ch'in obtained a position in the local survey commission that functioned under its aegis, as did other gentry members.[40] But Ch'ao-tung may well have exerted informal influence in tax matters, much as did his north Taiwanese peer, Lin Wei-yüan, who influ-

enced the governor in matters of the tea tax and the treatment of *ta-tsu* landlords, both of the greatest personal importance to him.[41]

If Ch'ao-tung played at best an indirect role in tax matters, he was directly involved in coping with the consequences of Liu's overly ambitious tax scheme. Disgruntled
over the high fee for the new land deeds, unsettled by the
prospect of sharply higher taxes, and baited by a high-
handed district magistrate, several thousand people re-
belled in Chang-hua in the fall of 1888. Rallying under a
respected local farmer, Shih Chiu-tuan, they had begun a
siege of Chang-hua city when Liu ordered Ch'ao-tung to
put the rising down. In a brief campaign, Ch'ao-tung approached the city at night, captured Pa-kua-*shan*, and dispersed the rebels.[42] The operation was in sharp contrast to
his father's heavy-handed pacification a quarter-century
earlier. Now there were no reprisals and no spoliations; the
troops maintained exemplary discipline. If anything,
Ch'ao-tung showed concern for the misguided rebels with
whose cause many wealthy landowners secretly sympathized.[43] Indeed, it was rich landlords like the Lins who
stood to gain most from the retreat on the tax issue which
the governor announced in the wake of the rising. As if this
was not reward enough, Ch'ao-tung earned his most signal
honor for this brief and essentially bloodless campaign: the
Yellow Riding Jacket, seldom awarded to one so relatively
junior in rank.[44]

Ch'ao-tung's ties to the governor brought him not only
personal honors but also an opportunity to mingle with
fellow-gentry from other parts of the island who gathered
in Liu's circle. It was through Liu, for example, that the
Wu-feng Lins first came to know their namesakes, the
powerful Pan-ch'iao Lins of north Taiwan.[45] Such contacts
and the work on island-wide reforms gave these notables a
broader political vision, a glimpse of the needs of Taiwan
as a whole. When Liu resigned in 1891, he left behind a
few prominent men who were learning to think in island-

wide terms. This was not the least of his legacies to Taiwan, or to the Lins.

The Last Stand of Ch'ing Taiwan

The new political vision was soon put to the test during the Sino-Japanese war of 1894-1895. Fought in Korea and north China, the war went badly for the Chinese, and a Japanese attack on Taiwan became a possibility in the spring.[46] At first, the prospects for defense seemed hopeful enough on the island. The local notables rallied around the acting governor, T'ang Ching-sung, raised braves, and prepared for resistance. Ch'ao-tung overcame his earlier reluctance to serve under Liu Ming-ch'uan's successors and responded to T'ang's call. He took his braves to their old battleground in the Keelung hills where they became the keystone of the anti-Japanese defense.[47]

Into this busy world of defense preparations, the news from Peking hit like a thunderclap in mid-April. Far from expecting the islanders to resist the despised "dwarf" barbarians, the throne was abandoning them; the Treaty of Shimonoseki ceded the island to Japan. On Taiwan, indignation soon turned to action as various groups sought to challenge the treaty terms.[48]

The highest official on the island, Governor T'ang himself, made secret contact with senior officials on the mainland who opposed the treaty terms and thought that Taiwan might yet escape annexation if a separate state were proclaimed on the island and a European sponsor for it found. Among the Taiwanese, important notables also began to agitate for a separate Taiwanese state, but on the premise that armed resistance, not diplomacy, would save Taiwan.

Ch'ao-tung, too, was drawn into this movement which was at its most vigorous in central Taiwan and whose leader was a brilliant young *chin-shih* from Chang-hua district, Ch'iu Feng-chia, a near neighbor of the Lins and a relative by marriage.[49] Ch'iu was indeed well-placed for such a role. Among his fellow-Hakkas, he was able to recruit numerous volunteers, while his contacts to the officials (Governor T'ang was a patron of the gifted young scholar-poet) promised success at the highest level. In the company of various notables from central and north Taiwan, including Ch'ao-tung,[50] Ch'iu approached the governor and persuaded him to become the island republic's first president. On May 25 T'ang was solemnly inaugurated in Taipei.

The solidarity between the notables and the new president and among the local leaders themselves was, however, deceptive. Ch'ing officials like T'ang, who had lent themselves to the republican scheme, and their Taiwanese backers had only papered over their real differences. T'ang and his advisers seem never to have envisaged an all-out battle against Japan; they counted on foreign intervention to save the island's independence.[51] Ch'iu and his supporters, on the other hand, were calling for battle, evoking memories of the independence which Taiwan had enjoyed under Koxinga's house.[52] The idea of republican government, too, was subject to different interpretations. T'ang proposed to run the island much as before, while the Taiwanese notables looked for a share of the ruling power. Personal relations between them and the new president, so important to the success of the republic, also failed to develop satisfactorily.

Nor were all the major notables united behind the republic. Some, like Lin Wei-yüan, withheld their support from the start, while others withdrew as T'ang's blunders antagonized them. A case in point was Lin Ch'ao-tung. Though he had helped persuade T'ang to lead the island republic, Ch'ao-tung's relations with the new president were, in fact, precarious. T'ang, a Kwangsi man who preferred Kwangtung braves for major military assignments, was being importuned by a Kwangtung commander whose troops were deployed in the Keelung hills near Ch'ao-tung's. Jealous of Ch'ao-tung as a rival for future honors, this man urged T'ang to transfer Ch'ao-tung back to mid-Taiwan; in late May, T'ang complied.[53]

T'ang's order confronted Ch'ao-tung with the first of many painful choices during that spring. To obey the governor-president was to abandon the most favorable battleground and to disappoint the many partisans of resistance who looked to him for military leadership. To defy T'ang and fight in the north was to undercut the authority of the new government and to oppose the will of the dynasty, in whose name T'ang appeared to be acting.[54] Ch'ao-tung obeyed and took his braves back to mid-Taiwan, but his allegiance to the new republic was severely shaken as T'ang allowed old-fashioned provincial preferences to interfere with his presidential duties.

When the Japanese landed near Keelung a few days later (May 29), they met a demoralized, worthless force, not Ch'ao-tung's valiant braves. They routed the Kwangtung troops and headed for Taipei, which T'ang abandoned. As the defeated soldiers straggled back to the capital, another weakness in the island's defenses became apparent. Blaming the "traitorous" Kwangtung soldiers for the defeat, the irate citizens of the capital attacked the braves, who in turn plundered the city.[55]

As T'ang attempted to organize a new resistance effort from nearby Tamsui, he turned to the man whose services he had just spurned. In early June, he sent urgent cables to mid-Taiwan, imploring Lin Ch'ao-tung to come north to fight the enemy. Ch'ao-tung's response was ambiguous; while he set his forces in motion northward, he allowed the troops to linger on the way. Possibly, he was awaiting T'ang's response to a concurrent proposal that the president come south to make a joint stand with the local leaders in mid-Taiwan.[56]

On his march north, Ch'ao-tung was not even half-way to Tamsui when he learned on June 11 that the Japanese had begun their advance south from Taipei and that

T'ang, far from joining the notables in mid-Taiwan, had fled the island.[57] The news forced Ch'ao-tung into another reappraisal. Was it still possible to organize an effective defense in the north, or would it be better to return home and prepare to defend mid-Taiwan? Unable to make a clearcut choice and temporarily out of touch with his vanguard, he allowed this advance unit to proceed north, where it would later contribute to the defense effort around Hsin-chu; he himself led the bulk of his troops back to Chang-hua district. Here, they had their hands full simply maintaining a semblance of order at a time when the exodus of many local officials and gentry was plunging the countryside into turmoil.

Ch'ao-tung himself must have considered the possibility of flight by this time. Already, on June 8, he had evacuated his family, sending the huge household under escort to Wu-ch'i and from there by boat to Ch'üan-chou. The Lin convoy was still so formidable that a number of officials and fellow-gentry joined it, trusting to Ch'ao-tung's braves for safe passage when the regular forces could no longer provide it.[58]

If Ch'ao-tung himself still held back, the events of the next two weeks helped him to make up his mind.[59] The frantic and ill-coordinated defense efforts in the north proved futile. In the Hsin-chu area, where remnants of the regular forces and local volunteers converged, the would-be defenders were at each other's throats. The remaining Kwangtung soldiers clashed with the native Taiwanese, and, among the islanders, the old communal tensions reappeared. When Hakka volunteers from the hill country descended into the plains to save Hsin-chu, the local people (mainly Fukienese) refused their request for food and supplies. Then the Hakkas proceeded to seize what they required, driving many of the local people straight into the arms of the Japanese.

Before the end of June, Ch'ao-tung seems to have concluded that resistance in mid-Taiwan would be equally futile and that a Japanese take-over was inevitable. In that case, his own course was clear. As a loyal subject of the throne, beholden to a patron like Liu Ming-ch'uan, he could not serve the new masters.[60] It remained to give final instructions for the safety of Wu-feng, where Ch'ao-hsüan, the most prestigious of Wen-ming's sons, and Wen-ch'in, head of the second branch, would remain behind. Ch'ao-tung ordered that they were to offer no resistance and avoid all provocation.[61] Weapons were to remain in hiding. The villages of the Lin turf were instructed to lie low as well. His old soldiers, too, must have received orders to melt into their native villages and return to civilian life. Then, late in June, Ch'ao-tung joined his family on the mainland.[62]

His instructions carried full weight after he was gone. When the Japanese moved into the Upper Valley in late August, they encountered no significant resistance. Though remnant forces from north and south Taiwan joined for a bloody stand at Chang-hua—the battle of Pa-kua-*shan* was the biggest Japan had to fight in Taiwan—the Lins played no part in the armed defense of mid-Taiwan.[63]

Unlike many other Taiwanese notables who fled in the panic of 1895 and returned later, Ch'ao-tung's departure was to prove final. Only his wife and sons returned to Taiwan, to claim their property and play a role in its economic and public life. Ch'ao-tung spent his remaining years on the mainland, where he held military office, was received in audience by the emperor, and managed his extensive business affairs.[64]

Ch'ao-tung's self-exile was symbolic of the change he had worked in the family's political stance. No longer a strongman, he had an overriding loyalty to the throne and to his patron, Liu. While he drew on the resources inherited from his forebears, he transcended their outlook. Gone were the brutality and violence of the strongmen days, gone also the personal heroism of Wen-ch'a, the general who climbed siege ladders and counted the heads he took in battle. If Ch'ao-tung saw the futility of a do-or-die stand against the Japanese, as his father and uncle might not, his life also lacked some of the color and savor of theirs, the strongman's fierce loyalty to place and people.

Ch'ao-tung, then, was a transitional figure. His career gave a more steady luster to the family than the Lins had known before, yet it also created untimely loyalties to a moribund dynasty. If 1895 forced a choice between his local power base and his broader political commitments, exile was the price he paid for the larger vision he had embraced. But we must not exaggerate the breadth of Ch'ao-tung's mind. He remained most comfortable in the web of dynastic and highly personal patron-client relationships that suffused the imperial polity. When he cooperated with a Hakka gentryman like Ch'iu Feng-chia, he proved the strength of their family ties and of gentry notions of collegiality. His soldiers had not transcended the communal enmities of the past.[65] A more inclusive Taiwanese consciousness would not emerge until the twentieth century. The "new" Taiwan in which Ch'ao-tung revived the fortunes of the family was still very much part of the old China.

CHAPTER 12

PILLARS OF THE COMMUNITY

The Lins as
Local Gentry, 1882-1895

*Since our family moved to Wu-feng, . . . it has
pursued farming and practiced the military arts;
Wen-ch'in alone was fond of learning and
exerted himself to be of service to the world. . . .
All the scholars who called on him and were his
followers paid their respects to him. Under an
imperial decree the officials presented him with
the plaque for those who "delight in goodness,
are fond of giving."*[1]

To love learning and virtue, to benefit the worthy and
enjoy the friendship of scholars—such, very nearly, has
been the ideal of the Chinese gentry for centuries. Newcomers to the gentry achieved this ideal, or at least the
reputation of gentility, by combining public service and
cultured leisure in their home communities. While Lin
Ch'ao-tung made the family famous throughout Taiwan,
other Lins engaged in local activities which had all the
patina of the gentry tradition.

By the late nineteenth century, thousands of newcomers
had swelled the Chinese gentry beyond previous limits.[2]
Sales of degrees and titles and lavish rewards to military
men had brought gentry status to many newcomers who
lacked degrees earned in examinations. In Taiwan, where

the elite had always been a less academic group, scores of landlords, grain merchants, entrepreneurs, and leaders of braves had gained admittance. The addition of another strongman family such as the Lins would hardly raise an eyebrow.

Notwithstanding its dilution, the gentry's privileged status, ample style of life, and social ethos were still intact. In joining the local gentry at the moment they did, the Lins therefore had the best of both worlds: ready access to an elite status which had as yet lost none of its privilege.

In their pursuit of respectability, the Lins enjoyed an ironic legacy from their most lawless days, for the ranks which several family members acquired in the 1850's and early 1860's had already conferred gentry standing on some segments of the family. For Wen-ch'a's immediate kinsmen, his posthumous honors assured gentry status beyond his lifetime. In the court records of the 1870's, his mother, Mrs. Tai, is invariably designated a "lady of the official class." Ch'ao-tung's inherited rank, *ch'i-tu-wei*, gave him something even more exclusive than gentry status: membership in China's only native hereditary nobility.[3] Since members of a household shared the legal status of its head, Ch'ao-tung's rank rubbed off on his brothers, too, though presumably not on his cousins, the sons of Wen-ming.

These other Lins, sons of the tainted Wen-ming and Tien-kuo, had to establish their own gentry credentials, either by purchase or as a reward for public-spirited donations to the government. Thus, Lin Ch'ao-hsüan, the most prominent of Wen-ming's six sons, acquired an expectant district magistrate title (Rank 7B) while Wen-ch'in, Tien-kuo's youngest son and after 1882 head of the second branch, collected a whole string of brevet titles, including an intendancy (Rank 4A) and other badges of honor.[4]

More significant than the pursuit of gentry credentials through purchase was the turn of several family members to the examination path. Here Wen-ch'in blazed the trail when he acquired a *sheng-yüan* degree in 1884 and topped it nine years later with the *chü-jen* degree. In the next generation, the *sheng-yüan* became *de rigueur* among the younger members. By 1895, four other members of the family had acquired it, and several others were in training for the examination.[5]

What are we to make of this odd assortment of titles, some inherited, others purchased or earned? Perhaps simply this: that individual family members followed their own bent in selecting a path into the gentry and that few aimed beyond a modest place in it. In Chang-hua, a *sheng-yüan* was *someone*. The higher degrees and the formal positions in the bureaucracy were beyond the family's ambitions.

With gentry standing came the externals of the gentry style of life, the spacious mansions, the large households, the lives of leisure. By the end of the century, the Lins surrounded themselves with all the accoutrements of their new status. They wore official dress and the roofs of their houses curved upwards in the manner reserved for the mansions of the gentry. When Ch'ao-tung travelled, carried by four sedan-chair carriers and with a second relay of four tagging along, no passerby could be in doubt that here was a personage of importance.[6]

Much of this no doubt was ostentation parading as a Confucian sense of rank. Enjoying the outward trappings of gentry rank, the Lins resembled thousands of social climbers who had preceded them into the gentry. To take a fuller measure of their transformation, we must examine whether they also came to practice the unostentatious, the inner virtues of the gentleman, his love of learning and moral endeavor, his code of loyalty and service.

The Lins and the Confucian Virtues

Looking at the younger generation, men born in the 1870's and 1880's, we see that gentry membership and the contacts it opened worked a slow but steady change in the values and interests of family members. Born too late to have acquired formal degrees before 1895, several of these young men developed a genuine love of literature, and particularly of poetry. An example was Lin Hsien-t'ang (1881-1956), Wen-ch'in's eldest son; he became a competent poet and turned out a great deal of the occasional verse expected of a Chinese gentleman. His antiquarian bent led to an interest in family and local history.[7] Several of his cousins loved books. Only one of this branch's scions, the alcoholic Wen-tien (1852-1877), Tien-kuo's middle son, disdained formal learning, though he was known to ex-

Fig. 14 A private tutor and his small charges (*Tien-shih-chai hua-pao*, East Asian Library, Columbia University).

press this contempt in Taoist allusions that paid a back-handed compliment to the learned tradition.[8]

It was in the senior branch, latecomers to learning, that there occurred a veritable explosion of literary talent which shed new luster on the Lin name. While its full flowering lies beyond our terminal date of 1895, it is clear that these men had spent their youth in a far more cultivated atmosphere than the family had ever maintained before. Wen-ming's posthumously adopted sixth son, Chün-t'ang (*ming*, or personal name, Ch'ao-sung, 1875-1915) and Ch'ao-hsüan's eldest son, Yu-ch'un (1880-1939) were among the leading poets of the early twentieth century, central figures in the island's cultural life.[9] Before 1895, they had made a name for themselves as ardent lovers of literature if not yet as poets in their own right. Early in the twentieth century, they helped found the *Li-she*, mid-Taiwan's major poetry society, where a whole generation of young Taiwanese expressed in classical verse its love of the Chinese heritage. Besides these two, Ch'ao-tung's second son, Tzu-ch'üan (*tzu*, or courtesy name Chung-heng, 1877-?) also became a well-known poet.[10]

Before 1895 the influence of these young men was necessarily limited; the family was dominated by older, less-educated men who were not yet at home with the responsibilities of a cultural elite. Characteristically, these older men even failed to preserve the written record of their own most distinguished member. Wen-ch'a's memorials were not printed, and perhaps not even collected,[11] a shocking omission in an older gentry family though understandable among recent strongmen. Private editions, hallmarks of the gentry as a cultural elite, did not make their appearance among the Lins until the twentieth century.

If the love of learning took hold only slowly, another gentry virtue, loyalty, was in evidence earlier, though the record is not without its ironies. Despite his abuses of the public trust, Lin Wen-ch'a gathered around himself the aura of the supremely loyal hero. As the family turned from the strongman past to the new gentry role, family myth-makers eagerly seized on selected highpoints of his career to fashion the image of a family uniquely devoted to the throne.[12]

The imperial government itself assisted in this pious fraud. Hoping to bind the gentry of the new province more closely to the dynastic center, the Manchus lavished ritual courtesies on the island. Shrines to local worthies blossomed while even Koxinga received belated accolades as an exemplar of dynastic fealty. In this atmosphere, the government authorized and built a temple for Wen-ch'a in Taichung in 1889.[13] Twice yearly, magistrates paid homage to the native son who had made the supreme sacrifice. What more convincing proof to the Lins and their neighbors that the family's fate was uniquely tied to the imperial house?

The touchstone of all such fine sentiments was, of course, 1895. As we have seen, Ch'ao-tung and his brothers followed in the footsteps of the Ming loyalists, abandoning their home and refusing to serve another ruler. Wen-ch'in, too, whose mother's health prevented his leaving, pointedly refused service under the new masters.[14] Loyalty, then, had become more than rhetoric. It impelled real sacrifices, at least for a time.

As moral exemplars for the wider society, gentry members were supposed to conduct their family life according to the highest moral standards. Without expecting an instant transformation, we may inquire whether entrance into the gentry brought with it a more conspicuous practice of such central virtues as filial piety and fraternal benevolence.

In fact, no clearcut pattern emerges. Both before and during the Lins's gentry days, manifestations of filial piety depended mainly on an individual's personal style. There were, in any case, numerous ways of being filial. Wen-ch'a had defied his grandfather's wishes in the matter of his education but later displayed exemplary filial piety in the pursuit of his father's killer. Similar inconsistencies occur later. Since so many fathers died young, many Lin sons were spared the key test of a son's filiality, his continued subordination, even as an adult, to paternal authority. Filial Lin sons instead bowed to mothers and grandmothers, but matriarchs were as easily defied or by-passed (as happened to Mrs. Tai toward the end of the lawsuit) as they were humored or obeyed.

Only Wen-ch'in made filial piety into a conspicuous virtue, submitting to his mother, Mrs. Lo, on sensitive questions of family ethics and translating her charitable impulses into good works. In 1890, he built the famous Lin garden, the *Lai-yüan* (Lai garden), as a birthday gift for his mother. Its very name expressed the intent, for Old Lai-tzu was one of the twenty-four paragons of filial piety, a seventy-year-old man who donned children's clothes and played childish games to amuse his ancient parents. As the genealogy reports, "Since [Wen-ch'in] had it always in mind to attain the spirit of Lai-tzu in his costumes, he built the *Lai-yüan* in the foothills of Wu-feng, complete with pavilions, terraces, flowers, and trees. The setting was extremely calm and profound. He kept a troop of players and in the spring and autumn, on fine days, he would raise the cup and have plays performed to entertain Mrs. Lo. There was nothing that he would not do to please her."[15]

Fraternal affection ranked as a companion virtue to filial piety. It, too, was in uneven supply among the Lins and flowed among individuals according to personal temperament and not in obedience to the moral law. Thus, strong individuals such as Ch'ao-tung had unquestioned authority over their younger brothers, while weaker individuals failed to command such deference. An older brother's care for younger brothers, too, depended mainly on the interplay of personalities. Thus, Wen-ch'a and his immediate descendants shared their wealth with the second brother, Wen-ming, and his offspring, but gave almost nothing to the third brother, Wen-ts'ai, and his descendants.[16]

Despite such vagaries of personality and a tendency to give short shrift to undistinguished or uncongenial brothers, the family as a whole was markedly successful in maintaining unity among several prominent brothers and the branches descending from them. This was true particularly of the branches descending from Ting-pang and Tien-kuo, the first and second branches in Wu-feng, and, within the senior branch, of the Wen-ch'a and Wen-ming segments. Both in strongman and in gentry days, these branches stood by each other. The Wen-ch'a segment contributed time and money to the lawsuit for Wen-ming's vindication, and the second branch made large, interest-free loans to the senior branch,[17] probably to help with legal expenses. On several occasions, brothers and cousins postponed the division of the inherited property. (See Ch. 14.) In maintaining large, jointly owned estates, the Lins honored the moral code even as they pursued the best interests of the family as they saw them.

Filial piety and fraternal benevolence transcended the span of a single lifetime, it was thought, and led to the veneration of remoter ancestors and the sense of solidarity with more distant kinsmen—the lineage spirit as defined by Confucian moralists of recent centuries.[18] This, too, was thought of as a gentry trait, expressed in ritual and institutional form by elite families. In fact, the lineage had little meaning for the Lins of the late nineteenth century. Since they depended on the broader surname group as a political power base, moral preachment alone could not breathe life into lineage institutions. There was, in the nineteenth century, neither a lineage temple nor a genealogy, neither a lineage code nor lineage self-government under the much-touted primogeniture system (*tsung-tzu*, rule by the eldest son of the oldest branch). In short, the Lins did little to institutionalize the lineage as a corporate group.[19]

Ancestral worship was conducted in domestic shrines. Their placement and the selection of the tablets underlined the importance of the branch, not of the lineage as a

Fig. 15 Male members of a gentry family honoring the ancestors (*Tien-shih-chai hua-pao*, East Asian Library, Columbia University).

whole. Thus, the descendants of Ting-pang worshiped to-gether, as did the offspring of Tien-kuo, but neither of these ritual groups maintained a special trust to defray the expenses of their founder's worship. Only in the 1890's, when the large, all-purpose estates of these branches were broken up, did each establish a small ritual trust in the name of each branch founder.[20]

Nor were earlier ancestors, common to both major Wu-feng branches, singled out as focal points of an emerging lineage. Neither Lin Shih nor his son, Sun, had a ritual trust. The only ritual trust that dates back before the 1890's had been established in honor of Chia-yin, evidently at the time he himself divided his estate among his sons.[21] But that trust's modest size—at most a few dozen *chia*, a mere fraction of the vast holdings of the living—underlined the family's reluctance to tie up land in entailed ritual trusts.

The gentry was expected not only to provide a moral example to the rest of the community, but to buttress the formal government by exercising informal leadership in the community. By the 1880's the Lins had begun to join the older gentry families in the discharge of such duties. The areas in which they chose to exert themselves were primarily two: local security and local communications. Not only did Ch'ao-tung and Wen-ch'in raise braves in the Sino-French war, as we have seen; Ch'ao-hsüan, Wen-ming's son, was an acknowledged expert in local security, consulted by Liu Ming-ch'uan on matters of aborigine and border warfare, and a leader of braves in his own right during the Shih Chiu-tuan rising.[22] In 1895, too, both Wen-ch'in and Ch'ao-hsüan were in the thick of local defense efforts. With other local notables, they raised militia (*lien-yung*) at government request and both served on the mid-island defense bureau which the local prefect established.[23] Amidst the incredibly confused resistance efforts of that spring and summer, the bureau was only a minor factor, yet one which showed how much local government had come to rely on the local gentry. Taxing and requisitioning powers, carefully guarded state monopolies in normal times, were turned over to bureau members among whom the Lins had a unique position as the only family represented by two individuals.

Communications was the other area in which the Lins exerted themselves. Given the poor state of the roads, this was indeed a vast field for gentry enterprise, and one in which Wen-ch'in took the initiative.[24] He had roads repaired and small bamboo bridges built, and he donated several small ferries. His most enduring contribution was a free ferry over the lower Ta-tu river near Wu-jih. This service operated for nearly half a century, until the Japanese built a bridge for general traffic in the 1930's. We hear less about exertions by the senior branch, though Ch'ao-tung is said to have contributed, along with Wen-ch'in, to a ferry over the Ta-chia river, the district's northern boundary, and there were undoubtedly other projects about which no information survives.

The concentration on local defense and communications must reflect long-standing family concerns, dating back to their strongmen days. Not student bursaries or private academies, but security and the roads preoccupied this recently gentrified strongman family. A broader concept of local leadership, transcending the family's background, emerged only in the next generation.

Relief of the needy was another duty of conscientious gentry members. Here, too, the second branch under Wen-ch'in took the lead.[25] He donated a piece of land, worth three hundred piculs a year, to an asylum for baby girls in Chang-hua. Other charities of this nature were confined to Wu-feng itself; here, Wen-ch'in gave free medicine to the sick, free rice to the poor, and free coffins to the dead. Several of the elderly Buddhist ladies in his household, especially his mother, Mrs. Lo, and Wen-tien's widow, Mrs. Ch'iu,[26] joined Wen-ch'in in these local charities.

On a broader stage, Wen-ch'in joined other notables in donating relief funds for the drought victims of Honan in 1889. Also on the mainland, he acted as a peacemaker among warring factions in Ch'üan-chou prefecture.[27] We know few details, except that he again spent a sizeable sum of money to help to compose an ancient feud. He may well have learned of this conflict during one of his business trips to the mainland and welcomed a chance to earn the good will of the large Ch'üan-chou element in mid-Taiwan.

Wen-ch'in's prominence among the philanthropists of the family raises questions of motive. More than others, he seems to have realized the need to live down the family's unsavory past. His own temporary disgrace, too, could be wiped out by such conspicuous good works. Many of Wen-ch'in's good deeds thus stemmed from his concern for his own good name. But this was not all. His mother, a lady of rare sweetness and generosity, inspired much of her son's giving; filial piety, if not the broader counsels of compassion, generated Wen-ch'in's philanthropy.

If a strongman with his trusty band could defy the local government and the local gentry, the gentry member needed their respect and approval to be effective. His power was the power to persuade, based on his influence within the intricate network of gentry connections. As the Lins sloughed off their strongman past and adopted the more legitimate, if devious, ways of the gentry, they also gained the approval of their peers with whom they rubbed shoulders on local committees and in social gatherings. It was their good standing among these fellow gentry which, along with imperial favors, finally validated the family's "gentrification."

One measure of a family's standing among their fellow notables was the ability to secure support for projects dear to their hearts. Here, the Lins scored well. In 1885, several prominent Taiwanese, among them Lin Wei-yüan of Pan-ch'iao, spoke to Governor Liu Ming-ch'uan in support of Lin Wen-ming's rehabilitation.[28] An even broader out-pouring of support for the family occurred a few years later when almost eighty notables, including several of the Taiwanese *chin-shih*, petitioned the government for the special temple to honor Wen-ch'a.[29]

The family's acceptance by their fellow notables regis-tered as well on the marriage market. By the last quarter of the century, the Lins exchanged brides with many gentry families from the district and beyond—degree holders, members of old elite families, and wealthy merchants, most of them residents of Chang-hua city or other towns in mid-Taiwan.[30] This was in sharp contrast to the pattern of the strongmen days, when the Lins intermarried with peasant families in the vicinity of Wu-feng or with an occasional strongman family from the Upper Valley.

The new ties with their fellow notables greatly eased the Lins's assimilation into gentry culture. But for these new friends, the family might not have moved so quickly from the crude world of a Tien-kuo or a Wen-ming to the vastly more cultivated world of their grandsons, a Hsien-t'ang or a Yu-ch'un. Among their new scholarly friends, Wu Te-kung of Chang-hua (1850-1924)[31] was a versatile literatus; only a middle-level degree-holder, he became a voluminous writer on local affairs. He had spent part of his youth in Wu-feng, where his teacher tutored the young Lin scions of the second branch and where Wu formed close ties with Wen-ch'in. Early in the twentieth century, the families joined together in business ventures and there were intermarriages as well. Another friend among the more conservative scholars was Chuang Shih-hsün (ca. 1854-1916),[32] a literatus from Lu-kang, a *chü-jen* of 1879, and a teacher at the *Wen-k'ai shu-yüan*, the district's major academy. The Lins greatly admired his character and his learning and invited him to Wu-feng as a tutor. Through Chuang, the Lins presumably had contact with the other luminaries of the *Wen-k'ai* circle, which included many recent arrivals from the mainland and at whose center was Ts'ai Te-fang, an 1874 *chin-shih* who stressed classical learning as a defense against Western threats.

The Lins also had contacts to the more progressive scholars. Among these we must count Ch'en Wang-tseng (1853-1929),[33] the Tainan *chin-shih* whom they had helped with travel money in 1874 and who later served with distinction in Kwangtung, where he contributed to economic development and municipal reform in Canton around the turn of the century. Since Wen-ch'in made frequent business trips to Hongkong and Canton, personal contact was easy to maintain; it was later strengthened by intermarriage. If we add to Ch'en's name that of the island's outstanding young reformist scholar, Ch'iu Feng-chia (1864-1912), the near neighbor from northern Chang-hua and a relative by marriage, or that of the Lüs,[34] another Chang-hua gentry connection by marriage and the owners of Taiwan's finest private library, we get a sense of the many cultivated friends who enriched the Lins in the late nineteenth century.

Not all their new friends were of scholarly bent, of course; there were connections, through marriage or otherwise, with several of the *nouveaux riches* of the district, with business dynasties such as the Shihs of Lu-kang,[35] with the wealthy Wus of Hsin-chuang-tzu,[36] or with the influential scions of the early frontier entrepreneurs, such as the Yangs of Chang-hua. Yang Chih-ch'en (1854-1930),[37] Ch'ao-tung's brother-in-law, was in fact a man after the heart of the earlier Lin strongmen, a leader of braves and a *kung-fu* (martial arts) expert. But while he himself may have lacked polish, he had ties to many of the older learned and professional families of the district city. Another of his brothers-in-law was a well-known painter and literatus and the son of one of the city's most renowned physicians.

The Lins's transition from local strongmen to local gentry had begun in the trying decade after Wen-ming's death and proceeded apace thereafter. The smooth passage can be credited to several circumstances. The new leadership in the family was most important. Vigorous in their own way, men like Wen-feng and Ch'ao-tung, Wen-ch'in and Ch'ao-hsüan had no taste for the unbridled and dangerous life of the strongman; they preferred to work within the established legal and political order. Circumstances of time and place worked in the family's favor, too. Eager to raise money and to bind the Taiwanese elite more closely to the center, the throne lavished honors and distinctions on the island which benefited wealthy would-be gentry families like the Lins. Finally, the older elite families welcomed the newcomers.

Their new status certified by official recognition and

gentry acceptance, the Lins went about the business, necessarily slow, of assimilating the values and style of life of a venerable cultural elite. Here too they had made notable progress by 1895, though a full flowering did not occur until after Taiwan had passed under Japanese rule.

The relative ease of the Lins's passage into the gentry can remind us, too, that for all their contrasts, strongmen and gentrymen had always had a good deal in common. Their power derived from similar sources: their ascendance in the local economy and their leading role in local group life, in the myriad clan and communal associations. If the strongman lacked the badge of learning, his martial values were not as foreign to the gentry mind as the traditional antithesis of *wen* (letters, culture) and *wu* (arms, force) would lead one to believe. Rightly viewed, the strongman's valor and his loyalty to friend and brave commanded the respect of the cultural elite. In becoming gentry members, the Lins therefore did not have to repudiate their entire past; they merely exorcised its darker features.

CHAPTER 13

AT HOME

Domestic Life in
the Late Nineteenth Century

Through the gate, I stepped into bright lamp light,
In the main hall, I paid respects to my mother.
Two or three of my brothers
Elegantly dressed, welcomed me.
Maidservants took the luggage
Sons and nephews arranged a welcome meal.[1]

Stepping through the ornate outer gate of a Lin mansion, one entered a private realm whose luxury mirrored the family's splendor in the larger world. It was mainly elite families like the Lins who maintained the much-touted "large households" of several generations, and many married brothers under the same roof.[2] They alone could afford the spacious quarters and the swarms of servants which distinguished the gentry mansion from the commoner's dwelling.

Until the middle of the nineteenth century, the Lins's domestic arrangements had been of the simpler type common among non-elite families. With each new generation, brothers had divided their patrimony and established their own households.[3] They kept the family size modest, usually under ten and often around five or six. No concubines—with the possible exception of Chia-yin—and few servants rounded out their commoner households.[4] The pattern persisted among the undistinguished Lins of the second half of the nineteenth century, among the descendants of Chia-yin's third and fourth sons, and of Ting-pang's obscure third son. Families here continued to be of the nuclear or stem type and there were fewer concubines and servants than in the households of those Lins who rose to eminence after mid-century.

The first large household had developed in 1848, when Ting-pang's sons kept their patrimony undivided after their father's death.[5] While the third son, Wen-ts'ai, kept a separate household[6]—supported, like the others, from a share in Ting-pang's estate—Wen-ch'a and Wen-ming maintained what the anthropologists call a fraternal joint family, a large joint household shared by the brothers, their wives, concubines, and children. The exceptional closeness of the brothers and their joint ventures as strongmen, supported from their inheritance and in turn replenishing it, must account for this development. Once Wen-ch'a had joined the government, his fame cemented the arrangement.[7] Wen-ming could only gain by sharing in an illustrious brother's household, even beyond 1864, when Wen-ch'a became merely an honored tablet in the household's domestic shrine.

When Wen-ming died in turn, however, a partial separation between the two segments took place.[8] Without as yet dividing their common estate, the two brothers' descendants arranged themselves into two separate households, each with its own cooking facilities, or stove, and its own budget, supported by each segment's share in the common estate. After the death of the two congenial brothers, the earlier joint arrangement had simply become too unwieldy. As it was, the household of Wen-ch'a's descendants alone numbered well over fifty persons.

Another large joint household emerged in the second branch, though somewhat later and for different reasons. When Tien-kuo went to jail in the mid-1860's, only Wen-feng had the experience and maturity to be in charge of a household; Tien-kuo's two other sons, Wen-tien and Wen-ch'in—born in 1852 and 1854, and of concubines, at that—were too young to head their own households. A property division was therefore postponed and Wen-feng presided over the joint household of the three brothers. When Tien-kuo died in 1880 and Wen-feng two years later, the situation repeated itself. Tien-kuo's middle son, the alcoholic Wen-tien, was already dead, and his and Wen-feng's sons were small boys. Only Wen-ch'in had the age and experience to preside over a household and manage its considerable assets. Property thus remained undivided and the household a joint one, shared by all of Tien-kuo's descendants.[9]

The Mansions

Having arranged themselves into several large households, the successful Lin branches built mansions to suit their enlarged needs and rising social status. Tien-kuo's descendants expanded their house until it had grown into a large L-shaped complex of buildings, covering more than half an acre.[10] Probably from its location on a small stream that flows through Wu-feng, the mansion and its denizens became known as the Upper House. Only a few hundred feet downstream, the Ting-pang branch constructed an entirely new and very spacious mansion for the joint use of the two related households, those of the Wen-ch'a and Wen-ming descendants. Built under Ch'ao-tung, probably in the 1880's, it covered more than an acre and a half of ground and ranked as a particularly handsome example of Taiwanese domestic architecture. Again from its location (and reversing the genealogical order), the mansion and its residents became known as the Lower House.

Both mansions were walled, as was typical of gentry houses, and both conformed to age-old principles of Chinese architecture, "the buildings . . . assembled around courtyards, with left balanced against right and the main

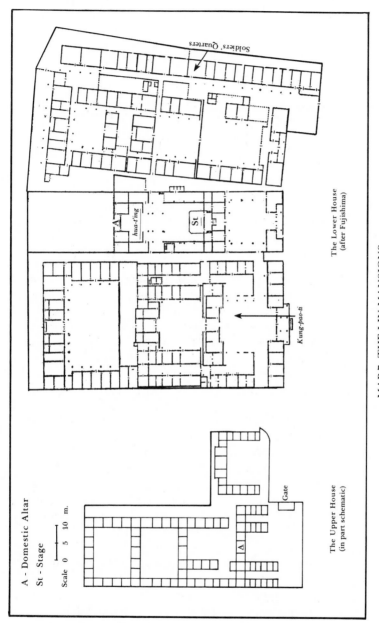

A - Domestic Altar

St - Stage

Scale 0 5 10 m.

The Upper House
(in part schematic)

Gate

A

Kung-pao-ti

hua-t'ing

St

Soldiers' Quarters

The Lower House
(after Fujishima)

MAP 7: THE LIN MANSIONS

hall on center at the rear. Along the main axis courtyards succeeded each other, with a corresponding increase in privacy."[11] Materials and workmanship were of the finest. Only bamboo for lumber and brick for certain walls were of local origin. Everything else was imported from the mainland, as were the artisans who carved, painted, and otherwise adorned the houses.[12] From their richly decorated main gates to their ornate roof brackets, both mansions proclaimed the success of the Lin family. As one of the young Lin poets later recalled,

> Between the buildings, horses could be ridden.
> An embellished hall, three stories high!
> Here, gentlemen could take their ease.[13]

The layout of the mansions reflected the internal patterning of the branches. This was most evident in the Lower House, newly built to accommodate the two related member households. This mansion consisted of three compounds, arranged side by side; the outer compounds served as residences for the two member households, the middle one as their joint ritual and social center.

Built around two courtyards on axis, this middle compound was dominated by a tall open pavillion at its rear, the *hua-t'ing* or Flower Hall.[14] Against the rear wall of the *hua-t'ing* stood the domestic altar with the tablets of Ting-pang and his descendants; here, the two member households gathered for periodic worship. In front of the altar stood the two facing rows of chairs typical of the Chinese parlor. On festive days, servants set a banquet table in the front part of the *hua-t'ing*. When they had been wined and dined, guests enjoyed operatic performances that were conducted on the rear courtyard's most remarkable structure, a free-standing stage.[15] With a wildly upward swerving roof resting on four columns, it resembled a gigantic four-poster bed. When guests included males from outside the family, the Lin women had to watch the performances from the second-floor galleries of the two pavilions that framed the courtyard on either side.

The two residential compounds flanked the shared middle compound. The honored place on the left was assigned to Wen-ch'a's descendants; in memory of their progenitor's most signal honor, they called this compound the *kung-pao-ti* (Residence of the Junior Guardian).[16] Like its counterpart on the right, the *kung-pao-ti* was built around three courtyards on axis. The buildings surrounding the first courtyard were relatively public and contained the offices and sleeping quarters of staff members and servants. Stepping into the second courtyard, one crossed the invisible line between the public and private quarters. As a rule, only male family members and male servants waiting on them proceeded into the family quarters that lay beyond. Brothers were assigned their living quarters in accord with the age hierarchy. In the *kung-pao-ti*, for instance, Ch'ao-tung's two brothers and their immediate families shared the middle courtyard, whereas Ch'ao-tung himself, with his wife, concubines, and children, inhabited the spacious quarters surrounding the most secluded, and most prestigious, third courtyard in the rear.

The Upper House of Tien-kuo's descendants was arranged according to similar principles. The domestic altar[17] stood in the main hall of the front courtyard on the long side of the L, while the residential quarters for the immediate families of Tien-kuo's three sons were arranged around the three courtyards that lay beyond. Brothers were treated more equally, each occupying a separate courtyard, though the age hierarchy was observed here, too; the Wen-feng segment, as befitted the eldest of the three brothers, was given the most honored rear courtyard. The short arm of the L, built around a separate courtyard, was set aside as the study quarters for the young men of the family, the five grandsons of Tien-kuo.

Matriarchs and Other Women

The Lin households appear in full plumage during the 1880's and 1890's, none more so than the *kung-pao-ti*. Very large by Taiwanese standards, the household of Wen-ch'a's descendants numbered well over fifty persons.[18] Ch'ao-tung's headship was of course unquestioned. His brothers, Ch'ao-yung and Ch'ao-tsung, were unassertive, content to enjoy the privileged ease which birth assured them. While Ch'ao-yung occasionally officiated for his absent brother on ritual occasions, the true ruler of the household in Ch'ao-tung's absence was his formidable wife, Mrs. Yang (1848-1935).[19] Descended from the early frontier entre-preneur Yang Chih-shen, she had the easy self-assurance of a member of Chang-hua's leading family. With a classi-cal education (most of the older Lin women were illiterate) and a domineering temper, she quickly made herself mis-tress of the kung-pao-ti.

Among the Lin women, few could in fact challenge her credentials for leadership. Ch'ao-tung's grandmother, old Mrs. Tai, was, to be sure, the senior matriarch; but much of the time she was away in Foochow to litigate her suit and by the early 1880's she had slipped into senility and then death. Of Wen-ch'a's generation, only two concubines sur-vived, women barely older than Mrs. Yang and of socially inferior background. Only one of them, the mother of Ch'ao-tsung, could even feel secure in the household.[20] Among the women of Mrs. Yang's generation, the wives of Ch'ao-tung's brothers were both much younger, though of similarly distinguished background. When they died young, both were replaced by second wives, probably former concubines of markedly lower social background. With unassertive husbands, such women were no threat to Mrs. Yang's primacy.

If the kung-pao-ti was nevertheless known for its quarrel-ing women, we may guess that tensions were most acute in Ch'ao-tung's own immediate family, among the denizens of the third courtyard. Here, Mrs. Yang was not as happily situated; though she enjoyed all the advantages of a main wife and of Ch'ao-tung's exceptional trust (it extended even to matters of public policy, an area into which a

Chinese wife seldom intruded) she lacked the chief element of a married woman's happiness, a son.[21] While two
of his concubines had presented Ch'ao-tung with sons,
Mrs. Yang bore none during the first twelve years of her
marriage. But when she finally had three sons in as many
years, the relations among Ch'ao-tung's womenfolk hardly
improved, for it now became Mrs. Yang's goal to establish
her eldest, Chi-shang, as the heir to his father's fortune
and position, at the expense of his two older half-brothers.
Luckily for her, custom gave more leeway in such matters
than did the letter of the succession law.[22] Death, too, has-
tened her designs, for in 1884 illness carried off Ch'ao-
tung's eldest son, a youth of sixteen. How the second son
was pushed aside we do not know, but when Ch'ao-tung
died early in the twentieth century, Mrs. Yang's eldest obtained control of his entire estate.

Tensions in the *kung-pao-ti* were not confined to Mrs.
Yang and her husband's concubines. Many of the young
women of the next generation also feared the iron-willed
matriarch who could transfix them with a single imperious
glance. A few learned to humor her and gained her favor
by being docile, or entertaining, or by spending hours with
her at the gaming table. Such favorites found Mrs. Yang a
generous though mercurial patron, one who would share
with them the bolts of silk and other finery which Ch'ao-
tung occasionally brought from Taipei.[23]

Among this younger generation, the fate of one young
woman illustrates the morals of the age and the tensions
that could arise between proud members of the same
household. From a collateral branch of the matriarch's own
family, young Miss Yang (1869-1895)[24] had been be-
trothed to Ch'ao-tung's eldest son. When death removed
the young man in 1884, Miss Yang considered her engagement binding, though the marriage had not yet taken
place. Following the highest canons of wifely fidelity, she
chose the life of a model Confucian widow, a virgin bride
and virtual recluse. Residing in the *kung-pao-ti*, she spent

her days in fasts and prayers and emerged from her room only long enough to pay the obligatory morning and evening calls on her parents-in-law. Only the crisis of 1895 broke her routine. As Ch'ao-tung's household prepared for flight, Miss Yang was found one day dangling from the rafters of her room, joined in death by a faithful woman servant.

The roots of this unhappy dénouement are variously described. The Lins's gentry friend, Wu Te-kung, counted Miss Yang as a moral paragon and included her in his roster of the model women of the district, explaining that she had feared for her virginity during the dangerous flight. Family and village gossip, on the other hand, holds that her suicide was not voluntary but that she was pushed into it when Ch'ao-tung and Mrs. Yang sent her a white scarf with which to hang herself (according to some), or (according to others) a choice of two scarves, one red for life, the other white for purity and death.[25]

In their separate compound in the Lower House, Wen-ming's descendants may have lived as a joint household for less than a decade, from just after Wen-ming's death until the end of the seventies. Then they seem to have split into several smaller households, perhaps as each of Wen-ming's sons reached maturity and married.[26] Fragmentation went even further as two of the sons (the third and fifth) left the mansion, and perhaps Wu-feng, altogether, along with their concubine-mother. The adopted sixth son moved out too, at least by 1893, when he became head of his own small household.[27] By 1895, therefore, only the first, second, and fourth sons lived under the same roof in their compound of the mansion, though no longer in a joint household. Lacking a single figure with Ch'ao-tung's stature in public life, this branch's fragmentation is not surprising; there simply was no one of sufficient weight to compel or to tempt the others to stay.

We know less about these brothers than about the strongly etched figures of the *kung-pao-ti*.[28] The first and fourth brother, living together in the middle section of the compound, had typical upper-class households, each with a wife, several concubines, and many children. Both wives died young and both brothers elevated former concubines to the status of main wife, though not without precipitating a bitter quarrel over the succession.

The domestic life of Wen-ming's second son, Ch'ao-hsüan, was more serene. The only son of Wen-ming's main wife—his mother lived with him—he occupied the favored rear courtyard of the Wen-ming compound and often acted as a spokesman for his branch of the family. He married a Miss Ho, a woman from Foochow, and, when she died, he married her sister. In an unusual arrangement, the wives' mother also resided in the Lin mansion. Along with one of Ch'ao-tung's concubines, Mrs. Chang, also known as *Fu-chou-ma* (Foochow mother), these Ho ladies were the only mainlanders in the Lin establishment. That a mainland wife added to her husband's prestige goes without saying, but whether she found happiness across the water is another matter. We know too little about the background of these women to guess at the kind of adjustment they made to the rich, if provincial, Lin household. The second Mrs. Ho appears as a graceful, markedly elegant woman on some photographs of the early twentieth century, open to such novelties as dark eye-glasses.[29]

Maintaining a single stove and an undivided estate, the descendants of Tien-kuo were second only to those of Wen-ch'a in prestige. With over forty persons in 1895,[30] this household too included several generations and the immediate families of several brothers. If Mrs. Yang set the tone of the *kung-pao-ti*, the Upper House reflected the personality of its senior matriarch, the saintly Mrs. Lo (1832-1921).[31] Initially Tien-kuo's concubine and maltreated by some of the women senior to her, she finally rose to the rank of main wife when Tien-kuo was already in jail. In the late nineteenth century, she was not only the mother of the household head, Wen-ch'in, but a remarkable figure in her own right. An illiterate peasant daughter from near Wu-feng, her reputation for warmth, generosity, and compassion contrasted with that of the *kung-pao-ti*'s imperious mistress. She refused to repay the hurts she had suffered earlier. Her treatment of children, too, was gentle, and she invariably placed the needs of the living over the strict demands of the moral code. When a young woman in her household, Wen-tien's tearful widow, threatened to commit suicide upon her husband's death, Mrs. Lo dissuaded her by speaking of the needs of the boy, Chi-t'ang, for a mother's care and affection.[32]

Mrs. Lo's humane attitude helped to resolve another domestic crisis, easily the Upper House's most scandalous episode. It involved the adultery of Wen-ch'in's wife, a woman who has of course been edited out of the genealogy.[33] She had borne Wen-ch'in two sons when she began an affair with a staff member, perhaps during one of her husband's frequent absences on a business trip. Wen-ch'in caught the couple *in flagrante* and proposed to put them both to death, as was his right and the almost universal custom.[34] But Mrs. Lo intervened on her daughter-in-law's behalf. While the hapless accountant *was* buried alive, the errant wife was allowed to return to her own family. Wen-ch'in later remarried, but his second wife never gained a significant position in the household nor, apparently, in her husband's affection. Wen-ch'in took a concubine, but for counsel on family matters he turned more and more to his mother.

Beyond the mansion, too, Mrs. Lo's name was associated with acts of charity to villagers in need. Her treatment of servants was also thoughtful and kindly, in contrast to the Lower House, where, villagers report, desperate maid servants committed suicide and then haunted the mansion as ghosts.

Living in the rear and center part of the mansion were the surviving members of Wen-feng's and Wen-tien's im-

mediate families.[35] The Wen-feng segment—once torn by
fierce quarrels among the concubines over the succession
to the status of main wife—had entered calmer waters.
Since the eldest boy, the sickly Lieh-t'ang, needed all his
mother's attention, her second boy, Teng-t'ang, was turned
over to a concubine to mother, an arrangement that
worked out well for the children and for the peace of this
contented little group.

In the immediate family of Wen-tien, there survived his
widow, his concubine, and his son, Chi-t'ang. Clearly, their
lives were overshadowed by the unhappy memories of
Wen-tien's final years. Mrs. Ch'iu, another widow who
lived as a near-recluse amid fasts and prayers, was constantly warning Chi-t'ang against his father's excesses. "She
often looked at him and wept, saying 'That your father did
not become an official was only because of the damage
done by drink. You should be prudent.' Chi-t'ang was
therefore careful of his health and prudent in his actions."[36] Along with such lessons, Mrs. Ch'iu also passed
along to the boy a sense of his obligation to the villagers.
Giving much to the local poor, she used Chi-t'ang as an intermediary, fostering in him too that sense of social responsibility which would later mark the Upper House off
from the Lower.

Aside from the crises of Wen-tien's dissipation and
Wen-ch'in's wife's adultery, the life of the Upper House
was sedate and on a more modest scale than that of the
kung-pao-ti. The older women were pious, filling their days
with good works and the chanting of sutras. Their foibles
were of the harmless sort, such as gambling, easily forgiven
in gentlewomen of otherwise impeccable conduct. But
above all it was the gentle matriarch, Mrs. Lo, who set the
tone of the Upper House and remained most vivid in the
memories of the young cousins who grew up in her household. They fondly recall her story-telling or the excitement
of her morning toilet, when many young women (there

were nine girl cousins to the five boys) would throng around the beloved grandmother, eager to be of assistance with brushes and face powders.

Daily Life in the Mansions

Custom assigned different activities to men and women, old and young, masters and servants. Clearly, the grown men were most free to do as they pleased. Ch'ao-tung's brothers and several of Wen-ming's sons stayed aloof from public life and pursued their private hobbies. Outdoor activities were popular among some of them, and they organized frequent hunting parties into the mountains, returning with their trophies and an appetite for further pleasures. As a somewhat censorious poet-friend of the younger Lins recalled,

> At night, the hunting grounds were lit by torches;
> At dawn, in the shooting boxes, bows drawn
> Spears, guns, knives, arrows are provided
> All around, balls of fire burst.
> In this way, they planned their pleasure.
> Then, relaxing the rules of drinking,
> They embraced the singing girls in the brothel,
> Drunken and lustful beyond all restraint.[37]

The younger men mixed the perennial male pleasures with some newly acquired gentry pastimes. Some collected books and art objects; others enjoyed taking walks and sharing scholarly hobbies with other young gentry scions ("at nightfall, lining up the lamps for a bright light, boiling well water for tea, we talk of past and present").[38] While they circulated in the wider gentry society of mid-Taiwan, they also had many diversions at home, including opportunities for sexual experimentation with attractive maid servants. Several of the young Lins formalized such liaisons and took concubines even before they acquired their main wives.

Fig. 16 A nursery in a wealthy household (*Tien-shih-chai hua-pao*, East Asian Library, Columbia University).

By comparison, the children and all the women were largely confined to the mansions themselves, the boys pursuing their education under a succession of tutors, the girls and the grown women held in the home by convention and domestic responsibilities.[39] While not obliged to do housework themselves, the women had to oversee large domestic staffs, educate daughters and very young sons, and tend to a few light chores, such as sewing and embroidering. Clearly, though, they enjoyed much leisure as well and they filled it according to personal taste, with religious devotions, with elaborate preparation of their toilette, with gambling, and with much visiting back and forth among the mansions, where gossip was traded over tea and waterpipes. Occasional outings took the women to their natal homes or to a local temple. But only as the men returned from trips to Taipei or Hongkong and brought back novelties—Western lamps and musical instruments, photographs—did the women receive an inkling of the material changes in the larger world outside.

Still, all such gadgets were marginal to the core of family life, which remained solidly Chinese. Near its center were the great feast days which brought all members of a huge household together: the numerous weddings (in all, a dozen young men and about twenty young women reached marriageable age during the last quarter of the century)[40] and the birthdays of the senior matriarchs. Mrs. Yang's birthday parties featured opera performances in the courtyard of the *hua-t'ing* and Mrs. Lo's were celebrated with banquets in the handsome Lin garden. It was in the garden, too—a five-minute walk from the mansions, elaborately arranged with hills and an artificial pond, pavilions and shaded walks—that the Lins entertained their many gentry friends, trading poetry with them in the pleasant afterglow of wine and food. That the food was, on the whole, more abundant than elegant may be deduced from a German visitor's account who enjoyed dinner in the *hua-t'ing* in 1898:

"We sat down at table. Lin-sho-do [Lin Shao-t'ang, i.e. Ch'ao-hsüan] had asked that the table be set in the European manner, and one of his two cooks, a man somewhat familiar with Western cuisine, had made a great effort. Several dozen bottles . . . were offered me so that I might make a choice. I opted for Japanese beer, brewed in the German manner, and cognac. We were served. . . . In between the individual courses, we helped ourselves from a large bowl in the center of the table which was filled with sugar cane and banana pieces; the peels were simply thrown under the table. . . . [From time to time] the servants swept up and removed these vegetable remains. . . . We had sweet and sour dishes and several soups, at the beginning, in the middle, and at the end of the banquet which consisted of no fewer than twenty or thirty courses. . . . The best course of the meal was the tangerines, roughly the size of oranges, which had a wonderful aroma and melted on the tongue like butter."[41]

To serve such banquets and perform other household chores, each mansion had a large staff of domestic servants, possibly more numerous than the family members themselves.[42] A key figure among the servants was the steward or manager (*kuan-shih*), their overseer, who also managed the day-to-day finances of the large household. It was he, for example, who supervised purchasing. While the common people relied on itinerant peddlers to bring merchandise to Wu-feng,[43] the Lin household's vast needs exceeded what the peddlers could carry. Lin servants therefore did much of the buying and hauling, trudging over the footpaths and through the fords of the Upper Valley, loads suspended from shoulder poles. They bought produce and other perishables on daily shopping trips to Ta-li-chi, staples and many non-food items on frequent excursions to Chang-hua city.

Household chores within the mansion were assigned to servants who were themselves ranked in hierarchic order. The coarse (*ts'u*) servants did the heavy work and the more unpleasant or routine chores for which no great skill was required. Here belonged such drudges as the water-carriers and the sedan-chair carriers. Among the women, coarse servants did the sweeping and washing. The refined (*hsi*) servants had close contact with their masters and mistresses. Here belonged the personal maids and men servants assigned to individual family members. They must have been numerous, to judge from the fact that one or two such maids were routinely assigned to each Lin daughter when she left her home to be married. Such personal servants ran errands, made beds, and waited on their masters or mistresses or their guests. Some maids may have functioned almost as companions to their ladies while yet others found favor with one or another of the young gentlemen and could rise to concubine status.

Cooking took place in a special kitchen area (perhaps somewhere behind the *hua-t'ing*) and had its own complex hierarchies. There was "coarse" food, served to the guards, to the remaining family braves, and to "coarse" servants. "Refined" food was for family members and for the "refined" servants. It was eaten at separate tables, servant groups of similar status eating together, while among the Lins, too, the immediate family of Ch'ao-tung, for example, ate separately from the families of his brothers.

The servants worked under a variety of legal arrangements. Male servants had contracts that stipulated pay and customary bonuses. The bulk of the maid servants were indentured, entering the Lin mansion around the age of eight and serving, without pay, for about ten years. At the end of that period, the family provided a dowry and married the girl off. While most such servants eventually left the family, some stayed on and became permanent members of the household, with a status halfway between that of servant and family member.[44] Here belonged several servant couples and some of the maid servants who had borne Lin children without being elevated to concubine status. In this category, too, were some of the indentured women servants who had never married but instead spent their declining years with the family, employed in various light occupations.[45] One encountered them particularly in Mrs. Lo's household. Here, too, belonged a few indigent female relatives from distant branches of the family who were taken in by their wealthy kinsmen and allowed to earn their keep by performing light domestic or supervisory chores.

In the late nineteenth century, the Lins's domestic life was of a piece with their new role in the public domain. In the one as in the other, they patterned themselves on the standards common to the higher gentry. Rendering public service in the community, men like Ch'ao-tung and Wen-ch'in presided at home over the large joint households extolled by Confucian moralists. While their marriages cemented alliances with other gentry families, their numerous concubines testified to the upper-class male's wealth and sexual prowess. Participating in the hierarchical structures of public life—the official ranking system, the rituals of patronage—these men observed rank order and symmetry in their domestic lives as well, as shown in the orderly layout of the mansions or the observed gradations among brothers, servants, and even foodstuffs.

Yet we can make too much of this patterning, this conformity to social expectations. In the private sphere no less than the public, individual taste and temperament was as important as the social code. Just as Ch'ao-tung and Wen-ch'in, the major figures of the age, exerted themselves along vastly different lines in their public careers, the households over which they presided differed markedly in atmosphere. Despite surface similarities in structure, Mrs. Yang and Mrs. Lo were able to impress their personal stamp on these establishments, with significant consequences for family members as well as for servants. Just as some brothers wrote poetry while others hunted, some concubines quarreled while others lived in harmony. Neither at home nor in the public domain had individual differences succumbed to prescribed social roles.

CHAPTER 14

WEALTH AND POWER

The Economic Foundations of a Gentry Family

Liu Ming-ch'uan appreciated Lin Ch'ao-tung's steady efforts on behalf of the public good and his disregard of private gain. So he spoke to him one day, saying: "Yin-t'ang, you are concerned for your country but you ignore your family. What will you bequeath to your sons and grandsons?"[1]

If Liu Ming-ch'uan was truly concerned about the Lin family's worldly goods—and his remarks prefaced the award of a large land grant to Ch'ao-tung—his worries were not only unfounded but more than a little suspect in their apparent naïveté. The Lins were quite wealthy, even without his largesse, and the governor cannot really have misconstrued the relation between public service and private wealth in a country where the one almost always led to the other. For of course Liu's own career illustrated this link[2] which was also acknowledged in a revealing remark by Li Hung-chang, Liu's old neighbor and patron, near the end of his long and rewarding life in office. "When Li met General Grant's son in New York in 1896, one of the first questions he asked him was whether or not he was rich. When Grant answered to the contrary, Li replied, 'Do you mean to tell me that your father was a General during a rebellion that lasted five years, and brought it to a successful conclusion, and that he was then afterwards twice elected Presi-

dent of the United States, and that yet you his son are
poor! Well, I do *not* understand how that could possibly
be!' "[3]

The Lins, too, would have been puzzled, for in their rise
to prominence access to public power had paved the way to
private wealth. It is these material fruits of their power, the
immense wealth that came from their strongmen and later
their official careers, that we must now describe.

Land and Water

In an economy based on wet rice agriculture, ownership of
land and water was the most important form of property.
By the year 1890, the three branches of the family descending from the three sons of Chia-yin owned close to 2,600
chia of cropland, most of it paddy. This enormous acreage
was unevenly divided among the branches, with the Lower
House holding the lion's share, around 1,700 *chia*[4] the
Upper House around 800 *chia*,[5] and the third branch
under 100 *chia*.[6] To this we must add a small trust of
perhaps a few dozen *chia* of ritual land jointly owned by the
three branches.[7] To put these figures in perspective, we recall that the average family farm in Taiwan measured
around 1.2 *chia*.[8]

With the exception of some 150 *chia* located in and
around the seaport of Wu-ch'i, the bulk of the land lay in
the middle section of the Upper Valley, in the old Lin turf.
Within this area, the highest concentrations of Lin-owned
land were reached in Wan-tou-liu (98 percent), Liu-Shu-
nan (92 percent), Wu-ts'o (84 percent), and Wu-feng itself
(77 percent). In an arc of villages to the west, northwest,
and north, concentrations ranged from 56 percent in
Nei-hsin to 14 percent in Ta-li-chi. If we take the total area
of cropland in the villages where the family owned such
land, the Lins's share amounted to roughly one-half.[9]

Almost all these holdings were in *hsiao-tsu* tenure. The
Lins thus occupied the most favorable position in Taiwan's

three-tier land system. *Hsiao-tsu* status now amounted to full ownership (formalized by Liu Ming-ch'uan), yet in Chang-hua the *hsiao-tsu* owners were able to evade the new tax payments which Liu imposed on them farther north.[10] While the old *ta-tsu* rights to income were still carefully recorded in the Lins's *hsiao-tsu* land deeds, it is unlikely that the family paid anything near the full amount owed to the assorted tribes and temples or to the descendants of earlier frontier entrepreneurs who held these *ta-tsu* titles.[11] The Lins therefore had the best of both worlds—great wealth without corresponding burdens.

Given these immense holdings, there may have been over four thousand tenant families renting some portion of their family farm from the mighty Lins.[12] What was the family's attitude toward their tenants and what were the Lins's practices as landlords? It may be significant that the local sources which refer to the family's depredations against their *hsiao-tsu* rivals never mention heavy burdens imposed on tenants.[13] The old bond of the strongman family and its followers may have persisted into the last third of the century to mitigate the lot of the Lin tenants at a time when tenancy elsewhere in Taiwan was becoming more onerous. But even if the Lins were among the better landlords, they still placed heavy burdens on their tenants, collecting sizeable rent deposits and a rental of perhaps half the crop.[14]

Unified management of the family's landholdings was achieved through the large family estates in which the bulk of the Lin lands were vested. Such an arrangement obviated the need for the "landlord bursaries" which provided centralized management elsewhere in China.[15] The day-to-day management of the estates involved large numbers of accountants and much detailed record-keeping. Over eight thousand separate rent payments (two a year per tenant) may have had to be logged, not to mention other dealings with tenants, such as requests for rent rebate, summonses to tardy tenants, and so forth. Besides keeping the books on rentals due and paid, staff members went on errands outside to inspect crop damage, re-survey fields after a flood, or oversee foremen and hired work crews who repaired roads and embankments.

If the paper work dealing with rent collection was massive, purchases and sales of land and payment of taxes and *ta-tsu* rents involved other kinds of record-keeping. *Hsiao-tsu* ownership itself could be documented in a number of ways, ranging from official attestations to purely private sales contracts.[16] For the most part, the Lins relied on written contracts to substantiate their land titles. Only at the time of Liu Ming-ch'uan's land survey did they finally bother to obtain official stamps of approval (*ch'i-wei*) on their private contracts or the new kind of title deed (*chang-tan*). How they substantiated title to the seized lands remains unclear but for these, too, the family obtained the title deeds issued under Liu.[17]

The importance of written contracts for Taiwanese landowners is vividly illustrated by the extreme care with which all pertinent documents were transmitted, preserved, and identified. When a parcel of land changed hands, it was customary to supply the buyer with all the past deeds of sale for that parcel, giving him a complete record of that land's occupance by Chinese. The documents pertaining to the parcel were then neatly folded and wrapped in a piece of white cloth, the bundle tied with a string and labelled with reference to the land's location. It is said that small landowners often carried such records on their persons for safekeeping. The Lins, like other big landlord families, devised ingenious filing systems and stored the entire collection in their well-guarded mansions.[18] Thus even a former strongman family, for whom possession had been the better part of the law, bowed to the prevailing tradition of written customary law.

As important as the title to the land, and no doubt reenforcing it, was the Lins's control over water. By the end of the century, the pattern of their water rights resembled the

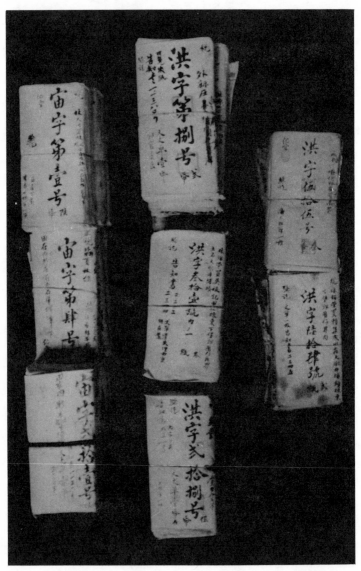

Fig. 17 Bundles of land deeds, wrapped in cloth and identified by location (Lin Land Records).

distribution of their landed property, with a high concentration in the southeast of their old "turf" shading off to partial but still significant control farther north. After seizing the Wu-feng *chün* from the Hungs in the 1860's, the Lins retained sole ownership into the twentieth century. The *chün* gave them control over the irrigation water for the roughly 1,000 *chia* of cropland in Wu-feng, Liu-shunan, and Wan-tou-liu, the three villages attached to the *chün*. Farther north, members of the Lower House owned rights in the T'ou-pien-k'eng *chün* (the remainder belonging to their T'ai-p'ing cousins) and of the Ju-pao *chün*, while members of the Upper House owned part of the Hu-lu-tun *chün*.[19]

In contrast to the centralized management of the land, *chün* management was decentralized. At least in the case of the Wu-feng *chün*, the Lins picked a few dozen men from among their tenants to act as headmen over particular sections of the *chün*. These men had to allocate the water and deliver the water rents to the family. An annual ceremony, followed by the obligatory banquet, honored the close relations between the *chün* masters and these important agents. The family alone remained responsible for periodic repairs and structural alterations in the facility.

Even though the annual income from a *chün* was small[20] compared with the *hsiao-tsu* rents, control over such a facility increased the income from and hence the value of the lands it watered. Beyond that, ownership of the Wu-feng *chün* not only reenforced the Lins's power over their tenants, it also gave them leverage over minor landlords and independent owner-farmers—the owners of that portion of the acreage in Wan-tou-liu, Liu-shu-nan, and Wu-feng which the Lins did not hold.

Considering the peasants' dependence on irrigation and the Taiwanese tradition of feuding over water rights, the combined land and water holdings of the family established their overwhelming predominance in the Upper Valley. While their tenants were not serfs in any technical sense, the economic preponderance of the Lins, added to the family's past history of armed private power, must have intensified the sense of personal dependence among the tenants. Given the crowding on the land and the tightening of landlord exactions elsewhere, few Lin tenants were in any real sense free to sever their ties with the Lin-owned land and water, except where urban employment held out better prospects. But the Lins's influence reached into the region's major trading centers and its export markets as well.

Business and Industry

Like many gentry families, the Lins were involved in several local and regional businesses. One such enterprise grew directly from their landlordism. Not content to sell their rent rice locally in Taiwan—and they could not possibly have consumed it—the Lins sent it via specially hired porters and rafts downriver to the coastal ports of Lu-kang and Wu-ch'i, and from there to the rice-deficient areas of mainland Fukien.[21]

The Lins's role in the rice export business involved them in a significant though often ignored branch of Taiwanese trade. Carried in junks from the mid-island ports (Lu-kang and Wu-ch'i between them handled almost 90 percent of Taiwan's rice export),[22] these shipments were overlooked in the commercial reports and trade statistics compiled by Westerners in the treaty ports. Yet the junk trade was the equal in volume of the treaty-port trade in modern ships.[23]

Furnishing perhaps as much as a tenth of the total mid-Taiwan rice export,[24] the Lins used a portion of the proceeds from the rice sales to purchase mainland goods for import to Taiwan. These commodities, largely foodstuffs and textiles, were then sold through family-owned retail shops in Ta-li-chi[25] and perhaps other outlets. Some of the purchased cloth underwent further treatment before re-sale (whether in a family-owned dyeing factory or through a putting-out system is unclear), the Lins taking advantage of the locally available indigo to give the cloth the strong colors so much admired by customers.[26]

All in all, the family's export-import business was an operation of some magnitude. Ta-li-chi was then still a major market town in the Upper Valley, and the Lin-owned shops, covering more than eight building lots, did business near the center of town.[27] The shops were run as a partnership between the two major Wu-feng Lin branches and a local family of Lin clansmen, who also contributed some capital and managed the day-to-day operations. Net profits were divided in proportion to the partners' investments, the reckoning being held on the fifth day of the new year in the common Chang-hua fashion.

Other business activities remain more shadowy. Some of the money realized in the export-import business may have been put to good use in money-lending, but we have no concrete information to that effect. Then, too, some of the profits from the rice sales on the mainland (and from the camphor sales discussed below) were probably never repatriated to Taiwan, but were used to buy urban real estate in coastal cities like Amoy, Foochow, and Shanghai.[28] In mid-Taiwan itself, urban real estate holdings were small—the Lower House at least owning only one town house in Chang-hua, one in Wu-ch'i and two or three others in small markets in the Upper Valley.[29] Not until the Japanese period did members of the family acquire substantial holdings in Chang-hua and Taichung real estate.

Somewhat better documented—though presented here only in outline—is the family's role in one of the major extractive industries of the late nineteenth century, the camphor industry. Initially used only for medicinal purposes, the demand for camphor grew in the last third of the century, when it became an essential ingredient in making celluloid and smokeless powder. By the 1880's, Taiwan provided well over half the world supply, and only Japan had camphor trees of similar quality.[30]

The Lins became involved in camphor making and marketing at a time when Taiwan's camphor exports underwent rapid expansion, climbing as they did from one to seven million pounds between 1890 and 1895. It was Liu Ming-ch'uan's land-opening grant (k'en-ch'i), bestowed on Ch'ao-tung in 1888, which gave the family an entry into this lucrative business.[31] Liu's grant was of the kind which the government had traditionally bestowed on the early frontier entrepreneurs. It covered several thousand chia in the hills and mountains east of the settled plain and stretched from the Ta-chia River in the north to the Cho-shui in the south, running, in short, the entire length of the old Chang-hua district. With large stands of virgin camphor, the area held out its chief promise not to the pioneer farmer but to the would-be camphor-maker.

The obstacles in the way were also the very ones which Ch'ao-tung, with his wealth and official connections, could best overcome. The area of the grant was largely aborigine territory over which only the recent campaigns and Ch'ao-tung's road-building had established a precarious control. Although Ch'ao-tung's posts in the Military Secretariat and the Pacification and Reclamation Bureau must have enabled him to direct government resources to the protection of his camphor workers, government troops were inadequate to safeguard the workers from aborigine attack. Ch'ao-tung therefore obtained official permission to set up a private force of two guard battalions.[32]

In addition to this outlay for the safety of the workers, capital was needed to set up the camphor stills and to hire and provision the workers. Ch'ao-tung therefore turned to his uncle Wen-ch'in and with him formed the so-called Lin Ho (Lin Cooperative), a company for the exploitation of the land-grant.[33] The arrangements between the two men are not known in detail, but it was probably an equal partnership, Ch'ao-tung providing the grant and the military expertise and government connection, Wen-ch'in supplying the bulk of the capital and marketing the camphor in Hongkong.

Since no records have survived, the full scope of the family's camphor enterprise can only be guessed at. The Lins were clearly preponderant in the mid-Taiwan camphor business and with five hundred or more guardsmen on duty, their camphor stills too may have numbered in the hundreds, allowing the family to produce perhaps as much as a tenth of the island's total output.[34] That the Lins's camphor operations were sizeable is borne out by a knowledgeable Western observer who reported that "the largest trade has been done by Chinese dealers in conjunction with capitalists, such as Lim Tsai Tang [i.e., Lin Ch'ao-tung]. These people have, for years, had men boiling camphor all along the western slopes of the hills, the produce being exported to Hongkong from the small junkports such as Lo-kang (Rokko) and Gochei [Wu-ch'i]."[35] On the ground, too, the Lin enterprise impressed a visitor who came upon it in the vicinity of Pu-li in 1898—the same gentleman who had dined in the *hua-t'ing* a few days earlier:

"A few minutes past the [police] station, the terrain rose steeply along the side of Yamata-yama. . . . Along [the path] which followed the bottom of a meandering valley, watch-towers had been placed every few hundred feet. The bamboo drums were sounding without pause, for we had no sooner been spotted by a guard than he gave the alarm. These guards—there are in this area some four hundred—are paid a total of 2,000 Yen annually from the Japanese government, but the larger part of their upkeep is provided by the rich Chinese Lin-sho-do [Lin Shao-t'ang, i.e., Ch'ao-hsüan] who owns camphor forests of immense extent in this area."[36]

The Lins's commitment to their camphor enterprise had been demonstrated a year or two earlier. When the Japanese first tackled the aborigine problem, they discovered that the only functioning border guards (*yai-yung*) operating in aborigine territory were the two Lin battalions.[37] Strung out in a line from east of Taichung to near Pu-li, these men not only protected the family's camphor operations, but aided the government with aborigine control in general, another demonstration of how closely family interests had become intertwined with government concerns[38] and how vigorously the family exercised quasi-official responsibilities during the interval between the end of Ch'ing power and the arrival of the Japanese on the aborigine border.

Estates, Trusts, and Personal Fortunes

The assets of what has loosely been called the Lin family were in fact either held jointly (in estates or trusts) or by individual family members. The term "estate" refers to the jointly held property of the male members of the family, which, in the normal course of events, will one day be divided among them by partition. The "trust" is also jointly held but is, at least in theory, indivisible, consisting of that portion of the family holdings which has been set aside to underwrite ritual, or sometimes educational, expenses.[39] Among the Lins, ownership of farmland was generally vested in estates and trusts. Water rights and houses were held either by estates or individuals. Thus, the Upper and Lower House estates jointly owned the Wu-feng *chün* while the Lins's shares in the other *chün* seem to have belonged to specific individuals.[40] Business and manufacturing too were conducted either by the estates or by individuals on their own accounts. It was the Lower House estate which owned at least some of the shops in Ta-li-chi. The *Lin Ho*, on the other hand, was a partnership of Ch'ao-tung, acting by himself, and Wen-ch'in, who may have acted in his own name or in that of the Upper House estate.

Normally, all the male descendants of an ancestor in whose name a trust was established shared in that trust equally, although certain kinds of adopted sons (*ming-ling-tzu*) were sometimes excluded.[41] Among the Lins, these ritual trusts were relatively small and were managed in rotation or on a more permanent basis by a less affluent though senior member who might then draw some personal income from the trust after providing for ritual expenses.

The estate, on the other hand, worked differently. It was not created by a specific act, but rather came into being when the sons of a father refrained from dividing his assets after his death and instead owned them jointly and used them to defray all their normal domestic, business, or political expenses. While all male descendants shared in an estate, they did not do so equally, some account being taken of their legal status or of their exertions on behalf of the family—whether they were, or were descended from, adopted sons, or eldest sons, or from members who had notably enlarged the holdings, and so forth. Among the Lins, the secular estates were infinitely larger than the ritual trusts. Estate management thus carried a grave responsibility for the welfare of an entire branch of the family and was therefore entrusted only to the most competent and well-connected member, whose managerial role in turn gave him vast power.

A brief overview of these joint holdings, starting with the secular estates, will clarify the situation:

(1) The Lower House's *Lin Pen-t'ang* was by far the largest estate, holding the lion's share of the Lower House's vast land holdings, some 1,600 *chia*.[42] It originated with Ting-pang's death in 1848, when his sons decided to keep their father's assets undivided; it was later greatly enlarged by Wen-ch'a and Wen-ming and continued to be jointly owned by Ting-pang's descendants until its dissolution in 1894. Management rested first with Wen-ch'a, then with Wen-ming, and finally with Ch'ao-tung. With an annual imcome of just over 40,000 piculs of rice, this estate provided for the upkeep of the Lower House's constituent households and for the political needs of its leading men.

(2) The Upper House's *Chin-jung-t'ang*. The name first appeared on Tien-kuo's land purchase records in the early 1860's; its use then may simply reflect the common south Chinese penchant for registering personal property in the

name of a *t'ang* (hall).[43] But when Tien-kuo died and his sons held the property undivided, the *Chin-jung-t'ang* became a true family estate. It was steadily expanded through land purchases under its two managers, Wen-feng and Wen-ch'in, until it reached some 800 *chia* in the early 1890's. It was dissolved in 1900 upon the death of Tien-kuo's youngest son, Wen-ch'in.

(3) The *Lin-yü pen-t'ang* came into existence in 1894, upon the division of the *Lin Pen-t'ang* when the descendants of Wen-ch'a decided to hold their share of the *Lin Pen-t'ang* together in a continuing, though smaller, joint estate rather than dividing it among Wen-ch'a's three sons. This estate was managed by Ch'ao-tung and supported the large joint household of the *kung-pao-ti*.[44]

The ritual trusts were more numerous but consisted of only a few dozen *chia* each, yielding at best 1,000 piculs of rice annually. In contrast to the secular estates, the trusts were not dissolved until later in the twentieth century and some indeed exist to this day. In roughly chronological order of their founding, they were:

(1) The *Chia-yin-kung*.[45] Established at the time Chia-yin's property was divided, it included farmland and the old homestead in Chia-yin-ts'un which was later converted into a family shrine. Undiminished until the early twentieth century, it was managed by the quintessential "poor relations," the descendants of Chia-yin's third son.

(2) The *Heng-tsu-kung*, in honor of Chia-yin's third son and presumably established soon after his death in 1842.[46]

(3) The *Yün-pu-t'ang*,[47] established by Wen-ch'a's descendants in his memory. In existence before 1894.

(4) The *Ching-t'ing-t'ang*, established by Wen-ming's descendants in his memory. In existence before 1894.

(5) The (new) *Lin Pen-t'ang*, also called the *Ta-kung*,[48] a ritual trust in memory of Ting-pang that was carved out of the original *Lin Pen-t'ang* at the time of its dissolution in 1894. It was managed in rotation by the branches descending from Ting-pang.

If the estates and trusts provided unified management and a defense against a premature dispersal of landed property, they did not prevent well-connected and powerful individuals from accumulating their personal assets outside the structure of joint holdings. Ch'ao-tung certainly did so and perhaps Wen-ch'in as well, though we know next to nothing about the latter's financial arrangements. Office perquisites and camphor profits were the likely sources of Ch'ao-tung's personal wealth. During the seven years of his friendship with the incumbent governor, and with large amounts of military pay, building funds, and perhaps camphor taxes passing through his hands, his extra income ("squeeze") from office may have been in the neighborhood of 20,000 to 30,000 *Taels* a year.[49] Camphor profits may have been 15,000 *Taels* yearly in the early 1890's.[50] All told, we have reason to believe that Ch'ao-tung's personal fortune stood in the vicinity of 200,000 *Taels* by 1894.[51]

Not only the men but the women also were able to accumulate sums of money under their personal control, although "fortune" would be too grand a word for the few hundreds of *Taels* which these women could call their own and which were presumably derived from their dowries, from "pin money" saved, from investments in pawnshops, and perhaps from the gaming table.[52]

Joint holdings and individual holdings, while discrete, were also interconnected. At times, estates or trusts collaborated with wealthy individuals in income-producing ventures; at other times, estates and trusts borrowed from each other or from individuals. Almost always, surpluses from ritual trusts flowed into individual pockets. To understand these complex relations among the property-holding units of the family, we must now consider their incomes in relation to their expenditures, for it was these, particularly the expenditures of the two large secular estates, which governed the flow of the monies and ultimately the life-span of the estates themselves.

Income, Expenditure, Indebtedness

In a country where the annual per capita income stood between seven and eight *Taels*,[53] the Lin family was obviously rich; it is equally plain that their financial health depended less on their absolute wealth than on their ability to live within their means. In the absence of account books, we must extrapolate from a few family records, from survey data, and from a general knowledge of prices a rough outline of the family's cost of living. Naturally, we shall treat the two major branches of the family separately and we shall also treat the early 1880's, when the lawsuits ended and the Lins began their political comeback, as a kind of watershed.

For the period 1871-1882, then, the annual income of the *Lin Pen-t'ang* is likely to have been around 60,000 *Taels*.[54] Its annual expenditures are much harder to gauge, but a number of items clearly must be included. Ordinary household expenses probably ran high because Ch'ao-tung's presence in Peking during some of these years, and Mrs. Tai's in Foochow, required the maintenance of separate residences, each with appropriate staff and quarters. Since the Lower House had a reputation for self-indulgence, we may assume that even the expenditures for food and clothing cannot have been small. Then there were at least minimal tax and *ta-tsu* obligations and the cost of Ch'ao-tung's small bodyguard and professional staff (private secretary, private tutor). Since these were also the years when the Lins sought the approval of their fellow gentry, sizeable expenditures (perhaps several thousand *Taels* a year) were no doubt incurred for the purchase of degrees and titles, for contributions to philanthropy, and subscriptions to public works, and for the benefactions to protégés and the other customary gifts that marked the way of life of the gentry. Nor could the Lins afford to skimp on the ceremonial expenditures common in the circles to which they now aspired, the costly weddings

(Ch'ao-tung's two brothers and Wen-ming's two eldest sons were married during this period) and elaborate funerals. A single funeral such as that of Wen-ch'a's wife—a lady of no mean rank, after all—could cost a few thousand *Taels*. All told, the relatively routine domestic expenses and the further expenditures dictated by the gentry way of life may have consumed as much as two thirds of the annual *Lin Pen-t'ang* income, or around 40,000 *Taels*.[55]

The remaining 20,000 *Taels* per year—and much more—went for the lawsuit, for Ch'ao-tung makes clear that the *Lin Pen-t'ang* had gone into substantial debt to finance the litigation.[56] Working backwards from the estate's debt in 1894, we arrive at a tentative figure of perhaps 100,000 *Taels* of indebtedness in 1882, of which some 30,000 may have gone for the interest on the remainder. This gives us a figure of upwards of a quarter-million *Taels* for the lawsuit (12 times 20,000 plus 100,000 *Taels*). If our estimates for the average current expenses during these years have been too high, that would mean that the total cost of the litigation was even higher, perhaps nearer half a million *Taels*. While such a figure appears astronomical at first sight, it is not out of line with other data on litigants' expenses.[57]

If the 1870's and early 1880's were overshadowed by the cost of the new respectability and the burdens of the lawsuit, the period from 1883-1894 saw a small increase in the *Lin Pen-t'ang*'s annual money income to around 70,000 *Taels*. This was largely due to the higher price of rice.[58] With this increase, and the end of the lawsuit, Ch'ao-tung might have paid off the debt had it not been for an even more expansive style of life and the new expenditures that arose in connection with the family's political comeback. In the preamble to the 1894 *Lin Pen-t'ang* estate division document (*chiu-shu*), Ch'ao-tung singles out the occasions for these large new expenditures: the raising of braves during the Franco-Chinese war (an item of conceivably 20,000 *Taels*);[59] the building of a family temple (its location, perhaps on the mainland, is unknown; anywhere from 5-10,000 *Taels* is plausible);[60] the splendid Lower House mansion (15,000 *Taels*?);[61] and expenses for emergency relief, philanthropy, and land-opening. Nor should we underestimate the continued heavy ceremonial expenses. There were in this twelve-year span three weddings of Lin sons and possibly ten of Lin daughters—all unions with other gentry families. There were, in addition, at least four important funerals, those of Mrs. Tai, of Wen-ming's main wife, and the wives of Ch'ao-tung's two brothers. Nor is it

Fig. 18 Private performance of an opera (*Tien-shih-chai hua-pao*, East Asian Library, Columbia University).

likely that the Lower House could reduce its expenditures for the "social investments" and the other amenities of gentry life—the lavish hospitality (a theatrical troupe, the large hunting parties, hobbies, some gambling), the gifts to protégés and subscriptions to charity that such a family owed to its station in society.

Given these large new expenditures and the relatively stagnant income of the *Lin Pen-t'ang*, it proved impossible to retire the old debt. On the contrary, growing at an average interest rate of 40 percent, the interest-bearing portion of the debt had climbed to the grand total of some 110,000 *Taels* by early 1894, while the interest-free debt had passed 40,000. Interest payments now consumed three-fourths of the estate's income and the time was not far off when interest alone would exceed the entire annual income.[62]

What was the Lower House to do? Attempts to refinance the debt seem to have failed,[63] and the selling of land, a possible option, was apparently ruled out. As in other crises, it was Ch'ao-tung who came to the rescue—but at a price. While he undertook to pay off the estate's debts out of his personal assets, he insisted that the *Lin Pen-t'ang* itself be dissolved.[64] Clearly this was not from a disenchantment with the idea of a family estate as such, for under Ch'ao-tung's direction the Wen-ch'a descendants placed their share from the *Lin Pen-t'ang* into a new estate. More likely, it was that Ch'ao-tung wished to shed the responsibility for the more distant branches of the Lower House, in particular Wen-ming's descendants.

In the division of the *Lin Pen-t'ang*'s assets, the legal statuses of the members and the merits of their forebears were considered.[65] Since Wen-ch'a and Wen-ming had done most to enlarge the estate, their descendants received the major shares, lands producing 15,000 piculs of rice annually each; Ch'ao-tung received in addition the customary (and sizeable) share due the eldest grandson (*tsung-tzu*), lands worth 8,000 piculs annually. The descendants of Ting-pang's third son, an adopted son who had done nothing on behalf of the estate, received lands worth under 2,000 piculs annually, while land producing 1,000 piculs was set aside for the new ritual trust in memory of Ting-pang.

Before we leave the financial affairs of the Lower House, a brief look at the interest rates paid and the sources of credit is in order. The *chiu-shu* provides us with the names of the creditors, the amounts lent, and, where applicable, the interest due. Invariably, the loans were recorded in dollars (*Yüan*) while interest was calculated in piculs of rice. It was the rising price of rice in the last years of the Ch'ing which accounts in part for the exceptionally high rate of interest. Ironically, the highest rates were paid on loans made by family members, especially the women, while the lowest came from unnamed sources in Taipei.

Among the interest-bearing loans, the largest single amount, some 12,000 *Taels*, came from Wu Luan-ch'i, the family friend, in-law, and *nouveau riche* gentry neighbor from Hsin-chuang-tzu. The Upper House's *Chin-jung-t'ang* contributed some 5,000 *Taels* and the small Lower House ritual trusts together just over 6,000 *Taels*. The ladies of the house furnished 2,300 *Taels*, with half the total coming from old Mrs. Ho, Ch'ao-hsüan's mother-in-law from Foochow. Other unidentifiable private persons lent some 6,000 *Taels* and assorted banks and stores together 29,000 *Taels*. Unnamed Taipei sources provided 34,000 *Taels* and a temple some 11,000 *Taels*.

Among the lenders of interest-free loans, the largest was the Upper House's *Chin-jung-t'ang*, with some 21,000 *Taels*. Some 14,000 *Taels* came from Ch'ao-tung, part from his personal assets, part from his "Tung Army" account. Various private persons and stores and the ritual trusts of the Lower House provided the other 6,000 *Taels*.

As for the income of the Upper House, it was always on a far more modest scale. In the 1870's the *Chin-jung-t'ang* may have yielded around 15,000 *Taels* annually,[66] but Wen-feng's frugal ways kept the expenditures well below that. The surplus went for the Upper House lawsuit, for the loans to the *Lin Pen-t'ang*, and a small but steady program of land purchases. With an expanding land base, the estate enjoyed rising incomes that may have reached 35,000 *Taels* a year in the early 1890's. To this we must add Wen-ch'in's share of the camphor profits, perhaps 15,000 *Taels* annually. With many fewer people to support than the *Lin Pen-t'ang*, the Upper House estate produced sufficient income to assure a comfortable living and to underwrite Wen-ch'in's philanthropy, his community roles, and his conspicuous filial piety. Even with further loans to the *Lin Pen-t'ang* and the expenses for weddings and funerals, the Upper House was able to buy more than 200 *chia* out of current income during the period 1883-1895.[67] In all, the more modest *Chin-jung-t'ang* enjoyed far better financial health than did the extravagant *Lin Pen-t'ang* before its demise.

In its economic underpinnings, the Lin family both resembled and differed from other wealthy gentry families. Like most others, they owed their wealth to their political prominence, and they used government connections to augment and protect their assets. As with other gentry families, too, most of the Lin wealth consisted of land, with lesser amounts invested in the more profitable but less esteemed business sector. Typically, too, the new wealth fostered ominous habits of luxury, at least in the Lower House, while the family estates could at most delay the recurrent property divisions among a growing number of sons.

Yet more instructive than the parallels are the differences, for they clarify what was distinctive about the Lins. The political prominence to which the family owed its wealth came not from the power of office exercised in a remote jurisdiction of the empire, but from private power at home sanctioned by the government, first under the peculiar circumstances of the mid-nineteenth-century crisis and later during the incumbency of an energetic governor.

And if the Lins expended less time and influence than the mainland gentry in manipulating tax rates to their advantage, this was chiefly because taxes in mid-Taiwan were already so low as to warrant little of their attention.

What remains most characteristic on the whole, though, was the local character of the family's economic operations, beginning with their landlordism and extending to their business, manufacturing, and borrowing of the late nineteenth century. Thus, the Lins never absented themselves from the land on which their tenants toiled; even their magnificent mansions were erected in Wu-feng and not in the district capital to which earlier *nouveaux riches* had repaired. Their export and import trade through the mid-Taiwan ports and the camphor operations in the eastern hills were so many local extensions outward from the old family turf into neighboring territory. The retail business in Ta-li-chi merely strengthened the family's presence in the commercial hub of the central Upper Valley. With the single exception of Ch'ao-tung, whose wider political horizons seem to have opened his eyes to the opportunities of the larger economic world (the big loan from Taipei, real estate in mainland treaty ports), the Lins gained and expended their wealth in the circumscribed region which sustained their political and social ambitions. So far from obeying some abstract notion of economic rationality— deploying their capital wherever it might produce the highest return—the Lins's economic decisions reflected the same ingrained localism that marked their strongman past and their gentry present.

CHAPTER 15

FRONTIERSMEN,
STRONGMEN, GENTLEMEN

An Overview, 1600-1895

*Although the people of mid-Taiwan tend to be
naturally contentious, on the other hand they all
are spirited and get things done.*[1]

As he tried to account for Lin Wen-ch'a's flawed performance in the Taiwan campaign, Tso Tsung-t'ang pinpointed
the characteristics of an entire people, the fiercely quar-
relsome yet remarkably enterprising and capable mid-
Taiwanese. While he may have had Wen-ch'a's failings
uppermost in mind, Tso's remarks do have a wider import,
for they touch on qualities in the local population that explain both the achievements and limitations of people like
the Lins and of the larger society in which they made their
way.

The people who settled mid-Taiwan were the product of
a particular subculture of mainland China, the southeastern littoral. Coastal Fukien and Kwangtung had been developing away from an older pattern of Chinese society for
some time. The area had experienced strong population
pressures and had responded creatively—with the large-
scale commercialization of its agriculture, the orientation
to overseas trade, the increased mobility of its people. If
China ever was a country of rooted and stolid peasants (a
view which may need to be reexamined), the southeastern

littoral, with its busy wharves and workshops, provided an alternative to the immobile peasant-bureaucratic empire of the past.[2]

The southeast was also riven by unusually bitter internal divisions. Whatever their remoter causes—a violent streak in the local populace, the mountainous terrain which encouraged a fierce localism, the recentness of much migration into the area, and its distance from the imperial center—these divisions produced an endemic state of violence as local groups armed themselves for self-defense and spoliation. Through lineages and communal organizations, the people of Fukien and Kwangtung provided for their own security, albeit at the price of a permanent militarization of their society.

It was these people—restless, inventive, clannish, pugnacious—who discovered Taiwan and colonized it after 1600. On the frontier, the southeastern heritage stood the settlers in good stead. With their entrepreneurial skills honed in the dynamic economy of the southeast, frontier developers assured the quick opening of large tracts of land, assembled the early settler parties, and undertook much of the initial irrigation work. In their wake came the many poor and middling peasants—they too products of a highly commercialized agriculture of the seaboard—without whose skills in farming and marketing Taiwan's agriculture could not have become so productive so soon nor so well integrated into the larger Chinese trading network. Their tradition of violence also contributed to the settlers' triumph on the Taiwanese frontier. Since most of them were used to armed fighting, their onslaught on the aborigines was swift and effective. After 1750, much of the Western plain was theirs for the taking.

If the southeastern heritage contributed much to Taiwan's colonization, it also complicated the islanders' relation to the Chinese state. For the enterprising spirit that urged the settlers overseas also took them beyond the orbit of government—to Taiwan when it was still outside the empire, and later into reserved aborigine lands or beyond the "earth cows." Advancing ahead of the state's own territorial expansion, the earliest settlers established their own rough-and-ready political arrangements: their pirate chiefs of the sixteenth and early seventeenth centuries, their "elders" of the Dutch period, their earliest frontier entrepreneurs. Thus, the frontier spawned local leaders with private power, including private armed power, who interposed themselves between the populace and the apparatus of a remote Chinese government. It was a custom which they would retain even after Taiwan was incorporated into the Chinese state.

Koxinga symbolized this kind of leadership, as he did so much else. Conquering Taiwan in the name of the defunct Ming house, he is, by a polite fiction, the earliest representative of a Chinese dynasty to govern a part of Taiwan. In reality, he represented mainly his family's tradition of private maritime power which flourished along the politically soft underbelly of the empire. If this son of a pirate chief was the first and undoubtedly the greatest of the many "overmighty subjects"[3] on the southeastern littoral, his true successors were the Taiwanese strongmen of a later day. Like the strongmen, the Chengs entered into ambivalent relations with the state, in turn challenging or acknowledging its official spokesmen and clothing schemes of personal aggrandizement in the rhetoric of dynastic fealty.

A Society Loosely Governed
Yet Tightly Bonded

In time, of course, the throne followed where private initiative had led. From 1683 to 1895 (for just over two centuries, a tenth of the empire's total duration),* Taiwan became a part of the centrally governed Chinese state. And

* Under a number of dynasties and with intervals of political division and foreign conquest, the Chinese empire lasted from 221 B.C. to A.D. 1912.

while that Chinese state was present in Taiwan not only
through its laws and officials but in the consciousness of the
Chinese settlers, we must ask ourselves how much of an
impact that state actually had on the developing frontier
society. No doubt, the eighteenth and nineteenth centuries
were crucial for Taiwan, for they completed the sinicization that had only begun in the seventeenth. Yet the
policies and institutions of government contributed far less
to this process than did the settlers themselves, working individually or through such private cooperative arrangements as they devised.

Most of the steps that made Chinese occupance possible
were achieved with scant or no aid from the government
and often in the teeth of official prohibitions—transporting
the settlers across the Strait, displacing the aborigines,
turning virgin land into paddy, lacing it with irrigation
canals, marketing the crops. The garrison outposts that
provided greater security to the near-by settlers or the occasional punitive expeditions against the tribes at best
speeded up a process that followed inexorably from the
land-hunger and the numerical preponderance of the
settlers themselves. And state laws concerning migration
and land-taking were notoriously irrelevant to the actual
settlement process.

What, then, about the government's role in shaping the
institutional framework of the emerging society? The state
was of course directly responsible for the territorial administration, the district and prefectural governments, but the
impact of these governments on society was limited. They
performed minimal services and imposed minimal burdens. Even such basic tasks as the administration of justice
and the maintenance of internal order rested largely with
private groups who settled such matters as best they
could—through community pacts, blood revenge, and
armed conflict. Unofficial groupings—clans, communal
groups, armed self-defense corps, secret societies, strongman bands—defined the political landscape of rural
Taiwan.

As with the political order, so with the economic. Basic institutions—the land tenure system, the system of private water rights—no doubt functioned under a legal umbrella upheld by the government, but their historical evolution and day-to-day operation went forward without reference to the state. A parcel of land might change hands half a dozen times before anyone bothered to register a purchase with the government.[4] Created by private effort, water rights were defended in like manner, by force if need be.

Under these circumstances, the class structure too was relatively immune from governmental influence, at least in the eighteenth century. The native elite consisted of the biggest landlords and merchants and those community leaders who had a grip on the clans and communal groupings. Except for some ta-tsu landlords and shippers who had benefited from government connections, these men owed little to the government. Only when the examination system came into wider use in the nineteenth century did the state gain a more systematic influence on the recruitment of the elite. Even so, this influence was diluted; financial need produced an indiscriminate selling of ranks and titles, once more opening high-status positions to the merely wealthy or privately powerful.

While the examination system thus had a limited impact on the class structure even in the nineteenth century, it did shape Taiwan's cultural evolution. For in channeling social aspirations, the examinations furthered the spread of classical culture which had initially been weak on the frontier. And even though Taiwanese holding office on the mainland were too few to create a significant bond with the imperial polity, educated Taiwanese henceforth shared the cultural values of their mainland peers. Here was one of the few government-sponsored programs that had a perceptible influence on Taiwanese society.

Taiwan in the Ch'ing period was thus a creation of its settlers, not an emanation of the state. Yet the weaknesses of the government on the Taiwanese frontier did not mean untrammeled freedom for the individual frontiersman.

Only rarely did the Taiwanese pioneer "go it alone." His neighbors and relatives were as crucial for success as was his ability to do the backbreaking labor on the land. From the ship's captain who smuggled him across the Taiwan Strait to the frontier entrepreneur who provided access to land, from the neighbor with whom he organized village defenses to the kinsman whom he joined in building an irrigation facility, the pioneer relied on the cooperation of others. Clanship and communalism in particular became the strongest bonds of the new society.

The lives of the early Lins—roughly the first three generations—illustrate the opportunities of the new land as well as the dependence on the clan group. Lin Shih settled in Ta-li-chi, already a gathering place of many Lins, and Lins from P'ing-ho at that. When his children and grandchildren scattered later, they remained well within the emerging Lin surname turf of the Upper Valley. Communalism entered these early Lin lives as well, as witness the community pact which Shih and Sun helped devise and their exposure to communal conflict later.

For ambitious and hardworking men who cultivated the necessary ties to clan and communal group, to patrons and peers, Taiwan held out far brighter prospects than could be realized at home on the mainland. This too is borne out by the early Lin lives and especially by the two remarkable ascents to affluence within three generations, each within a single lifetime. The successes of Shih and Chia-yin bore the stamp of each man's age. Arriving in the mid-eighteenth century, Shih benefited from the plentiful supply of good land; from pioneer farming he branched into landlordism, the grain trade, and money-lending. Half a century later, Chia-yin began in trade, and then expanded into manufacturing (charcoal) and from there into land-opening and landlordism.

But if the cooperation of one's kinsmen and communal group members was vital for success, it carried dangers as well, as the Lins were to discover also. It was fear of entanglement in communal violence which sent Lin Sun back to the mainland, and it was Lin Shih's kinship ties to the rebel leader which entangled him in the Lin Shuang-wen rebellion. Bonds that had been vital for success turned into fetters, for guilt-by-kinship or by communal affiliation was simply the obverse of the tightly protective group networks which the settlers had developed in the absence of effective local government.

The Lin Shuang-wen episode thus underlines a further ironic aspect in the relation of state and society on the frontier: Taiwan's remote and feckless government had reserve powers that were immense. When mobilized, these powers could make or break any individual. The spirited and successful pioneer ancestor fell victim to one of these spasmodic government exertions, the hapless "little man" caught in the wheels of a government machine whose workings he barely understood.

Local Violence and the Strongmen

If the first three Lin lives belong to the history of a particular Chinese frontier, the story of the next two generations—the men who dominated the middle third of the nineteenth century, Ting-pang and Tien-kuo, Wen-ch'a and Wen-ming—illustrates the peculiar opportunities that arose for ambitious men when Taiwan's local turbulence became caught up in China's larger crisis. In a decisive first step, Chia-yin's two eldest sons—the first of the family to be born in Wu-feng—had become local strongmen, foci of private armed power in the rural hinterland. Everything else followed from this: the increasingly bitter conflicts with local rivals and the violent deaths that ended so many Lin lives; the family's growing power in its native village, and Wu-feng's power in the Upper Valley; the rewarding opportunities for government service and the exceptional temptations this placed in the family's way.

Students of the Chinese local elite have weighed the relative role played by men of learning and men of wealth in running local affairs. Whatever we may yet learn about these matters, it is time to add a third type, the man of private armed power, to the other two. It has taken time for the local strongman to come into focus. He belongs to that sphere of local militarization which official sources largely ignore or else capture only in moments of crisis and rebellion, times which polarize not only the society but the very idiom of the observer. Birds of a feather, Tai Wan-sheng, Lin Wen-ch'a, Lin Jih-ch'eng and the Hung brothers, appear in the official record under entirely different rubrics, some as rebels, others as loyal subjects, as if that was all that mattered. It is in correcting such distortions that the local perspective of this study has been most helpful, for it has revealed the underlying similarity of their operations.

With their roots in local groupings—the clans and communal groups that had been so important from the beginning of the Taiwanese frontier—the strongmen organized private albeit unstable systems of rural power. Unlike the wealthy landlords who merely hired gangs of toughs, strongmen went into battle themselves. Fighters and leaders of fighting men, their ascendancy rested not only on the pay and booty they secured for their followers, but also on the personal qualities with which they inspired their men—bravery, generosity, resourcefulness, and tact. At the other extreme, we must distinguish the strongmen from the leaders of roving bandit gangs, outsiders with no ties to the society on which they preyed, and from Hobsbawm's "social bandits" who fought both the state and the rich on behalf of the local poor. It was of the essence of the Taiwanese strongman that he represented a local, but economically differentiated, group and that he combined personal prowess, local prestige, wealth, and at least marginal legitimacy in the eyes of the government.

Among recent studies in mainland social history, Philip Kuhn's *Rebellion and Its Enemies in Late Imperial China* delineates local power configurations that resemble those I found in mid-Taiwan. Though the book focuses on moments of major crisis and on the gentry's role in coordinating the defense against rebellion, Kuhn shows that initial militarization at the local and intermediate levels (what he calls the simplex and multiplex scales of organization) often arose from private and a-political feuding which antedated rebellion. And while he does not specifically focus on the strongman, he mentions many local figures who appear to meet the definition and whose political ambiguity also resembles that of the Taiwanese specimen. What makes Kuhn's findings so important is the fact that most of his data come from Hunan and Anhui, mainland provinces beyond the southeastern littoral. If many local rebels and local rebel fighters in these older mainland provinces arose from among the leaders of initially a-political armed groupings, we may discover that rural violence and the strongmen which it bred were far more common in imperial China than has yet been recognized.

If many students have concentrated too much on the major crises to appreciate the endemic low-level violence and the patterns of local power it spawned, other students of rural China have focussed too exclusively on class conflict to see the world of the strongman for what it was: one in which men frequently struggled over economic issues but seldom aligned on the basis of economic status. Instead, ties of loyalty ran vertically, between wealthy leaders and poorer followers, within such distinct segments of society as clans and communal groups. Men did not associate on the basis of class and across clan or communal ties. Nor can we salvage the notion of class conflict by making the contestants out to have been poor and rich clans or communal groups. While there were undoubtedly differences of wealth between competing strongmen and the groups from which they drew their strength, far more evident was the economic differentiation within each strongman turf.

Only further studies can clarify how widespread this pattern was, but they must avoid automatic assumptions about the priority of class conflict.

Preoccupation with the class model of social conflict also tends to obscure the many non-economic but no less real issues over which the armed feuds of the countryside erupted: the personal slights and insults, and the violations of sexual or religious tabus over which men resorted to arms. Only on the theory that all human endeavor can be reduced to the pursuit of economic interest will such issues appear trivial or incapable of explaining the hostilities that ensued.

If Taiwan's rural violence and the strongman cannot be understood simply in terms of class conflict or the pursuit of gain, an explanation may be found in the realm of culture and especially in the heroic tradition which forms a neglected part of Taiwanese, and of the larger Chinese, culture. Here too the dominant historiography has painted a misleading picture, one of a profoundly pacified country in which men of distinctly civilian ethos ruled by cultural guidance over a population that purportedly loathed violence, where the man of the brush was always mightier than the man of the sword. In fact, Chinese contempt for soldiering was reserved for the mercenary armies of the recent dynasties; it did not extend to the great warrior-emperors nor to the other heroes whose deeds of valor adorn the historical record. Down to the present, China has embraced a heroic tradition alongside the civilian ethos with which her historians have made us familiar.

The heroic outlook flourished not only in the realm of popular culture. High culture and popular culture in China were intertwined, and both inherited the martial strain directly from the classical age. Nor is this surprising. After all, China's philosophically formative age had been an era of warrior aristocrats who cultivated the knightly arts along with ritual purity and courtly manners. The Confucians did not repudiate these values, even as they added an emphasis on moral endeavor and book learning. In the *Book of Songs* and many of the early histories China had her own primers of the heroic style of life.

Nor did the advent of a unified empire destroy the martial values of the feudal age. The imperial state, to be sure, strove for a monopoly of armed power and looked askance at those who lived heroic lives in defiance of government writ, such as the knights-errant. Yet there was always room for heroes within the state structure itself. During the early imperial dynasties, the aristocratic families furnished officers for the army, a most honorable calling. It was the early imperial period, too, which established the figure of Kuan Yü, the paragon of Chinese heroes, forever in the Chinese imagination. Only from the Sung on, with the rise of the examination-based meritocracy, did the ruling class become more distinctly civilian in outlook. But the heroic strand was not lost even then. It reasserted itself in times of foreign crisis when Kuan Yü was raised to the status of a god of war and when heroes like Yo Fei led the resistance against the barbarians. Nor did the great soldier-statesmen die out in the later dynasties, as witness the careers of Wang Yang-ming and Tseng Kuo-fan, Confucian gentlemen who excelled on the battlefield as much as in the study or the *yamen*.

Popular culture, to be sure, embraced the martial ideal with particular fervor. Deeds of valor figured in many popular plays and magical swordsmen performed at country fairs. Boxing societies appealed to the young and whole generations were nourished on the story of the heroic outlaws of Liang-shan moor. Lodges and brotherhoods reenacted the peach blossom oath, symbol of the fabled blood brotherhood of the Three Kingdoms heroes.

We have undoubtedly much to learn about this heroic tradition and how it interacted with other elements in Chinese culture. But perhaps enough has been said to suggest that the strongman with his pride and prowess was no freak, no outsider to the Chinese tradition. Instead, he represented an element that was widely diffused in the civilization and found a particularly congenial lodging on the Taiwanese frontier.

The Perils of Political Ambition

If strongmen were perennial figures in the rural landscape, each individual strongman functioned in a narrowly bounded space, the "turf" from which he drew his strength. Yet there was a contradiction between a strongman's finite base and his often soaring ambition. In a period of major crisis such as the mid-nineteenth century, this contradiction was bound to sharpen, for the times promised to reward the strongman who ventured beyond his turf. If he were tempted, or pushed, into rebellion, he might become a rebel "king" or "prince," lording it over a considerable stretch of the countryside. But rebellions were seldom successful and almost always fatal for rebel leaders. It took rare political skill for a strongman-turned-rebel to bargain his way back into the good graces of the government, though the feat was occasionally accomplished.

The Lin story makes plain that it was almost as dangerous for a strongman to take the opposite course, to align himself with the state and against the rebels. The rewards of such a course were obvious, to be sure—official ranks and funds, a chance to recruit a larger force and to throw one's greater weight around. But there was a price to pay for all this added power and glory. As he recruited more widely and campaigned farther from home, the strongman stood to lose touch with his local base, to dilute his force (as happened in Wen-ch'a's last campaign) or, finally, to put dynastic loyalty ahead of local ties (as was the fate of Lin Ch'ao-tung later).

What made for even more serious trouble, however, was the strongman's inexperience in handling the formidable powers of the state. To entrust a Lin Wen-ch'a with the emergency powers of the 1864 campaign could not but aggravate pacification and Wen-ch'a's own standing with the authorities. With his moral training confined to the strongman code of prickly pride and blood revenge, inexperienced in the measured exercise of public power, such a strongman was bound to overplay his hand, as did, in their lesser ways, both Tien-kuo and Wen-ming. The higher he rose, the greater the strongman's opportunity to abuse public power, and the greater the depth to which he could subsequently fall. Had Wen-ch'a lived to face the consequences of his actions in 1864, his punishment might easily have been as severe as Tien-kuo's, the less gifted man who came to grief over pettier spoliations.

If the long arm of imperial justice did not reach him, the machinations of personal enemies probably would. For, complicating the strongman's relations to the state was his penchant for making enemies among the officials almost faster than he made friends. Clearly, individuals varied in their political finesse as they climbed the ladder of success. To have been locally successful in the first place, a strongman must have had some basic political skills, skills which Wen-ch'a certainly commanded in his relations with local officials and garrison commanders in the 1850's. But when a strongman rose as steeply to greater heights as Wen-ch'a did later, success often went to his head. He became overbearing and alienated former patrons without necessarily gaining new friends; some former friends resented his success. The highest commanders under whom such a strongman might serve either looked on him as a rival, as did Ch'i-ling, or they retained doubts about his temperament and unsavory associates, as did Tso Tsung-t'ang.

In short, the Lins provide a striking example of a family which succumbed to nearly all the temptations of unaccustomed power and tasted to the full both glory and humiliation in their relation to government. What is more, they managed to extricate themselves from the pitfalls into which they had stumbled; in the process, they provide us with yet another insight into the relations of state and society.

Government, it seems, affected the people in its power not so much through its general policies—these were often enough a dead letter—but through the *ad hoc* decisions of individual officeholders. The favors shown to Wen-ch'a in connection with his trial and on subsequent campaigns, the vendettas of hostile officials against the Lin family later, and the role of personal connections in the lawsuit demonstrate not only the vast discretionary power of officeholders but also the vigor with which they intervened for or against particular men.

Clearly, local officials in the Ch'ing were never as aloof from their districts as they have been pictured. They were, of course, outsiders of a sort, natives of another province. But so far from being simply whisked in and out of their jurisdictions without becoming familiar with the locale, many bureaucrats served long stints in one and the same or in a neighboring jurisdiction or returned to it after being rotated elsewhere. They had ample time to develop local contacts and to enter deeply into the contests of competing local groups and strongmen. In Chang-hua district, a case in point is Tseng Yü-ming, a powerful figure with years of service in mid-Taiwan as a *pei-lu* garrison commander and finally Taiwan brigade general. He was close to several of the major local strongmen and, hoping to coopt rather than challenge, sought good terms with all of them and even attempted to mediate their internal feuds. Another example is Ting Yüeh-chien, a man who had built such good relations with the Tan-shui notables in the 1850's that he was still able to mobilize them for pacification when he returned as an intendant a decade later. That he and several of his colleagues entered intimately into the affairs of the Lin family and their strongmen rivals we have seen.

From the vantage point of this study, then, it appears that we must revise our picture of the relations between local officeholders, civilian and military, and the community in their keeping. It was not simply that educated magistrates had a natural affinity for the local degree-holders, that officials could be bribed, or that new incumbents were tipped off about the powerful local families on whose interests they must not encroach. In addition there developed personal friendships and enmities between officials and locals, reflecting the vagaries of individual temperament and years of close acquaintance. If China's was a government of men rather than of laws, as has sometimes been said, the individual subject's dependence, not on an impersonal bureaucracy, but on the "human, all too human" frailties of specific powerholders underlines that point at the local level.

The Predicament of the Late Ch'ing Gentry

Strongmen families who survived the perils of state service usually entered the gentry. A convenient arrangement, it assured Peking of the gratitude of powerful subjects while giving them a badge of status which only the throne could bestow. Coming on top of the massive sales of gentry titles begun earlier, this cooptation of loyal strongmen and other notables diluted the gentry far beyond its original core group, the examination-tested scholar-gentry. By the late nineteenth century, the local elites in much of China included a wide range of families, some scholarly, some martial, others simply wealthy.[5]

In Taiwan, where the local elite had always been a mixed group, the dilution was probably felt less keenly than elsewhere. This may explain why Chang-hua's gentry families welcomed the Lins so openly, despite the atrocities charged to Wen-ch'a or Wen-ming's shameful death. In a mainland district with older, prouder gentry families, the Lins might not have become so respectable so soon.

While the family's passage into the gentry thus raised few eyebrows, it was in effect a remarkable event. For the Lins were not content with the change in their formal status. With the zest they had once devoted to the expansion of their turf, they now threw themselves into the traditional gentry activities. In the process, they modified their relations to the surrounding community and the manner in which family power was exercised. Ch'ao-tung, whose recruiting of braves still smacked of the strongman world, did not use his force for private feuds and was adroit in his relations with government. Wen-ch'in and Ch'ao-hsüan went beyond him, discontinuing the use of a permanent private force altogether and assuming new tasks of community leadership and philanthropy.

As the new generation abandoned the ways of their strongmen-fathers, the region over which the Lins exercised a significant influence widened. The old strongman turf stood out less sharply from the rest of the Upper Valley, though the sense of clan cohesion survived. Except in the case of Ch'ao-tung, wealth rather than armed power became the key to the continued ascendancy of the Lins— now simply the Upper Valley's major landlords, waterlords, employers and entrepreneurs. Perhaps not coincidentally, the management of family business appears to have claimed a growing share of the senior men's time in the 1880's and 1890's. Beyond the Upper Valley, Wen-ch'in's gentry activities and the new marriage pattern created ties to mid-Taiwan as a whole, and especially to its elite families, while Ch'ao-tung's exertions on the provincial level made the Lins a force to reckon with far beyond Chang-hua district.

Yet as the family acted in the gentry mode and over a wider area, their ties to followers and clients weakened. The close mutual dependence between a strongman family and the people of its turf could not be sustained outside the context of armed feuding, where each bloody battle reaffirmed the sense of a shared destiny and the strongman's growing power enhanced his people's security. A mild paternalism replaced the strongman's charismatic leader-

ship. Without underrating his generosity, we may doubt
whether Wen-ch'in's ties to his beneficiaries were as close as
Wen-ch'a's to his fighting men. And who, after all, were the
beneficiaries of the family's latest good works? The travel-
lers crossing the Lower Ta-tu on Wen-ch'in's free ferry?
Orphan girls in the Chang-hua asylum? Or all the people
of mid-Taiwan on whose behalf the mid-island defense
bureau labored in the spring of 1895? And what sentiments beyond a vague gratitude could they feel toward
their distant benefactor? Characteristically, when Wen-
ch'in raised local braves in 1895 he quickly lost control over
the undisciplined force.[6] For all his benefactions to a wider
world, Tien-kuo's son no longer held the key to power that
his father once possessed: personal control over armed
fighting men.

The Lins's transformation from strongmen into gentlemen thus deprived them of the older and vital function of
war-leaders, of organizing their people for the use of force
and leading them into battle. For all his military merits in
the province at large, even Ch'ao-tung failed the local
people on this score in 1895. The gentry tasks which the
Lins embraced instead, and discharged with such vigor and
distinction, rendered no comparable service to the larger
community for which they spoke in the late nineteenth
century. Only effective leadership in the self-strengthening
effort could have done that, and here the local gentry—to
judge from the Lins—lacked either the vision or the institutional setting for bold and independent action. Wen-
ch'in's private benefactions brought marginal improvements but hardly addressed the major questions of the day.
And Ch'ao-tung's semi-official exertions, while more relevant to the self-strengthening program, remained singularly dependent on the patronage of a reform-minded
governor. Besides, the gentry's capacity for political leadership suffered from the continuing fragmentation of
Taiwanese society. When a supreme challenge loomed, as

in 1895, the lingering division into communal groups, and the notables' ties to these groupings, prevented them from leading a unified and effective defense. Not until the twentieth century, when these cleavages had begun to heal and when Japanese colonialism presented a new political challenge, did a member of the family once more champion a cause of vital importance for his people. But before Lin Hsien-t'ang could lead the Taiwanese autonomy movement, he had to go beyond late Ch'ing notions of gentry politics to embrace a broader vision of Taiwanese patriotism.

If the gentry's political capabilities in late Ch'ing Taiwan failed to match the needs of the hour, their cultural leadership appeared, at first glance, more secure. In adopting the gentry style of life, the Lins testified to the continuing attraction of the traditional gentry ideal, with its notions of self-cultivation, moral leadership, and public service. With many brothers under a single roof, hierarchically arranged in their symmetrical mansions, with chaste widows and with many concubines to provide sons, with the young immersed in "the *Rites* and the *Music*, . . . the *Odes* and the *History*,"[7] the family's domestic life suggested that all was still well with the old order, with fraternal good feeling and filial piety, with the place of women and the prestige of traditional learning. We cannot tell whether the Lins had already sensed the tremors that would soon shake this seemingly placid order; their literati friends at the *Wen-k'ai shu-yüan* were aware of the West's cultural challenge well before 1895 and the Lins too would feel the winds of change blowing through the land as soon as a modernized Japan took over.

The Lins, then, joined the gentry at the very moment when its political and cultural *raison d'être* began to be put in doubt. Too independent to enslave themselves to every prescription of the gentry code, they nevertheless benefited from it, broadening their concept of community beyond the strongman's narrow idea of "turf." In adapting to an ancient but embattled tradition, the Lin gentlemen of the late nineteenth century thus paved the way for the patriots of the twentieth.

Epilogue: The Lins in the Twentieth Century

This story of the Lin family ends logically in 1895, when Taiwan was cut loose from the Chinese body politic and became a colony of Japan. What made 1895 important was not so much the fact that the islanders exchanged one distant master for another, but rather that the Japanese colonial regime possessed many more of the attributes of the "modern state" than did the Great Ch'ing dynasty. The conditions that had shaped family history up to this point—the lawlessness and localism that had favored the assertion of private power—disappeared as the Japanese imposed an effective police system reaching down to the local level and as they greatly improved transportation. Moreover, the vigorous economic development pursued by the Japanese and the spread of primary education and other modern systems helped reshape Taiwanese society enough to alter the ways in which any family of local notables could henceforth behave.

To underline the new departures after 1895 is merely to argue that the Lins of the twentieth century deserve a study of their own. Such a work would in fact encompass one of the most significant chapters in the history of this distinguished family and should prove of equal value to students of Japanese colonialism and of Chinese modernization. In tracing the family's modernizing role under an effective if authoritarian regime, such a study would tell us much about the modernizing potential of China's traditional elite, a potential seldom realized under the quite different political conditions of the mainland in the first half of the twentieth century. This brief epilogue, however, cannot address the issues that a book on the Lins of the twentieth century would raise; it can merely supply a few highlights of recent family history.

First of all, then, in a period of considerable geographic mobility, the Lins remained the Lins of Wu-feng. Most family members retained their residence there even as the large households of the late nineteenth century broke up and some of the new, smaller households moved out of the old mansions and into more modern single-family houses. Only a few family members took up residence in Taichung, the rising city to the north, and entered into its business and civic life.

Social change was pervasive, especially in the area of family life. Mothers ceased binding their daughters' feet[8] in the same mansion where Miss Yang had just affirmed the highest ideals of traditional womanhood. Girls began to receive a formal education and some Lin wives even took an interest in the social movements of the new century,[9] an unheard-of role for a gentlewoman under the old order. Young men nourished on the *Odes* and the *History* travelled around the world or sought knowledge at foreign universities. Large households dissolved as brothers established their independent households and an occasional one or two even embraced the ideal of monogamous marriage. Clearly, it was a polite fiction to speak of Mrs. Lo's harmonious household as a bastion against social disorder, as did the Lins's distinguished houseguest, Liang Ch'i-ch'ao, in a poem celebrating the matriarch's eighty-first birthday.[10]

Economically, the family retained its strength throughout the Japanese period, resting it on their unchallenged control of land and the survival, with but minor changes, of Taiwanese landlordism. Their economic ascendancy was enhanced by their role in the Chang-hua Bank, an important institution in the island's modern economic life, in which several family members were active as directors or stockholders. Some of the entrepreneurial activities begun in the late nineteenth century also expanded, such as the family interest in camphor production. Thus, the Japanese household registers refer to the major male figures as either landlords or camphor producers.

There were some exceptions, to be sure, to this record of continuing prosperity. Ch'ao-tung's son Chi-shang (1878-1925), who assumed control of his father's assets upon Ch'ao-tung's death in 1904, seems not to have been a wise steward of his branch's wealth. He squandered much through ill-timed land sales, partly to raise funds for his political adventures on the mainland (see below).[11] Others from the Lower House, too, lived beyond their means. Thus, the fortunes of this major segment of the family had already declined, probably below the level of the continuingly prosperous Upper House members, well before the Nationalist government resumed control of Taiwan in 1945.

In the early 1950's, as the rent reduction and land-reform programs wiped out Taiwanese landlordism and created a new class of small owner-farmers, the Lins lost the bulk of their land. What use family members made of the compensation offered in lieu of the land is not clear, but for some these payments may have eased the transition into new careers (in banking or insurance) in which they hold positions now. Clearly, though, the family registered a drastic economic decline after mid-century.

In these more straitened circumstances, the Lins today still bask in the afterglow from the fame of the Lin patriots and poets who gave their house enduring luster during the Japanese period. It is the lives of some of these men we must now briefly recall, for they reveal a modern sense of patriotism and civic responsibility that grew directly out of the gentry legacy of the late Ch'ing. In adapting this earlier tradition to a new age, these Lins of the twentieth century retraced the footsteps of their forebears whose public service had either taken them to the mainland or kept them in Taiwan itself. Two lives will illustrate these modes of modern patriotism.

In the footsteps of his father, Ch'ao-tung, and his grandfather, Wen-ch'a, Lin Chi-shang expressed his political commitment through military service on behalf of the Nationalist cause on the mainland.[12] He had returned to Taiwan after the flight of 1895, only to leave again in 1913 and take up residence in Amoy. It was from there that, a few years later, he developed ties to the struggling movement of Sun Yat-sen. He raised volunteers in Chang-chou and (significantly, in view of the older communal jealousies) also in Ch'üan-chou and made them available for Sun's Canton-based government in the years after 1917. He apparently led his troops in action and—shades of the 1860's—recovered several district capitals in Fukien. During peaceful interludes, he held civilian offices, including that of provincial water conservancy director in Fukien. In 1925, he died, apparently in action, at the hands of a subordinate of Sun Ch'uan-feng, the northern warlord who was then contesting Fukien with the Nationalist forces. Forty years later, the Kuomintang honored Chi-shang as a hero in its cause.

By contrast, the most important scion of the Upper House during the Japanese period, Lin Hsien-t'ang, rendered his public service in Taiwan itself, and not in the military field.[13] This too reflected the tradition established by his father, Wen-ch'in. Just fourteen when Taiwan passed to the Japanese, Hsien-t'ang had grown up under the influence of his scholarly father and of Wen-ch'in's mother, the legendary Mrs. Lo. As an adult, he played the role of the socially responsible aristocrat while adapting it to the changing conditions of the twentieth century. Co-founder of the island's first modern high school and advocate of a higher education for his fellow-Taiwanese, he not only financed a Japanese university education for gifted young protégés but presided over a vast expansion of the family's civic activities. In the Lin garden, where his father had entertained local notables, Hsien-t'ang welcomed guests of international stature, such as Liang Ch'i-ch'ao and Itagaki Taisuke. In the gentry tradition of representing local interests before a remote government, he led the Taiwanese home-rule movement and the many cultural and modernizing currents it embraced. Thus, he presided over the Taiwan Cultural Association and the many young patriots who gathered under its wings, and used his immense influence and prestige to work for greater local autonomy and social betterment for his fellow-Taiwanese. Only from the 1930's, when a more radical nationalist movement arose among the younger generation, was he even challenged as a spokesman for the Taiwanese patriots. Even then, though, he remained so clearly the first citizen of Taiwan that many islanders believe that he would easily have won election as Taiwan's first president had such a choice been open to the Taiwanese after 1945.

Lin Hsien-t'ang initially supported the return of Taiwan to Nationalist China and led a delegation to Nanking in September of 1945 to help smooth the transition. He continued active in public life but became increasingly disenchanted with the policies of the Nationalist government—the bloody repression of the 1947 riots and perhaps the gathering assault on the landlords as well—and chose self-exile in Japan, leaving Taiwan in 1950 and dying in Tokyo six years later. Younger relatives have continued to work within the political structures available on the island, some serving as members of national bodies or in such local offices as district magistrate.

Like the soldierly Chi-shang and the civic-minded Hsien-t'ang, the major poets of the Lin family—Wen-ming's adopted sixth son, Chün-t'ang, and Ch'ao-hsüan's eldest son, Yu-ch'un—expressed their new patriotism in an older idiom. In verse that appears conventional in mood and imagery, these scions of a mighty house interwove themes of familial pride and patriotic shame, of nostalgia for lost grandeur and protest against an unworthy present. A few lines from a poem by Lin Chün-t'ang, written after a visit to his uncle Wen-ch'a's special temple in Taichung,[14] may stand as a token of their achievement and an epitaph to the story told in this book:

> For ten years, his memory was honored only in domestic rites,
> Yet the fame of a hundred battles lives on among the people.
> Now the sun shines on the vile deeds of Fu-sang*
> A big tree in a whirlwind, the general's house is breaking up.
> I cannot bear to remember his worthy example of loyal service;
> Tears wet my blue gown as I take the cup to offer sacrifice.

* Japan.

Notes

Complete references to the works cited will be found in the Bibliography. The following abbreviations have been used in the notes:

CHHCK   *Chang-hua-hsien chih-kao*
HTHAHL   *Hsin-tseng hsing-an hui-lan*
TCSL   *T'ung-chih shih-lu*
TWSTCK   *T'ai-wan-sheng t'ung-chih-kao*

Notes to Chapter 1

1. From a 1685 work by a Chinese official in Taiwan, quoted in Thompson (1964), p. 179.

2. On the geography, I have consulted Chen (1956), Hsieh (1964), and the atlas by Chang (1963). The early history after Haguenauer (1930a), who summarizes the three-volume work by Ino Kanori, *Taiwan bunka shi*.

3. Thompson (1964), p. 163.

4. See the references to the *Sui-shu* account in Hirth and Rockhill (1911), p. 164.

5. On the Chinese advance into Fukien, see Bielenstein (1959); on the Sung maritime policy, Lo (1955).

6. That the expeditions added little to China's knowledge of Taiwan is clear from Needham (1959), Figure 231. On Cheng Ho's visit, Haguenauer (1930a), p. 41.

7. The per capita average was 3.5 *mou* or .531 acres. See Perkins (1969), p. 225, Table B5.

8. Details on this "commercial revolution" in Ho (1959), pp. 199-200 and Rawski (1972), pp. 64-67.

9. Boxer (1948), pp. 18, 42.

10. On the ban and its effects, see Wiethoff (1963) and Wiethoff (1964).

11. On the leading role of the Chinese among the so-called "Japanese pirates," see So (1975).

12. Thompson (1964), p. 177.

13. Ts'ao (1962), p. 8.

14. On early Japanese contacts with Taiwan, I follow Haguenauer (1930b).

15. Thompson (1964), p. 178, n. 39. This name later evolved into "Taiwan."

16. On the early Europeans in Taiwanese waters, see Davidson (1903), Chs. II and III.

17. Details in Wills (1974), pp. 22-23.

18. This is the thesis of Ch'en (1962). Particulars on the growing Chinese presence on the island from Campbell (1903), *passim*, a work based on original Dutch sources.

19. Campbell (1903), p. 385.

20. Ch'en (1966), p. 12.

21. Quoted material in this paragraph from Campbell (1903), pp. 210, 231, 306, 386, 392-393 and 461.

22. On the Cheng family, see biographies in Hummel (1943-1944), pp. 108-112.

23. Ch'en (1966), p. 12. Economic developments after Haguenauer (1930a), p. 41.

24. Political developments after Lien (1962), pp. 133-134 and cultural trends according to Davidson (1903), p. 58.

Notes to Chapter 2

1. *Chu-lo hsien-chih*, p. 88.

2. His biography in Hummel (1943-1944), p. 653. Other details on Shih Lang's role in the conquest of Taiwan in Fu (1966), I, 34-35, 60-61, and Kuo (1973), p. 172.

3. Lee (1970), p. 35.

4. K'ang-hsi's concerns in Fu (1966), I, 72.

5. On the emigration ban, see TWSTCK, Vol. II, *Jen-min chih, Jen-k'ou p'ien*, p. 122, and Chuang (1962), pp. 84-85. On the prohibition of land purchases and rentals, Hui (1959), p. 97.

6. On the military dispositions, see TWSTCK, Vol. III, *Cheng-shih chih, Fang-shu p'ien, passim*. Further details on the *pei-lu* garrison in *Chu-lo hsien-chih*, pp. 42-44.

7. Tung (1962), pp. 27-28, an eighteenth-century source.

8. *Chu-lo hsien-chih*, pp. 127-133.

9. Details after Lan Ting-yüan, an early eighteenth-century source translated in Bridgman (1838), p. 425. Nineteenth-century conditions after Lamley (1964), pp. 60-61.

10. The administrative divisions are detailed in TWSTCK, Vol. III, *Cheng-shih chih, Hsing-cheng p'ien*, p. 35.

11. See Whitney (1970), p. 86.

12. Details from Lien (1962), p. 464.

13. Haguenauer (1930a), p. 43.

14. This was Chou Chung-hsüan, a Kueichow man.

15. Treatment of the aborigines after Haguenauer (1930a), pp. 80-82.

16. On abuses in the interpreter system, Bridgman (1838), p. 426.

17. Chu's biography in Hummel (1943-1944), pp. 181-182.

18. On Lan, see *ibid*., pp. 440-441, and the translation of his essay by Bridgman (1838).

19. On the censors, see *T'ai-wan t'ung-chih*, p. 344, and on the new administrative divisions, *ibid*., p. 348, and TWSTCK, Vol. III, *Cheng-shih chih, Hsing-cheng p'ien*, p. 35.

20. See Chuang (1962), pp. 84-85; Chang (1962b), p. 19; and Hui (1959), p. 87.

21. On this step, see Chang (1962b), p. 19, and Okamatsu (1900), pp. 48, 53.

22. On the uprisings and the increase in garrison strength, see Lien (1962), pp. 66-67, 295. On the *pao-chia*, Hsiao (1960), p. 48.

23. Chuang (1962), pp. 84-85 and TWSTCK, Vol. II, *Jen-min chih, Jen-k'ou p'ien*, p. 122.

24. Hui (1959), pp. 100, 97.

25. For policies pursued on the mainland, see Miyakawa (1960).

26. On the tribe's sinicization, see Chang (1955b) and Liu (n.d.). The detail on the gardener is from a document in the T'ai-ta P'an Collection.

27. On this policy, see Haguenauer (1930a), pp. 80-85.

28. For information on the siting of the "earth cows" in mid-Taiwan, I am indebted to Mr. Hung Min-lin of the Taiwan Historical Commission, a specialist in mid-Taiwanese history. In the Upper Ta-chia valley, the village of T'u-niu near Shih-kang recalls one such site. On the outskirts of the village, a stone stela records the magistrate's prohibition of 1761 against entering the interior.

29. *Chang-hua hsien-chih*, p. 71.

Notes to Chapter 3

1. Lin (1936), Biography of Lin Shih.

2. On the rivers, see *Chang-hua hsien-chih*, p. 15, and Hsieh (1964), pp. 20, 41, 79. Modern maps show only the river beds to which the rivers were confined when the Japanese built a series of great embankments in the 1930's.

3. The Reverend George Candidius in Campbell (1903), p. 9.

4. *Chu-lo hsien-chih*, pp. 30-31.

5. Chang (1951) and Ferrell (1969) provide schemes for the classification of the tribes.

6. Comments by a Chinese businessman who visited Taiwan in 1697, translated in Thompson (1964), p. 193.

7. *Ibid.*, pp. 187-188, for this and the next quotation.

8. Lien (1962), p. 44.

9. *Chu-lo hsien-chih*, pp. 30, 32, 117.

10. On this major irrigation project, see TWSTCK, Vol. IV, *Ching-chi chih, Shui-li p'ien*, pp. 14, 199-200.

11. "T'ai-chung-hsien chih-kao," Chronology, entry for 1701.

12. Lien (1962), p. 64.

13. "T'ai-chung-hsien chih-kao," Chronology, entries for 1721 and 1722.

14. Lien (1962), p. 157.

15. See *Chu-lo hsien-chih*, p. 30; *Chung-hsiu fu-chien t'ai-wan fu-chih*, pp. 79-80; *Hsü-hsiu t'ai-wan fu-chih*, pp. 73-75; *Chang-hua hsien-chih*, pp. 43-51.

16. Ch'en (1966), p. 8.

17. These colloquial expressions from Skinner (1957), p. 96.

18. *Ibid.*, p. 95.

19. Biographies in Lien (1962), pp. 807-808, and CHHCK, Vol. x, *Jen-wu chih*, pp. 2-4.

20. Biographies in Lien (1962), pp. 806-807, and CHHCK, Vol. x, *Jen-wu chih*, pp. 1-2. He shares the middle element of his name with Shih Lang's sons and may thus have been a nephew of the admiral. A Lu-kang tradition holds that relatives of Shih Lang settled there. See De Glopper (1974), p. 51.

21. Biographies in Lien (1962), p. 809, and CHHCK, Vol. x, *Jen-wu chih*, pp. 4-5.

22. Biographies in Lien (1962), pp. 808-809, and CHHCK, Vol. x, *Jen-wu chih*, p. 4.

23. Numerous references to such settler-groups in "T'ai-chung-hsien chih-kao" and in TWSTCK, Vol. II, *Jen-min chih, Shih-tsu p'ien, passim.*

24. Legal and historical aspects of land tenure after Okamatsu (1900), Kawada (1928), and Hui (1959).

25. On the origins of Chinese *ta-tsu* ownership, see especially Okamatsu (1900), pp. 48-53, and Hui (1959), pp. 96-97. On size of holdings, see *Chang-hua hsien-chih*, pp. 164-169.

26. Okamatsu (1900), p. 94.

27. On the condition of tribal *ta-tsu* rights, see Mid-Taiwan Local Records Collection and Lin Land Records.

28. On the changing status of the *hsiao-tsu* holders, see Okamatsu (1900), pp. 80-83.

29. Taiwanese prices in the 1750's and 1760's from documents in Lin Land Records and Ch'en Han-kuang's Facsimile Reprints. Mainland prices after Chang (1962a), p. 138.

30. Calculated from land deeds in Lin Land Records and T'ai-ta P'an Collection.

31. Their conditions are reconstructed from some three dozen tenant contracts from the Ch'ien-lung period in the

P'an Collection. The An-li tribe rented directly to Chinese tenants, acting as both *ta-tsu* and *hsiao-tsu*.

32. Okamatsu (1900), pp. 114-115.

33. Figures are approximate and based on my own calculations. Yields according to *Rinji taiwan tochi chosa kyoku* (1904), pp. 140-143; rice prices according to Wang (1958) and taxes according to Okamatsu (1900), p. 25. A nineteenth-century yardstick of what it required to lead a life of leisure is in Chang (1962a), p. 133. I have adjusted this for inflation and taxes. The per capita income *ibid.*, p. 328.

34. To build their live bamboo palisades, the settlers used the species Bambusa stenochachya Hackel, commonly known as *Tz'u chu* or thorny bamboo. Breeding grounds of disease-bearing mosquitoes, these bamboo stands were cut down by the Japanese around the turn of the century.

35. See Lin Shih's story in Ch. 4 below. In I-lan, a more recent frontier, this continued to be true in the late nineteenth century. See Warburg (1889), p. 381.

36. Lists of irrigation projects and their sponsors in *Chang-hua hsien-chih*, pp. 54-58, and in Lin (1954b).

37. On the lineage in southeastern China see Freedman (1958) and Freedman (1966). On conditions in Taiwan, Ch'en (1966), p. 14, and Pasternak (1969), pp. 553, 557.

38. On surname clusters in general see Jordan (1972), pp. 12-26. On the clustering of Lins and Hungs in adjacent parts of the Upper Valley, see Lin (1936) and *Hung-shih tsu-p'u, passim*. Despite much recent migration, the outlines of these clusters are still visible on the modern surname maps in Ch'en and Fried (1970).

39. Also called speech-groups. On such clustering in the early eighteenth century, see Huang (1957), pp. 38-39. The author was one of the censors who visited Taiwan in the 1720's.

40. See *Chang-hua hsien-chih*, pp. 157-158, and TWSTCK, Vol. 1, *T'u-ti chih, Sheng-chi p'ien*, pp. 94-100.

41. In Chang-hua district armed feuding became

marked enough by the early 1780's to attract official attention. See Ch. 4 below.

42. On the aborigine trade, see "T'ai-chung-hsien chih-kao," Chronology, entries for the 1770's and 1780's.

43. Lien (1962), p. 72. The earliest rice shipment from Lu-kang is noted in the *Chung-hsiu fu-chien t'ai-wan fu-chih* of 1742, p. 84.

44. On the various small industries, information from manuscript sources such as P'an Documents and T'ai-ta P'an Documents and from local informants.

45. Their growth was marked between the 1760's and the 1830's. Compare the lists of such towns in *Hsü-hsiu t'ai-wan fu-chih* (1763), pp. 88-89, and in *Chang-hua hsien-chih* (1834), pp. 39-42.

46. The following details from *Chang-hua hsien-chih*, pp. 35-37, 51-60, and from TWSTCK, Vol. I, *T'u-ti chih, Sheng-chi p'ien*, pp. 87-95.

47. Local graduates above the *sheng-yüan* level are listed in *Chang-hua hsien-chih*, pp. 232-239.

48. See TWSTCK, Vol. I, *T'u-ti chih, Sheng-chi p'ien*, pp. 94-100.

49. Lien (1962), p. 279.

50. Grousset (1958). Ch. II is entitled "The expansion of a race of pioneers."

Notes to Chapter 4

1. From a popular song, "Hsin-k'an ch'üan-jen mo-kuo t'ai-ke," in *T'ai-wan su-chü chi*.

2. Unless otherwise indicated, all details of the pioneer ancestor's life are taken from Lin (1936), Biography of Lin Shih and Genealogical Tables.

3. This and the next quoted passage from an early nineteenth-century source quoted in Hsiao (1960), p. 362. The tense has been changed.

4. See "Hsin-k'an ch'üan-jen mo-kuo t'ai-ke" in *T'ai-wan su-chü chi*.

5. Lin (1936), preface.

6. On its location and early history, see Yoshida (1911-1913), VI, 71. The Taiwan portion of this geographical dictionary was prepared by Ino Kanori. On the presence of the Lin surname, see the eighteenth-century source, *Ch'in-ting p'ing-ting t'ai-wan chi-lüeh*, p. 159, which speaks of the "Lin clan of Ta-li-chi" in the context of the early 1780's. Many Ta-li-chi Lins are also mentioned by name in documents of that period in Mid-Taiwan Local Records Collection, especially in Document Chia III, 16.

7. See *ibid.*, for An-li complaints against the villagers.

8. Shih's eldest son, Lin Sun, is described as summoning "tenant farmers" (*tien-nung*) in ca. 1780. See Lin (1936), Biography of Lin Sun.

9. *Ibid.*

10. Yoshida (1911-1913), VI, 71. On the term "chi," communication from local informants.

11. Unless otherwise indicated, details from Lin Sun's life are taken from his biography and from Genealogical Tables in Lin (1936).

12. Lin (1936), Biography of Lin Shih. On the functions and powers of these sub-bureaucrats, see Ch'ü (1962), Ch. III.

13. On the initial presence of the Hakka element, see Yoshida (1911-1913), VI, 71. On the Hakka/Fukienese fighting, *ibid.*, p. 82, entry "Mao-lo-pao."

14. On such pacts, see Hsiao (1960), pp. 201-205 and Freedman (1966), pp. 82-94. A nineteenth-century pact from neighboring Tan-shui is in Lou (1961), pp. 162-164.

15. Yamazaki and Murakami (1927), p. 221.

16. Lin (1936), Biography of Lin Sun, for this and subsequent quotations in this paragraph.

17. His biography in Hummel (1943-1944), pp. 253-255.

18. *Ibid.*, p. 369, entry "Hung-li" (i.e., Ch'ien-lung).

19. See his treatment in TWSTCK, Vol. VII, *Jen-wu chih*, III, 25-29. I have been told that Sun Yat-sen praised Lin as a precurser, but have not found the *locus classicus*.

20. On the society's introduction to Taiwan, see Lien (1962), p. 819. Its Chang-chou orientation, despite some leaders' efforts to reach out more widely, is clear from *Ch'in-ting p'ing-ting t'ai-wan chi-lüeh*, pp. 124, 128, 187, 199, 217, and from Hummel (1943-1944), pp. 23-24, entry "Ch'ai Ta-chi."

21. His biography and a full sketch of the rebellion in Lien (1962), pp. 819-827.

22. Particulars in *Ch'in-ting p'ing-ting t'ai-wan chi-lüeh*, p. 159.

23. On the burning and looting, see *ibid.*, pp. 128, 187. On Lu-kang's pro-loyalist stance, *ibid.*, pp. 124, 146, and Wu (1959a), p. 15.

24. *Ch'in-ting p'ing-ting t'ai-wan chi-lüeh*, p. 241.

25. Lin Shih and Lin Shuang-wen are once referred to as fellow-*tsung* members, twice as fellow-*tsu* members. Both terms can mean either lineage or clan, as understood by modern anthropologists.

26. Outside the Lin genealogy, only Lien (1962), p. 820, and Izumi (1929), p. 22, mention this matter. Since Lien was a friend of the Lins, and Izumi had access to Lien, the family tradition may be the only source for this detail.

27. A ban on the departure of rebels and their associates was already in effect. See *Ch'in-ting p'ing-ting t'ai-wan chi-lüeh*, p. 159. Perhaps Mr. Huang merely invoked it to serve his own purposes. The quotation is from Shih's biography in Lin (1936).

28. Statutory penalties for rebel relatives in Boulais (1966), p. 465, and Staunton (1966), p. 270. In addition, personal scores would most likely be settled during the forthcoming "pacification."

29. Shih's biography explains that "Ho Ao would often borrow money and even when he was given some, he wanted more and was forever dissatisfied."

30. Cases from Chang-hua and neighboring Tan-shui in Lien (1962), p. 811, and in TWSTCK, Vol. VII, *Jen-wu chih*, II, 89.

31. On this practice, see Staunton (1966), p. 435, section "Supply of food and clothes to prisoners."

32. He had "a reputation for unscrupulousness second only to that of Ho-shen," the notoriously corrupt favorite of Ch'ien-lung. Hummel (1943-1944), p. 254.

Notes to Chapter 5

1. Lin (1936), Biography of Lin Sun.

2. This detail and the move to T'u-ch'eng, *ibid*.

3. See Lin (1936), Ta-li branch edition, biography of Lin Ch'ing. On the high proportion of dry land, as late as 1900, see "T'u-ch'eng-chuang t'u-ti shen-kao-shu."

4. This and the next quoted passage from Lin (1936), Biography of Lin Sun.

5. Such troubles are vividly detailed in the P'an Collection.

6. Like several of the Lin wives, she receives a few lines in her husband's biography; no woman has a biography of her own.

7. This and the other quotations in this paragraph from Lin (1936), Biography of Lin Sun. On the custom of blaming family quarrels on feuding females, see Freedman (1958), p. 21.

8. Personal communication from family members. According to the Genealogical Tables in Lin (1936), no Huang girls married into the family (excepting the Wu-feng branch) between the 1790's and 1870. Marriages of Lin daughters are not recorded.

9. Information on births and deaths from Lin (1936), Genealogical Tables.

10. Quotation and details in this paragraph from Lin (1936), Biography of Lin Shih.

11. Estimates by Ta-li (the old Ta-li-chi) officials and family members. On the high ratio of government-owned land, see "Ta-li-chi-chieh t'u-ti shen-kao-shu."

12. This detail from Lin (1936), Biography of Lin Sun.

13. The quotation *ibid.*, Biography of Lin Shih. Information on sons and their descendants from Lin (1936), Genealogical Tables, and personal communications from family members.

14. Lin (1936), Biography of Lin Wu-hsiang.

15. The move presumably occurred a few years after the end of the rebellion. The preface to Lin (1936) states the move to Wu-feng occurred "more than one hundred forty years ago," i.e., prior to 1796. On the early history of Wu-feng, see Izumi (1929), p. 20, and Wu-feng (1941).

16. The name was bestowed by the then governor of Taiwan, Liu Ming-ch'uan. See Lien (1964), pp. 209, 220.

17. On the fortified outpost, see "T'ai-chung-hsien chih-kao," Chronology, entry for 1735. On the diverse settler groups, Yoshida (1911-1913), VI, 81-82, "Mao-lo-pao;" on the tribe's renting practices, see a modern handwritten copy of a 1753 cultivation contract between the tribe and one Cheng I, in Lin Land Records. The document appears to have been transcribed and preserved from historical interest. On the Lins from Ta-li-chi, Yoshida (1911-1913), VI, 82. On the origins of the Wu-feng *chün*, see Lin (1954b), p. 187, and personal communication from staff members of the Ts'ao-t'un *shui-li-hui*.

18. Liu-shu-nan was two miles to the west, Ta-li-chi three miles to the northwest. Central Taiwan did not have the clearly demarcated, discrete "standard marketing areas" of the Skinnerian scheme. See Crissman (1972), p. 238.

19. On the bamboo palisades, communications from staff members of the Wu-feng *hsiang-kung-so*.

20. Communications from villagers and family members. On geomantic beliefs, see Freedman (1966), Ch. v.

21. Lin (1936), Biography of Lin Sun.

22. See remarks by an early nineteenth-century magistrate from Tan-shui, quoted in Lou (1961), p. 163.

23. On the move, Lin (1936), Biography of Lin Chia-yin.

On the fate of his descendants and the subsequent relations of the two branches, personal communications from a descendant of Ch'ung-yao.

24. Unless otherwise indicated, details and quotations relating to his life are from Lin (1936), Biography of Lin Chia-yin.

25. Besides the wild land he opened up, he also bought *hsiao-tsu* titles to cultivated paddy land. Lin Land Records contains the deeds for two parcels he acquired, in 1815 and 1836 respectively, both in Chan-ts'o-yüan, southwest of Ta-li-chi.

26. The customary law in matters of estate division is discussed in Tai (1963), pp. 11-17. Professor Myron Cohen of Columbia University, who has studied many such estate division documents (*chiu-shu*), tells me that the language used here, "he ordered his sons . . ." is standard phraseology. On the disagreements over the division, personal communications from family members.

27. On the fourth son's status, see Lin (1936), Genealogical Tables. The term *ming-ling-tzu* goes back to a phrase in the *Book of Songs*. Such an adopted son may have been the son of his father's mistress or concubine who for some unknown reason did not qualify for the status of a full son. Or else he may have been adopted from outside the surname group. See Tai (1963), pp. 9, 13.

28. Lin (1936), Biography of Lin Wen-ch'a.

29. On economic developments, see Kuo (1973), p. 182.

30. Native degree-holders and their careers in *Chang-hua hsien-chih*, pp. 232-234.

31. On the local academies, see CHHCK, Vol. VIII, *Chiao-yü chih*, pp. 12-13, and Vol. X, *Jen-wu chih*, p. 11. On the mainland scholars, *ibid.*, *passim*. On the district gazetteer and its editors, *ibid.*, pp. 6-7.

32. Ho (1962), p. 182 mentions massive sales of the *chien-sheng* degree at this time; such degrees were particularly numerous among Chang-hua's elite and were, I presume, largely purchased.

33. Two such lists, from 1840 and 1850, in *T'ai-wan chung-pu pei-wen chi-ch'eng*, pp. 133-136 and 144-148.

34. Their role in local defense in CHHCK, Vol. x, *Jen-wu chih, passim,* and as temple sponsors in Lien (1962), pp. 278-281.

35. TWSTCK, Vol. III, *Cheng-shih chih, Chien-chih p'ien,* p. 18.

Notes to Chapter 6

1. Lin (1936), Biography of Lin Tien-kuo.

2. TWSTCK, Vol. IV, *Ching-chi chih, Shui-li p'ien,* pp. 175-177.

3. Their role in local violence in neighboring Tan-shui after Lou (1961), p. 163.

4. On the tradition of private feuding (*hsieh-tou*) see Freedman (1958), pp. 105-113 and Freedman (1966), pp. 104-117.

5. *Chang-hua hsien-chih,* pp. 157-158 and TWSTCK, Vol. II, *Jen-min chih, Tsung-chiao p'ien,* pp. 189-192. Also personal communications from two local historians, Liu Chih-wan and Hung Min-lin.

6. A catalogue of such occasions, many from southeast China, is in Hsiao (1960), pp. 419-433, and contains many useful translations from primary sources.

7. The major incidents are listed in TWSTCK, Vol. II, *Jen-min chih, Jen-k'ou p'ien,* pp. 190-193.

8. On the exodus of the aborigines, Yoshida (1911-1913), VI, 82. Izumi (1929), p. 20, mentions the retreat of two surname groups, presumably Hakkas, from the Wu-feng area to Tung-shih, a Hakka enclave in the district's northeast corner. Major clashes between Hakkas and Fukienese occurred in Chang-hua district in 1809 and 1826 and in Tan-shui in 1826 and 1834. TWSTCK, Vol. II, *Jen-min chih, Jen-k'ou p'ien,* pp. 190-193. Major clashes between Chang-chou and Ch'üan-chou settlers took place in the district in 1806, 1809, and 1844 and in Tan-shui in 1809 and 1833. *Ibid.*

9. On the arrival of new Lins, Izumi (1929), p. 20, and on the Nei-hsin temple, Lin (1962), Part A, p. 149.

10. Lin (1936), Biography of Lin Tien-kuo. On the Hungs, see *Hung-shih tsu-p'u*, *passim*, and on the Lais (clustering around Chiu-she, some six miles north of Ta-li-chi), Ting (1959), p. 582.

11. Thus, Lin landlords built and controlled the T'ou-pien-k'eng *chün* near the center of the emerging Lin turf in the Ta-li-chi area. See Lin (1954b), p. 187. Preferential renting of land to fellow-members of a landlord's communal group is mentioned in a case from the early 1860's in TCSL, p. 14.

12. This is reconstructed from the history of land sales pertaining to sixty-three parcels of land in the emerging Lin turf where ownership can be traced back to 1800. See Lin Land Records.

13. Evidence for this summary view of the *genus t'u-hao* will be found below in the narrative sections on the Lin strongmen and their rivals.

14. I have found no evidence on this matter for Taiwan, but mainland parallels suggest this was the case. It has been said that the hiring of braves provided a species of "outdoor relief" for the rural poor. See Kuhn (1970), p. 160 and *passim*.

15. This is suggested by an episode in Li (1935), p. 250, and by personal communications from Wu-feng residents.

16. Description of a strongman lair from neighboring Chia-yi in the 1870's in Campbell (1915), pp. 87-88, 93. One of the cannons used in the defense of Wu-feng in 1862-1863 is on display in the Lin garden. That the people of Wu-feng manufactured their own, and very excellent, guns was asserted later in the century. See Liu (1969), p. 54. On the fierce dogs that patrolled the lairs, *T'ai-wan shih-ch'ao*, p. 374. On two town-based strongmen who made their last stand in small rural lairs, see the accounts of Hung Ts'ung and Tai Wan-sheng in Ch. 8.

17. On the heroic strand in Chinese culture, see Ruhlman (1960) and Liu (1967).

18. An important proviso, suggested by Professor Myron Cohen, who has discovered similar live-and-let-live arrangements between officials and private power-holders in his research area in south Taiwan.

19. Such tacit alliances must be inferred from the continued flow of the agrarian surplus into the coastal ports, a trade nexus in which both rural strongmen and urban merchants and rentiers had an interest.

20. On the very similar political ambiguity of mainland strongmen, see also Kuhn (1970), *passim*, and especially pp. 170, 199.

21. See Lien (1962), pp. 897-901, and CHHCK, Vol. x, *Jen-wu chih*, p. 75.

22. Unless otherwise indicated, details and quotations relating to his life from Lin (1936), Biography of Lin Tien-kuo.

23. Unless otherwise indicated, details and quotations relating to his life from Lin (1936), Biography of Lin Ting-pang.

24. The term headman (*tsung-li*), used for the leaders of both private and semi-public groupings, *ibid*. In Lien (1962), p. 894, and in Takatori (1919), p. 6a, he is called the head of a rural *chia*, presumably in the *pao-chia* organization.

25. This stipulation from an official source from the Tan-shui area, quoted in Lou (1961), p. 164.

26. Takatori (1919), p. 6a.

27. Lien (1962), p. 894. On the species in general, see Liu (1967).

28. A list of these men who were rewarded for their services is in *Ch'ou-pan i-wu shih-mo hsüan-chi*, pp. 68-69. Mid-Taiwan became peripherally involved in the war through the incident over the brig *Ann*. For details, see Davidson (1903), pp. 103-109, and Yen (1965), pp. 28-43.

29. Details of the incident in Lin (1936), Biography of Lin Ting-pang, and in Takatori (1919), pp. 2a-5b.

30. This detail from a popular tradition is in Li (1935), p. 236.

31. This detail in Takatori (1919), p. 5a, is probably based on the now lost Chinese source he consulted.

32. *Ibid.*, p. 4a.

33. *Ibid.*, pp. 4a-b.

34. This and other details in this paragraph from Lin (1936), Biography of Lin Wen-ch'a.

35. According to Takatori (1919), p. 4a, he succeeded in the first round but came to grief later; according to Lin (1936), Biography of Lin Wen-ch'a, he simply did not take the examination.

36. Lin (1936), Biography of Lin Wen-ch'a.

37. Ch'ü (1961), pp. 78-87, provides a general discussion of blood revenge, including on p. 79 a translation of the *locus classicus* from the *Li Chi*: "A son should not live under the same sky with the enemy of one's father. He should sleep on straw with the bare earth as his pillow. He should resign any official post he might have and concentrate all his energies on seeking vengeance." Lien (1962), pp. 1001-1003, reveals the views of a modern Taiwanese intellectual on the subject.

38. Slightly differing versions of this sequence of events in Lien (1962), p. 894, and Takatori (1919), p. 6b.

39. Details and quotations in this and the next paragraph from Lin (1936), Biography of Lin Wen-ch'a.

40. Personal communication from a Wu-feng resident.

41. Lin (1936), Biography of Lin Wen-ch'a. Local informants report that Ho-shang's exceptionally beautiful young son was also put to death.

42. Lin (1936), Biography of Lin Wen-ch'a. According to Takatori (1919), pp. 7a-b, Wen-ch'a surrendered voluntarily without pressure from a lawsuit. Lin (1936), Biography of Lin Wen-ch'a, credits his release to one Magistrate Kao. Elsewhere it is credited to K'ung Chao-tz'u, a Shantung *chin-shih* and descendant of Confucius then serving in Taiwan. See K'ung's biography in *Ch'ing-shih*, pp. 5314-5315, and in *Ch'ing-shih-kao t'ai-wan ts'ai-liao chi-chi*, p. 947.

43. On the Keelung campaign of 1854, he took two hun-

dred men. See Lin (1936), Biography of Lin Wen-ch'a. Fighting on the mainland eight years later, he took two thousand troops over from Taiwan. See Ch. 7.

44. The connection between geographic mobility and the professionalization of braves is discussed in Kuhn (1970), pp. 166-167. The move within Wu-feng must have been made by 1851. This was revealed by a Wu-feng resident who shared the general amazement that Wen-ch'a's eldest son, born in 1851, enjoyed exceptional success even though he was not born in the auspicious northern palisade.

45. Ts'ai (1964), p. 50, in relation to the early 1860's. This corresponds to the area extending from Wu-feng in the south to at least Ta-li-chi in the north.

46. An observer of the early 1860's describes Wen-ch'a's force as composed of "young fellows from his clan" (Ch'in-tsu tzu-ti). See Ting (1959), p. 581.

47. I have found no systematic listing, but their names crop up in several of Wen-ch'a's biographies and in accounts of his mainland fighting. In addition to several Lins we count three Ch'ens, one Hsieh, one Feng, and one Lai.

48. On this intervention, see Takatori (1919), pp. 8a-b.

49. This was the Fu-hsing-kung. See Ta-li hsiang-kung-so files.

50. Lin (1936), Biography of Lin Wu-hsiang.

51. In 1862, the government conscripted two hundred of his braves. See ibid., Biography of Lin Tien-kuo. Two years later, an official spoke of "several hundred bullies" under his command. See Ting (1959), pp. 582-583. On his feud with the Lais, see Lien (1962), p. 897.

52. Details on these rivalries in Ch. 8. A truce is mentioned in Hung-shih tsu-p'u. Others may be inferred from the fact that Wen-ch'a was able to leave the district and campaign far away.

53. This is mentioned in a memorial by Tso Tsung-t'ang on the reorganization of the Taiwan garrison. Tso (1960), p. 11.

54. Such rebellions are mentioned in *Hsien-feng shih-lu*, *passim*, and in TWSTCK, Vol. II, *Jen-min chih, Jen-k'ou p'ien*, pp. 192-193.

55. The Keelung campaign after Takatori (1919), pp. 7b-8a. The 1858 campaign is the earliest mentioned in Wen-ch'a's official biographies. See *Ch'ing-shih kao*, ch. 216, p. 3b, and *Ch'ing-shih lieh-chuan*, ch. 51, p. 9a.

56. I have evidence for his receiving government funds only for the 1863-1864 Taiwan campaign, for which see Ting (1959), p. 581, and Tso (1960), p. 87. For the earlier years, such support must be assumed. Braves in the Canton area received six dollars and up per month in the 1850's. See Wakeman (1966), pp. 25, 37, 140. Taiwanese braves may well have received more. On cost-of-living differentials later in the century, see Speidel (1967), p. 180.

57. *Ch'ing-shih lieh-chuan*, ch. 51, p. 9a.

58. On concubines, see Lin (1936), Genealogical Tables.

Notes to Chapter 7

1. Takatori (1919), Preface by Shimomura Hiroshi. The "wind and clouds" refers to the Ch'ien diagram of the *I Ching*, emblematic of the elements that bow to the superior man.

2. It had come in the spring from Wang Yi-te, then Min-Che governor-general. See *Ch'ing-shih lieh-chuan*, ch. 51, p. 9a, and Takatori (1919), Chronology.

3. Ting's biographies in Lien (1962), pp. 896-897, and *Huai-ning hsien-chih*, ch. 18, pp. 48b-49b. See also Ting (1959), pp. 3-4.

4. I have found no biography, but he wends his way in and out of the state papers of the 1850's and 1860's. See especially *Hsien-feng shih-lu* and *T'ung-chih shih-lu*, *passim*. On his recommending Wen-ch'a, Lien (1962), p. 894, and Lin (1936), Biography of Lin Wen-ch'a.

5. On Wang's retirement because of illness, see *Hsien-feng shih-lu*, p. 57. On his successor's prior service in Fukien, *ibid.*, *passim*.

6. Their skill is mentioned in *Chung-hsing chiang-shuai pieh-chuan*, ch. 19 *hsia*, p. 6a.

7. Lien (1962), p. 894.

8. On the borrowing of the uniforms, see *Chung-hsing chiang-shuai pieh-chuan*, ch. 19 *hsia*, p. 6a. The figure of 2,000 men relates to the year 1861 and appears in *Ch'ing-shih kao*, ch. 216, p. 4a, and in *P'ing-che chi-lüeh*, ch. 8, p. 1a. On numbers left in Wu-feng, Lin (1936), Biography of Lin Wen-feng.

9. Several sub-commanders are mentioned in *P'ing-che chi-lüeh*, ch. 8, *passim*. Wen-ming's rank in 1862 was lieutenant-colonel. See *Ch'ing-shih lieh-chuan*, ch. 51, p. 10a.

10. On this man, see Lien (1962), p. 896.

11. The Fukien campaigns are mentioned briefly in Wen-ch'a's biographies in Lin (1936), in *Ch'ing-shih kao*, and in *Ch'ing-shih lieh-chuan*, and more fully in Takatori (1919), pp. 8b-14a.

12. According to Ting's biography in Lien (1962), p. 897, they quarreled over military matters; on the credit for the T'ing-chou recovery, see *Ch'ing-shih kao*, ch. 216, p. 4a and *Huai-ning hsien-chih*, ch. 18, p. 49a.

13. The *Min-chün's* exploits in Chekiang are detailed in *P'ing-che chi-lüeh*, ch. 8. Size of the total force calculated from given sizes of various sub-units, *ibid., passim*.

14. General background on the strategic situation in Michael (1966), pp. 164-168.

15. *Ibid.*, p. 167.

16. On Tso's strategy, see Bales (1937), pp. 131-132, 136.

17. The official correspondence concerning the *Min-chün* in TCSL makes this clear.

18. Hummel (1943-1944), p. 764, and Bales (1937), especially map on p. 130.

19. *Ch'ing-shih lieh-chuan*, ch. 51, p. 10a.

20. Such a waiver became virtually necessary since braves fought only under the commanders that had recruited them. The point is brought out in a memorial of Governor-General Ch'ing-tuan in TCSL, p. 23.

21. The major sources such as Wen-ch'a's biographies in

Ch-ing-shih kao, *Ch'ing-shih lieh-chuan*, and *Chung-hsing chiang-shuai pieh-chuan*, and Takatori (1919) as well as *P'ing-che chi-lüeh*, are in agreement on the basic facts although each has its characteristic emphases and omissions.

22. Governor-General Ch'ing-tuan's reports and the throne's responses in TCSL, pp. 21, 27, 31. On Tseng's knowledge, *Ch'ing-shih lieh-chuan*, ch. 51, p. 10a. On the promotions, TCSL, pp. 26, 30.

23. On the transfer, *ibid.*, p. 36. On the minor victories, *P'ing-che chi-lüeh*, ch. 4, p. 1a, which credits him with the recovery of Wu-yi.

24. Takatori (1919), p. 16a.

25. The imperial edict in response to Fukien governor Hsü Tsung-kan's request in TCSL, p. 27.

26. Ch'ing-tuan's dismissal, *ibid.*, p. 28, and criticism of him earlier on pp. 7-8, 10-11. Charges and counter-charges between the two men, pp. 30-32. On Ch'i-ling's bias, pp. 31, 34.

27. *Ibid.*, p. 34.

28. Tso (1960), p. 5; Takatori (1919), p. 16a and Lin (1936), Biography of Lin Wen-ch'a.

29. On the new command, TCSL, p. 40. Takatori (1919), Chronology, gives the date of his return to Fukien as the second month (March 19-April 17).

30. TCSL, p. 43, for the change in the governor-generalship. On Tso, see his biographies in Hummel (1943-1944), pp. 762-767, and Bales (1937).

31. On Tso's assignment, TCSL, p. 32. His views on Wen-ch'a in a letter to Governor Hsü, Tso (1960), pp. 81-82.

32. On Tso's campaign plans, Bales (1937), pp. 153-154. On the new assignment, Takatori (1919), pp. 16b-17a. See also Tso's views on army reform in letters to Wen-ch'a and Governor Hsü, Tso (1960), pp. 3, 85-88.

33. Tso's letter of thanks to Wen-ch'a and orders to the provincial treasurer for another shipment in Tso (1960), pp. 86-87, 89-90.

34. This can be inferred from Tso's reply to the complaints of the deputy-governor of Fukien, Chang Yu-chih. Tso (1960), pp. 90-91.

35. Tso's dissatisfaction with the pace of the Taiwan campaign in letters to Governor Hsü in Tso (1960), pp. 81-86, and memorials paraphrased in TCSL, pp. 48-50. The recommendation of Wen-ch'a to the throne (jointly with Hsü) in Tso (1960), pp. 4-6. Imperial edict confirming the appointment, under date of TC 2/8/15 (September 27, 1863), *ibid.*, pp. 6-7.

36. Michael, in Spector (1964), pp. xxxii-xxxiii, maintains that the rule of avoidance applied only to the officers and not the enlisted men of the Army of the Green Standard. It was certainly not enforced in the Taiwan garrison, many of whose officers were natives of Fukien. See *T'ai-wan t'ung-chih*, pp. 263-338.

37. Tso (1960), p. 5. The court agreed with this line of reasoning. See TCSL, p. 49.

38. Tso (1960), p. 87.

39. Entitled "P'ing-t'ai yao-yen" and dated September 6, 1863, the essay is reprinted in Ting (1959), pp. 417-420.

40. Tso's reply in Tso (1960), pp. 90-91, from which Chang's objections can be inferred.

41. Edict in response to Governor Hsü's memorial in TCSL, p. 52. The initial appointment of early October, some seven weeks earlier, *ibid.*, pp. 49-50.

42. On Wen-ch'a's appointment, see *supra*. The date of Ting's appointment is unknown, but on TC 2/8/25 (October 7, 1863), an edict referred to his recent appointment. See TCSL, p. 50. That Hsü recommended Ting for the post is stated in their respective biographies in Lien (1962), pp. 867 and 896, and seems natural in view of their longstanding patron-client relationship.

43. Fairbank and Teng (1961), p. 25, Table 1.

44. Except for Marsh (1960) and Marsh (1961), I know of no systematic study of this subject.

45. See Hummel (1943-1944) on the background of Liu

Ming-ch'uan, a former salt smuggler, and of Ch'eng Hsüeh-chi and Feng Tzu-t'ai, two ex-rebels, all of whom reached general's rank.

Notes to Chapter 8

1. Ts'ai (1964), p. 54.

2. Kuhn (1970), pp. 117, 153, 164.

3. On his background and role in the rebellion, see his biography in Lien (1962), pp. 883-894, which, along with Wu (1959a) and Ts'ai (1964), is a basic work on the rebellion.

4. Lien (1962), p. 883, speaks of a quarrel with people from Wu-feng; Wu (1959a), p. 55, mentions a quarrel over land with the Lin clan (*Lin hsing*); and Ts'ai (1964), p. 11, speaks of a quarrel between Lin Tien-kuo and the Tais.

5. According to Lien (1962), p. 888, Tseng once tried, in vain, to mediate the Lin-Tai dispute, a fact which suggests that he was on good terms with both sides.

6. Wu (1959a), p. 4, reports the revival of the fighting band under the *T'ien-ti-hui* label, possibly as late as 1861. On the conscription by the magistrate, *ibid.*, and TCSL, p. 1. According to Lien (1962), p. 883, the force was then some three-hundred men strong.

7. Wu (1959a), p. 4.

8. See the folk ballad "Tai Wan-sheng fan-ch'ing ke," in Liao (1960), pp. 23-24.

9. The omens in Wu (1959a), p. 4. The debate in the Chang-hua *yamen* in Liao (1960), pp. 25-26.

10. On his antecedents, see Wu (1959a) and Ts'ai (1964), *passim*.

11. This was Ch'iu Yüeh-chin, then Tan-shui magistrate, who had been posted to Chang-hua to help in the suppression of Tai. Some time earlier, when Ch'iu had held the Chang-hua magistracy as a temporary post, he had tried to apprehend Lin Jih-ch'eng and failed. On this episode and the hatred it left behind in the strongman, see Wu (1959a), p. 5, and Ts'ai (1964), p. 3.

12. On his feuds with Wen-ch'a and Tien-kuo, see Ts'ai (1964), pp. 11, 18, 54, and the folk ballad in Liao (1960), pp. 25-26, 34. Also Wu (1959a), pp. 5, 50, and Lin (1936), Biography of Lin Wen-feng.

13. Ts'ai (1964), p. 18 mentions the colonel's attempt to mediate between him and the Wu-feng strongmen. On his government service, Lien (1962), p. 884. Lin Jih-ch'eng at the time had a force of four-hundred men.

14. On Lin's ability, see Wu (1959a), p. 56. On his political goals, Lien (1962), p. 886.

15. See especially Wu (1959a), pp. 8, 15.

16. Lo's biography in Lien (1962), pp. 905-906.

17. Background on the Hungs in Liu (1959a), pp. 42-63, and *Hung-shih tsu-p'u*. The Hungs joined the rebellion in the fifth month (May 28-June 26).

18. The background of the feud from *Hung-shih tsu-p'u* and from local informants.

19. On the *Szu-ta-hsing*, see *Hung-shih tsu-p'u*. On its temple, built in 1807, TWSTCK, Vol. 1, *T'u-ti chih, Sheng-chi p'ien*, p. 80. On the Hung clan temple, personal communication from Hung Min-lin. It was located in Hsin-chuang, northwest of Ts'ao-t'un.

20. On the *Wan-an-chü*, see *Hung-shih tsu-p'u*, section "Great men of the clan." According to Hung informants, Hung braves had been recruited for service on the mainland.

21. Lin (1936), Biography of Lin Tien-kuo.

22. See Wu (1959a), p. 10. Particulars and quotations in this and the next paragraph from Lin (1936), Biography of Lin Wen-feng. At the time of the siege, Wu-feng is said to have had only seventy-two able-bodied men left.

23. Personal communication from a member of the Lin family. This detail evidently belongs to an oral family tradition. On the role of women in rebel ranks, see also Liao (1960).

24. Lin (1936), Biography of Lin Wen-ch'a.

25. On their help to Wu-feng, Lin (1936), Biography of Lin Wen-feng, and Wu (1959a), p. 44.

26. Details and quotations in this and the next paragraph from Lin (1936), Biography of Lin Wen-feng.

27. The throne had instructed him to do so. See edict of TC 2/10/9 (November 19, 1863) in TCSL, p. 50. Ting's progress southward can be charted from his memorials in Ting (1959) and from edicts acknowledging them in TCSL, *passim*.

28. Lien (1962), p. 891, says this occurred on January 11, 1864 (TC 2/12/3).

29. Wen-ch'a's movements after *Ch'ing-shih lieh-chuan*, ch. 51, p. 11a, and Takatori (1919), pp. 18a-19b. On the number of his braves, see edict of TC 3/1/27 (March 5, 1864), TCSL, p. 58.

30. Wen-ch'a's memorial reporting the victory is summarized in an edict of TC 2/12/29 (February 6, 1864), TCSL, pp. 56-57.

31. Ting's report on the conference in Ting (1959), pp. 444-449. Wen-ch'a's memorials have not survived, but his biography in *Ch'ing-shih lieh-chuan*, ch. 51, p. 11a, gives him credit for the Chang-hua victory on these grounds, suggesting that he himself may have claimed such a feat. *Ch'ing-shih kao*, ch. 216, p. 4a, and Takatori (1919), pp. 18b-19a, merely claim that he contributed troops to the Chang-hua battle. On Ting's counter-charge, see Ting (1959), pp. 447-448.

32. This is reconstructed from the pattern of their associations and mutual support over the next few months. See Ting (1959) and TCSL, *passim*.

33. In an edict of TC 2/12/29 (February 6, 1864), TCSL, p. 56.

34. Ting's memorial, acknowledged in an edict of TC 3/1/27 (March 5, 1864), TCSL, pp. 57-58.

35. See Liao (1960), pp. 34-35, for details of the siege, including the quoted material.

36. See his memorial summarized in an edict of TC 3/3/8 (April 13, 1864), TCSL, p. 61.

37. Wen-ch'a's complaint and the promotion in TCSL, pp. 61-62.

38. Edict of TC 3/3/8 (April 13, 1864), TCSL, p. 61.

39. From Ting's undated letter to Tso, Ting (1959), p. 568.

40. This is suggested by the fact that others acted much like Wen-ch'a and with apparent impunity. For instances, see Wakeman (1966), p. 149, and Perkins (1969), p. 93.

41. Ting often presented charges against Wen-ch'a in private letters to his superiors, Hsü and Tso, weeks before he made them official in a memorial. Compare his letters and the memorial in Ting (1959), pp. 567-568, 570-573, and 462-466.

42. See Tso's letter to Hsü, Tso (1960), p. 92.

43. The May memorial in Ting (1959), pp. 462-466, and especially pp. 463-464. The June follow-up memorial *ibid.*, pp. 467-471.

44. Edict of TC 3/7/18 (August 31, 1864), TCSL, pp. 77-78.

45. The joint memorial by Tso and Hsü is summarized in an edict of 3/8/15 (September 15, 1864), TCSL, pp. 80-81. Tso further sought to calm the waves by urging Hsü to remind Ting "to keep the over-all situation in mind and not to let personality differences create friction." Tso (1960) p. 92. Peking's insistence on the examination in the above edict. Ting's most detailed charges against Wen-ch'a in a letter to Tso, probably of late September, Ting (1959), pp. 580-585.

46. In an anonymous memorial, summarized in the edict of TC 3/8/15 (September 15, 1864), TCSL, pp. 80-81.

47. Peking's earlier orders that troops be returned in TCSL, especially pp. 57-60, 64-66, 68, and 69-71. Wen-ch'a's memorial on the new rebel upsurge in an edict of TC 3/5/11 (June 14, 1864), TCSL, p. 74. Ting's views in a letter to Hsü, Ting (1959), p. 573.

48. Edict of TC 3/8/24 (September 24, 1864), TCSL, pp. 81-83.

49. Governor Hsü's memorial, reporting Wen-ch'a's arrival, is summarized in an edict of TC 3/9/8 (October 8, 1864), TCSL, p. 83.

50. They are in Li (1935), pp. 229-254. Local informants maintain that the Lins tried to prevent the publication of this material.

51. See the "T'u-ti shen-kao-shu" for Wu-feng and adjacent villages. Also Map 6.

52. Li (1935), p. 240, and Lin (1954b), p. 187. As the sequel will show, the Lins are not likely to have had the means to buy or seize these lands after 1870. Acquisition in the 1860's is thus most likely, with the lion's share seized during pacification.

53. The earliest reference to the Lins as owners relates to the period after 1862, when they are said to have repaired the damages to the *chün* sustained in that year, most likely in connection with the hostilities. See Lin (1954b), p. 187.

54. This can be inferred from the high percentage of land the family later owned in Wu-ts'o, the administrative area which encompassed Szu-k'uai-ts'o. According to a personal communication from Hung Min-lin, many of Lin Jih-ch'eng's followers who had been despoiled joined the Hungs in their final stand at Pei-shih-nan.

55. Li (1935), pp. 235-239.

56. For this, we have only the word of Ting Yüeh-chien. See his letters to Governor Hsü and Governor-General Tso and memorial in Ting (1959), pp. 573, 582-583, and 463.

57. Ting's letter to Tso, *ibid.*, especially pp. 583-584. On "Millionaire" Wang, information from Lin relatives in Chang-hua city.

58. Ting (1959), p. 584.

59. *Ibid.*, p. 583.

60. The appropriate statute in Boulais (1966), p. 465. The charges in Ting (1959), p. 584.

61. Personal communication from Wu-feng residents. The Lin Land Records, especially documents T'ien 4 and Ti 11, suggest that the family did take advantage in this way but later made amends. These purchases, at below market prices, occurred in 1854 and 1867 however and cannot be linked directly to the pacification of 1864.

62. The story in Li (1935), p. 240.

63. Examples in Li (1935), pp. 239-240.

64. In a letter to Tso, Ting (1959), p. 584.

65. On details of land holdings and titles, see Ch. 14 below. Since a member of the family served on the local commission which conducted the land survey of 1886-1887, the Lins may have had an opportunity to manipulate the cadasters and make their claims appear *bona fide*. See Ch. 11 below. On average holdings of large landlords elsewhere in China, see Feuerwerker (1969), p. 13.

Notes to Chapter 9

1. Liu (1958), pp. 384-385, an 1885 memorial by Taiwan governor Liu Ming-ch'uan requesting that Wen-ming's case be reopened.

2. On their incursion into Fukien, Michael (1966), pp. 178-179, and Fan (1959), p. 217.

3. Hsü's memorial is summarized in a rescript of TC 3/10/1 (October 30, 1864), TCSL, p. 83, which granted his request. On Wen-ch'a's meeting with the governor, see also *Ch'ing-shih lieh-chuan*, ch. 51, p. 11a, and Takatori (1919), p. 13a.

4. On the two hundred braves, see *Ch'ing-shih lieh-chuan*, ch. 51, pp. 11b-12a, quoting Hsü's and Tso's memorials, which speak of the inadequate number of Wen-ch'a's troops and his hurried recruiting on the mainland. Family sources maintain that friction among the newly recruited braves contributed to the subsequent defeat.

5. The engagement at the pass according to *Ch'ing-shih lieh-chuan*, ch. 51, p. 12a, and Lin (1936), Biography of Lin Wen-ch'a. On the date, I follow Lin (1936), which is consistent with the imperial edict of TC 3/12/1 (December 29, 1864), acknowledging news of Wen-ch'a's death. *Ch'ing-shih lieh-chuan* and Takatori (1919) give slightly differing dates.

6. Lin (1936), Biography of Lin Tien-kuo.

7. On the attempt to flee, personal communication from a family member. On the gunshot wound, see Tso's memorial quoted in TCSL, p. 87. Stories of torture from family members and local informants.

8. The honors are detailed in *Ch'ing-shih kao*, ch. 216, p. 4a, and the other official biographies. Also in TCSL, p. 90.

9. Governor Liu Ming-ch'uan, as quoted in note 1 above.

10. HTHAHL, ch. 12, p. 2a. Tien-kuo's biography in Lin (1936) hints at trouble with the authorities over disbandment pay but stops short of admitting his incarceration. Instead, it claims that Tien-kuo decided on his own not to return to Wu-feng since so many of its sons had died under him.

11. Unless otherwise indicated, details and quotations bearing on Wen-feng's life are from Lin (1936), Biography of Lin Wen-feng.

12. *Ibid.*, Biography of Lin Tien-kuo.

13. Personal communication from family members.

14. *Ibid.*

15. *Ibid.*

16. Before leaving Taiwan, Wen-ch'a had turned over certain pacification duties to Wen-ming, an assignment which the throne routinely noted in an edict of TC 3/8/24 (September 24, 1864), TCSL, p. 82. Responding to a memorial by Ting which had criticized Wen-ming's pacification measures, the throne in an edict of TC 3/10/5 (November 3, 1864) cancelled Wen-ming's assignment. TCSL, p. 84.

17. Li (1935), pp. 250-251, speaks of a family force of "several thousand" in the spring of 1870, just after Wen-ming's death. The lack of official funds and the fact that Wen-ming did not operate far from home points to the largely part-time, semi-professional character of his army.

18. Details in Li (1935), *passim*.

19. On the local manufacture of rifles, see a statement from the 1880's in Liu (1969), p. 54. Most likely, this skill had been developed earlier. On the cannon in the hillsides, HTHAHL, ch. 12, p. 1b.

20. See the story in Lien (1962), pp. 1001-1003, presumably from the late 1860's.

21. On the Hungs, see *Hung-shih tsu-p'u* and information from Hung clan members. On the Shu-tzu-chiao strongman and his offering refuge to Wu-feng's enemies, personal communication from a descendant.

22. On Wen-ming's role in this project as well as details concerning Lin Wu-hsiang, see Lin (1936), Biography of Lin Wu-hsiang. On the origins of the Lin clan temple, Lin (1962), Part A, p. 149.

23. On this Lin branch's control of the *chün*, see Lin (1954b), p. 187. On Lin Wu-hsiang's association with Wen-ch'a during the pacification, see Ting (1959), p. 583.

24. Details in Wu (1961), pp. 32-33.

25. Ta-li (1938).

26. The episode is described in Lin (1936), Biography of Lin Wen-feng.

27. See a memorial by Fukien governor Ting Jih-ch'ang in *Peking Gazette*, May 8, 1877.

28. Li (1935), p. 235.

29. Biographical data in CHHCK, Vol. x, *Jen-wu chih*, pp. 62-63. Assessments of his character in Wu (1959a), p. 31, and Ts'ai (1964), pp. 23, 25. On his quarrel with Wen-ch'a, Li (1935), pp. 241-246. On his Feng-shan post, *Feng-shan-hsien ts'ai-feng ts'e*, p. 197.

30. On Wen-ming's removal, see citations in note 16 above and Ting's memorial in Ting (1959), pp. 472-474. Ting's role in the arrest of Tien-kuo is mentioned in HTHAHL, ch. 12, p. 2a.

31. His title of *wei-yuan ibid., passim*.

32. Ting's biography in *Huai-ning hsien-chih*, ch. 18, p. 49b, states that he lived in Nanking when his tour of duty in Taiwan was over. That he served in Fukien, if only briefly, is implied in Lien (1962), pp. 896-897, and in CHHCK, Vol. x, *Jen-wu chih*, p. 72.

33. Ling's initiative is described in Li (1935), pp. 246-247. The chance encounter according to a Wu-feng resident.

34. Date and charges are mentioned in a later appeal by Wen-ming's mother, quoted in *Shen-pao*, p. 754. Lien (1962), pp. 896-897, reports that Hungs and Lais also sued. A somewhat different version of the charges is in a memorial by Governor-General Ying-kuei, TC 9/5/6 (June 4, 1870), TCSL, p. 126. The plaintiff's name is here given as Lin Ying-yüan.

35. The family's defense against the charge in Mrs. Tai's appeal quoted in *Shen-pao*, pp. 605-606.

36. Li (1935), p. 236.

37. Details in TCSL, pp. 99, 105.

38. HTHAHL, ch. 12, p. 1b, mentions the appointment but without throwing light on how it came about. Lien (1962), pp. 896-897, and CHHCK, Vol. x, *Jen-wu chih*, p. 72, state that Ting arranged for the appointment. Li (1935), p. 247, maintains that Ling obtained the post through a bribe.

39. His earlier positions in Fukien from TCSL, *passim*.

40. Ying-kuei's verdict from his memorial that is summarized in an edict of TC 9/5/6 (June 4, 1870), TCSL, p. 126. According to HTHAHL, ch. 12, p. 1b, Ying-kuei's decision was more cautious; he ordered the apprehension and trial of the law breaker. The steps leading up to Ying-kuei's verdict and the assignment to Li Chao-t'ang from HTHAHL, ch. 12, p. 1b.

41. Li's background from the biography in the gazetteer of his native district in Kwangtung, *Shun-te hsien-chih*, ch. 18, pp. 17b-21a. While holding the Taiwan post, Li summarily executed a fellow-provincial from Kwangtung, a military officer stationed in Taiwan, in what looks like a personal vendetta. Details in TCSL, p. 127; *Ch'ou-pan i-wu shih-mo hsüan-chi*, pp. 376-379; and Pickering (1898), pp. 94-96.

42. The term is used in Li (1935), p. 250, and in the appeal by Wen-ming's mother quoted in *Shen-pao*, p. 864.

43. Ts'ai (1964), p. 35, reports this episode in a context completely divorced from the Lin story.

44. On his Chang-hua assignment, see HTHAHL, ch. 12, p. 1b and Li (1935), p. 248. According to Li (1935), it was Intendant Li who made this assignment in view of Ling's familiarity with the district.

45. On the Hungs and Ts'ao-hu Lins, Li (1935), p. 248. Some members of the Hung clan still express pride in their ancestors' role in this act of revenge.

46. This version in Li (1935), p. 229, and in Mrs. Tai's appeal quoted in *Shen-pao*, p. 754.

47. See HTHAHL, ch. 12, p. 1b, for the picture conveyed to Intendant Li, presumably by Ling.

48. Text of the proclamation in the appeals by Mrs. Tai quoted in *Shen-pao*, pp. 605, 754. On delaying its publication to a suitable moment, HTHAHL, ch. 12, p. 1b.

49. The government's final official version of the case (HTHAHL, ch. 12, p. 1b) claims that Intendant Li at this point contacted the governor-general, requesting that Ying-kuei impeach Wen-ming and ask to have him stripped of his official rank preparatory to his execution. It does not claim that Ying-kuei carried out this request or that the intendant's proclamation was insufficient to sanction Wen-ming's execution. Indeed there is no evidence in TCSL that Li or Ying-kuei sought a broader authorization than the proclamation for putting Wen-ming to death. Ying-kuei's first communication to the throne in the matter occurred *after* Wen-ming had been slain. See his memorial summarized in an edict of TC 9/5/6 (June 4, 1870), TCSL, p. 126.

50. On procedural safeguards, see Bodde and Morris (1967), p. 131, "Noteworthy, and probably a heritage from Confucianism, is the insistence in Chinese law on careful scrutiny of every capital case at the highest level, including imperial ratification, before life may be taken."

51. The emergency provisions and the debate about their abolition can be reconstructed from memorials and edicts in *Peking Gazette*, in particular the issues of June 17, August 28, September 3, 10, 26, October 9-10, 30, Novem-

ber 6, 30, 1874; November 19, December 3, 11, 1881; January 7, 14, 25, February 4, 6, March 19, April 1, 7, 23, May 14, June 1, 30, July 12, 1882. The subject has not been studied except for a student paper done under professor Randle Edwards of the Columbia Law School, who made the paper available to me and provided a number of clarifications on this and the next chapter.

52. From a censor's memorial quoted in *Peking Gazette*, September 3, 1874.

53. The episode from Li (1935), pp. 229, 248-250. It is not clear what festival this was. The birthday of Ma-tsu on 3/23 (April 23 in 1870) falls too late to fit the events.

54. On the visit, Li (1935), pp. 229-230, and Mrs. Tai's appeals quoted in *Shen-pao*, pp. 605, 754, and 863. HTHAHL, ch. 12, p. 1b, agrees that Ling's "guidance" resulted in Wen-ming's court appearance, but differs in other respects.

55. On this detail, see Li (1935), p. 230, and Liu Ming-ch'uan's memorial in Liu (1958), p. 385. The family made much of this point as proof of Wen-ming's peaceable intent.

56. Li (1935), pp. 230-232, from which the following account is taken. Its basic agreement with the family version of the events is all the more significant since the source is by no means pro-Lin family and gives very graphic details of the depredations of the Lin strongmen. Some of the themes of the story, such as that of the doors shutting and separating the villain from his men, have been used elsewhere in Chinese fiction, such as the stories that deal with the good and clever judge Pao-kung.

57. On this punishment, see Bodde and Morris (1967), p. 97.

58. Li (1935), p. 232, and Mrs. Tai's appeals quoted in *Shen-pao*, pp. 605-606, 754, and 863.

59. The mood of the city in Li (1935), p. 232.

60. On their failure to press for restoration of the stolen property, see Ch. 10. Their slanted reporting to their

superiors began almost immediately, as we can reconstruct from the earliest known official account, Governor-General Ying-kuei's memorial, summarized in the edict of TC 9/5/6 (June 4, 1870), TCSL, p. 126. Ying-kuei seems to have been told that Wen-ming had attacked the *yamen*, but not that he was dead. This report, predictably, evoked his order for Wen-ming's execution. It looks, then, as if the officials not only misrepresented the story of who attacked first, but reported the facts selectively so as to obtain Ying-kuei's legitimation for an "execution" that had already taken place.

Notes to Chapter 10

1. From a *Shen-pao* editorial on the Wen-ming case, February 15, 1878. *Shen-pao*, p. 762.

2. Lin (1936), Biography of Lin Wen-feng.

3. Credit for restraint goes to Wen-feng, see *ibid.*, and to Mrs. Tai in HTHAHL, ch. 12, p. 2b. Li (1935), pp. 250-251, credits a local *tsung-li* from near Chang-hua with turning the troop back en route.

4. See his biography in Lin (1936).

5. See HTHAHL, ch. 12, p. 3a, where Ling Ting-kuo and Wang Wen-ch'i, the regular Chang-hua magistrate, are criticized for their failure to press this matter.

6. See Ying-kuei's memorial summarized in the edict of TC 9/5/6 (June 4, 1870), TCSL, p. 126. This account is not only incomplete, as we have noted above, but is in important respects at variance with the later official version in HTHAHL.

7. Boulais (1966), pp. 465-466, gives the statutory provisions. That the law was no dead letter is clear from the *Peking Gazette* of November 28, 1877, which reports that the young son of a convicted and executed rebel was statutorily castrated upon reaching puberty.

8. On his stay in Peking and post with the Board of War—he was a *lang-chung* or department director, with rank 5A—see Lin (1936), Biography of Lin Ch'ao-tung.

9. Mrs. Tai's personal presence in Foochow is mentioned in her appeals quoted in *Shen-pao*, pp. 605, 754, and 865. Family members report that Ch'ao-hsüan similarly spent time in the provincial capital in connection with the litigation.

10. The descendants of Tien-kuo, by then also enmeshed in the litigation (see below), established ties with Liu Ao through Wen-ch'in, Wen-feng's youngest brother. Ch'ao-tung established ties with Governor Ts'en and exerted himself on the Ta-chia marsh draining project. See Lin (1936), Biography of Lin Ch'ao-tung. On his approach to the governor in the matter of the lawsuit, see HTHAHL, ch. 12, p. 2b.

11. Tso (1960), a collection of his letters and memorials concerning Taiwan, contains nothing relating to the lawsuit.

12. P'eng's role as intercessor in Li (1935), p. 254. His biography in Hummel (1943-1944), pp. 617-620. Whether he had ever met Wen-ch'a or Wen-ming on the mainland is unknown. There may have been a connection between P'eng and the Lin brothers through Li Yüan-tu, like P'eng a member of Tseng Kuo-fan's circle, and whom Wen-ch'a seems to have known during the Chekiang fighting in the winter of 1861-1862. See TCSL, p. 11.

13. Personal communication from family members. The man's biography in TWSTCK, Vol. VII, *Jen-wu chih*, II, 188-189.

14. A conclusion based on negative evidence—the absence of any references to a Lin force in contemporary local records.

15. See Lin (1936), *passim*, and personal communications from family members.

16. Lin Land Records, Document T'ien 4. The compensation payment was made in 1878. Other such cases date from the 1880's, after the end of the litigation.

17. The subscription list and related data in *T'ai-wan chung-pu pei-wan chi-ch'eng*, p. 158.

18. My reconstruction of how this system worked is

based on memorials in the *Peking Gazette, passim*. I have also reviewed the subject with Professor Randle Edwards. The discussion in Bodde and Morris (1967) often fails to distinguish between the automatic review procedure mandated by law and the appeals procedure initiated by a private appellant.

19. One such reiteration is in *Peking Gazette*, April 8, 1877. Professor Edwards informs me that this prohibition had been issued repeatedly earlier, apparently without effect.

20. *Peking Gazette*, August 18, 1875. Similar views on July 20 and December 18, 1875.

21. Metzger (1973), pp. 276-287 discusses the types of offenses and their punishments.

22. On the unhealthy prisons, see censors' complaints in *Peking Gazette*, July 20, 1875; January 25-28, 1876; and March 13, 1881. On the risk of torture and punishments for an unsuccessful appeal, see Bodde and Morris (1967), pp. 97-98, 118.

23. For categories of persons privileged at the bar of justice, see Boulais (1966), pp. 32-33; on the privileges extended to the old, see *ibid*., pp. 716, 74-75. Because of these exemptions from the full rigor of the law, Professor Edwards tells me, Mrs. Tai should actually have been precluded from acting as an appellant. Why she was nevertheless allowed to appeal is unclear.

24. On the types of expenses likely to arise for a Chinese litigant, see Van der Sprenkel (1962), pp. 70, 138. On the family's financial sacrifices in connection with the lawsuit, see the memorial by Liu Ming-ch-uan, Liu (1958), p. 383, personal communications from family members, and Ch. 14 below.

25. Bodde and Morris (1967), p. 118.

26. I have only checked out the more accessible translated novels such as *Chin P'ing Mei, Dream of the Red Chamber, The Scholars*, and *The Travels of Lao Ts'an*. Leaving out plain attempts at the bribery of a judge, instances of such personal approaches to judges occur in *Chin P'ing*

Mei, pp. 128, 180, 308, 399, 783; in Ts'ao (1958), pp. 526, 544, 546; in Wu (1957), pp. 553-554; and in Liu (1952), pp. 48, 167, 179, 216. On the importance of personal connections when faced with a lawsuit, see also Folsom (1968), pp. 37-38.

27. See TCSL, *passim* on personnel changes at the provincial level.

28. This first appeal is the only one for which I have not found the full text. A summary appears in an edict of TC 10/9/9 (October 22, 1871), TCSL, pp. 135-136, and references to it are in the later appeals.

29. There is no suggestion in the relevant memorials or edicts of the 1870's that this or the subsequent appeals were in any way procedurally defective. Nevertheless, the case was eventually placed in the *yüeh-su* (Cases improperly presented at the highest tribunals) section of HTHAHL.

30. The delays and their causes are mentioned in HTHAHL, ch. 12, p. 3a, and in Mrs. Tai's later appeals as quoted in *Shen-pao*, especially pp. 754 and 864. The turnover of judicial officials from TCSL, *passim*.

31. This is mentioned in Mrs. Tai's second appeal, *Shen-pao*, p. 605. One has to assume that she would not misrepresent such a simple matter, easily verified by the Censorate.

32. A charge made in Mrs. Tai's second appeal, quoted *ibid.*, p. 606. The available documentation is too sparse to permit a definitive confirmation of such tampering, but indirect evidence points strongly in that direction. Thus, the discrepancies between Ying-kuei's memorial of June 1870 and the final official version of 1882 (in HTHAHL) probably resulted from an attempt, on the part of the implicated officials, to adapt the official record to whatever was required in the light of the family's accusations as presented in successive appeals.

33. The text is presumably the same that we find in HTHAHL, ch. 12, p. 1b.

34. A charge made in Mrs. Tai's second appeal, *Shen-pao*, p. 606. There is no evidence that such a charge had ever

been levied against Wen-ming during his lifetime. Mrs. Tai argued that the officials pinned this crime on her son when the charges stemming from the 1867 lawsuit had been successfully refuted by her and when the officials were therefore anxious to find grounds for the extraordinarily harsh punishment (as they called it) of Wen-ming. The multiple murder charge had the advantage, from their point of view, that this crime was punishable, as was rebellion, as one of the "ten abominations." Wen-ming's exposed head could thus be justified as due punishment for a multiple murderer.

35. The memorial is summarized in an edict of TC 13/8/1 (September 11, 1874), TCSL, p. 163.

36. His negligence in the case would presumably fall under the rubric of the lighter offenses. See Metzger (1973), pp. 278, 300.

37. His positions in the 1870's from *Ch'ing-shih*, Vol. IV, Tables of Metropolitan Officials, and *Peking Gazette*, September 10, 1874.

38. See his biographies in *T'ai-wan t'ung-chih*, p. 351 and in *Shun-te hsien-chih*, ch. 18, pp. 17b-21b. On his removal from the Taiwan post, edict of TC 10/4/10 (May 28, 1871), TCSL, p. 134.

39. Shen's biography in Hummel (1943-1944), pp. 642-644.

40. I have found no evidence in Li's biographies or anywhere else for the statement in Folsom (1968), p. 174, that Li became acting Taiwan intendant during the Taiwan crisis of 1874-1875.

41. See Li's biography in *Shun-te hsien-chih*, ch. 18, p. 20a. On the importance of this post, see Spector (1964), pp. 136-138, and Folsom (1968), p. 173.

42. Examples in Feuerwerker (1958), p. 156; Spector (1964), p. 58; and Folsom (1968), pp. 117-118, 152.

43. A memorial of Ting Jih-ch'ang from June 1876 explains that Ling had held the post since 1874. *Shen-pao*, pp. 616-617.

44. Wang K'ai-t'ai, acting governor of Fukien from 1870

to 1874, was close to Li Hung-chang. See Spector (1964), pp. 63-64, 318; and Kuo (1973), p. 188. Hsia Hsien-lun, the Taiwan intendant from 1873 to 1879, was part of the shipyard circle around Shen Pao-chen. See Rawlinson (1967), pp. 54, 105-106. Chou Mou-ch'i, the prefect from 1871 to 1876, later served in the naval yard and subsequently under Li Hung-chang in Tientsin. See Rawlinson (1967), p. 224, n. 27, and Folsom (1968), p. 177.

45. Her two appeals are reproduced fully in the memorials of the censors which in turn were reprinted in *Shen-pao*, pp. 605-607 and 753-755.

46. Under the date of KH 4/1/14 (February 15, 1878), *ibid.*, pp. 761-763.

47. His official biography from *Ch'ing-shih kao* is reprinted in *Ch'ing-shih kao t'ai-wan ts'ai-liao chi-chi*, pp. 865-866. See also *Ch'ing-shih*, pp. 5029-5030. On his ties to Li Hung-chang, Folsom (1968), pp. 74, 167. The Lins thought him hopelessly biased because of his *t'ung-hsiang* ties to Li Chao-t'ang—both men were from Shun-te district. On the family's attitude, see Liu (1958), p. 383.

48. *Shun-te hsien-chih*, ch. 18, p. 20b.

49. This is charged by Mrs. Tai in her third appeal, *Shen-pao*, p. 754.

50. We find Mrs. Tai defending the family against the new charges in her fourth appeal of the summer of 1879 (*Shen-pao*, pp. 864-865) but not in her third appeal of late 1877. This helps to fix the date of the renewed litigation. Compared with the 1867 suit, Lin Ying-shih's charges of land robbery against the Lins had now been recast. He more than doubled the figure for his loss, from 6,000 to 14,000 *Yüan*, and he no longer connected the robbery with the pacification.

51. Summary in an edict of KH 4/12/26 (January 18, 1879) in *Kuang-hsü shih-lu*, p. 52. Judging from Wen-feng's personality, the new charges had little merit.

52. Lin (1936), Biography of Lin Wen-feng.

53. The list of Wen-ming's crimes was substantially re-

tained in the final official verdict on the case, HTHAHL, ch. 12, pp. 2a-b. The finding on Wen-feng and the report to Foochow, *ibid*., p. 2a.

54. Compare the case of Wen-ming's alleged abduction of Lin Ying-shih's sister-in-law in HTHAHL, ch. 12, p. 2a, and in Li (1935), pp. 238-239. Hsia's simplistic reporting is evident.

55. Wen-feng's disappearance in HTHAHL, ch. 12, p. 3a. According to a censor's memorial quoted in *Shen-pao*, p. 865, the complaining brother was Lin Wen-luan, identified as a son of Tien-kuo and brother of Wen-feng. This same individual is mentioned in HTHAHL, ch. 12, p. 3a, as making an appeal on behalf of the jailed Tien-kuo. His identity remains unclear since the genealogy lists no such person, but rather describes Wen-feng himself as defending his father in court, and family interests in Peking.

56. Lin (1936), Biography of Lin Wen-feng.

57. The particulars in a memorial by Ho Ching, *Peking Gazette*, September 28, 1879.

58. Lin (1936), Biography of Lin Wen-feng.

59. The story is still told locally.

60. Concerning Ho's reliance on Lin and Ling, see HTHAHL, ch. 12, p. 2a.

61. His memorial in *Peking Gazette*, November 12, 1879.

62. The petition by *chü-jen* Ch'iu Min-kuang and others is summarized in an edict to the cabinet of KH 6/3/29 (May 7, 1880), *Kuang-hsü shih-lu*, p. 69.

63. I know of no treatment of the topic of change of venue in the relevant literature. I have reconstructed official attitudes from memorials in *Peking Gazette*, January 10 and February 8-9, 1876; March 19, 1877; and February 10-11 and 24, 1881.

64. *Peking Gazette*, May 8, 1880.

65. Divisions in the family are described in Liu Ming-ch'uan's memorial requesting that the case be reopened. See Liu (1958), p. 383.

66. Li (1935), p. 254, mentions P'eng's role. The inter-

cession by the Han-lin compiler, Ho Ch'in-shou, and by two censors, Wu Hung-en and K'ung Hsien-ku, is mentioned in Liu (1958), p. 384, though without indication of a date.

67. HTHAHL, ch. 12, p. 2a, indicates that Ch'ao-tung had accepted the final formula before Ho Ching submitted it to Peking.

68. They are embodied in Ho Ching's memorials as reprinted in HTHAHL, ch. 12, pp. 1a-3a. An edict approving the terms and reprinted in *Peking Gazette*, August 26, 1882, allows us to pinpoint the date.

69. The term is "*kuo-tang.*" See HTHAHL, ch. 12, p. 2b.

70. Information from local informants, including a descendant of Lin Ying-shih.

71. So did his colleague, the Taiwan brigade general, Yang Tsai-yüan, who had co-signed the proclamations against Wen-ming. Since the Lins in their appeals did not dwell on his responsibility, I have not pursued his role in the conspiracy or the cover-up. He seems to have had an unsavory career in the Taiwan garrison, including two dismissals for embezzlement and other offenses. Ho Ching brought him back into the service. Mention of him in *Shen-pao*, pp. 9, 639, 688; in Ho's biography in *Ch'ing-shih kao t'ai-wan ts'ai-liao chi-chi*, p. 866, and in *Kuang-hsü-chao tung-hua hsü-lu hsüan-chi*, p. 55.

72. *Shun-te hsien-chih*, ch. 18, p. 18b.

73. HTHAHL, ch. 12, p. 3a. On Ling's disgrace for embezzlement on the An-p'ing job, see details in *Peking Gazette*, May 7 and 23, 1876, and *Shen-pao*, pp. 616-617.

74. Liu (1958), p. 384.

75. Awards in HTHAHL, ch. 12, pp. 2b-3a, and *Peking Gazette*, August 26, 1882.

76. HTHAHL, ch. 12, p. 2b.

77. The response to Liu's intercession in Liu (1958), p. 385.

Notes to Chapter 11

1. Lin (1936), Biography of Lin Wen-ch'in.

2. Yen (1965), Gordon (1970), and Kuo (1973) provide highlights.

3. See *ibid.* and Gordon (1965).

4. Kuo (1973) and reform memorials in *Peking Gazette*, *passim*.

5. Hsü (1975) provides an overview; Eastman (1967) a detailed analysis of Chinese policy.

6. A brief biography is in Hummel (1943-1944), pp. 526-528. His achievements in Taiwan are detailed in Ch'u (1963), Speidel (1967), and Speidel (1976).

7. Hummel (1943-1944), p. 526, mentions Liu's heading "a band of freebooters" engaged in salt smuggling and his murder of a rich villager. A local pattern which connects private power and feuding with salt smuggling and political dissidence can be gleaned from references in Chiang (1954), pp. 15-20 and from Kuhn (1970), pp. 179-180. None of Liu's biographers has delved into this early period.

8. I use the Western term to refer to the treaty port near Taipei and the Wade-Giles transliteration, Tan-shui, to refer to the sub-prefecture.

9. See Liu (1969), pp. 53-54.

10. Lin (1936), Biography of Lin Wen-ch'in. Action in the southern theater according to Davidson (1903), pp. 235-236. The political consequences for Wen-ch'in are mentioned below.

11. Lin (1936), Biography of Lin Ch'ao-tung.

12. Details *ibid.*, and in Liu (1958), pp. 181-197, 374-377.

13. Concerning such efforts, see a contemporary poem which contrasts Liu's ineffectual leadership with the bravery of the Lin soldiers, in Lai (1958b), p. 40. By a patriotic poet from Chia-yi, it may have been connected with Liu Ao's attack on Liu Ming-ch'uan.

14. Speidel (1967), p. 66.

15. His rewards in *Kuang-hsü shih-lu*, p. 197. On his wife's honors, see the biography of her son in TWSTCK, Vol. VII, *Jen-wu chih,* III, 9.

16. Liu's reform efforts have been discussed in Ch'u (1963), Speidel (1967), and Speidel (1976).

17. See Speidel (1967), pp. 186-187. On the dismissals, *ibid.*, p. 210, n. 5, and Liu (1958), pp. 339, 379.

18. The terms "Tung battalions" and "Tung Army" occur in Liu Ming-ch'uan's memorials and elsewhere. According to Takatori (1919), p. 25a, the Tung Army on occasion included as many as thirteen battalions.

19. The force's loyalty was to Ch'ao-tung personally, yet he did not use it for private vendettas and spoliations. Hence the term "semi-private."

20. *Ch'ing-shih kao*, ch. 216, p. 4a and *Chung-hsing chiang-shuai pieh-chuan*, ch. 19 *hsia*, p. 3b, refer to his troops as *"chia-ping,"* "house-soldiers"; Lai (1958b), p. 40, calls them *"Lin-chia hsiang-yung,"* "local braves of the house of Lin"; Liu Ao's call for recruits had spoken of Lin clansmen. See Liu (1969), p. 54. Among sub-commanders, I have identified a son, a brother-in-law, two cousins, and assorted notables from the district, both Lins and non-Lins. See Wu (1959a), pp. 97, 101-102; Wu (1959b), pp. 41-42, and Liu (1958), p. 190.

21. Lin (1936), Biography of Lin Ch'ao-tung. On the Secretariat, Speidel (1967), pp. 174 and 208, n. 45.

22. Wu (1959b), p. 49, and communications from family members.

23. Speidel (1967), p. 276.

24. Detailed reports in Liu (1958), pp. 199-201, 204-208.

25. *Ibid.*, especially pp. 207-208.

26. *Ibid.*, pp. 209-216, 219. Also Liu (1969), p. 267.

27. Speidel (1967), p. 291.

28. Rewards for the first and second campaign in *Kuang-hsü shih-lu*, pp. 214, 219-220. For Ch'ao-tung, they included raises in rank and military decorations like the

Baturu title. On Liu's tarnished image, Speidel (1967), pp. 306-307.

29. Details in Liu (1958), pp. 222-223.

30. Lists of such bureaus in Lien (1962), pp. 476-479, and Speidel (1967), pp. 106-109. Service in such bureaus was exempt from the "law of avoidance" which otherwise forbade official service in one's native province.

31. Takatori (1919), p. 25a, states that Ch'ao-tung did not serve under Liu's successors. I have found evidence of only one minor service rendered in connection with aborigine control after Liu's departure and before the crisis of 1895. See *Kuang-hsü-chao tung-hua`hsü-lu hsüan-chi*, pp. 157-158. On his loyalty to Liu as a factor in the 1895 decision, Liu (1958), p. 40.

32. See Liu (1958), pp. 439-440. The titles Wen-ch'in lost were probably minor purchased ones. An account of the entire Liu-Liu imbroglio in Speidel (1967), pp. 53-58, and, more favorably to Liu Ao, in Lien (1962), pp. 921-924.

33. See Speidel (1967), p. 447.

34. Liu (1969), pp. 100-102, has details. On the road pattern, see Speidel (1967), p. 118.

35. Lien (1962), p. 261. A detailed history of the development of the city is in Pannell (1973).

36. Speidel (1967), p. 120.

37. From a poem on the deserted site in Lai (1958a), p. 72.

38. Kuo (1973), p. 232.

39. On Ch'ao-tung's post, see Lin (1936), Biography of Lin Ch'ao-tung and Lien (1964), p. 220. On camphor and the government camphor monopoly, see Davidson (1903), Ch. XXIV.

40. Lin (1936), Biography of Lin Wen-ch'in. On the role of the gentry in the land survey, Speidel (1967), p. 222, and Lien (1962), p. 904.

41. Lin Wei-yüan's influence on the governor in Speidel (1967), p. 249.

42. The background and course of the rebellion in Lien (1962), pp. 877-882, and Wu (1959a). Ch'ao-tung's campaign in Wu (1959a), pp. 101-102, and Lin (1936), Biography of Lin Ch'ao-tung.

43. On landlord sympathies, see Speidel (1967), pp. 231-232.

44. Lin (1936), Biography of Lin Ch'ao-tung, maintains that he was the only expectant *tao-t'ai* in China to earn this honor, a claim I have not attempted to verify.

45. Communication from family members.

46. See Hsü (1975), Ch. XIV, for an overview of military and diplomatic developments.

47. Woodside (1963), pp. 165-166; Lamley (1964), pp. 166, 178-180; and Lamley (1970), pp. 32-33.

48. On the complex maneuvers of the next few weeks, I have consulted the works cited in the previous note as well as Lamley (1968) and, among Chinese sources, Wu (1959b), Hung (1959), Lin (1954a) and *Chung-jih chancheng*.

49. Biographies in Hummel (1943-1944), pp. 171-172, and in CHHCK, Vol. x, *Jen-wu chih*, pp. 174-175. His home was in northeastern Chang-hua, near Feng-yüan. On his ties to the Lins, personal communication from a family member.

50. Lin (1954a), p. 189.

51. Their hopes must have been buoyed by the Triple Intervention of late April in which Russia, France and Germany demanded that Japan retrocede the Liaotung peninsula to China. Details in Hsü (1975), p. 422.

52. Local followers in mid-Taiwan urged Ch'iu to assume the title of *"tung-tu ta-wang"* (Great King of the Eastern Capital) in direct succession to Koxinga. Woodside (1963), p. 187.

53. On this episode, see Wu (1959b), p. 32; Woodside (1963), p. 181; and Lamley (1964), pp. 149, 166-167.

54. Ch'ao-tung's feelings according to Hung (1959), p. 4.

55. On the chaos in Taipei, Lin (1954a), p. 192, and Lamley (1964), pp. 175-176.

56. T'ang's cables and Ch'ao-tung's response in Wu (1959b), pp. 39-40. Ch'iu Feng-chia too was being asked to come north once more. The concurrent proposal to T'ang, though not originating with Ch'ao-tung, was probably known to him. See Woodside (1963), p. 184.

57. He had reached Hou-lung, one of the towns whose garrison he had commanded under Liu Ming-ch'uan. This and Ch'ao-tung's subsequent moves reconstructed from Wu (1959b), p. 43. By a gentry member from Chang-hua, this account gives the best mid-Taiwanese perspective on this turbulent period.

58. On the family's evacuation, *ibid.*, p. 42. A poem by Ch'ao-tung's eldest son, commemorating the flight, is in Lamley (1964), p. 240. Concerning the Lin convoy, Hung (1959), p. 5, explains in one of his characteristically barbed references to the Lins that the Lin soldiers behaved in such exemplary fashion only because they had recently received their government pay.

59. These events reconstructed from Hung (1959), pp. 5-6.

60. On his motives, see Lin (1936), Biography of Lin Ch'ao-tung, and Liu (1958), p. 40.

61. Details in Hung (1959), pp. 13, 31. The author comments in a critical tone on the Lins's reluctance to join the anti-Japanese resistance, especially in view of the provocative behavior of the Japanese during their takeover of Wu-feng. Wen-ch'in remained behind, due to his mother's inability to travel. The rest of his household, counting upwards of forty persons, had left for Ch'üan-chou, led by Wen-ch'in's eldest son, the fourteen-year-old Lin Hsien-t'ang. See Yeh (1960), entry for 1895.

62. The date is approximate. Wu (1959b), p. 49, and *Chung-jih chan-cheng*, Vol. I, p. 133, point to June 24 or 25.

63. On the Japanese take-over of the Upper Valley,

Hung (1959), pp. 13, 31. Only in T'an-tzu, north of the Lin family turf, did a minor strongman, one Lin Ta-ch'un, offer resistance. See Wu (1959b), pp. 58, 63. On the battle of Pa-kua-*shan*, *ibid*., p. 59.

64. Lin (1936), Biography of Lin Ch'ao-tung. The Japanese resented the exiles' failure to return. Lamley (1964), p. 457.

65. The Tung Army units which reached Hsin-chu joined in the fight against the Kwangtung braves there. See Hung (1959), p. 6, and Wu (1959b), p. 42.

Notes to Chapter 12

1. Lin (1936), Biography of Lin Wen-ch'in.

2. Chang (1955a), pp. 100, 111. On the gentry's legal privileges, see Ch'ü (1961), pp. 128-154, 178-183.

3. On this rank and its heritability, see Brunnert and Hagelstrom (1911), No. 944, and Ho (1962), p. 24. Ch'ü (1961), pp. 152-153, 185 on the extension of privilege to family members.

4. On these titles, see Lin (1936), Genealogical Tables and Biography of Lin Wen-ch'in.

5. Degrees and studentships, *ibid*.

6. On styles of dress, see family photographs. The mansion is discussed in Ch. 13. On the sedan-chair carriers, communication from a local informant.

7. See Yeh (1960) and Boorman (1967-1971), II, 372-373.

8. On the cousins, see their biographies in TWSTCK, Vol. VII, *Jen-wu chih*, II, 181, 198. On Wen-tien, Lin (1936), Biography of Lin Wen-tien.

9. Their biographies and selections from their poetry in TWSTCK, Vol. VI, *Hsüeh-yi chih, Wen-hsüeh p'ien*, III, 97-105, 150-160. Lin Chün-t'ang's collected poems have been published in the *T'ai-wan wen-hsien ts'ung-k'an* collection, Vol. 72.

10. One of his poems is reprinted in TWSTCK, Vol. VI, *Hsüeh-yi chih, Wen-hsüeh p'ien*, III, 18.

11. The evidence is negative. Family members today neither own nor know of such a collection.

12. Wen-ch'a's loyalist side was obviously stressed in the legal appeals. Late nineteenth-century works such as *P'ing-che chi-lüeh* and *Chung-hsing chiang-shuai pieh-chuan* reenforced the point, as did Liu Ming-ch'uan's memorials. Wen-ch'a's biography in Lin (1936) marks the full flowering of this interpretation.

13. The temple in Lien (1962), p. 261. On other temples, *Peking Gazette, passim*, especially in the 1870's.

14. Lin (1936), Biography of Lin Wen-ch'in. On the practice of political seclusion under the early Japanese occupation, see Lamley (1964), pp. 259-260, 354, and in China in general, Mote (1960). The benefits of collaboration are detailed in Lamley (1964), pp. 260, 334-335.

15. Lin (1936), Biography of Lin Wen-ch'in.

16. See the estate-division document (*chiu-shu*) discussed in Ch. 14.

17. *Ibid*.

18. On the lineage's role in Confucian moral thought, see Twitchett (1959) and Liu (1959b); on the lineage as a political organization in southeast China, see Freedman (1958) and Freedman (1966).

19. The only exception seems to have been Wen-ch'in, who compiled a hand-written genealogy. See Lin (1936), "Directions to the Reader."

20. On the domestic shrines and the absence of ritual trusts, information from family members. See also Ch. 13 on the placement of tablets within the mansions, and Ch. 14 on estate divisions and ritual trusts.

21. Information from family members, especially from a descendant of Chia-yin's third son, whose branch administered the trust.

22. On his local defense activities, see Lin (1936), Supplement to List of Officeholders, p. 33b.

23. On the recruitment of militia, Wu (1959b), pp. 41, 62. On the mid-island defense bureau, *ibid.*, p. 47.

24. Particulars in Lin (1936), Biography of Lin Wen-ch'in. On the free ferries, information from older local residents who recall using them.

25. Details from Lin (1936), Biography of Lin Wen-ch'in, and local informants.

26. On her charities, see Lin (1936), Biography of Lin Wen-tien.

27. On the Honan relief, *ibid.*, Biography of Lin Wen-ch'in. Peace-making activities in mainland Fukien, *ibid.*

28. Liu (1958), p. 384.

29. *Ibid.*, pp. 295-296.

30. Lin (1936), *passim* and personal communications from family members.

31. See CHHCK, Vol. x, *Jen-wu chih*, pp. 19-20, and Lamley (1964), pp. 256, 433. Also personal communications from his descendants.

32. See CHHCK, Vol. x, *Jen-wu chih*, p. 13 and TWSTCK, Vol. vii, *Jen-wu chih*, ii, 181-188. Also Lamley (1964), pp. 359, 372, 380, 414, 493.

33. TWSTCK, Vol. vii, *Jen-wu chih*, ii, 188-189.

34. This famous family was from San-chiao-tzu, about ten miles north of Wu-feng. See in particular Wu (1959c), pp. 54-56. Wen-ch'in's daughter married a Lü. See Yeh (1960), entry for 1881.

35. Biographies of family members in CHHCK, Vol. x, *Jen-wu chih*, pp. 13-15, 31-32. Also Lamley (1964), pp. 418, 424-425, 497.

36. Further details on this connection in Ch. 14. *T'ai-wan lieh-shen chüan*, p. 195, on Wu Luan-ch'i, a son of the Wu Ching-ch'un who had died with Wen-ch'a in the last Fukien campaign. The link with the Wus thus goes back to the strongman days.

37. His biography in CHHCK, Vol. x, *Jen-wu chih*, pp. 33-34, and in TWSTCK, Vol. vii, *Jen-wu chih*, ii, 195-196. I have also spoken with some of his descendants.

Notes to Chapter 13

1. From the poem "Homecoming" by Lin Chün-t'ang, Wen-ming's sixth son, and reproduced in Mao (1955), p. 43.

2. On household sizes and structures, see Freedman (1964). According to Tai (1963), p. 1, the average household size in Taiwan in 1900 was 5 persons.

3. Such divisions are mentioned, at times obliquely, in the biographies in Lin (1936).

4. On family sizes and make-up, see the admittedly incomplete—no daughters are listed—tables in Lin (1936).

5. The division finally took place in 1894. See Ch. 14.

6. Personal communication from family members. That he received income from the common estate may be deduced from the fact that he was given a small share of the estate when it was finally divided.

7. Freedman (1958), p. 30, on this centripetal force.

8. It cannot be dated, but is described by family members. The pattern suggested—separate cooking facilities and households financed from separate branch-shares in the common estate—appears to have been common among the gentry. See Freedman (1958), pp. 25, 29, and Liu (1959c), pp. 65-66.

9. Family members describe these arrangements for the period down to the late 1890's, when this branch's estate was divided after Wen-ch'in's death. According to the Japanese household registers, the sons of Wen-feng and Wen-tien established independent households upon the deaths of their fathers, in 1882 and 1877, respectively. I do not know what criteria the Japanese used to define an independent household, and therefore follow the family tradition.

10. Personal communication from family members. I have found no records bearing on the history of either of the two mansions. Brief descriptions may be found in

Fujishima (1948) and in Lin and Kao (1966). A discussion of Taiwanese gentry mansions is in Lin (1963).

11. Sickman and Soper (1960), p. 221.

12. Information from family members and from Miss Hsiao Mei, then a graduate student in architecture at Tunghai University and a specialist in Taiwanese domestic architecture who accompanied me on a walking tour of the mansions in 1965.

13. Lin Chün-t'ang in Mao (1955), p. 43.

14. On the hall and its furnishings, information from family members and from Fischer (1900), pp. 112-113, a German author who visited there at the end of the nineteenth century.

15. A photograph is in Fischer (1900), p. 112. The stage had decayed and had already been removed before I saw the mansion.

16. On the arrangement of living quarters, personal communications from family members. My oldest inform-ant was Mrs. Hung, a concubine of Ch'ao-tung's second brother, who joined the household in the late 1880's.

17. It housed not only the tablets of Upper House forebears such as Tien-kuo but also of the common (be-tween Upper and Lower Houses) ancestors such as Shih, Sun, and Chia-yin, and thereby hangs a tale. According to local informants, the Upper House had once been accused of violating the sumptuary laws concerning residential dwellings. It was at that point that the tablets of these re-moter ancestors, and especially that of Chia-yin, who had received the posthumous rank of *chen-wei chiang-chün* (Rank 1B)—presumably on account of Wen-ch'a's merits—were moved into the Upper House. Their pres-ence there now legalized what would otherwise have been an illegal luxury. On the sumptuary laws, see Ch'ü (1961), pp. 141-143. Chia-yin's title from Lin (1936), Genealogical Tables.

18. Its size reconstructed from Lin (1936) and the household registers of the successor households. Unless otherwise indicated, particulars on the domestic arrange-

ments from family members, particularly some of the older women I interviewed, who were born or married into the Lin households in the late nineteenth century.

19. Lin family members and members of the Yang family convey much the same impression of her personality.

20. On the status of the concubine, see Lang (1946), pp. 51, 220, and Ch'ü (1961), pp. 123-127. Comparisons of the Lin genealogy and the Japanese household registers bear out the marginal status of several concubines who are listed in the latter, for example, but not in the former.

21. On a wife's barrenness and its possible consequences, see Ch'ü (1961), pp. 118-120.

22. On the law, see Tai (1963), pp. 11-17.

23. Details above from family members.

24. Her story in Wu (1961), pp. 69-70, and in Lien (1962), pp. 1024-1025. CHHCK, Vol. x, *Jen-wu-chih*, p. 172, reports that her tablet was placed in the Temple for Chaste and Filial Women in Chang-hua.

25. See also the interesting discussion of involuntary suicide in Ch'ing China in Bodde and Morris (1967), p. 190.

26. Information from family members. Again, this seems to have been the separation into "stoves" which appears in the Japanese household registers as a division into separate households.

27. Birth and death dates for the third and fifth sons and their concubine-mother are missing in Lin (1936), suggesting a rupture in relations. The date of their move is unknown. On the sixth son, communication from family members.

28. Details below from Lin (1936) and personal communications from family members.

29. Photograph in the family album.

30. Yeh (1960), entry for 1895.

31. Particulars about her life and personality from Lin (1936) and personal communications from family members, family friends, and villagers.

32. Lin (1936), Biography of Lin Wen-tien.

33. Her sons are attributed to Wen-ch'in's second wife, the only wife acknowledged in the genealogy. This episode has been confirmed by friends of the family.

34. On his legal rights, see Boulais (1966), p. 688, and Ch'ü (1961), pp. 110, 198. The custom still flourished as late as the 1940's when one of Wen-ch'in's nephews put an unfaithful wife to death. Information from local informants, again including family friends.

35. Details from Lin (1936) and from family members and local informants.

36. Lin (1936), Biography of Lin Wen-tien.

37. Hung (1972), p. 305. A friend of Yu-ch'un and Chün-t'ang, Hung was critical of the family's strongman past and of Ch'ao-tung's failure to fight in 1895. This may explain his surprisingly critical tone in a *fu* (prose-poem) dedicated to Chün-t'ang.

38. *Ibid.*, p. 281.

39. What follows is based on the personal recollections of some of the older family members.

40. Calculated from Lin (1936) and personal communications from family members.

41. Fischer (1900), pp. 113-114.

42. Data on servants from family members and from Japanese household registers.

43. On the role of peddlers in the marketing structure of Chang-hua, see Crissman (1972), p. 254.

44. They are listed under the category of "co-residents" (*t'ung-chü-jen*) in the Japanese household registers.

45. They were affectionately known as "aunties" or "grannies" (*lao-p'o*).

Notes to Chapter 14

1. Lin (1936), Biography of Lin Ch'ao-tung.

2. See Hummel (1943-1944), p. 526.

3. From Mrs. Archibald Little's biography of Li quoted in Folsom (1968), p. 105.

4. This total was composed of some 1,600 *chia* in the Lower House estate (see *Lin Pen-t'ang* below) and ca. 100 *chia* in two ritual trusts. The *chia* figure was calculated by taking the rice rental amounts from a number of villages listed in the *Lin Pen-t'ang chiu-shu* (estate division document) and dividing this by the known number of *chia* owned by the *Lin Pen-t'ang*, or its successors, in these same villages (according to the "T'u-ti shen-kao-shu"). The resulting figure of 25 piculs/*chia* (actually 25.2) has been used throughout to convert rents into acreage and vice versa, and thus to obtain either set of data where only the other was known. The 25 piculs/*chia* is consistent with data in Okamatsu (1900), p. 99, and in Chang (1962a), p. 299. Unless otherwise indicated, all figures refer to unhulled rice.

5. This figure is based on the total Upper House holdings in those villages for which I examined the "T'u-ti shen-kao-shu," plus an estimated 50 percent for holdings in villages whose cadasters I did not inspect. The 50 percent increment was arrived at by analogy with the *Lin Pen-t'ang*, two-thirds of whose income came from villages whose "T'u-ti shen-kao-shu" I examined.

6. This figure was calculated in the same fashion as the Upper House figure and accords with information from family members.

7. Information from family members.

8. Wickberg (1969), p. 2.

9. I examined the "T'u-ti shen-kao-shu" for the villages of Ch'i-hsin, Han-ch'i, K'e-li, Liu-shu-nan, Nei-hsin, T'ai-p'ing, Ting-t'ai, Ts'ao-hu, T'u-ch'eng, Wan-tou-liu, Wu-ch'i, Wu-feng, and Wu-ts'o and for the town of Ta-li-chi. Other localities where both major branches owned land were Chan-ts'o-yüan, Ch'iao-tzu-t'ou, and Wai-hsin-chuang. Localities in which at least one of the major branches owned land were Li-t'ou-tien, Pei-kou, Pei-t'ou-pu, San-shih-chang-li, Szu-k'uai-ts'o, and Ting-szu-chuang. In the villages for which I have "T'u-ti shen-kao-shu" data, the Lin-owned share averages out to 58 percent. Including

the other localities, the percentage may be somewhat lower.

10. See Speidel (1967), p. 233, and Ch. v, *passim* for the land survey and land tax reform.

11. See Lin Land Records for recorded *ta-tsu* obligations. On the weakening of the *ta-tsu*'s ability to collect his rents, see Wickberg (1969), p. 3.

12. A statistical average based on the assumption that, the Lins owning half the cropland in the villages where they owned land, all tenants rented half their land from the Lins. In reality, of course, some tenants rented all and some very little of their land from the Lins.

13. I am thinking of local informants and of the folk traditions gathered in Li (1935), pp. 229-254.

14. On the evolution of tenancy, see Okamatsu (1900), pp. 92, 116. I am assuming that the Lins' rental rates were close to the prevailing 50 percent, but that tenants might have had greater security and perhaps a smaller rent deposit. I have seen no Lin tenancy contracts and assume that they were, as elsewhere, in oral form.

15. The estates are discussed in more detail below. On landlord bursaries, see Muramatsu (1966). On the day-to-day management of Lin lands, I have used information from a former accountant and from family members.

16. Details in Okamatsu (1900), pp. 41-46.

17. The Lin Land Records show a preponderance of private contracts. Official *ch'i-wei* stamps, while always available, were generally not obtained until the time of Liu's land survey. For the villages where seizures are likely to have been heaviest (Wan-tou-liu, Wu-ts'o, Liu-shu-nan), the Lins secured the title deeds (*chang-tan*) which Liu issued. These were submitted to the Japanese surveyors for documentation. See T'u-ti shen-kao-shu.

18. This paragraph is based on a study of the Lin Land Records, a more cursory examination of similarly organized records in the possession of the Pan-ch'iao Lin family, and information from local informants.

19. Data in this and the next paragraph from Lin (1954b), pp. 187-188, 193, and files of the Feng-jung and Ts'ao-t'un Irrigation Offices (*shui-li-hui*). I have also spoken with staff members of both offices.

20. A late Ch'ing booklet recording water-rents shows a standard rate of 0.4 *Taels* per *chia* of irrigated land. See Feng-jung Irrigation Office.

21. The annual per capita consumption was 3 piculs of hulled rice (six unhulled); at that rate, the Lower House might have consumed 600 of its 41,625 piculs of rice; details on transportation and trade routes from family members and the former accountant.

22. *Rinji taiwan kyukan chosa kai* (1905), Vol. 1, pp. 41-44, 213-214.

23. Speidel (1967), p. 39.

24. The total annual rice export from Lu-kang and Wu-ch'i in the late 1890's was 570,000 piculs. Between them, the Upper and Lower Houses had rice rental incomes in the vicinity of 50,000 to 60,000 piculs.

25. Information from family members, from relatives of the Lins's former business associate in Ta-li-chi, Lin Ch'iu-ch'in, and from staff of the Ta-li *hsiang-kung-so*.

26. On the dye industry, information from *hsiang-kung-so* staff in Ta-li. On the quality of the dye, see Colquohun (1884-1885), p. 191. The plant which yields the indigo color is still brought to the attention of the visitor in Ta-li today.

27. Details in this paragraph from descendants of the Lins's former business associate in Ta-li-chi; the eight lots in *Lin Pen-t'ang chiu-shu.*

28. Family members mention that Ch'ao-tung had such property when he lived as an exile on the mainland. Such assets are more likely to have been acquired when Taiwan was still part of the Chinese empire than later, unless Ch'ao-tung bought them from office income generated on the mainland during the post-1895 period.

29. According to the *Lin Pen-t'ang chiu-shu.*

30. Unless otherwise indicated, information on the camphor industry is from Davidson (1903), Ch. xxiv, "The Formosan Camphor Industry."

31. On the grant, see Lin (1936), Biographies of Lin Ch'ao-tung and Lin Wen-ch'in. Also Lien (1962), p. 371.

32. Lien (1962), p. 371 mentions a Lin force of two battalions with a total of five hundred men. The cost of such *yai-yung* (border guards) must have been around five *Taels* per man per month.

33. Lien (1962), p. 371 calls the *Lin Ho* a company (*kung-szu*); further details from family members and local informants.

34. With a minimum of perhaps three hundred stoves, each producing twelve piculs a year, the Lins's total output would have been 3,600 piculs or 478,000 lbs. Between 1890 and 1895, the Taiwanese production rose from one to almost seven million lbs. See Davidson (1903), p. 423, on productivity and p. 442 on total exports.

35. Mitchell (1900), p. 52.

36. Fischer (1900), p. 124. Ch'ao-tung's absence explains Fischer's references to Ch'ao-hsüan as the head of the Lin family.

37. See Government of Formosa (1911), pp. 12-13.

38. There are tantalizing hints of other ways in which Ch'ao-tung may have exploited his government posts (which may at one time have included the mid-Taiwan camphor office) for the benefit of his private business, but to unravel the whole complex camphor story did not seem worthwhile.

39. I use the definitions as established in Freedman (1966), pp. 49-52. The distinction coincides with one made by my Taiwanese informants who stress the differences between the ritual trusts (*kung-yeh*, with *kung* as in "*T'ien-hsia wei kung*") and the secular estates (*kung-yeh*, with *kung* as in *Kung-ch'an-tang*).

40. On the Wu-feng *chün*, see the significant fact that both in the mid-1860's and again in 1890 it was the man-

agers of these two estates who undertook the *chün* repairs. Lin (1954b), pp. 187-188. On the other *chün*, I am also relying on circumstantial evidence. Thus, the Lin share of the Hu-lu-tun *chün* belonged, in the twentieth century, to Lieh-t'ang and Teng-t'ang, suggesting an inheritance from their father, Wen-feng. The other partial shares seem to have belonged to Ch'ao-tung personally. See Feng-jung *shui-li-hui* records.

41. This happened to Chia-yin's fourth son, as we have seen.

42. For calculation of acreage figures, see note 4 above. Since the *Lin Pen-t'ang* had already been dissolved by the time of the Japanese survey which produced the "T'u-ti shen-kao-shu," I have calculated *Lin Pen-t'ang* holdings on the basis of the holdings of the various joint or individual owners who succeeded to the estate, such as the *Lin-yü pen-t'ang* and the sons of Ch'ao-tung and Wen-ming who are individually listed in the cadasters. Uses to which the *Lin Pen-t'ang* income was put from the preamble to the *chiu-shu*.

43. The estate's first mention and gradual expansion from Lin Land Records. Calculations of acreage as explained in note 5 above. Again, since this estate had been dissolved and does not appear in the "T'u-ti shen-kao-shu," its holdings have been reconstructed from those of the five heirs, the grandsons of Tien-kuo, among whom the *Chin-jung-t'ang*'s assets were divided.

44. Its holdings of 800-850 *chia* are much in evidence in the "T'u-ti shen-kao-shu."

45. "*Kung*" stands for "*kung-yeh*."

46. Information from a member of the third branch.

47. This and the next trust appear in the *Lin Pen-t'ang chiu-shu* as lenders of several thousand *Taels*. Function according to Lower House informants.

48. *Ta-kung* is the term used in the *chiu-shu*. Family members also refer to it as the *Lin Pen-t'ang* but it is clearly different from the nineteenth-century estate of that name.

49. Chang (1962a), pp. 15-34, discusses the extra income from office. Ch'ao-tung handled, at a minimum, the funds for his Tung battalions while they were on the government payroll (and lent some of these funds to the beleaguered *Lin Pen-t'ang*). He also administered the quarter-million *Taels* involved in the Taichung building project as well as some camphor taxes. Davidson (1903), p. 408, calculates the substantial amounts of camphor tax that were syphoned off by unnamed mandarins.

50. The difference between production costs and sales price was about 25 *Yüan* per picul. On 3,600 piculs, the *Lin Ho* should have shown a profit of some 90,000 *Yüan* or a little over 60,000 *Taels*. If we deduct the cost of the border-guards (500 men times 5 *Taels* per month) we get a net profit of 30,000 *Taels*, to be divided between Ch'ao-tung and Wen-ch'in. On production costs and sales prices, see Davidson (1903), pp. 407, 442.

51. See Ch'ao-tung's willingness to assume the *Lin Pen-t'ang*'s debt of some 160,000 *Taels*. Details below.

52. The *Lin Pen-t'ang chiu-shu* shows several women in the family making loans to the estate in amounts ranging from 100 to 300 *Taels*. Mrs. Ho, Ch'ao-hsüan's mother-in-law from Foochow, lent a little over 1,000 *Taels*. The sources of these assets are conjectural.

53. Chang (1962a), p. 296.

54. The following considerations went into making this estimate and have been applied to the estimates of income for the other estates as well: The *Lin Pen-t'ang*'s known annual income (1894 *chiu-shu*) was 41,625 piculs of rice, a figure that seems to have varied little from year to year. I assume that the bulk of this, say 40,000 piculs, was sold at a retail price of 1.25 *Taels* per picul, for a total price of 50,000 *Taels*. If half of this amount was invested in the import business and yielded a profit of 20 percent, we get an additional income of 5,000 *Taels*. Assuming a rent deposit of half the annual rental and a 20 percent interest rate on

it, we obtain another 5,000 *Taels*. The water-rent for the Wu-feng *chün* (1,000 *chia* of irrigated land) would be 400 *Taels*, half of it going to the *Lin Pen-t'ang*.

55. This figure is conjectural. Systematic work on cost-of-living dates only from the twentieth century and has focussed more on ricksha coolies than gentry members. Incidental references in biographies and in realistic works of fiction provide only rough guidelines. We know that prices in late nineteenth-century Taiwan were higher than on the mainland. See Speidel (1967), p. 180. The importance of gifts for persons in government circles is stressed in Folsom (1968), p. 107. The costs of a funeral could run from a thousand to several thousand *Taels*, depending on the location of the burial site and the quality of the coffin wood. Information from Professor Fang Chao-ying.

56. The heavy debt that arose in connection with the litigation is stressed in the preamble to the 1894 *chiu-shu*. Size of debt, interest rates, and sources of credit in a subsequent tabulation in the same document. In estimating the debt at its 1882 level, I have assumed some payment of interest in the 1882-1894 period, as well as further borrowing to carry the heavy interest charges.

57. The legal secretary of a *hsien* magistrate in Shantung in the 1890's received 2,000 *Taels* for handling a locally important lawsuit. See Pruitt (1967), p. 137. Considering the length of the Lins's litigation and the many levels of government where they sought influence, the figure I suggest seems reasonable. See also the table in Chang (1962a), p. 40, suggesting customary annual amounts of "extra income" for prefects, circuit intendants, judicial commissioners, and governors. Plaintiffs like the Lins would have been a prime source of such "squeeze" which ranged from 52,000 *Taels per annum* in the case of a prefect to 180,000 for a governor.

58. I have assumed a wholesale price roughly .25 *Taels* below the retail prices given in Wang (1958), p. 5.

59. This is my estimate, based on the known figure of 500 men, serving at an estimated 6 *Taels* per month for 6-7 months.

60. I know of no such temple built in mid-Taiwan during the Ch'ao-tung years, but family members speak of such construction in the old family home in P'ing-ho. Cost of such a temple in Shantung in the 1890's was 5,000 *Taels*. See Chang (1962a), p. 24.

61. The few prices for mansions I discovered ran from 4,000 to 25,000 *Taels*. See Chang (1962a), p. 318, and Folsom (1968), p. 104. Lin family members speak of the very high cost of their mansion, due to the fact that most of the material and labor were brought over from the mainland.

62. Figures in the *Lin Pen-t'ang chiu-shu* are given in *Yüan* which I have converted into *Taels*. The interest, calculated in rice, stood at 32,519 piculs out of a total income of 41,625 piculs.

63. If the list of creditors is in chronological order, as seems likely, a recent loan of 34,000 *Taels* from Taipei sources at 30 percent interest may constitute an attempt to refinance the earlier, even more expensive loans.

64. Since Ch'ao-tung was by far the strongest member of the Lower House, both in terms of political stature and outside assets, the division could hardly have taken place without his initiative and strong support.

65. The document does not acknowledge this explicitly, but the division formula speaks for itself. Figures rounded off to nearest 1,000.

66. I have used the Lin Land Records (which relate to a portion of the *Chin-jung-t'ang*) to reconstruct the rate at which this estate grew in the late nineteenth century, and have estimated land holdings of approximately 400 *chia* in the early 1870's, 600 in the early 1880's, and 800 by the mid-1890's. Income has been calculated according to the formula explained in note 54 above.

67. The estimated 225 *chia* bought by the *Chin-jung-t'ang* in the period 1883-1895 would have cost around 50,000

Taels. The Lin Land Records indicate an average price of 210 *Taels* per *chia*, a surprisingly low figure.

Notes to Chapter *15*

1. Tso Tsung-t'ang in a letter to Hsü Tsung-kan. Tso (1960), p. 92.

2. On the polarity of littoral and hinterland, and the littoral's role in modernization, see Cohen (1974), Part IV.

3. J. H. Hexter discusses their role in English history in his "A New Framework for Social History." See Hexter (1961).

4. This ratio was calculated from the transactions recorded in Lin Land Records and applies to the first half of the nineteenth century.

5. For Szechuan, this has been established by Schoppa (1973), who found that some sixty percent of the men who functioned as local elite were not even degree-holders. His study covered the third quarter of the nineteenth century.

6. Details in Wu (1959b), pp. 41, 62.

7. Lien (1962), p. 901.

8. The household registers show that Lin daughters and Lin wives (from similarly situated families) born after around 1900 no longer had their feet bound.

9. According to local informants, this was true of Lin Hsien-t'ang's wife, another daughter of the Chang-hua Yang family.

10. Reprinted in Huang (1965), pp. 56-57.

11. Information from local informants, including family members.

12. On Chi-shang's exploits, information from family members and biography in TWSTCK, Vol. VII, *Jen-wu chih*, III, 9-11.

13. See Yeh (1960) for details of his career.

14. Lai (1958b), p. 56.

Bibliography

Part A. *Oral Sources*

A significant part of my evidence comes from interviews and conversations with a variety of local informants, most of them conducted in Hokkien through my Taiwanese research assistant. In all, some four dozen persons made themselves available, among them family members from Wu-feng and neighboring localities, residents of Wu-feng (including former Lin tenants and employees), in-laws and friends of the family from all over mid-Taiwan, as well as members of local families who had once been "at war" with the Wu-feng Lins.

With the family members, I went over portions of the genealogy to clarify and expand certain points and to gain further insight into the relations of the different segments of the family to each other. It was important to learn from them certain details not recorded in the genealogy biographies nor in the public record and bearing on personal habits, tastes, and idiosyncrasies of my subjects. I also listened to the reminiscences of some of the older Lins, particularly the women, concerning the domestic life in the mansions at the turn of the century.

With the Wu-feng residents and the many other informants from the Upper Valley I explored various aspects of the family's more public life; they had a good deal to say on the Lins's former glory and present decline and they spoke as well about the earlier conditions—of roads, rivers, settlements, and fortifications—in Wu-feng. Some allowed themselves to be drawn into a discussion of the old feuds in which the family was entangled in the middle of the nineteenth century. Families related by marriage or the more distantly related branches descending from the pioneer ancestor were able to throw light on the relations of their families to the Wu-feng Lins and on some of the more vivid personalities on either side.

With almost all of my informants it took time before they felt free enough—if they ever did, and some did not—to discuss the more sensitive aspects of family history. Others, and this included descendants of some of the Lins's former enemies, welcomed the chance to tell me their family's side of the old feud. Given the particular history of the Lins, it was not surprising to find a range of views expressed by my informants, both as to the substance of what they had to say and the candor with which they approached certain matters. In this situation, it was important to know whom to trust, and how far.

I cannot claim to have taken the precise measure of each witness; but the opportunity to conduct repeated interviews with some of my key informants and to test their story for consistency allowed me to develop a fair idea of each informant's trustworthiness. Clearly, some had far better memories or stronger biases than others, and informants differed as well in their ability to bring something like a sense of history to bear on their accounts, an awareness that one's grandfathers and greatgrandfathers must be judged by the standards of their own time, not necessarily by ours. In sum, I worked out my own conclusions as to which informants provided me with relatively "hard" or with comparatively "soft" data and I have tried to indicate in my narrative or in the notes just how much faith I put into their testimony.

A final point became clear: in a country suffused with the written and the printed word (all my informants except for one or two of the older women were literate) there occurs a continuous osmosis between written and oral accounts of the past—folkstories are committed to writing only to be read and to inspire new oral versions. Thus, it was nearly impossible to say that any oral testimony that matched available written evidence was a truly independent confirmation of the written record. On balance, then, the oral information remained most valuable where it supplemented the written record rather than paralleled it.

PART B. *Manuscript Sources*

China has long been the land *par excellence* of the printed word and her historians have made far less use of manuscript sources and archival records than have the historians of other nations; a word is therefore in order concerning the manuscript materials used in this research. They are indeed a miscellaneous lot, some being of private and some of official provenance. The large majority of the manuscripts have this in common: they record some administrative, legal, or other formal transaction.

The authenticity of the manuscripts was easily established since most of them were located precisely where one would expect to find them—household registers in the local *hsiang-kung-so*, the second copy of the *chiu-shu* among the papers of a member of the Lower House's second (Wen-ming) branch, and so forth. Even where this was not the case, as in the now widely scatted collection of the P'an family papers, I gathered sufficient background on the history of the collection to convince myself of the authenticity of this material as well. Moreover, the physical appearance of the documents and their general conformity to type—the similarity of the Lin Land Records to land records from elsewhere in Taiwan, of the formulaic expressions in the *chiu-shu* to those found in other such estate division documents—convinced me that these documents were actually what they purported to be.

As for their reliability, I could very nearly rule out the customary questions about subjective bias since all but one of the collections express no personal views on historical events or personages. Being records of formal transactions—sales, loans, estate divisions, government surveys—the documents naturally have other shortcomings, some inherent in the biases or limitations of the persons or institutions who prepared them. The censuses and land surveys, for example, are subject to many hazards that may introduce an upward or downward bias in the data, hazards which have been amply discussed by students of Chinese demography (Ho [1959]). In the long tradition of population and land censuses in China, the

Japanese surveys of the early twentieth century actually stand up very well. The household registers are highly accurate on almost all matters of family composition, with the exception of actual residence of individuals, and the land surveys have also proven of much greater accuracy than the preceding survey that had been carried out in the 1880's.

The private documents may on the whole have even fewer limitations. True enough, the quantitative data from many of the documents in the Lin Land Records probably understate family holdings (as we know from the time of Liu Ming-ch'uan's survey when the Lins obtained official title deeds [*chang-tan*]; in almost all cases the holdings were seen to be significantly larger than the older private sales contracts showed them to be). But the corrective is built right into the collection, which includes the title deeds issued by Liu. Elsewhere, moreover, quantitative data are very precise, as in the *Lin Pen-t'ang chiu-shu*, the accuracy being demanded by the situation that produced the document itself. Naturally, it would be foolish to extend one's credence uncritically to all aspects of such a document, and the sincerity of many of the sentiments expressed in the *chiu-shu* preface must be doubted. But the fact that the Lins subscribed to such ideologically flavored expressions of Confucian familism is itself, of course, a historical fact.

Finally, much of the information I gleaned from the manu-script materials was incidental to the concerns which prompted the making of the documents; hence the information is likely to be highly reliable, particularly where it is consistent with data from elsewhere in Taiwan or from other contemporary Chinese sources.

The following collections have been used:

CH'EN HAN-KUANG'S FACSIMILE REPRINTS

A set of some forty facsimile reprints of original documents, largely from the nineteenth century and relating to land-ownership in different parts of Taiwan. Provenance unknown. Made available by the late Ch'en Han-kuang 陳漢光 , a member of the *T'ai-wan-sheng wen-hsien wei-yüan-hui* 臺灣省文獻委員會.

CH'EN HAN-KUANG'S MID-TAIWAN DOCUMENTS

A collection of some fifty original documents, largely from Chang-hua district and the nineteenth century, with a few going back to the eighteenth. They record miscellaneous transactions, particularly concerning land. Provenance unknown. In the custody of the late Mr. Ch'en.

FENG-JUNG IRRIGATION OFFICE RECORDS

Public and private records from the Ch'ing period in the custody of the Feng-jung Irrigation Office (*T'ai-wan-sheng feng-jung nung-t'ien shui-li-hui* 臺灣省豐榮農田水利會) in Tai-chung. They deal with miscellaneous transactions (sales, rentals, rent collection, *chün*-building, etc.) chiefly in the northeastern part of the old Chang-hua district.

HOUSEHOLD REGISTERS

Under the title *Pen-chi hu-k'ou t'iao-ch'a-pu* 本籍戶口調查簿 , these registers were set up for the households existing in 1906, and thereafter as new households were formed. Births, deaths, marriages, and adoptions were entered as they occurred. I consulted the household registers in the Wu-feng *hsiang-kung-so*.

LIN LAND RECORDS

A collection of almost five hundred documents in the possession of Mr. Lin Hao-nien 林鶴年, great-grandson of Lin Tien-kuo. The records relate to some sixty-odd parcels of land and generally trace a complete history of each parcel's ownership from the beginning of Chinese occupance. All parcels are located in the old Lin "turf" and came into the possession of the Upper House during the nineteenth century.

LIN P'AN-LUNG PAPERS

Miscellaneous papers in the possession of Mr. Lin P'an-lung 林攀龍, eldest son of Lin Hsien-t'ang. They include rent collection records from the early twentieth century and an occasional piece going back to the nineteenth, such as the *chü-jen* essay of his grandfather, Lin Wen-ch'in.

LIN P'EI-YING PAPERS

Miscellaneous papers in the possession of Mr. Lin P'ei-ying 林培英, greatgrandson of Lin Wen-ming. The most important item was the estate division record (*chiu-shu*) of the Lin Pen-t'ang. The collection also includes family photographs and other mementos.

MID-TAIWAN LOCAL RECORDS COLLECTION

Entitled *T'ai-wan chung-pu ti-fang wen-hsien ts'ai-liao* 臺灣中部 地方文獻資料, this is a twentieth-century handwritten transcript of original documents once in possession of the P'an family (the An-li tribal chieftains) and now deposited in the Taiwan Museum in Taipei. It encompasses 237 separate items, equivalent to many hundreds of pages of original documentation, and extends from the K'ang-hsi to the Kuang-hsü reigns. The collection includes both private and public records, covering such items as genealogies, registers of tribal militiamen, tribal complaints to magistrates, and copies of official decisions affecting the tribe. It is an invaluable source on the changing tribal life under pressure of sinicization and on the relations between the tribe and the Chinese authorities and settlers. Since the tribe's allotted area extended into the Ta-li vicinity, it provides contemporary information on the environment in which the Lin ancestor settled. The work was made available to me by Mr. Chang Yao-ch'i 張耀錡, a Taita graduate in anthropology and then manager of the Taichung Central Bookstore.

P'AN COLLECTION

The remainder of a once vast record collection which remains in the possession of the P'an family. Consisting of some 320 items, the collection is kept in the home of Mr. P'an Che-chou 潘啓洲 in Ta-she 大社 , near Feng-yüan, and was made available to me there. The documents consist largely of leases of tribal land to Chinese cultivators and other financial transactions between the An-li chiefs and the Chinese. Extending from the 1750's to the late nineteenth century, the records cluster in the Ch'ien-lung (102 items) and Chia-ch'ing (141 items) periods.

SHEN-PAI T'AI-CHENG 神牌臺帳

A list of the individual tablets that have been placed in the Taichung Lin clan temple, with the date of each tablet's admission and the name of the chief worshiper. Made available by the custodian of the temple, the document has been useful in identifying denizens of the Lin turf and genealogical relationships not covered by the Lin genealogy.

TA-LI HSIANG-KUNG-SO RECORDS

A collection of miscellaneous folders with historical materials in the *hsiang-kung-so* of Ta-li, the former Ta-li-chi.

"T'AI-CHUNG-HSIEN CHIH-KAO" 臺中縣志稿

A manuscript version of a projected local gazetteer made available to me in the Feng-yüan office of the *T'ai-chung-hsien wen-hsien wei-yüan-hui*.

T'AI-TA P'AN COLLECTION

Part of the now dispersed collection of the An-li chieftain's family, these some 150 documents are now in the Library of Taiwan University (T'ai-ta). Made available by Mssrs. Lai Yung-hsiang 賴永祥 and Ts'ao Yung-ho 曹永和 of the Library staff, the records relate chiefly to land transactions and money-lending between the mid-eighteenth and mid-nineteenth centuries.

TAIWAN MUSEUM COLLECTION

This includes many of the originals of the documents described above under Mid-Taiwan Local Records Collection, as well as other historical records and maps relating to Mid-Taiwan.

TS'AO-T'UN IRRIGATION OFFICE RECORDS

Miscellaneous records pertaining to the irrigation facilities in the southeastern part of the old Chang-hua district, including materials on the history of the Wu-feng *chün*, kept in the *T'ai-wan-sheng ts'ao-t'un nung-t'ien shui-li-hui* 臺灣省草屯農田水利會

T'U-TI SHEN-KAO-SHU 土地申告書

Registers of the land survey carried out by the *Rinji taiwan tochi chosa kyoku* in 1898–1903. Filed under the then existing administrative divisions (villages, *chuang* 莊 and towns, *chieh* 街) these records are kept in the *T'ai-wan-sheng ti-cheng-chü* 臺灣省地政局 in Taipei. I had access to several volumes bearing on villages in the old Lin turf. Other data from the collection were made available by the branch office in Wu-feng.

WU-FENG HSIANG-KUNG-SO RECORDS

Miscellaneous records bearing on the Ch'ing and early Japanese period.

PART C. *Printed Works in Chinese and Japanese*

Chang Fan-ch'ien 張奮前 , 1962b. "T'ai-wan shan-ti chih pao-liu-ti," 臺灣山地之保留地 (Reserved Lands in Taiwan's mountain areas), *T'ai-wan wen-hsien*, XIII, i, 19–28.

Chang-hua hsien-chih 彰化縣志 (Gazetter of Chang-hua District) ("T'ai-wan wen-hsien ts'ung-k'an" series, No. 156). Taipei: Taiwan Bank. 1962. 3 *ts'e*. Orig. publ. 1834.

Chang-hua hsien-chih kao 彰化縣志稿 (Draft Gazetteer of Chang-hua District). Chang-hua: Chang-hua wen-hsien wei-yüan-hui, 1960–1961.

Chang Yao-ch'i 張耀錡. 1951. *P'ing-pu tsu-she ming-tui chao-pao* 平埔族社名對照表 (Table of Names of the Plains Tribes). Taipei: T'ai-wan wen-hsien wei-yüan-hui.

Chang Yao-hun 張耀焜. 1955b. "An-li ta-she yü t'ai-chung p'ing-yeh chih k'ai-fa," 岸裡大社與臺中平野之開發 (The An-li Tribe and the Opening of the mid-Taiwan Plain), *Chung-hsien wen-hsien*, I, 4–28.

Chin-shen ch'üan-shu 縉紳全書 (Complete Roster of Civil and Military Officials). Peking: privately printed, quarterly.

Ch'in-ting p'ing-ting t'ai-wan chi-lüeh 欽定平定臺灣紀略 (Imperially Commissioned Account of the Pacification of Taiwan) ("T'ai-wan wen-hsien ts'ung-k'an" series, No. 102). Taipei: Taiwan Bank, 1961. 6 *ts'e*. Orig. publ. ca. 1788.

Ch'ing-chi shen-pao t'ai-wan chi-shih chi-lu 清季申報臺灣紀事輯錄 (Selected Items Concerning Taiwan from the *Shen-pao* of the Late Ch'ing Period) ("T'ai-wan wen-hsien ts'ung-k'an" series, No. 247). Taipei: Taiwan Bank, 1968. 8 *ts'e*.

Ch'ing mu-tsung shih-lu hsüan-chi 清穆宗實錄選輯 (Selections from the Veritable Records of the Ch'ing Mu-tsung Reign) ("T'ai-wan wen-hsien ts'ung-k'an" series, No. 190). Taipei: Taiwan Bank, 1963.

Ch'ing-shih 清史 (History of the Ch'ing Dynasty). Taipei: Kuo-fang yen-chiu-yüan, 1961. 8 *ts'e*.

Ch'ing-shih kao 清史稿 (Draft History of the Ch'ing Dynasty). Chao Erh-sung 趙爾巽 et al. eds. 1927.

Ch'ing-shih kao t'ai-wan ts'ai-liao chi-chi 清史稿臺灣資料集輯 (Collection of Materials Relating to Taiwan from the Draft History of the Ch'ing Dynasty) ("Tai-wan wen-hsien ts'ung-k'an" series, No. 243). Taipei: Taiwan Bank, 1968. 6 *ts'e*.

Ch'ing-shih lieh-chuan 清史列傳 (Collected Biographies from Ch'ing History). Kuo-shih-kuan ed. 1928.

Ch'ing te-tsung shih-lu hsüan-chi 清德宗實錄選輯 (Selections from the Veritable Records of the Ch'ing Te-tsung Reign) ("T'ai-wan wen-hsien ts'ung-k'an" series, No. 193).

Taipei: Taiwan Bank, 1964. 2 *ts'e.*

Ch'ing wen-tsung shih-lu hsüan-chi 清文宗實錄選輯 (Selections from the Veritable Records of the Ch'ing Wen-tsung Reign) ("T'ai-wan wen-hsien ts'ung-k'an" series, No. 189). Taipei: Taiwan, Bank, 1964.

Ch'ou-pan i-wu shih-mo hsüan-chi 籌辦夷務始末選輯 (Selections from the Complete Record of the Management of Barbarian Affairs) ("T'ai-wan wen-hsien ts'ung-k'an" series, No. 203). Taipei: Taiwan Bank, 1964. 3 *ts'e.*

Chu-lo hsien-chih 諸羅縣志 (Gazetteer of Chu-lo District) ("T'ai-wan wen-hsien ts'ung-k'an" series, No. 141). Taipei: Taiwan Bank, 1962. 2 *ts'e.* Orig. publ. 1717.

Chuang Chin-te 莊金德 . 1962. "T'ai-wan li-shih feng-wu ts'ung-t'an," 台灣歷史風物叢譚 (Collection of Taiwanese Historical Customs), *T'ai-wan wen-hsien,* XIII, ii, 74–89.

Chung-hsing chiang-shuai pieh-chuan 中興將師別傳 (Unofficial Biographies of Commanders-in-Chief of the Restoration Period), Chu K'ung-chang 朱孔彰 ed. 1897.

Chung-hsiu fu-chien t'ai-wan fu-chih 重修福建臺灣府志 (Revised Gazetteer of Taiwan Prefecture, Fukien) ("T'ai-wan wen-hsien ts'ung-k'an" series, No. 74). Taipei: Taiwan Bank, 1961. 4 *ts'e.* Orig. publ. 1742.

Chung-jih chan-cheng 中日戰爭 (The Sino-Japanese War). Shanghai: Shang-hai jen-min ch'u-pan-she. 1971. 7 *ts'e.*

Feng-shan-hsien ts'ai-feng ts'e 鳳山縣採訪冊 (Gazetteer of Feng-shan District) ("T'ai-wan wen-hsien ts'ung-k'an" series, No. 73). Taipei: Taiwan Bank, 1960. 3 *ts'e.* Orig. comp. 1894.

Fujishima Gaijiro 藤島亥治郎 . 1948. *Taiwan no kenchiku* 台湾の建築 (Taiwanese Architecture). Tokyo: Shokukusha.

Hsien-feng shih-lu. See *Ch'ing wen-tsung shih-lu hsüan-chi.*

Hsin-tseng hsing-an hui-lan 新增刑案滙覽 (New Supplement to the Conspectus of Penal Cases). Preface dated 1886.

Hsü-hsiu t'ai-wan fu-chih 續修臺灣府志 (Revised Gazetteer of Taiwan Prefecture) ("T'ai-wan wen-hsien ts'ung-k'an" series, No. 121). Taipei: Taiwan Bank, 1962. 6 *ts'e.* Orig. publ. 1763.

Huai-ning hsien-chih 懷寧縣志 (Gazetter of Huai-ning District). 1915.

Huang Shu-ching 黃叔璥. 1957. *T'ai-hai shih-ch'a lu* 臺海使槎錄 (Account of a Mission to Taiwan) ("T'ai-wan wen-hsien ts'ung-k'an" series, No. 4). Taipei: Taiwan Bank.

Huang Te-shih 黃得時. 1965. "Liang jen-kung yu-t'ai k'ao" 梁任公遊臺考 (Notes on Mr. Liang Jen's Trip to Taiwan), *T'ai-wan wen-hsien*, XVI, iii, 1–68.

Hui Ts'un 惠邨. 1959. "Ch'ing-tai t'ai-wan te tsu-fu" 清代臺灣的租賦 (Rent and Taxation in Taiwan in the Ch'ing Period), *T'ai-wan wen-hsien*, x, ii, 91–147.

Hung Ch'i-sheng 洪棄生. 1972. *Chi-hao chai hsüan-chi* 寄鶴齋選集 (Collected Writings from the Chi-hao Studio) ("T'ai-wan wen-hsien ts'ung-k'an" series, No. 304). Taipei: Taiwan Bank.

————. 1959. *Ying-hai hsieh-wang chi* 瀛海偕亡記 (Record of Those Deserted in the Great Sea) ("T'ai-wan wen-hsien ts'ung-k'an" series, No. 59). Taipei: Taiwan Bank.

Hung-shih tsu-p'u 洪氏族譜 (Genealogy of the Hung Family), Chang-hua: Hung-shih tsu-p'u pien-tsuan wei-yüan-hui, 1964.

Izumi Furo 泉風浪. 1929. *Chubu taiwan wo kotowaru* 中部台湾を語る (Stories from Central Taiwan). Taichung: Nanying hsin-pao.

Kuang-hsü-chao tung-hua hsü-lu hsüan-chi 光緒朝東華續錄選輯 (Selections from the Continuation of the *Tung-hua-lu* of the Kuang-hsü Period) ("T'ai-wan wen-hsien ts'ung-k'an" series, No. 277). Taipei: Taiwan Bank, 1969. 2 *ts'e.*

Kuang-hsü shih-lu. See *Ch'ing te-tsung shih-lu hsüan-chi.*

Lai Tzu-ch'ing 賴子清. 1958a. "T'ai-wan chih hsieh-ching shih" 臺灣之寫景詩 (Nature Poetry of Taiwan) *T'ai-wan wen-hsien*, IX, ii, 53–88.

————. 1958b. "T'ai-wan yung-shih shih" 臺灣詠史詩 (Historical Poetry of Taiwan) *T'ai-wan wen-hsien*, IX, iv, 27–60.

Li Hsien-chang 李獻璋 ed. 1935. *T'ai-wan min-chien wen-hsüeh chi* 臺灣民間文學集 (Collection of Taiwanese Folklore). Taichung: T'ai-wan hsin-wen hsüeh-she.

Liao Han-ch'en 廖漢臣. 1960. "Chang-hua-hsien chih ke-yao," 彰化縣之歌謠 (Popular Songs from Chang-hua District) *T'ai-wan wen-hsien*, XI, iii, 16–41.

Lien Heng 連橫. 1962. *T'ai-wan t'ung-shih* 臺灣通史 (General History of Taiwan) ("T'ai-wan wen-hsien ts'ung-k'an" series, No. 128). Taipei: Taiwan Bank. 6 *ts'e*. Orig. publ. 1916.

———. 1964. *Ya-t'ang wen-chi* 雅堂文集 (Collected Writings of Ya-t'ang) ("T'ai-wan wen-hsien ts'ung k'an" series, No. 208). Taipei: Taiwan Bank.

Lin Heng-tao 林衡道. 1963. "T'ai-pei-shih te ku-hsien chu-chai" 台北市的古先住宅 (Old Houses of Taipei City), *T'ai-pei wen-hsien*, III, 74–128.

——— and Kao Erh-kung 高而恭. 1966. "Wu-feng lin-chai chih chien-chu" 霧峰林宅之建築 (Architecture of the Wu-feng Lin Mansions), *T'ai-wan wen-hsien*, XVII, iii, 167–72.

Lin Hsien-t'ang 林獻堂 ed. 1936. *Hsi-ho lin-shih tsu-p'u* 西河林氏族譜 (Genealogy of the Lin Family of Hsi-ho). Taichung. Variant editions for the branches at Shu-tzu-chiao, Ta-li-chi, T'ai-p'ing, and Wu-feng were printed, all sharing the same early record. Unless otherwise indicated, citations refer to the Wu-feng edition.

Lin Hsiung-hsiang 林熊祥 ed. 1954a. *T'ai-wan wen-hua lun-chi* 臺灣文化論集 (Collected Essays on Taiwanese Culture). Taipei: Chung-hua wen-hua ch'u-pan shih-yeh wei-yüan-hui. 3 *ts'e*.

Lin Lan-ya 林蘭芽. 1954b. *T'ai-wan-sheng ke-ti shui-li wei-yüan-hui kai-huang* 臺灣省各地水利委員會概況 (Outline of Irrigation Organizations in Various Localities of Tai-wan). Taipei: T'ai-wan-sheng shui-li wei-yüan-hui lien-ho-hui.

Lin-shih tsu-p'u pien-chi wei-yüan-hui 林氏族譜編輯委員會. 1962. *Lin-shih tsu-p'u* 林氏族譜 (Genealogy of the Lin Clan). Taichung: Jui-ch'eng yin-shu-chü.

Liu Chih-wan 劉枝萬. n.d. "I-ke hsiao wang-kuo: an-li ta-she," 一個小王國：岸裡大社 (A Small Kingdom: The

An-li Tribe), *T'ai-chung chang-hua shih-hua*. No place, no publisher.

————. 1959a. *Nan-t'ou-hsien ke-ming chih-kao* 南投縣革命志稿 (Draft History of Revolutions in Nan-t'ou District) ("Nan-t'ou wen-hsien ts'ung-chi," Vol. 7), Nan-t'ou (?): Nan-t'ou-hsien wen-hsien wei-yüan-hui.

Liu Ming-ch'uan 劉銘傳. 1958. *Liu chuang-su-kung ts'ou-i* 劉壯肅公奏議 (Memorials of Liu Ming-ch'uan) ("T'ai-wan wen-hsien ts'ung-k'an" series, No. 27). Taipei: Taiwan Bank. 3 *ts'e*.

————. 1969. *Liu ming-ch'uan fu-t'ai ch'ien-hou tang-an* 劉銘傳撫臺前後檔案 (Complete archives of Liu Ming-ch'uan's Governorship). ("T'ai-wan wen-hsien ts'ung-k'an" series, No. 276). Taipei: Taiwan Bank, 2 *ts'e*.

Lou Tzu-kuang 婁子匡. 1961. "Tao-kuang tan-shui-t'ing t'ung-chih lou yün te shih-chi t'iao-ch'a," 道光淡水廳同知婁雲底事蹟調查 (Survey of the Achievements of the Tan-shui Prefect Lou Yün in the Tao-kuang Period), *T'ai-wan wen-hsien*, XII, iv, 156–64.

Mao I-po 毛一波. 1955. "Lin Ch'ih-hsien chih shih," 林癡仙之詩 (Poetry of Lin Ch'ih-hsien) *T'ai-wan wen-hsien*, VI, i, 37–50.

P'ing-che chi-lüeh 平浙紀略 (Account of the Pacification of Chekiang). Preface dated 1874.

P'ing-ho hsien-chih 平和縣志 (Gazetteer of P'ing-ho District). Taipei: Ch'eng-wen Publishing Company. Photographic Reprint of the 1889 ed. Orig. publ. 1719.

Rinji taiwan kyukan chosa kai 臨時臺灣舊慣調查會 (Temporary Commission of the Taiwan Government-General for the Study of Old Chinese Customs). 1905. *Dai-nibu chosa keizai shiryo hokoku* 第二部調查經濟資料報告 (Second Section: Report on the Survey of Economic Materials) Vol. I. Taipei.

Rinji taiwan tochi chosa kyoku 臨時臺灣土地調查局 (Temporary Commission of the Taiwan Government-General, Bureau of Land Investigation). 1904. *Dai-sankai jigyo hokoku* 第三回事業報告 (Report on the Affairs of the

Third Section). Taipei.

Shen-pao. See *Ch'ing-chi shen-pao t'ai-wan chi-shih chi-lu*

Shun-te hsien-chih 順德縣志 (Gazetteer of Shun-te District).
1929.

Ta-li 大里. 1938. *Ta-li-chuang kuan-nei kai-huang chi shih-wu kai-
yao* 大里莊管內概況及事務概要 (Survey of Village Or-
ganizations and Outline of Operations in Ta-li Village).
No place: no date. A pamphlet available in the Ta-li
hsiang-kung-so.

Tai Yen-hui 戴炎輝. 1963. "Ch'ing-tai t'ai-wan chih chia-
chih chi chia-ch'an" 清代臺灣之家制及家產 (Family
System and Family Property in Ch'ing Taiwan) *T'ai-
wan wen-hsien,* XIV, iii, 1–19.

T'ai-wan chung-pu pei-wen chi-ch'eng 臺灣中部碑文集成 (Collection of Inscriptions from Central Taiwan) ("T'ai-wan
wen-hsien ts'ung-k'an" series, No. 151). Taipei: Taiwan
Bank, 1962.

T'ai-wan lieh-shen chüan 臺灣列紳傳 (Lives of Taiwanese
Notables). Taipei, 1916.

T'ai-wan min-tsu yün-tung shih 臺灣民族運動史 (History of the
Taiwanese Popular Movement) Edited by Ts'ai P'ei-huo
蔡培火 at al. Taipei: Tzu-li wan-pao ts'ung-shu, 1971.

T'ai-wan-sheng t'ung-chih-kao 臺灣省通志稿 (Draft Gazetteer of
Taiwan Province). Taipei: T'ai-wan wen-hsien wei-
yüan-hui, 1950–52. 54 *ts'e.*

T'ai-wan shih-ch'ao 臺灣詩鈔 (Preliminary Collection of Taiwanese Poetry) ("T'ai-wan wen-hsien ts'ung-k'an" series,
No. 280). Taipei: Taiwan Bank, 1970.

T'ai-wan su-chü chi 臺灣俗曲集 (Collection of Taiwanese Folk
Songs). No compiler, no place, no date. A volume in the
Taiwan Branch Library, National Central Library.

T'ai-wan t'ung-chih 臺灣通志 (General History of Taiwan)
("T'ai-wan wen-hsien ts'ung-k'an" series, No. 130). Taipei: Taiwan Bank, 1962. 4 *ts'e.*

Takatori Taichiro. 鷹取田一郎. 1919. *Rin bunsatsu den* 林文察
傳(Biography of Lin Wen-ch'a). Taipei: Taiwan nichi
nichi.

Ting Yüeh-chien 丁曰建. 1959. *Chih-t'ai pi-kao lu* 治臺必告錄 (Necessary Information About Governing Taiwan) ("T'ai-wan wen-hsien ts'ung-k'an" series, No. 17). Taipei: Taiwan Bank. 4 *ts'e*. Orig. publ. 1869.

Ts'ai Ch'ing-yün 蔡青筠. 1964. *Tai-an chi-lüeh* 戴案紀略 (An Account of the Tai Incident) ("T'ai-wan wen-hsien ts'ung-k'an" series, No. 206). Taipei: Taiwan Bank. Orig. publ. 1923.

Tso Tsung-t'ang 左宗棠. 1960. *Tso Wen-hsiang-kung tsou-tu* 左文襄公奏牘 (Memorials of Tso Tsung-t'ang) ("T'ai-wan wen-hsien ts'ung-k'an" series, No. 88). Taipei: Taiwan Bank.

Tung T'ien-kung 董天工. 1962. *T'ai-hai chien-wen-lu* 臺海見聞錄 (Account of Things Seen and Heard in Taiwan) ("T'ai-wan wen-hsien ts'ung-k'an" series, No. 129). Taipei: Taiwan Bank. Orig. publ. 1753.

T'ung-chih shih-lu. See *Ch'ing mu-tsung shih-lu hsüan-chi.*

Wang Shih-ch'ing 王世慶. 1958. "Ch'ing-tai t'ai-wan te mi-chia," 清代臺灣的米價 (The price of rice in Ch'ing Taiwan) *T'ai-wan wen-hsien* IX, iv, 11–20.

Wu-feng 霧峰. 1941. *Wu-feng-chuang kuan-nei kai-huang chi shih-wu kai-yao.* 霧峰莊管內概況及事務概要 (Survey of Village Organizations and Outline of Operations in Wu-feng Village). No place: no date. A pamphlet available in the Wu-feng *hsiang-kung-so.*

Wu Te-kung 吳德功 1959a. *Tai-shih liang-an chi-lüeh* 戴施兩案紀略 (Account of the Tai and Shih Incidents) ("T'ai-wan wen-hsien ts'ung-k'an" series, No. 47). Taipei: Taiwan Bank. Orig. publ. 1892.

———. 1959b. "Jang-t'ai chi" 讓臺記 (Record of the Surrender of Taiwan) in *Ko-t'ai san-chi* 割臺三記 (Three Accounts of the Cession of Taiwan) ("T'ai-wan wen-hsien ts'ung-k'an" series, No. 57). Taipei: Taiwan Bank.

———. 1961. *Chang-hua chieh-hsiao ts'e* 彰化節孝冊 (Roster of Chaste and Filial Women of Chang-hua District) ("T'ai-wan wen-hsien ts'ung-k'an" series, No. 108). Taipei: Taiwan Bank. Orig. publ. 1919.

Wu Tzu-kuang 吳子光. 1959c. *T'ai-wan chi-shih* 臺灣紀事 (Historical Events of Taiwan) ("T'ai-wan wen-hsien ts'ung-k'an" series, No. 36). Taipei: Taiwan Bank.

Yamazaki Shigemura 山崎繁樹 and Tadayuki Murakami 野上矯介 1927. *Taiwan shi* 臺灣史 (History of Taiwan). Tokyo: Hobun-kan.

Yeh Jung-chung 葉榮鐘 ed. 1960. *Lin hsien-t'ang hsien-sheng nien-p'u* 林獻堂先生年譜 (Chronological Biography of Mr. Lin Hsien-t'ang). Taichung.

Yoshida Togo 吉田東伍. 1911–1913. *Dai nihon chimei jisho* 大日本地名辞書 (Geographical Dictionary of Greater Japan). Tokyo: Fuzambo.

PART D. *Printed Works in Western Languages*

Bales, W. L. 1937. *Tso Tsung-t'ang: Soldier and Statesman of Old China.* Shanghai: Kelly and Walsh.

Bielenstein, Hans. 1959. "The Chinese Colonization of Fukien until the End of the T'ang," in *Studia Serica Bernhard Karlgren Dedicata.* Copenhagen: E. Munksgaard.

Bodde, Derk and Clarence Morris. 1967. *Law in Imperial China: Exemplified in 190 Ch'ing Dynasty Cases.* Cambridge: Harvard University Press.

Boorman, Howard L. and Richard C. Howard, eds. 1967–1971. *Biographical Dictionary of Republican China.* 4 vols. New York: Columbia University Press.

Boulais, Le Père Guy. 1966. *Manuel du Code Chinois.* Reprinted Taipei: Ch'eng-wen Publishing Company. Orig. publ. 1924.

Boxer, C. R. 1948. *Fidalgos in the Far East, 1550–1770.* The Hague: Nijhoff.

Bridgman. E. C. 1838. "Remarks on Formosa, Respecting the Rebellion of Choo Yikwei, with Suggestions for Quelling Insurrections and for the Improvement of the Island: From the Works of Luh-chow," *Chinese Repository,* VI, 418–427.

Brunnert, H. S., and V. V. Hagelstrom. 1911. *Present-Day Political Organization of China.* Shanghai: Kelly and Walsh.

Campbell, William. 1903. *Formosa under the Dutch.* London: Kegan, Paul.

———. 1915. *Sketches from Formosa.* London: Marshall Bros.

Chang Chi-yun. 1963. *National Atlas of China.* Vol. i, *Taiwan.* (In English and Chinese) Yang-ming-shan: National War College.

Chang Chung-li. 1955a. *The Chinese Gentry: Studies of their Rôle in Nineteenth-Century Chinese Society.* Seattle: University of Washington Press.

———. 1962a. *The Income of the Chinese Gentry.* Seattle: University of Washington Press.

Chen Cheng-siang. 1956. "The Geographic Regions of Taiwan," *T'ai-wan yen-chiu: Studia Taiwanica*, i, 21–30.

Ch'en Shao-hsing. 1962. "The Migration of Chinese from Fukien to the Philippines under the Spanish Colonization and to Taiwan under the Dutch Colonization," *International Association of Historians of Asia: Second Biannual Conference: Proceedings*, pp. 459–468.

———. 1966. "Family, Lineage, and Settlement Pattern in Taiwan," Paper Submitted to the Conference "Kinship in Chinese Society," Greyston House, Riverdale.

———and Morton Fried, 1970. *The Distribution of Family Names in Taiwan.* New York: Columbia University, East Asian Institute.

Chiang Siang-tseh. 1954. *The Nien Rebellion.* Seattle: University of Washington Press.

Chin P'ing Mei: The Adventurous History of Hsi Men and His Six Wives. New York: Capricorn Books, 1960.

Ch'u, Samuel C. 1963. "Liu Ming-ch'uan and Modernization of Taiwan," *Journal of Asian Studies*, xxiii, i, 37–53.

Ch'ü T'ung-tsu. 1961. *Law and Society in Traditional China.* The Hague: Mouton.

———. 1962. *Local Government in China under the Ch'ing.* Cambridge: Harvard University Press.

Cohen, Paul A. 1974. *Between Tradition and Modernity: Wang T'ao and Reform in Late Ch'ing China*. Cambridge: Harvard University Press.

Colquohun, A. R. 1884–85. "A Sketch of Formosa," *China Review*, XIII, 161–207.

Crissman, Lawrence W. 1972. "Marketing on the Chang-hua Plain, Taiwan," in W. E. Willmott, ed. *Economic Organization in Chinese Society*. Stanford: Stanford University Press, pp. 215–259.

Davidson, James W. 1903. *The Island of Formosa*. New York: Macmillan.

De Glopper, Donald R. 1974. "Religion and Ritual in Lukang," in Arthur P. Wolf, ed. *Religion and Ritual in Chinese Society*. Stanford: Stanford University Press, pp. 43–69.

Eastman, Lloyd E. 1967. *Throne and Mandarin: China's Search for a Policy During the Sino-French Controversy, 1880–1885*. Cambridge: Harvard University Press.

Fairbank, John K. and S. Y. Teng. 1961. *Ch'ing Administration*. Cambridge: Harvard University Press.

Fan Wön-lan. 1959. *Neue Geschichte Chinas*. Berlin: Deutscher Verlag der Wissenschaften. A translation of his *Chung-kuo chin-tai shih*.

Ferrell, Raleigh. 1969. *Taiwan Aboriginal Groups*. Nankang: Academia Sinica, Institute of Ethnology.

Feuerwerker, Albert. 1958. *China's Early Industrialization: Sheng Hsuan-huai (1844–1916) and Mandarin Enterprise*. Cambridge: Harvard University Press.

———. 1969. *The Chinese Economy, ca. 1870–1911*. Ann Arbor: University of Michigan, Center for Chinese Studies.

Fischer, Adolf. 1900. *Streifzüge durch Formosa*. Berlin: E. Behr's Verlag.

Folsom, Kenneth E. 1968. *Friends, Guests and Colleagues: The Mu-fu System in the Late Ch'ing Period*. Berkeley: University of California Press.

Freedman, Maurice. 1958. *Lineage Organization in Southeastern China*. London: Athlone Press.

———. 1964. "The Family in China, Past and Present," in

Albert Feuerwerker, ed. *Modern China*. Englewood Cliffs: Prentice-Hall, pp. 27–40.

———. 1966. *Chinese Lineage and Society*. London: Athlone Press.

Fu Lo-shu. 1966. *A Documentary Chronicle of Sino-Western Relations, 1644–1820*. Tucson: University of Arizona Press.

Gordon, Leonard H. D. 1965. "Japan's Abortive Colonial Venture in Taiwan, 1874," *Journal of Modern History*, xxxvii, ii, 171–185.

———. "Taiwan and the Powers, 1840–1895," in Leonard H. D. Gordon, ed. *Taiwan: Studies in Chinese Local History*. New York: Columbia University Press, pp. 93–116.

Government of Formosa. 1911. *Report on the Control of the Aborigines in Formosa*. Taipei: Bureau of Aboriginal Affairs.

Grousset, René. 1958. *The Rise and Splendor of the Chinese Empire*. Berkeley: University of California Press.

Haguenauer, M. C. 1930a. "Formose depuis les origines jusqu' à son annexion par le Japon," *Bulletin de la Maison Franco-Japonaise*, ii, iii–iv, 37–92.

———. 1930b. "Les Japonais à Formose." *Bulletin de la Maison Franco-Japonaise*, ii, iii–iv, 93–106.

Hexter, J. H. 1961. *Reappraisals in History*. New York: Harper.

Hirth, Friedrich, and W. W. Rockhill, eds. 1911. *Chau Ju-kua: His Work on the Chinese and Arab Trade in the Twelfth and Thirteenth Centuries, Entitled Chu-fan-chi*. St. Petersburg: Printing Office of the Imperial Academy of Sciences.

Ho Ping-ti. 1959. *Studies on the Population of China, 1368–1953*. Cambridge: Harvard University Press

———. *The Ladder of Success in Imperial China: Aspects of Social Mobility, 1368–1911*. New York: Columbia University Press.

Hsiao Kung-chuan. 1960. *Rural China: Imperial Control in the Nineteenth Century*. Seattle: University of Washington Press.

Hsieh Chao-min. 1964. *Taiwan: Ilha Formosa: A Geography in Perspective*. Washington: Butterworth.

Hsü, Immanuel C. Y. 1975. *The Rise of Modern China*. 2nd ed. New York: Oxford University Press.

Hummel, Arthur, ed. 1943–1944. *Eminent Chinese of the Ch'ing*

Period. Washington, D.C.: Government Printing Office.

Jordan, David K. 1972. *Gods, Ghosts, and Ancestors: The Folk Religion of a Taiwanese Village.* Berkeley: University of California Press.

Kawada, Shiryo. 1928. "The Tenant System of Formosa," *Kyoto University Economic Review,* III, 86–146.

Kuhn, Philip. 1970. *Rebellion and Its Enemies in Late Imperial China: Militarization and Social Structure, 1796–1864.* Cambridge: Harvard University Press.

Kuo Ting-yee. 1973. "The Internal Development and Modernization of Taiwan, 1683–1891," in Paul Sih, ed. *Taiwan in Modern Times.* New York: St. John's University.

Lamley, Harry J. 1964. "The Taiwan Literati and Early Japanese Rule, 1895–1915." Doctoral Dissertation, University of Washington.

————. 1968. "The 1895 Taiwan Republic," *Journal of Asian Studies,* XXVII, iv, 739–62.

————. 1970. "The 1895 Taiwan War of Resistance: Local Chinese Efforts Against a Foreign Power," in Leonard H. D. Gordon, ed. *Taiwan: Studies in Chinese Local History.* New York: Columbia University Press, pp. 23–77.

Lang, Olga. 1946. *Chinese Family and Society.* New Haven: Yale University Press.

Lee, Robert. 1970. *The Manchurian Frontier in Chinese History.* Cambridge: Harvard University Press.

Liu Hui-chen Wang. 1959b. "An Analysis of Chinese Clan Rules: Confucian Theories in Action," in David S. Nivison and Arthur F. Wright, eds. *Confucianism in Action.* Stanford: Stanford University Press, pp. 63–96.

————. 1959c. *The Traditional Chinese Clan Rules.* Locust Valley, N.Y.: J. J. Augustin.

Liu, James J. Y. 1967. *The Chinese Knight Errant.* Chicago: University of Chicago Press.

Liu T'ieh-yün (Liu E). 1952. *The Travels of Lao Ts'an.* Ithaca, N.Y.: Cornell University Press.

Lo Jung-pang. 1955. "The Emergence of China as a Sea Power During the Late Sung and Early Yüan Periods," *Far*

Eastern Quarterly, xiv, iv, 489–503.

Marsh, Robert M. 1960. "Bureaucratic Constraints on Nepotism in the Ch'ing Period," *Journal of Asian Studies*, xix, i, 118–132.

——. 1961. "Formal Organization and Promotion in a Pre-Industrial Society," *American Sociological Review*, xxvi, 547–556.

Mendel, Douglas H. 1970. *The Politics of Formosan Nationalism.* Berkeley: University of California Press.

Metzger, Thomas A. 1973. *The Internal Organization of Ch'ing Bureaucracy.* Cambridge: Harvard University Press.

Michael, Franz in collaboration with Chang Chung-li. 1960. *The Taiping Rebellion: History and Documents.* Vol. i. Seattle: University of Washington Press.

Mitchell, Charles Archibald. 1900. *Camphor in Japan and Formosa.* London: Chiswick Press.

Miyakawa Hisayuki. 1960. "The Confucianization of South China," in Arthur Wright, ed. *The Confucian Persuasion.* Stanford: Stanford University Press, pp. 21–46.

Mote, Frederick W. 1960. "Confucian Eremitism in the Yüan Period," in Arthur F. Wright, ed. *The Confucian Persuasion.* Stanford: Stanford University Press, pp. 202–240.

Muramatsu, Yuji. 1966. "A Documentary Study of Chinese Landlordism in Late Ch'ing and Early Republican Kiangnan," *Bulletin of the School of Oriental and African Studies*, xxix, 566–599.

Needham, Joseph with the collaboration of Wang Ling. 1959. *Science and Civilization in China*, Vol. iii, *Mathematics and the Sciences of the Heavens and the Earth.* Cambridge: At the University Press.

Okamatsu, Santaro. 1900. *Provisional Report on Investigations of Law and Customs in the Island of Formosa Compiled by the Order of the Governor-General of Formosa.* Kobe: Kobe Herald Office.

Pannell, Clifton W. 1973. *T'ai-chung, T'ai-wan: Structure and Function.* Chicago: University of Chicago, Department of Geography.

Pasternak, Burton. 1969. "The Role of the Frontier in Chinese Lineage Development," *Journal of Asian Studies*, XXVIII, iv, 551–61.

Peking Gazette. Shanghai: Reprinted from the *North China Herald and Supreme Court and Consular Gazette.*

Perkins, Dwight. 1969. *Agricultural Development in China, 1368– 1968.* Chicago: Aldine.

Pickering, William A. 1898. *Pioneering in Formosa.* London: Hurst and Blackett.

Pruitt, Ida. 1967. *A Daughter of Han: The Autobiography of a Chinese Working Woman.* Stanford: Stanford University Press. Orig. publ. 1945.

Rawski, Evelyn Sakakida. 1972. *Agricultural Change and the Peasant Economy of South China.* Cambridge: Harvard University Press.

Rawlinson, John L. 1967. *China's Struggle for Naval Development, 1839–1895.* Cambridge: Harvard University Press.

Ruhlman, Robert. 1960. "Traditional Heroes in Chinese Popular Fiction," in Arthur F. Wright, ed. *The Confucian Persuasion.* Stanford: Stanford University Press, pp. 141– 176.

Schoppa, R. Keith. 1973. "The Composition and Functions of the Local Elite in Szechwan, 1851–1874," *Ch'ing-shih wen-t'i*, II, iv, 7–23.

Sickman, Laurence and Alexander Soper. 1960. *The Art and Architecture of China.* Baltimore: Penguin Books.

Skinner, G. William. 1957. *Chinese Society in Thailand.* Ithaca, N.Y.: Cornell University Press.

So Kwan-wai. 1975. *Japanese Piracy in Ming China During the Sixteenth Century.* n.p. Michigan State University Press.

Spector, Stanley. 1964. *Li Hung-chang and the Huai Army: A Study in Nineteenth Century Chinese Regionalism.* Seattle: University of Washington Press.

Speidel, William M. 1967. "Liu Ming-ch'uan in Taiwan, 1884–1891." Doctoral Dissertation, Yale University.

———. 1976. "The Administrative and Fiscal Reforms of Liu Ming-ch'uan in Taiwan, 1884–1891: Foundations of

Self-Strengthening," *Journal of Asian Studies*, xxxv, iii, 441–459.

Staunton, Sir George Thomas. 1966. *Ta Tsing Leu Lee: Being the Fundamental Laws and A Selection from the Supplementary Statutes of the Penal Code of China.* Reprinted Taipei: Ch'ingwen Publishing Company. Orig. publ. 1810.

Thompson, Laurence G. 1964. "The Earliest Chinese Eyewitness Accounts of the Formosan Aborigines," *Monumenta Serica*, xxiii, 163–204.

Ts'ao Hsüeh-chin. 1958. *The Dream of the Red Chamber: A Chinese Novel of the Ching Period.* New York: Pantheon Books.

Ts'ao Yung-ho. 1962. "Chinese Overseas Trade in the Late Ming Period," *International Association of Historians of Asia: Second Biannual Conference: Proceedings*, pp. 429–458.

Twitchett, Denis. 1959. "The Fan Clan's Charitable Estate, 1050–1760," in David S. Nivison and Arthur F. Wright, eds. *Confucianism in Action.* Stanford: Stanford University Press, pp. 97–133.

Van der Sprenkel, Sybille. 1962. *Legal Institutions in Manchu China: A Sociological Analysis.* London: Athlone Press.

Wakeman, Frederic, Jr., 1966. *Strangers at the Gate: Social Disorder in South China, 1839–1861.* Berkeley: University of California Press.

Warburg, Dr. O. 1889. "Über seine Reisen in Formosa," *Verhandlungen der Gesellschaft für Erdkunde zu Berlin*, xvi, 374–87.

Whitney, Joseph B. R. 1970. *China: Area, Administration, and Nation Building.* Chicago: University of Chicago, Department of Geography.

Wickberg, Edgar. 1969. "The Tenancy System in Taiwan, 1900–1939." Seminar Paper, University Seminar on Modern East Asia: China, Columbia University.

Wiethoff, Bodo. 1963. *Die chinesische Seeverbotspolitik und der private Überseehandel von 1368 bis 1567.* Wiesbaden: Harassowitz.

———. 1964. "Tribut und Handel: chinesische Seeräuber

und Überseehändler im 16. Jahrhundert," *Saeculum*, xv, 230–248.

Wills, John E., Jr. 1974. *Pepper, Guns, and Parleys: The Dutch East India Company and China, 1622–1681.* Cambridge: Harvard University Press.

Woodside, A. B. 1963. "T'ang Ching-sung and the Rise of the 1895 Taiwan Republic," *Papers on China*, xvii, 160–191.

Wu Ching-tzu. 1957. *The Scholars.* Peking: Foreign Languages Press.

Yen, Sophia Su-fei. 1965. *Taiwan in China's Foreign Relations, 1836–1874.* Hamden, Conn.: The Shoe String Press.

Glossary

Of Proper Names and Special Terms Used in Text and Notes

Commonly used terms and names of persons listed in Hummel (1943–44) have been omitted.

A-chao-wu 阿罩霧
A-shu 阿束
an-ch'a-shih 按察使
An-li 岸裏
An-p'ing 安平
Baturu (*pa-t'u-lu*) 巴圖魯
Chan-ts'o-yüan 詹厝園
Chang-chou 漳州
Chang-hua 彰化
Chang, Mrs. 張氏
Chang Ta-ching 張達京
chang-tan 丈單
Chang Yu-chih 張佑之
Ch'ang-shan 常山
chen 鎮
chen-wei chiang-chün 振威將軍
Ch'en 陳
Ch'en, Mrs. 陳氏
Ch'en Ta-shih 陳大忝
Ch'en Wang-tseng 陳望曾
Cheng I 鄭遺
Ch'i-hsin 溪心
Ch'i-ling 耆齡
ch'i-tu-wei 騎都尉
ch'i-wei 契尾
chia 甲

chia-ping 家兵
Chia-yi 嘉義
Chia-yin-kung 甲寅公
Chia-yin-*ts'un* 甲寅村
Chiang-shan 江山
Ch'iao-tzu-t'ou 橋仔頭
chieh 街
chien-sheng 監生
Chien-yang 建陽
Chin-jung-t'ang 錦榮堂
ch'in-tsu tzu-ti 親族子弟
Ching-t'ing-t'ang 荊庭堂
Ch'ing-tuan 慶端
Chiu-she 舊社
chiu-shu 鬮書
Ch'iu Min-kuang 邱敏光
Ch'iu, Mrs. 邱氏
Ch'iu Yüeh-chin 秋日覲
Cho-lan 卓蘭
Cho-shui 濁水
Chou Chung-hsün 周鍾瑄
Chou Mou-ch'i 周懋琦
Chu-lo 諸羅
Ch'u-chou 處州
chü 局
Ch'ü-chou 衢州

Ch'üan-chou 泉州
chuang 莊
Chuang, Mrs. 莊氏
Chuang Shih-hsün
chün 圳
Fan-tzu-liao 番子寮
Fang 方
Feng-jung 豐榮
Feng-shan 鳳山
Feng-yüan 豐原
fu 府
fu 賦
Fu-chou-ma 福州媽
Fu-hsing-kung 福興宮
Fu-ning 福寧
Fu-sang 扶桑
Han-ch'i 旱溪
Heng-tsu-kung 恒足公
Ho Ao 何傲
Ho Ch'in-shou 何金壽
Ho Ching 何璟
Ho, Mrs. or Miss 何氏
Hou-lung 後龍
hsi 細
Hsia Hsien-lun 夏獻綸
hsiang-kung-so 鄉公所
hsiang-yüeh 鄉約
Hsiao Mei 蕭梅
hsiao-tsu 小租
Hsieh 謝
Hsieh Ying-su 謝穎蘇
Hsin-chu 新竹
Hsin-chuang 新莊
Hsin-chuang-tzu 新莊仔
hsing 姓
Hsing-hua 興化
Hsü Tsung-kan 徐宗幹

Hu-lu-tun 葫蘆墩
Hu-wei 虎尾
hua-t'ing 花廳
Huang 黃
Huang, Mrs. 黃氏
Hung Fan 洪箸
Hung Hou 洪厚
Hung Min-lin 洪敏麟
Hung, Mrs. 洪氏
Hung Ts'ung 洪欉
Ju-pao-chün 入寶圳
Kao, Magistrate 高邑主
K'e-li 喀哩
k'en-ch'i 墾契
k'en-shou 墾首
kuan-shih 管事
Kuan-yeh-hui 關爺會
Kuan Yü 關羽
kung-pao-ti 宮保邸
kung-szu 公司
kung-yeh 公業
kung-yeh 共業
K'ung Chao-tz'u 孔昭慈
K'ung Hsien-ku 孔憲穀
Kuo-hsing-yeh 國姓爺
kuo-tang 過當
Lai 賴
Lai, Mrs. 賴氏
Lai-tzu 萊子
Lai-yüan 萊園
lang-chung 艮中
lao-p'o 老婆
li 里
Li Chao-t'ang 黎兆棠
li-fan t'ung-chih 理番同知
Li Hao-nien 李鶴年
Li-she 櫟社

Li Shih-hsien 李世賢
Li-t'ou-tien 犂頭店
Lien-ch'eng 連城
lien-yung 練勇
Lin Ch'ao-ch'ang 林朝昌
Lin Ch'ao-hsüan 林朝選
Lin Ch'ao-sung 林朝崧
Lin Ch'ao-tsung 林朝宗
Lin Ch'ao-tung 林朝棟
Lin Ch'ao-yung 林朝雍
Lin Chi-shang 林季商
Lin Chi-t'ang 林紀堂
Lin-chia hsiang-yung 林家鄉勇
Lin Chia-yin 林甲寅
Lin Ch'ing 林請
Lin Ch'iu-ch'in 林秋金
Lin Chung-heng 林仲衡
Lin Ch'ung-yao 林瓊瑤
Lin Chün-t'ang 林俊堂
Lin Ho 林合
Lin Ho-shang 林和尚
Lin Hsien-t'ang 林獻堂
Lin hsing 林姓
Lin Jih-ch'eng 林日成
Lin Kang-min 林剛愍
Lin Lieh-t'ang 林烈堂
Lin Pen-t'ang 林本堂
Lin Shao-t'ang 林紹堂
Lin Shih 林石
Lin Shuang-wen 林炎文
Lin Sun 林遜
Lin Ta 林大
Lin Ta-ch'un 林大春
Lin Teng-t'ang 林澄堂
Lin Ti 林棣
Lin Tien-kuo 林奠國
Lin Ting-pang 林定邦

Lin Tzu-ch'üan 林資銓
Lin Wei-yüan 林維源
Lin Wen-ch'a 林文察
Lin Wen-ch'in 林文欽
Lin Wen-feng 林文鳳
Lin Wen-luan 林文鸞
Lin Wen-ming 林文明
Lin Wen-tien 林文典
Lin Wen-ts'ai 林文彩
Lin Wu-hsiang 林五香
Lin Yin-t'ang 林蔭堂
Lin Ying-shih 林應時
Lin Ying-yüan 林應源
Lin Yu-ch'un 林幼春
Lin Yu-li 林有理
Lin-yü pen-t'ang 林裕本堂
Ling Ting-kuo 淩定國
Liu Ao 劉璈
Liu-shu-nan 柳樹湳
Lo Kuan-ying 羅冠英
Lo, Mrs. 羅氏
Lu-kang 鹿港
Lu-kang-pu 鹿港埔
Lü 呂
lü-ying 綠營
Ma-tsu 媽祖
Mao-lo 猫羅
Miao-li 苗栗
Min 閩
Min-chün 閩軍
ming-ling-tzu 螟蛉子
mu-yu 幕友
nan-lu 南路
Nei-hsin 內新
nei-shan 內山
Pa-kua-hui 八卦會
Pa-kua-*shan* 八卦山

pa-pao-chün 八保圳
Pai-sha shu-yüan 白沙書院
Pan-ch'iao 板橋
Pan-hsien 半線
P'an 潘
pao 保
Pei-kou 北溝
pei-lu 北路
Pei-shih-nan 北勢湳
Pei-t'ou 北投
Pei-t'ou-pu 北投埔
pen-ti 本地
P'ing-ho 平和
"*P'ing-t'ai yao-yen*" 平台藥言
Pu-li 埔里
P'u-p'ing-she 莆坪社
San-chiao-tzu 三角仔
San-shih-chang-li 三十張犁
Shen-pao 申報
sheng 生
Shih 施
Shih Chiu-tuan 施九緞
Shih-kang 石岡
shih-li 勢力
Shih Shih-pang 施世榜
shu 熟
Shu-tzu-chiao 樹子腳
shui-li-hui 水利會
Shun-te 順德
Sui-ch'ang 遂昌
Sung-tung 楝東
Sung-yang 松陽
Sung-yin 松陰
Szu-chang-li 四張犁
Szu-k'uai-ts'o 四塊厝
Szu-ta-hsing 四大姓
Ta-chia 大甲

ta-kung 大公
Ta-li-chi 大里杙
ta-tsu 大租
Ta-tu 大肚
Ta-tu-*shan* 大肚山
Ta-tun 大墩
Ta-yüan 大員
Tai, Mrs. 戴氏
Tai Wan-sheng 戴萬生
T'ai-p'ing 太平
T'ai-yung 台勇
Tan-shui 淡水
T'an-tzu 潭子
tang-yü 黨羽
t'ang 堂
T'ang Ching-sung 唐景崧
tao-t'ai 道台
t'i-tu 提督
tien-jen 佃人
T'ien-ti-hui 天地會
Ting-szu-chuang 頂四莊
Ting-t'ai 丁台
Ting Yüeh-chien 丁曰健
T'ing-chou 汀州
Tou-liu 斗六
T'ou-pien-k'eng 頭汴坑
Ts'ai Te-fang 蔡德芳
Ts'ao-hu 草湖
Ts'ao-t'un 草屯
Ts'en Yü-ying 岑毓英
Tseng Yü-ming 曾玉明
Tseng Yüan-fu 曾元福
tsu 族
tsu-jen 族人
ts'u 粗
tsung 宗
tsung-li 總理

tsung-tzu 宗子
T'u-ch'eng 塗城
t'u-hao 土豪
t'u-niu 土牛
T'u-ti kung-hui 土地公會
t'u-ti shen-kao-shu 土地申告書
t'uan-yung 團勇
Tung-shih 東勢
Tung-shih-chiao 東勢角
tung-tu ta-wang 東都大王
t'ung-chü-jen 同居人
t'ung-hsiang 同鄉
t'ung-shih 通事
tz'u-chu 莿竹
Wai-hsin-chuang 外新莊
Wan-an-chü 萬安局
Wan-sung 萬松
Wan-tou-liu 萬斗六
Wang Ch'ien-wan 王千萬
Wang K'ai-t'ai 王凱泰
Wang Wen-ch'i 王文棨
Wang Yi-te 王懿德
wei-yüan 委員
Wen-k'ai shu-yüan 文開書院
Wu 吳

Wu-ch'i 梧棲
Wu Ching-ch'un 吳景春
Wu-feng 霧峰
Wu Hung-en 吳鴻恩
Wu-jih 烏日
Wu Lo 吳洛
Wu Luan-ch'i 吳鸞旂
Wu (River) 烏
Wu Te-kung 吳德功
Wu-ts'o 吳厝
Wu-yi 武義
yai 隘
yai-yung 隘勇
Yang Chih-ch'en 楊吉臣
Yang Chih-shen 楊志申
Yang, Mrs. or Miss 楊氏
Yang Tsai-yüan 楊在元
Ying-kuei 英桂
ying-wu-ch'u 營務處
Yo Fei 岳飛
Yüan 元
Yüan 圓
yüeh-su 越訴
Yün-lin 雲林
Yün-pu-t'ang 芸圃堂

Index

LIBRARY OF CONGRESS CATALOGING IN PUBLICATION DATA

Meskill, Johanna Margarete Menzel, 1930-
A Chinese pioneer family.

Bibliography: p.
Includes index.
1. Lin family.   2.   Taiwan—Genealogy.   I.   Title.
CS1169.L5   1979   929'.2'0951249   78-70308
ISBN 0-691-03124-X